GENERAL ARRANGEMENT

2⁵⁰

Bridge-Deck

Boat-Deck

Main-Deck

D0951924

Tween-Deck

Hold

Christine

Zchng. Nr.: SKR 109

29.6.54

Also by Nicholas Gage

GREEK FIRE

GREEK

The Story of Maria Callas and Aristotle Onassis

FIRE

NICHOLAS GAGE

Alfred A. Knopf   New York   2000

THIS IS A BORZOI BOOK
PUBLISHED BY ALFRED A. KNOPF

www.aaknopf.com

Knopf, Borzoi Books, and the colophon are registered trademarks of Random House, Inc.

Library of Congress Cataloging-in-Publication Data
Gage, Nicholas.
Greek Fire : the story of Maria Callas and Aristotle Onassis / Nicholas Gage.
p.   cm.
Includes bibliographical references and index.
ISBN 0-375-40244-6
1. Callas, Maria, 1923–1977.   2. Onassis, Aristotle Socrates, 1906–1975.   I. Title.
ML420.C18G23   2000
782.1'092—dc21   00-040553
[B]

Manufactured in the United States of America

FIRST EDITION

TO JOAN

for the first thirty years

It was as if a fire was devouring them both.

Giovanni Battista Meneghini
on the passion of Maria Callas
and Aristotle Onassis

*Happy are the fiery natures which burn themselves out, and
glory in the sword which wears away the scabbard.*

Camille Saint-Saëns
writing about nineteenth-century
soprano Pauline Viardot

*Callas . . . blazed through the skies and was burned
out early, but what years those were!*

Harold Schonberg,
New York Times music critic,
on the death of Maria Callas

Contents

Onassis Family Tree

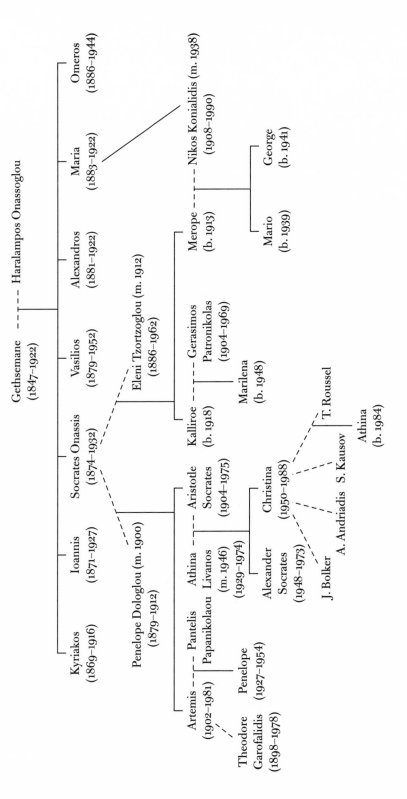

Foreword

Just how difficult it is to write biography can be reckoned by anybody who sits down and considers just how many people know the real truth about his or her love affairs.

Rebecca West, *The Art of Skepticism*

"All biography," a college professor of mine liked to say, "is a kind of murder." Until I began the research for this book, I had no idea how true this aphorism could be.

Maria Callas and Aristotle Socrates Onassis are the two most famous Greeks of the twentieth century. As the bibliography at the end of this book suggests, an astonishing number of people have chronicled their lives. It seems that everyone who ever met Onassis or Callas felt compelled to put pen to paper.

Onassis is the subject of books by one of his secretaries, his masseuse, an assistant steward on his yacht, one of his first lovers, and half a dozen reputable journalists, biographers both authorized and unauthorized. All portray him as the most colorful of the Greek shipping tycoons—the one who transformed a conservative and secretive fraternity with his innovative and controversial business deals usually funded with Other People's Money. They detail his penchant for acquiring famous playmates and priceless toys while enjoying an international lifestyle that kept his name in the headlines and inspired such terms as "jet set." All agree he capped his high-profile exploits in 1968 when he married Jacqueline Kennedy, earning the epithet "Daddy O"—for him the ultimate coup in a life devoted to collecting tokens of status.

For her part, Maria Callas inspired books written by her sister, her mother, her estranged husband, a personal assistant, a cousin, even the wife of an ex-lover. And then there is the mountain of critiques, appreciations, and discographies by dozens of music scholars, critics, and adoring fans celebrating the unequaled singing voice and persona of La Divina. Her skills as a singer and actress so completely reinvigorated and transformed her art that her admirers now speak of all opera as Before Callas or After Callas. Michelle Krisel, the artistic director of the Washington Opera, called her "the performer who changed the standard by which all other opera singers are judged." Leonard Bernstein went even further, dubbing Callas "the greatest artist of the world." The director Luchino Visconti considered Callas "the greatest tragedienne since Duse," and after witnessing one of her performances at Covent Garden, Noël Coward wrote in his diary, "She is one of the few great artists that I have ever seen in my life." Her most fervid fans worshiped her as a near deity, and many shared the sentiments of the Italian musicologist Attila Csampai, who wrote: "During the ten years of her unquestioned reign, between 1949 and 1959, she bestowed upon the lost souls of the world—disoriented and bewildered by the war—more music, more art, more humanity and warmth than any other individual of this century."

Today Callas devotees and scholars still argue passionately about the quality and eventual deterioration of her singing and have described her every performance, evaluated every recording, and analyzed each occasion the diva reached for a high note with her ravaged voice and missed.

With such a plethora of biographical material about these two renowned figures, one would think that the basic facts of their lives had been reliably established and were beyond argument. At least that's what I thought when I started researching this book.

I met Onassis only twice, once socially and later when I interviewed him for the *Wall Street Journal.* I never met Maria Callas. Yet as an American journalist who was born in Greece and has written half a dozen books on Greek themes, I felt that there was an untold story in the fifteen-year relationship of Onassis and Callas, and that only someone who truly understood their world could write it. I speak Greek, and while serving as the *New York Times* correspondent in Athens from 1977 until the end of 1980, I came to know many friends and relatives of both Callas and Onassis. For sixteen years, until I left journalism to write the book *Eleni,* about the life and death of my mother in the Greek Civil War, I worked as an investigative reporter for the *Times,* the *Wall Street Journal,* the *Boston Herald-Traveler,* and the Associated Press. For this book about Callas and Onassis, I traveled to England, France, Italy, Greece, and Turkey to seek out and verify information about the pair, and I have rigorously maintained the standards of an investigative reporter, validating each fact with at least two independent sources—two individuals who concur but don't know each other—or an original document.

Before beginning my own research, I read virtually everything in print about Onassis and Callas.

I will never read a biography with the same faith again.

It quickly became evident that almost all published books about Onassis or Callas are studded with errors. Everything from their birth dates to the causes of their deaths—and especially the details of their relationship—has been reported with inaccuracies that range from the hilarious to the appalling. In many cases, I realized, an incorrect detail was incorporated by one reporter and then picked up by ensuing authors until it became part of the canon. Glaring pieces of misinformation about their lives, their love affairs, their careers are now accepted as fact.

To be fair, it's not possible to achieve absolute accuracy when telling the story of two people so obscured by fantasies and legend as Onassis and Callas. Biographers and chroniclers of the pair are not entirely to blame for all the inaccuracies and outright fairy-tales that have become accepted as fact. Both Onassis and Callas compounded the problem because they loved to embroider and edit the details of their lives.

Onassis was a brilliant raconteur in all of the five languages he spoke fluently. He suffered from insomnia and it was his practice to pass the long nights regaling anyone willing to listen—guests on his yacht or local fishermen in a Greek harborside taverna—with his stories. Randolph Churchill, the journalist who was Sir Winston's son, once described in the *London Evening Standard* Onassis' Homeric gift for oral narration: "He is a born orator with a poetic sense and can build up a list of adjectives in an ascending order of emphasis and weight which are as perfect as a phrase of music."

In his own tales of a thousand and one nights, Onassis liked to portray himself in heroic terms—the intrepid lad who prevailed over childhood tragedy, poverty, and physical danger; who defeated all challengers to become one of the richest men in the world. He would often push the envelope of poetic license, as when he described the scene of the Turkish atrocities in his native city of Smyrna in 1922. It's true that the Onassis family were driven from their home and suffered greatly during the Turkish massacre of Greeks and Armenians in Anatolia. It's also true that thousands of Smyrna's inhabitants crowded along the harbor of the burning city, many throwing themselves into the water only to drown trying to swim to the foreign ships lying at anchor. But it is not true that the youthful Aristotle Onassis was among those wretched souls swimming through the darkness past floating corpses under a hail of bullets. Nevertheless, that's the way he often liked to tell it.

Onassis even changed the year of his birth when it served his purposes, and the resulting confusion followed him to the grave. The date carved on the marble cover of his tomb on Skorpios, 1906, is at odds with one appearing on many official papers he signed, including his first passport: 1900. In fact, both dates are wrong and no book or article published thus far lists his real birth date, which I deduced from research described later in these pages.

While Onassis changed facts to make himself appear younger, poorer, more imperiled, and, ultimately, triumphant over ever greater odds, Maria Callas had her own objectives in rewriting her life. She always sought to paint herself as a victim, cravenly exploited and betrayed by everyone around her. This impulse seems to have stemmed from her unhappy relationship with her mother, Evangelia, to whom Callas refused to speak for the last twenty-six years of her life. Maria was the chubby, myopic younger daughter of a cold, neurotic social climber who was a classic stage mother. Evangelia, or "Litsa," as she was called, saw her younger daughter's precocious musical talent as the key to winning wealth, status, and independence from a husband she despised. Maria felt, rightly, that she could win Litsa's love only when she sang.

Throughout her life Maria saw this pattern repeated with lovers, relatives, and colleagues. No one, she believed, esteemed her for herself. Everyone cared only about Callas the Diva—her remarkable voice and the profit it would bring. "Only my dogs will not betray me," she once cried in despair. This lifelong insecurity, even paranoia, created a dichotomy in Maria's mind between her real self and La Callas—the insecure, unloved child versus the regal, temperamental, even arrogant star. She often verbalized this feeling of having a split personality, complaining at one point, "Callas is killing me."

Although there was truth in this perception of being exploited, Maria's habitual reimagining of her life sometimes drove her to tell friends of injustices done to her that in fact never happened. Her goal was to camouflage her faults, errors, and misbehavior and to win sympathy, and she always portrayed herself as more of a victim than she really was. For example, when she was five years old, Maria was struck by a car while running across a Manhattan street toward her mother and her older sister, Jackie. When Callas told the story over the years, the distance she was dragged lengthened and the seriousness of her injuries increased. She often told friends that she had been in a coma for days and hovered near death for weeks. But her sister disputes the account. "I recall that we were terrified at first," Jackie Callas remembered, "but as soon as we arrived at St. Elizabeth's

Hospital on Fort Washington Avenue, we were reassured that she had only had a nasty bump and a bad shock and that she would be all right."

In fact, both Callas and Onassis embroidered their own legends to such a degree that a biographer needs to muster the skills of a detective, an archaeologist, and a Diogenes to determine in each case which among the many stories available is the truth.

The most-reported—and the most egregiously inaccurate—part of their story is the account of the cruise on the yacht *Christina,* beginning on July 22, 1959, when Aristotle and Tina Onassis hosted Maria and her husband, Giovanni Battista Meneghini, on a three-week vacation that also included such celebrated guests as Sir Winston Churchill and his wife, Lady Clementine. During the course of that odyssey, Maria and Aristotle fell in love and the Meneghini and Onassis marriages dissolved before the alarmed eyes of their fellow passengers and crew. By the time the *Christina* docked back at Monte Carlo on August 13, the world press was getting wind of the events on board, and soon entire forests were being wiped out to supply newsprint to cover the ensuing drama.

Every published account of this cruise is inaccurate from beginning to end. I first began to suspect this when I read over and over again that the passengers disembarked at Mount Athos, in northern Greece, where they visited the Greek patriarch, who gave a blessing to Onassis and Callas that seemed to observers like a sacrament for their extramarital union. Any Greek knows that the disembarkation at Mount Athos as reported by several biographers of Onassis and Callas, including her husband, Meneghini, was impossible. Mount Athos is an independent enclave of Orthodox monasteries from many countries. Callas and the women aboard could never have set foot on the Holy Mountain because, as Anthony Montague Browne, Churchill's private secretary, dryly notes in his memoir, *Long Sunset,* "No female creature was allowed on Mount Athos, not even bees." The blessing did take place, I learned, but it occurred in Istanbul, where the Patriarchate, the Greek Orthodox equivalent of the Vatican, is located.

As I was to discover, even the names of the passengers on the *Christina*'s cruise have been continually misstated. After reading repeatedly that the Italian auto magnate Umberto Agnelli and his wife, Antonella, were aboard (or, in many cases, Gianni Agnelli and his wife, Marella), I wrote to Umberto asking for an interview. He wasn't invited on the cruise, he wrote back; it must have been his brother. I secured an interview with Gianni Agnelli and flew to Turin to meet him at the Fiat headquarters. He received me graciously and shared with me fond memories of Onassis, but pointed out that he, too, was not present on that fateful cruise.

I then flew to Athens and met Kostas Anastasiades, who served as captain of the *Christina* from 1953 until Onassis' daughter gave the ship to the Greek state after her father's death in 1975. He checked the ship's log, which he keeps at his home in the Athens suburb of Neo Psychiko, and found that no Agnellis were on the cruise in question.

Just as one Agnelli or another is consistently included among the passengers (even by Meneghini, Maria's cuckolded husband, who should have known better, since he was present), so Lord Moran, Churchill's doctor, and his wife, Lady Moran, are inevitably named among the reported guests. In London, I interviewed Anthony Montague Browne and his ex-wife Nonie, now Lady Sargant, who were among the most helpful surviving passengers. Anthony Montague Browne served for thirteen years as Churchill's personal assistant and accompanied the British elder statesman on eight cruises aboard the *Christina*. Nonie kept a diary of all the cruises— actually a series of short notes covering each day's destination and activities—and her record is invaluable in verifying and re-creating the events on board. Montague Browne used his ex-wife's notes and his own sharp memory as a basis for his wry and witty reflections on Onassis in *Long Sunset*, his memoir of life with Churchill.

Having gone on so many trips on the *Christina*, neither Montague Browne nor his former wife could recall for certain whether Lord and Lady Moran were on this particular cruise, but there is another surviving passenger—Celia Sandys, Sir Winston's granddaughter—who was along, accompanying her mother, Diane Sandys. At the time, Diane's marriage to Duncan Sandys was dissolving and Sir Winston thought it might ease his daughter's pain to travel on Onassis' luxurious yacht. Though biographers of Onassis and Callas commonly cite passengers on the cruise who weren't there, like the Agnellis and the Morans, most don't even mention Celia Sandys. But Celia, then sixteen years old and possessing the acuity of an impressionable teenager, remembers the trip vividly. She has provided details about the events on board that have not been reported before, including the fact that Churchill's elderly doctor was not among the guests, a point about which she was quite positive.

The book *Churchill: Taken from the Diaries of Lord Moran*, published by Houghton Mifflin in 1966, confirmed what Celia Sandys told me: Lord Moran wasn't on the *Christina* in July of 1959 but in England (although he was with Churchill on another important outing on the yacht, in March of 1960). When Lord Moran was supposed to be lounging on the deck of the *Christina* with Onassis, Callas, and the Churchills, he was in fact lunching at his home, Birch Grove, with Prime Minister Harold Macmillan.

The alleged presence of the Agnellis and the Morans on the cruise when Maria and Aristotle fell in love was just one of the many inaccuracies in nearly every biography. One might expect accuracy at least from Giovanni Battista Meneghini, Maria's hapless Italian husband, who was one of the protagonists in this byzantine tale of infidelity and lost love. He was, after all, an eyewitness as, day by day, his wife's affections were transferred from him to their host. But in his book *My Wife Maria Callas,* Meneghini perpetuated the most flagrant errors. (He even described Sir Winston's beloved pet, Toby, who shared the great man's stateroom, as a "little dog." In fact, Toby was a green parakeet, or budgerigar, who would bitterly grieve his owner a year later when he flew out the window of Churchill's penthouse suite of the Hôtel de Paris in Monte Carlo and disappeared.)

Perhaps, though, poor Meneghini had a better excuse than anyone else for recasting the truth. Speaking only Italian, he had difficulty communicating with the other guests, and spent most of the time miserably seasick and alone in the cabin he shared with Maria. As he was increasingly ignored and humiliated by his wife, he pitifully tried to "improve his acquaintance" with the ladies seated beside him at dinner, according to Montague Browne and Lady Sargant, by playing footsie with them under the table, staining their evening gowns with his pipe-clay white shoes. No wonder Tina Onassis, the hostess, scornfully dubbed him "Meningitis." In his book Meneghini not only misreported the various ports of call of the *Christina,* he also described a shipboard life that sounded like a Hollywood fantasy: "The women, and also the men, often sunbathed completely nude and fooled around in broad daylight, in front of everyone. In simple and precise words, I had the impression of finding myself in the middle of a pigpen." The suggestion that this kind of behavior would be allowed in the presence of the very proper Churchills so outraged Anthony Montague Browne that he sued Meneghini for libel and won.

Thanks to the Montague Brownes, Celia Sandys, and the *Christina*'s captain, Kostas Anastasiades, all of whom provided detailed notes and mutually corroborating memories, I'm convinced that the day-to-day account of the voyage of the *Christina* in July of 1959, when the romance between Callas and Onassis began, is told accurately and fully in these pages for the first time.

Both protagonists in this love story have become even more famous in death than they were in life. Maria, especially, stares back at us with her great, sorrowful Byzantine eyes from Greek postage stamps and American billboards advertising Apple computers (the latter bearing the grammatically challenged slogan "Think different"). Her record sales have soared since the last year of her life, 1977, when 280,000 albums were sold: in 1997, the twentieth anniversary of her death, 750,000 CDs were purchased.

Like all iconic figures, Onassis and Callas assume our own fears and longings, and as a result of all we've read about them, we feel we know them. In the popular mind Onassis has evolved into the image of a modern Midas. Through his cleverness and ambition, the legend goes, he turned everything he touched to gold, only to see his life and his hopes collapse with an irony worthy of any tragedy told by Euripides: his only son falling from the sky to perish like Icarus; his child-bride marrying his archrival, then dying of an overdose of pills; his last marriage—to the revered widow-queen of the United States—becoming an empty, unloving union that he desperately tried to escape. After his own end, his remaining child died at thirty-seven in mysterious circumstances, leaving his fortune in the potential control of the French playboy father of his only grandchild, a girl who knows nothing of the Greek language, country, or religion that meant so much to Onassis.

Maria Callas, too, has been turned into an icon, the archetype of the volcanic prima donna, prone to hysterical cancellations of her performances and terrifying temper tantrums, pouring all her energy obsessively into her art until she met a man who could ignite passionate love in her for the first time. But because of this love, her devotees believe, she squandered her unique talent, only to be rejected by her insensitive paramour and end her life a recluse dependent on sleeping pills, until her body gave out and she died at fifty-three, her voice ruined by excess and disuse. By losing sixty-five pounds at the height of her career and transforming herself from an awkwardly overweight soprano into a sylphlike diva with the face and form of a goddess, Callas came to embody yet another one of our favorite cultural archetypes: the ugly duckling turned swan.

All these perceptions of the tycoon and the diva are of course clichés forged by decades of misinformation and inaccuracies published about them. We create the gods and goddesses and cultural icons that we need. Though there is in every cliché a core of truth, these two people were far more complicated and vulnerable than their legends suggest. To perpetuate the popular perception of Callas as a tragic artist destroyed by a fickle and cruel philistine who consistently did her wrong is to cheat both these talented individuals of their humanity and to turn them into two-dimensional figures of melodrama.

Their love affair was quite different from the legend, the accepted but inaccurate story that "everybody knows." In fact, although their relationship was certainly tempestuous, for both of them it was the deepest and longest-lasting emotional commitment of their lives. And the devotion was not all on Maria's side, as is popularly believed.

Then there is the abortion, which has become the central fact that "everyone knows" about the Onassis-Callas romance. Maria, characteristically representing herself as victim, spoke to her closest friends of an abortion in 1966, forced upon her by Onassis after he persistently and cruelly refused to marry her. This terminated pregnancy is the emotional climax of the award-winning play *Master Class,* by Terrence McNally.

But what Maria did not tell her friends and what none of her previous biographers discovered is that at 8 a.m. on March 30, 1960, in Milan, eight months after she first slept with Aristotle Onassis during the cruise on the *Christina,* Maria gave birth by cesarean section to a living baby boy. Because the premature infant was in trouble, the doctor had it rushed by ambulance to a better-equipped clinic. On the way there, in the ambulance, a nurse christened the boy after one of Onassis' favorite uncles. The child died on the same day he was born, but before he was buried in a Milan cemetery, he was photographed. For months after his death Maria would visit the child's grave and kneel there to pray. In later years, when she lived in Paris, she would fly to Milan with her devoted maid, Bruna Lupoli, to visit the grave. Thirteen years after the baby's death, when twenty-four-year-old Alexander Onassis, named for another of his father's favorite uncles, died in the crash of his private plane, an inconsolable Aristotle Onassis flew to Maria in Paris. Their tears mingled as he said to her, "My boy is gone. There's nothing left for me!" and she cried, "If only our son had lived!"

The love child of Maria Callas and Aristotle Onassis, who was born and died on March 30, 1960, is only part of the story of their tragic relationship that has never been told, until now.

GREEK FIRE

1

THE LAST DEAL

*Call no man happy until you know the nature of
his death; he is at best but fortunate.*

Solon, from Herodotus, *History, Book I*

On February 6, 1975, Aristotle Socrates Onassis set out on his final journey, on foot.

Stelios Papadimitriou, his private attorney and the director of his shipping empire, had been summoned to the Boss's villa in the Athens suburb of Glyfada with the news that he was sinking fast. His myasthenia gravis, a degenerative neuromuscular disease, had been complicated by a case of influenza and an infection of the gallbladder. Foreign doctors and family members were gathering at his bedside and arguing about his medical treatment.

In the two years since his son Alexander had died in a plane crash, Onassis had lost the will to live. He was negligent in taking his medications. Six weeks earlier, on Christmas Day, 1974, he had given each member of his household staff ten thousand drachmas (about three hundred dollars), an unusually large Christmas gift, which seemed to them to be his way of saying good-bye.

In the months of December and January, Onassis lost forty pounds. Not even his sister Artemis, who prepared Anatolian delicacies for him, could coax him to eat. His daughter, Christina, still believed that the doctors she had summoned from Paris and New York might be able to save her father, but Papadimitriou suspected, as he climbed the front steps to the villa on that overcast February morning, that the news would not be good.

After being received by the Onassis retainer Panayiotis Konidiaris and greeting the shipowner's worried sisters in the parlor, Papadimitriou hurried up the stairs toward the second-floor bedroom. He found Onassis' twenty-four-year-old daughter huddled near the top of the stairs, sobbing. She told him that she couldn't convince her father to go to Paris, to the American Hospital in Neuilly, in the company of the French surgeon Dr. Jean Caroli, who wanted to remove Onassis' inflamed gallbladder. (The American doctor who flew in with Jacqueline Kennedy Onassis from New York felt that the rigors of such an operation would kill him.) Christina begged Papadimitriou to convince her father to go. There was a car and driver waiting outside to take him to the airport, but he wouldn't budge.

As they spoke, Papadimitriou, then a heavy smoker, burst into a fit of coughing and Onassis heard him through the door. *"Irthe o Kephalas,"* Onassis called out with derisive affection, "Big Head has come." (The nickname means "pig-headed," stubborn.) Papadimitriou let himself into the bedroom and found his boss looking weak and shockingly emaciated. "You should take Christina's advice and go to the American Hospital in Paris," the attorney suggested.

"You want me to go die in Paris?" Onassis asked. "I'm either going to die here or in Paris. It doesn't make any difference."

Papadimitriou protested that he was being foolish and would soon be well again. Onassis, ever the negotiator, spied the prospect of a deal and brightened. "What are you going to give me if I go to Paris?" he asked his aide. "Do you hear my daughter crying outside? I want your word on my deathbed that if I go to Paris you will promise me that you'll stay with Christina until the bitter end, whatever she does to make it difficult for you. Is it a deal?"

Papadimitriou nodded his assent, and Onassis told him to call his daughter inside. She came in weeping. Onassis took her hand and that of his employee and said, *"Chryso mou* [my treasure], Stelios will look after you no matter what you do to him, so try not to be too hard on him." All the suicide attempts, rash love affairs, and impetuous decisions that had marked Christina's tumultuous young life couldn't have been far from his thoughts.

The only one who still believed her father could be cured, Christina nodded, relieved that he was giving in to her pleadings.

Onassis looked at Stelios and said, "From now on, Christina is your sister. Now bend to kiss me."

The press had gathered like carrion birds outside the villa. Papadimitriou and Christina helped the invalid down the stairs to the side door, where his car had pulled up. His sister Artemis draped a coat over his shoulders against the damp winter chill. Waiting in the back seat of the car was his wife, Jacqueline Kennedy Onassis.

Onassis could barely walk, Papadimitriou recalls, but when the door opened and he saw the crowd outside, "He shrugged his shoulders, letting the coat fall to the ground, pulled himself up, and walked to the car like a *palikari* [warrior]. In the car he slumped down and looked very feeble, but when we pulled up to the plane, he took off the coat again and walked up the stairs alone, refusing to be helped."

Onassis ultimately regretted the last deal he made. "At one point in the hospital," Papadimitriou says, "when he couldn't talk anymore because he was hooked up to machines, with tubes down his throat, he wrote Christina a note which said in big letters, 'PLEASE,' then in smaller letters, 'Let me die.' But they didn't let him die and he suffered for some time after that."

Born and raised in Alexandria, Egypt, Papadimitriou first met the man with whom he would have a volatile but devoted working relationship in 1954, when the young lawyer was one of only two Greeks qualified to practice law in Egyptian courts. He was summoned from Alexandria to Jeddah to be considered with seven others competing for a lucrative contract with a stranger named Onassis. After he met the mysterious Greek in Jeddah, Papadimitriou was required to translate from Arabic to Greek at meetings between Onassis, the Egyptian minister of commerce, and the king of Saudi Arabia. Then Onassis engaged him in an all-night drinking contest, which ended up back at the Jeddah airport at the first light of dawn. When Onassis' plane was announced, Papadimitriou still didn't know whether he'd won the job or not, but as the tycoon headed onto the tarmac he turned around and said, according to Papadimitriou: " 'We will be together until one of us departs,' meaning, until one of us dies."

The stocky sixty-eight-year-old lawyer, now the president of the Alexander S. Onassis Public Benefit Foundation, paused and stared at the floor, remembering the sight of his employer as, twenty-one years later, he climbed the stairs to another plane—his private Learjet waiting to take him to the American Hospital in Neuilly. "When he got on that plane for Paris, that was the last time I ever saw him."

Of all Onassis' innumerable possessions, jewels and priceless objets d'art, the only one that he chose to take with him on his last journey, toward death, was a small red cashmere Hermès blanket that he had been given a month earlier, for his birthday. It was a gift not from his wife, Jackie, but from the woman whom he had loved more deeply and for more years than any other in his life: Maria Callas.

When Onassis and his wife and daughter reached Paris, he insisted on going to his apartment at 88 Avenue Foch, saying he had work to do, and that he'd enter the hospital tomorrow. He rode in a separate limousine from Jackie and Christina, arriving thirty minutes before them. This time there was a veritable army of press as well as five television crews waiting outside his apartment. Onassis once again summoned the energy to walk through the crowd on his own, rejecting any offer of help from his chauffeur as his gaunt image was recorded for the last time in the artificial daylight of the flashbulbs.

Inside the apartment, from his bed, Onassis made a phone call to a Paris number he didn't have to look up. The phone rang at 36 Avenue Georges Mandel, only a few blocks away. It was the home of Maria Callas, who had been waiting for his call. The phone was answered by her butler, Ferruccio Mezzadri. "They talked for a while in Greek," Ferruccio told me, "and after she hung up she told us the Signore was going to the American Hospital. She was very upset."

Maria later told friends that she had begged to see Onassis right away, but he told her that "*e Hira,*" the Widow, was with him. But he knew that Jackie was eager to leave him behind as soon as she could—a complaint that Maria had heard before. As soon as his wife headed back to New York, Aristo promised, he would try to find a way to get her into the hospital. It wouldn't be easy to evade the press and his sisters, anxious to avoid any scandal, but they had to try. He needed to talk to her, he said. Maria promised him she would stay in her apartment until he called.

After Jackie and Christina arrived, Onassis slept for a while, then he asked for a capsule of Pyridostigmine, a slow-release anticholinergic agent that would give him a burst of energy through the night so that he could find the strength to deal with a few last items of business. He called for his closest aides to be brought into the bedroom one by one.

The next morning Onassis was driven to the American Hospital in Neuilly. While Jackie and Christina distracted the press at the main entrance, Onassis entered through a side door with several aides. When one of them offered a wheelchair, he waved it off, according to one of his young assistants from New York, Nicholas Papanikolaou. "No, I'll go in on my own steam," he said, "but it's going to take four to bring me out."

Meanwhile, at 36 Avenue Georges Mandel, Maria Callas sat by the phone and waited.

2

A MEETING IN VENICE

All things are produced by Fate.

Zeno

There are some who say that Maria Callas and Aristotle Socrates Onassis may have first met in the late 1930s in the streets of Manhattan, where Mary Anna Callas, as she signed her schoolwork, was attending P.S. 189 in Washington Heights at 188th Street and Amsterdam Avenue. "Onassis had met Maria in New York in the late 1930s—she was a classmate of one of his nieces," maintains one Onassis biographer. In fact, Onassis was then living in Europe, and his only niece at the time never visited the United States.

Maria attended school only until she was thirteen. At her eighth-grade graduation ceremony on January 28, 1937, she sang a musical selection from Gilbert and Sullivan's *H.M.S. Pinafore,* just as she had performed other popular airs at previous school ceremonies, leaving her teachers awestruck at her surprisingly adult-sounding voice. A shy, awkward child, Mary Anna modestly inscribed her fellow students' autograph books after the ceremony with the hackneyed couplet: "Being no poet, having no fame / Permit me just to sign my name."

A month later, she sailed with her mother, Evangelia, to join her older sister, Jackie, in Greece. Evangelia Kalogeropoulos (the surname of Maria's parents when they immigrated to the United States), a woman of boundless ambition and unfulfilled dreams, planned to return to her native land to launch Maria's singing career with lessons financed through the largesse of admiring relatives. But the extended family proved less than eager to help, and the mother and two girls found themselves destitute and trapped in the beleaguered country for eight years amidst the hardships of World War II and the Greek Civil War that followed.

During the 1930s, Onassis was a young, newly rich shipowner living in London and Buenos Aires and conducting an affair with an older Norwegian woman, Ingeborg Dedichen, until the outbreak of war convinced him and many of the London Greek shipping community to move to New York City in 1940. Even if the thirty-something Onassis had visited New York City in 1937 and for some reason had attended a grade-school ceremony in Washington Heights, it is unlikely that the ambitious playboy shipowner would have noticed or remembered a tall, stocky, bespectacled, pimply preteen with a lovely voice who sang at school events but had no friends and was escorted to and from school every day by her mother.

Their first real meeting took place much later, at a glittering all-night ball held in the Hotel Danieli on the canals of Venice, after Maria had completed her metamorphosis from unhappy schoolgirl, exploited by her neurotic stage mother, to the world-famous soprano who had virtually re-created the art of opera. Her singing career had begun with controversy in Greece when she was only fifteen. After the war, when she was twenty-one, Maria returned to the United States, but she failed to find employment there. Two years later, in 1947, penniless, she borrowed money and sailed to Italy for a singing engagement in Verona that would pay her only $240 dollars for four performances. There she met a balding, pudgy Veronese businessman and opera buff more than twice her age named Giovanni Battista Meneghini; he befriended her, then married her and guided her career until she became the reigning deity of La Scala in Milan.

With his brothers, Meneghini had made a fortune in the construction business in Verona—"When I met my wife, I . . . owned twelve factories"— and he was sometimes referred to disparagingly as a "brick salesman." On the day they met, June 29, 1947, Battista was fifty-three—thirty years older than the fledgling singer. He was well known in the city as a mentor and protector of aspiring singers, and although his aged mother and brothers never approved of his association with "a woman of the stage," Battista dedicated himself to Maria's career almost from the moment he met her. He devoted his time, money, and energy to providing her with lessons and auditions and convinced her to stay in Italy even after she was initially rejected by La Scala.

Meneghini wrote in his memoir, *My Wife Maria Callas*, that when he was introduced to Callas she was sitting at a table at the restaurant above which he lived, and when she arose from the table, "I was moved to pity. Her lower extremities were deformed. Her ankles were swollen to the size of calves. She moved awkwardly and with effort." Nevertheless, Meneghini insisted on showing the nearby city of Venice to the new arrival—an invitation she at first refused "for personal reasons." In Venice their friendship began to bloom, and he ultimately learned that Maria had been reluctant to accept his invitation because she had no other clothes than what she was wearing when he met her. Hoping his intentions would not be misunderstood, Meneghini recalled, he eventually made her an offer: "It's six months until the first of the year. During that period I will take care of all necessities—hotel, restaurants, wardrobe, everything. You will concern yourself only with singing and studying with the *maestri* that I choose for you. At the end of this year, we will evaluate the results. If we are both satisfied, we will draw up an agreement that will cover our future professional relations."

Although there were several disappointments at the beginning, including the rejection by La Scala, ultimately Callas proved to be a wonder, and Meneghini devoted himself full-time to managing her career. With her peerless voice and range, she resurrected operas that had been neglected for decades for lack of performers able to do them justice. Then, in 1953, another near miracle: Callas suddenly dropped sixty-five pounds from her amazonian frame and emerged as an exotic, willowy beauty who soon drew the attention not only of opera lovers but of international society as well.

She had always been shy and ill at ease in social situations, and her drearily bourgeois, rotund husband, who could speak only Italian, and that with a strong Veronese accent, was little help in this connection. (Once he dozed off at a dinner party in London in the company of the Queen Mother.) But emboldened by her new slim form and undoubtedly still conditioned by her mother's lifelong social aspirations, Maria quickly determined to make her way in the beau monde. Toward this end she courted and won the passionate friendship of Elsa Maxwell, then the doyenne of international society.

Maxwell, who had broken into café society playing piano at private parties, was an unlikely social arbiter. Born in 1883, she described herself as "a short, fat, homely piano player from Keokuk, Iowa, with no money or background, [who] decided to become a celebrity and did just that." She parlayed a modest gift for music and a great one for organizing outrageous parties with other people's money into a long career as the author of an influential gossip column on international society. Maxwell followed the winds of fashion every year, from the couture shows to the races at Ascot, the opening of the opera season in New York, the film festival in Venice, tea with the Windsors in Paris, and drinks with film stars at El Morocco in Manhattan—wherever the elite found amusement and scandal.

Elsa Maxwell's annual ball was the highlight of the Venice film festival every autumn, and it was at one of these balls, given in Maria's honor on

September 3, 1957, that the seventy-four-year-old Maxwell, whom Callas' husband described as "the ugliest woman I have ever seen," introduced her protégé to Aristotle Onassis.

Maria had won the affection and protection of Elsa Maxwell only a year earlier with a simple but effective ploy. On October 29, 1956, Maria made her debut at the Metropolitan Opera in New York, a nine-week run that was marked by controversy and criticism. For years her famous temper tantrums and walkouts and her husband's demands for unprecedented fees had made the Met's general manager, Rudolf Bing, reluctant to hire her, but finally terms were agreed on and all New York hurried to buy tickets to Callas' debut in Bellini's *Norma*. The *New York Times* reported that "never had so many Americans tried to pay so much money to hear an opera."

Just days before that performance, a blistering cover story on Maria appeared in *Time* magazine. It featured her mother's tales of the singer's ingratitude and coldheartedness, including the infamous letter in which Callas replied to her mother's request for cash: "If you can't make enough money to live on, you can jump out of the window or drown yourself." By opening night, during an unseasonably hot October, the New York audience was so hostile and the diva so frightened that she had to be literally pushed onto the stage by the stage director. But by the end of her performance the skeptics had been won over and roared their adoration through sixteen curtain calls.

"Her voice had flaws, as the critics eagerly pointed out," *Time* reported. "But in the low and middle registers she sang with flutelike purity, tender yet sharply disciplined, and in the upper reaches—shrill or not—she flashed a swordlike power that is already legend."

Not so easily charmed, however, was Elsa Maxwell, who was a devoted friend and admirer of Maria's rival, the soprano Renata Tebaldi. "The great Callas left me cold," the columnist wrote after the debut. While the two sopranos traded veiled insults in the press, Maxwell continued to snipe at Maria in her column throughout the New York run, which also included Puccini's *Tosca* and Donizetti's *Lucia di Lammermoor*. After *Lucia* Maxwell wrote: "I confess the great Callas' acting in the Mad Scene left me completely unmoved."

Maxwell's public criticisms were hurting Maria, and she made a decision to beard the social lion in her den. A few days before leaving for Milan, Callas and her husband attended a dinner dance given for the American Hellenic Welfare Fund at the Waldorf-Astoria. The host was the Greek film tycoon Spyros Skouras, and Maria asked him to introduce her to Elsa Maxwell. The portly, grim-faced gossip columnist condescended to be led over to the diva but greeted her with the icy words: "Madame Callas, I would have imagined myself to be the last person on earth that you would have wished to meet." Maria mustered her most winning smile and, as Maxwell wrote in her next column, replied, "On the contrary, you are the first one I wish to meet, because, aside from your opinion of my voice, I esteem you as a lady of honesty who is devoted to telling the truth."

Instantaneously, Elsa Maxwell felt herself wounded by Eros, or, as she wrote in her column, "When my hand was grasped warmly by Miss Callas, and I looked into her amazing eyes, which are brilliant, beautiful and hypnotic, I realized she is an extraordinary person. Thus we buried the hatchet. I was amazed at her lack of animosity toward me." From that moment, the smitten Maxwell was constantly by the diva's side. Callas quickly realized that the older woman's interest was more than maternal and tried to avoid being left alone with her, but she nevertheless gloried in the heady new social milieu that Maxwell so easily opened to her.

Flying back to New York in January of 1957 for another ball at the Waldorf-Astoria, this time in costume, Maria wore three million dollars' worth of emeralds (borrowed from Harry Winston) as part of her elaborate masquerade as the Egyptian queen Hatshepsut. Elsa Maxwell dressed as Catherine the Great, with a starched lace ruff that seemed ready to carry her aloft, given a strong enough wind. In April at La Scala in Milan, when Maria opened in Donizetti's *Anna Bolena* and broke the house record for solo curtain calls during twenty-four minutes of applause, Elsa Maxwell was among the most ecstatic fans. Maria was photographed at the Milan airport embracing Maxwell as her mentor flew in to attend her rehearsals of Gluck's *Iphigénie en Tauride*.

As soon as *Iphigénie* was over, Maxwell escorted Callas on a three-day tour of Paris, including tea with the Windsors, cocktails with the Rothschilds, dinner at Maxim's, and visits to the racetrack with Prince Aly Khan, for whom Maxwell had long done unpaid public relations. It was, for Maria, an intoxicating but exhausting social triumph.

The hectic pace and a heavy schedule of concerts, coupled with Callas' lifelong problem of low blood pressure, left her at the end of her strength. When she traveled to her native Greece in late July to sing at the Herodes Atticus Theater, below the Acropolis, she found herself greeted with controversy. She had offered to perform for free, but the directors of the festival took offense and told her they were capable of paying her a proper fee, whereupon her husband asked for the same amount Callas had received from the Met. Opponents of the then Greek government denounced this as excessive. Depleted and frightened, Maria vacillated, and in the end she canceled her performance only an hour before curtain time, driving her fellow Greeks into a rage. Five days later, on August 5, she finally sang in the ancient theater at the foot of the Acropolis and was a great success, but she returned to her home in Milan near collapse. She was determined to perform with La Scala at the Edinburgh Festival, beginning August 19, despite her doctor's advising against it.

Elsa Maxwell was planning a ball in Maria's honor in Venice immediately after her last performance at Edinburgh. Although unwell, the diva sang Bellini's *Sonnambula* four times in the cold, wet Scottish city. Then the director of La Scala, Antonio Ghiringhelli, decided to schedule a fifth performance, expecting that Maria would rage and protest but ultimately concede to appear. To his surprise, despite his pleas to "save La Scala," Maria simply left for Venice and Maxwell's ball. The British press blew up the episode into a front-page scandal as ANOTHER CALLAS WALK-OUT. Maxwell tried to praise Maria in her column, but only made things worse by writing: "I must precede this with an account of wonderful friendship shown by the great and only Maria Callas. I have had many presents in my life, beautiful gifts from rich and important people, but I have never had any star give up a performance in an opera house because she felt she was breaking her word to her friend." The besotted journalist's rhapsodizing succeeded only in further damaging the reputation of her beloved, because it implied that Maria had indeed walked out on a prior commitment in order to be with Maxwell, when the truth was that she had not agreed to a fifth performance.

In Venice, Maria appeared at Maxwell's ball wearing a gown with a tight black bodice, a white satin cummerbund, and a voluminous skirt of white polka-dotted satin. Her arms were encased in long black gloves. The guests were expected to come in some kind of fantasy headdress, and they had taxed their imaginations trying to outdo one another. One *comtesse* created a balloon, enveloping herself in a striped paper sphere, and the marquise de Cadava (at the time the first lady of Portugal) managed to construct on top of her head a miniature Venetian campanile. Elsa Maxwell looked like some sort of medieval gnome in an embroidered lace dress, mink stole, and pointed fifteenth-century doge's cap. Princess Forta Ruspoli was unrecognizable as a white Persian cat and won second prize for her costume. The white feathered headdress of Tina Onassis stretched like an egret's crest two feet high, but was not spectacular enough to win her the first prize of a brooch, which went to Baroness La Monaco, who, according to Elsa Maxwell, came as "an elderly bride with a great nose: she was quite the funniest and best thing I have ever seen."

*Callas with her social champion and hostess, Elsa Maxwell, at the
Hotel Danieli the night Maria first met Aristotle Onassis*

In comparison, Maria was dressed simply, but she still managed a nod
to the theme of the evening by twining her necklace of large teardrop emeralds into her upswept hair (although by the end an emerald had been lost
and found and the necklace was back around her neck).

Around 5 a.m., after a breakfast of spaghetti was served, Elsa played
the piano as Maria sat casually on the platform nearby, her arms clasping
her knees as she hummed along to "Stormy Weather." Maxwell was beside
herself. She wrote in her column: "It seems immodest, but frankly, I have
never given a better dinner and ball in my life. It had a flare of such joy and

happiness. Even two princesses who hated each other were found exchanging smiles, while another comtesse who couldn't remain in the same room with Merle Oberon stayed until 5 a.m."

Maxwell's self-congratulations about the magic of her party, the friendships and reconciliations it engendered, omitted the most significant and ultimately the most notorious friendship that began there. On that night of Tuesday, September 3, 1957, in the Hotel Danieli in Venice, Elsa Maxwell introduced, as she said, the "two most famous living Greeks in the world": Aristotle Onassis, then fifty-three, and Maria Callas, thirty-three.

Their acquaintance began inconspicuously enough. Onassis found a seat next to Maria and engaged her in conversation; soon thereafter his twenty-eight-year-old wife, Tina, in her jeweled and feathered headdress, joined them.

Though there is no record of exactly what was said when Maxwell introduced them, based on the common threads of what Onassis and Callas later told friends, it is possible to weave an account of their first conversation. Maria was known for saying exactly what she thought, without any seasoning of tact or humor. After the introduction Onassis started speaking to her in rapid-fire, unaccented Greek. Surprised, Maria gazed at him and remarked, "Ah, I see you're not a *Tourkosporos,* like they say."

Onassis bristled at the insult—the word means "sperm of a Turk" and was often applied to Greek refugees from Anatolia by their mainland countrymen, who looked down on the wretched survivors crowding over their borders after the 1922 massacres of Greeks in Turkey. Heatedly, he began listing for Maria all the notable Greeks, from Homer to Herodotus, who like him had originated in Asia Minor.

Maria assured him that she wasn't trying to insult him, but was simply surprised, considering the international society he traveled in, that he was still so Greek.

"They can take me as I am, or take a walk," he retorted. "Can you imagine me acting like a *psefto-Anglos* [fake Brit] in a tight suit, like some shipping Greeks I know?" He cocked his head, threw out his chest, and pursed his lips to impersonate the affected manners of a would-be English aristocrat, mercilessly evoking the overrefined manner and lisping speech of his rival, Stavros Niarchos. Maria couldn't help laughing at the imitation.

"No, you'd better stay a Greek," she told him, while their fellow revelers wondered what these two, rattling on in their peculiar language, found so amusing. Meneghini, if he did try to eavesdrop, was helpless in anything but his native Italian. Tina Livanos Onassis was 100 percent Greek, but she had been born a British citizen and brought up like an American princess: she had attended boarding schools in England, Montreal, and Greenwich,

*A fishy snack is shared by Onassis and Callas during the first week
of their acquaintance, as Meneghini and Elsa Maxwell join in.*

Connecticut, and her family maintained homes in Oyster Bay on Long
Island, in London, and at the Plaza Hotel in Manhattan. She once said to
her friend Lady Caroline Townshend, "I learned to speak in England, think
in New York, and dress in Paris." Tina spoke serviceable Greek with an
American accent, but was much more comfortable in English or French.

Maria, on the other hand, like "Aristo," as she began to call him, could
swear with the ease and creativity of a Greek sailor when her temper flared.
From their first encounter in the grand ballroom of the Hotel Danieli, the
two famous Greeks began to discover that they had much more in common
than just a language.

Later Maria told Korinna Spanidou, a physical therapist for the couple,
who became a friend as well, "Even if my path and Aristo's divide, there will
always be mutual respect between us. We have the same roots. We are
Greeks—the same stubborn race. We started from zero and reached the top
only thanks to our own will and our own abilities. We do not reflect others'
light; we radiate our own."

Their meeting was congenial, and no one thought anything of it when Onassis offered to put his motorboat and two crewmen at Maria's disposal for the rest of her stay in Venice. For the next few days of what Elsa Maxwell dubbed "Callas Week," Maria and her husband were seen everywhere in the company of Onassis and his wife—attending another all-night ball (this one given by Count Volpi), drinking at Harry's Bar, dining at Florian's, strolling on the Lido with the Henry Fondas, having cocktails on the yacht *Christina*.

In the same column trumpeting the success of her fabulous ball and the ensuing social activities of "Callas Week," Elsa Maxwell described how she and the Meneghinis had been invited aboard the *Christina* (which she spelled *Cristina*). She described Onassis with considerable naiveté:

> *I can't tell you how fond I have grown of Aris (as we call him), good-looking and profound. He is a very interesting man, quiet, happy with a few friends, not socially ambitious at all, and I was delighted when he asked Maria Callas, her husband Battista and me to go on a cruise next year to Greece. We accepted at once. . . . He is a great guy. I think he knows me better than most anybody else. It is nice to feel you are understood by a man like Onassis. His wife Tina, the gayest, blondest, cutest thing in the world, he regards as his baby. He says, "She's my baby doll. I love her." What more could any girl ask for?*

When photographs of these revels appeared in the tabloids, the British were enraged at La Callas for having fled chilly Edinburgh and her starring role in *La Sonnambula* to sing "Stormy Weather" and sip Bellini cocktails in Venice with the likes of Elsa Maxwell and Aristotle Onassis. But at that time, no one suspected that the seeds had been sown for a love affair that would ultimately shatter the lives of all those taking their ease in the warm Venetian sun on the deck of the *Christina*.

3

THE RULES OF THE GAME

Love is not to be purchased
And affection has no price.

St. Jerome, Letter 3

Aristotle Socrates Onassis married Athina "Tina" Livanos, younger daugh-
ter of Stavros Livanos, the patriarch of the Greek shipping world, in New
York on December 28, 1946, when she was only seventeen years old and
Onassis was forty-two (although he maintained he was forty). The *New York
Daily News* reported the event under the headline MAGNATE'S DAUGHTER
DROPS DEBUT IN FAVOR OF MARRIAGE, noting that the "strikingly hand-
some" bride "had planned a December debut—the . . . notion thrown into
the discard by yesterday's ceremony."

The wedding took place in the Greek Orthodox Cathedral of Holy
Trinity on East Seventy-fourth Street with Archbishop Athenagoras, the
primate of the Greek Orthodox church in the Americas, personally officiat-
ing. The reception was held in the Terrace Room of the Plaza Hotel, where
the bride's parents maintained one of their many residences. Tina's older
sister, Eugenia, was the maid of honor, and seated nearby, looking very
British in his well-tailored cutaway, was Onassis' rival, the rising Greek
shipowner Stavros Niarchos, then thirty-seven.

Livanos was at first outraged when Onassis asked for his younger
daughter's hand, since it was Greek tradition—and his intention—to marry
off his older daughter first. But Onassis liked nothing better than a challenge, and the lively blond teenage daughter of the prominent shipowner
appealed to him more than her quiet brunet sister, Eugenia. When he first
stated his intentions and Livanos grumbled, citing custom, Onassis replied

Union of two Greek shipping dynasties, old (Livanos) and new (Onassis),
at the Plaza Hotel, December 28, 1946

blithely, "Your daughters aren't ships, Mr. Livanos. You don't dispose of the first of the line first." Then he added his lifetime motto: "The only rules are that there are no rules."

There followed a year of intense and flattering courtship by Onassis. (He even attached a streamer reading T.I.L.Y—for "Tina I Love You"—to trail behind his boat as he sped by the family's Oyster Bay mansion.) Livanos was besieged by all the pleading and tears of a teenaged daughter who found the middle-aged Onassis dangerous and exciting. Eventually the father grudgingly gave his blessing to the marriage. The dowry he furnished his daughter was a Liberty ship (less a prize than it seemed, because it carried an outstanding $400,000 mortgage) and a town house at 16 Sutton Square, situated in the exclusive East Side neighborhood favored by the shipping Greeks. Tina said some time later, "Greek marriages are not infrequently arranged. It would have been the usual thing in my case, too. But my marriage to Ari was 'arranged' only by Eros, the god of love."

Livanos was somewhat appeased a year later when Stavros Niarchos asked for the hand of the elder daughter, Eugenia. The marriage of Livanos' two daughters to Onassis and Niarchos may not have been the matches he would have preferred—he considered both men publicity-seeking arrivistes—but he recognized that the alliances were very good business deals, linking three of the largest shipping fleets in Greek or any other hands.

In marrying Tina, Onassis gained entry into the traditional Greek shipping fraternity, which had regarded him with suspicion ever since he purchased his first ships fourteen years earlier. Having made his first millions in Argentina by importing tobacco, he noticed that the shipowners who brought the tobacco to him made more money carrying it than he did selling it. Onassis decided to study the shipping business.

His first opportunity to break into the business came in 1932 when he learned that the Canadian National Steamship Company was forced to lay up ten freighters. He bought six of them at $30,000 each—essentially their scrap value—and kept them working throughout the Depression. As it abated, he recognized the growing demand for oil, and began building new tankers in Sweden. When World War II began, Onassis had the largest tanker fleet afloat, but neutral Sweden seized two thirds of his ships and held them for the duration of the war. At first furious, Onassis turned out to be lucky, because his ships were not subjected to attacks at sea, which decimated the fleets of other Greek shipowners.

After the war, the established owners used the upstart tycoon's lack of wartime losses as an excuse to cut him out of the distribution of ninety-eight surplus Liberty ships that the U.S. Maritime Commission allocated to Greece. The seven-thousand-ton freighters were offered at the bargain price of $125,000 each and were financed with loans guaranteed by the Greek government. Onassis exploded and sent a blistering letter to the Greek Shipowners Association.

"I began from zero, without being the offspring of a shipowner," he wrote. "I worked and succeeded without exploiting either the name, or the flag, or the guarantee of the Greek people and I am proud of that." By contrast, he charged, the established shipowners were making huge profits "with the signature of all the Greek women and children dressed in rags, and without paying one penny," and were buying new ships under foreign flags with the money while their countrymen went hungry. "You owe everything—all—to the nation, which owes you nothing and moreover has treated you with scandalous favor." (His outrage was not mere pique at being cut out of the windfall. Throughout his life Onassis demonstrated a strong attachment to Greece, and he became one of the first shipowners to make major investments in the country after the war.)

Onassis' attack did not seem to bother his father-in-law, Stavros Livanos, who received twelve Liberty ships, nor Tina, who took no interest in the controversy.

There's no doubt that Onassis came to love his pampered and rather frivolous young bride, whom he called "my baby doll." Until they divorced, after thirteen years of marriage, he often liked to say that he had three children: his son, his daughter, and Tina, who until her death in 1974 at the age of forty-five maintained a girlish, even childlike quality. But for Aristotle Onassis, the marriage to Tina was calculated foremost as a deal—a triumphant incursion into the snobbish Greek shipping establishment, which had scorned him at every opportunity. On his wedding day Onassis, with typical Greek chauvinism, considered his seventeen-year-old bride to be clay that he would mold into the perfect consort for a rising entrepreneur.

Tina would not disappoint this ambition. Blithe and model-thin, well schooled in fashion and the social graces, she proved to be with no self-consciousness the perfect hostess and trophy wife. She loved to shop and to ski, and followed the social whirl from London to Paris to Rome to New York, moving with the seasons. Although she was not as successful as a mother as she was in society, she did soon produce, on April 30, 1948, the all-important son and heir.

In spite of Greek tradition, which calls for naming a firstborn son after one's father, Onassis called the boy not Socrates but Alexander, for one of his favorite uncles who was hanged by the Turks in 1922. "He didn't slight our father, because he gave him Socrates as a middle name," Aristotle's middle sister, Merope, told me. "He wanted the boy to have the same initials as he did, A.S.O., which was the name of the holding company for all his operations. The initials spell out the Greek word for 'ace,' the top of the deck, which is how he thought of himself and wanted his son to be too."

In evolving his dynastic mythology, Onassis also took pride in possessing and giving to his son the Greek initials alpha and omega. He often cited Revelation 22:13—"I am Alpha and Omega, the beginning and the end, the first and the last." These intertwined letters, a symbol of God, are found in every Greek Orthodox church, and one of his childhood friends told me that when Aristotle was a boy in Smyrna, the other boys used to joke: "Your father is so rich he's put your initials in all the churches." Alexander Onassis would indeed be the first and the last, but not in the manner his father had planned.

Tina became pregnant again in 1950. By then she was still only twenty-one. Some biographers report that she never wanted a second child. Tina herself told Reinaldo Herrera, who later became her lover, that it was Onassis who didn't desire another child, as it would have compelled him to divide his fortune. He wanted it all for Alexander, who was adored by both his parents. Tina told Herrera that Onassis beat her when he found out that she was pregnant again. Her brother, George Livanos, rejects this, however. "It's not true that Onassis didn't want a second child," he told me, echoing the words of the Onassis family friend Lilika Papanikolaou. "He was very happy when Christina was born." Livanos also denied that Onassis was

Daddy O: Alexander on Onassis' left knee, Christina with her legs on his shoulders, and his favorite niece, Marilena Patronikola, on his right knee

ever physically abusive to his sister: "No. Absolutely not. Mentally, maybe, but physically, no."

At the time of Tina's second pregnancy the couple was living on the French Riviera, but Onassis made arrangements for his wife to return to New York in time for the birth, on December 11, 1950, of a dark-eyed little girl. He wanted to make sure that both his children, unlike him, had American passports. Only American citizens were qualified to take advantage of the bargain-basement sale of used Liberty ships then being conducted by the U.S. government, and Onassis wanted to be able to pass on to his children controlling interest in the company he had set up with American fronts to buy seven of the cheap vessels.

Again Onassis ignored Greek tradition in not naming his daughter after his mother, Penelope. This time the reason, according to relatives, was that both his mother and his eldest niece, who was named after her, had had difficult lives and died young. Onassis, being deeply superstitious, didn't want to give his daughter a name that had been unlucky for his family. He later told Greta Garbo that he took the name Christina for his daughter from Garbo's film *Queen Christina,* which he saw while he was in Sweden to place an order for his first new ship. That order proved very fortunate, he said, and he wanted his daughter to have a name associated with good luck. The name did not finally prove auspicious, however, for Christina Onassis would die suddenly at thirty-seven, only four years older than her unfortunate grandmother Penelope had been.

Tina, like Ari, favored her son over the sad-eyed little girl who had inherited her father's dark, Levantine looks and none of her mother's fair-haired beauty. But in either case, nursing babies and staying home was not the way Tina intended to spend the remainder of her youth, and the children were brought up by an array of nannies, tutors, and servants under the supervision of Ari's older sister, Artemis, who focused all her maternal affection on her nephew and niece after her only daughter's death.

In 1953, looking for a centrally located base of operations with a promising fiscal climate and a benevolent tax situation, Onassis acquired a controlling interest in Monaco's Société des Bains de Mer et Cercle des Etrangers (SBM for short), which controlled most of Monte Carlo, including the casino, the Hôtel de Paris, and the famous gardens. His initial stake cost him three million dollars—about the price of one of his tankers. When the newspapers dubbed Onassis "The Man Who Bought the Bank at Monte Carlo," Prince Rainier III did not complain. He knew his principality needed an infusion of new money, and indeed, Onassis quickly revitalized the playground of the international set. After Onassis took over the Old Sporting Club on the Avenue d'Ostende for the offices of his shipping company, Olympic Maritime, and his own private living quarters, Prince Rainier would often dine with him or go sailing on his yacht, and the two remained friends until they fell out a decade later.

Onassis' coup in Monte Carlo aroused an envy among other Greek shipowners that had been building ever since he entered the business; it also provoked a heated row with Stavros Niarchos, his brother-in-law. Niarchos claimed that he had given Onassis money for an interest in SBM, but Onassis maintained that the funds were payment for expenses he had incurred in other business involvements with Niarchos. Eventually the dispute was arbitrated and Onassis paid his brother-in-law $132,428 to settle the matter, but Niarchos was hardly appeased and the already growing friction between the two tycoons intensified.

The rivalry between Onassis and Niarchos, once close friends, began as business one-upmanship, but soon after Ari and Tina's wedding it became intensely personal as well. In the early days Onassis said of Niarchos, "In business, we cut each other's throats, but now and then we sit around the same table and behave—for the sake of the ladies."

There are many theories as to why Onassis' hatred of Niarchos became so bitter. Some say that Tina mischievously fanned the flames by telling her sometimes indifferent husband that Niarchos flirted with her, or worse. Others report that Onassis had originally wanted Eugenia for his bride, was rebuffed by her, and only then turned his attentions to Tina. The society columnist Doris Lilly holds with this theory and adds, in her book *Those Fabulous Greeks:* "Greek shipowners present [at Niarchos' wedding] were whispering among themselves that Onassis' absence had something to do with the dowry. And, in fact, it did. . . . Nobody knew how much Papa Livanos gave Eugenia. Nobody but Onassis, who was less than pleased that it was considerably more than his wife had received."

(Stavros Livanos was famously tight-fisted, as illustrated by an anecdote recounted to me by Reinaldo Herrera: "Once Tina and I were having lunch at Maxim's and her father, Stavros, was having lunch with J. Paul Getty, who was notoriously stingy too. Tina said to me, 'Watch, they'll each try to wait each other out so neither picks up the check.' About four o'clock she called over the waiter and told him to put their lunch on her tab, and she sent her father a note: 'Papa, you can both leave now. I've paid the bill.' ")

The old Greek shipping families are a secretive and proud fraternity. Their founders began as sailors and sea captains who played a major role in freeing Greece from four hundred years of Turkish occupation during the War of Independence in 1821. They are notoriously clannish and conservative, marrying among themselves and avoiding publicity at all costs.

Both Niarchos and Onassis were considered "nouveau" by these families, but Niarchos ranked slightly higher, coming from a marginally better background than the uneducated refugee from Turkey. Stavros Niarchos was the son of a prosperous Greek couple who owned a small restaurant and ice cream parlor in Buffalo, New York, until they returned to Greece only four months before his birth on July 3, 1909. Stavros was educated as a lawyer at the University of Athens and after graduation went to work for his uncle's flour-milling company. In 1935, when the harbor of Piraeus was clogged with idle ships as a result of the worldwide depression, Stavros persuaded his uncles to buy some of the vessels to carry grain from Argentina and thus cut the company's freight bills. Within a year, he started his own shipping firm.

Whereas Onassis was known for his personal charm and sense of humor, Niarchos was notoriously humorless and formal. He had a speech impediment that sounded like a lisp, and his conversation, sprinkled with phrases like "old chap," sounded affected even for a Briton, which he was not.

Both Onassis and Niarchos introduced profitable innovations to the shipping business, including the building of supertankers (Onassis) and the practice of arranging long-term charters with oil companies, then using these contracts as collateral to borrow money to buy the ships to fulfill the contracts. As their fortunes grew, so did their competitive megalomania. Niarchos bought the world's largest privately owned sailing vessel, the *Creole*. Onassis converted a frigate into the *Christina*, the "world's most luxurious yacht." Niarchos assembled a priceless art collection that included an El Greco, and so did Onassis (although the *Madonna and Angel* that hung so prominently on his yacht was either a copy or from El Greco's school, as the yacht's captain, Kostas Anastasiades, learned from Onassis himself). Both filled their homes with celebrities like Greta Garbo and Aly Khan, the Windsors and Elsa Maxwell. Both built more and better supertankers and both became major investors in their homeland. Niarchos won the concession to build Greece's first shipyard; Onassis won the national airline, which he turned into the profitable Olympic Airways.

The feud reached its height in early 1954 when Onassis managed to negotiate the biggest deal in the history of shipping. Using intermediaries with close ties to the royal family of Saudi Arabia, he signed an agreement with the Saudi government that gave him first option to transport all the petroleum produced annually in the Middle East (then some forty-two million tons) by the Arabian American Oil Company (ARAMCO). It was immediately opposed by ARAMCO executives, most European countries with major interests in Middle East oil, and other shipowners with tanker fleets, including Niarchos. He took the lead in the international effort to scuttle the deal, calling it "a political crime and economic monstrosity," and hired a former FBI agent, Robert Maheu, to prove the rumor that Onassis had bribed high officials in the Saudi government.

Maheu, who later became a top aide to Howard Hughes and participated in CIA plots to assassinate Fidel Castro, set up investigative teams with the CIA in New York, Athens, Rome, and Saudi Arabia, and they employed all conceivable means, including unauthorized electronic surveillance of the Onassis apartment at the Pierre Hotel in Manhattan, to monitor every move the shipowner made. Eventually Maheu found a Greek friend of Onassis' who charged that the tycoon had agreed to pay one million dollars to the brother of the Saudi finance minister plus a bonus for every ton of oil shipped on Onassis tankers, but this "friend" was unable to provide documentation. Maheu tried to leak the story to several European newspapers anyway, but they refused to publish it without evidence. He then approached the Athens daily, *Ethnos,* which printed the allegations.

Other newspapers picked up the report, now that they could attribute it, and shortly afterward, King Saud met with ARAMCO executives to terminate the entire agreement with Onassis. The collapse of the deal cost Onassis several billion dollars in potential profits, and he never forgave Niarchos for it. Onassis, however, would ultimately trump his rival as a shipping visionary when Lloyd's List, the bible of the industry, selected him posthumously as Man of the Century.

In the course of building vast real estate holdings, Onassis and Niarchos both bought homes in Manhattan, St. Moritz, Paris, Athens, and London, on Long Island, and on the Riviera. The race never ended. When Onassis rented the sumptuous Château de la Croë in Cap d'Antibes, with its two dozen servants, twenty-five acres of land, tennis courts, and a drawing room with a retractable roof to allow for indoor sunbathing, Niarchos rented the slightly less sumptuous Château de la Garoupe nearby. But he would not have to suffer the lesser accommodations for long.

Tina was basking in the sun at the Hôtel Eden Roc in Cap d'Antibes when she was recognized by an old school chum, Jeanne-Marie Rhinelander. They renewed their friendship and Jeanne helped Tina pass the many days and nights when Ari was far away. But when Tina impulsively drove to her friend's home one afternoon to complain yet again about her absent husband, she was chagrined to discover him there in Jeanne's arms. A few months later, when the Château de la Croë came up for sale, in the spring of 1954, Tina told her husband that she would never live in it if he bought it; she was sick of Cap d'Antibes. As soon as the Onassis family left, Stavros Niarchos bought the estate and settled his growing family in.

Onassis was perfectly happy to move to a lavishly appointed apartment in Monte Carlo above his offices, since the principality was now his base of operations. Tina kept busy too, jetting to international watering spots. She was often photographed in the company of attractive men closer to her age than Ari, who almost never seemed to be on the same continent as his wife. After a time, that was fine with Tina, for she found his tendency to meld business with his personal life increasingly difficult to endure. "I don't like dining with somewhere between twenty and eighty people every night," she told her husband's insurance agent one evening. "This life is killing me."

"For the first five years of the marriage they were very happy together," Onassis' half sister Merope told me, "but then things started to unravel." Why did the marriage break down? "Onassis fooled around almost from the beginning," his lawyer and aide, Stelios Papadimitriou, says, echoing the general opinion of Onassis' friends as well as Tina's, "and when she found out about it, she repaid him in kind."

According to Peter Evans, whose biography of Onassis is one of the most detailed, a friend of the couple's was sitting near Tina at a dinner party when, somewhat in her cups, Tina remarked to the table at large about her marriage: "I think it's beastly that we still sleep together. It makes me feel soiled." Ari replied insouciantly, "We are all soiled. We live in a soiled society."

At dinner parties Onassis may have feigned indifference to his wife's infidelities, but like a typically macho Greek, he found the thought that she was cuckolding him insupportable. The fact that he himself had been cheating on Tina since the early months of their marriage, on the other hand, was considered perfectly normal in their world of rich Greeks, as long as he behaved discreetly. (One of his alleged amours in the first six months after his wedding was the first lady of Argentina, Eva Perón. They had an assignation on the Italian Riviera. When she personally cooked him an omelet, he gave her a donation of ten thousand dollars for her favorite charity and later commented that it was the "most expensive omelet I ever ate.")

In 1956, the twenty-seven-year-old Tina met Reinaldo Herrera, twenty-two, the scion of a prominent Venezuelan family, at a Rothschild ball in Paris and began an affair with him. Reinaldito, as his friends called him, was heir to a fortune in South American land holdings and a skilled skier (unlike Ari, who joked, "I do most of my skiing on my backside").

Tall, slender, and boyish, Reinaldo Herrera was endowed with qualities that cannot be acquired, only inherited: easy cosmopolitan charm, sultry good looks, and a pedigree that stretched back to the sixteenth century. He was born in Venezuela and attended the exclusive St. Mark's school in Massachusetts, then Harvard and Georgetown, but owing to his mischievous escapades he never graduated from college, as he told me when I interviewed him in his Manhattan townhouse in early 1999. "I did horrendous things, like bringing a horse to class one day. Then I got a very high paying job as an intern at Standard Oil, and the moment 1 came into my trust at twenty-one, I sent them a wire and resigned."

Reinaldo first met Tina Onassis at the coming-out party for Alain Rothschild's daughter Beatrice in Paris in 1956. "Tina was there alone," he told me. "Ari at the time was in Monte Carlo, I think. She said to me, I remember distinctly, 'Are you going to Aly Khan's party tomorrow? . . . Why don't we go together?' " At the time, Herrera said, he was engaged to a French girl and Tina was having an affair with the Dominican diplomat and playboy Porfirio Rubirosa. After Tina refused to leave Ari and marry Rubirosa, according to Herrera, he married another heiress: Barbara Hutton.

It was after the Rubirosa-Hutton marriage that Tina and Reinaldo began their affair. "This was in the summer of 1956," Reinaldo told me. "I went to Monte Carlo and we saw each other at various social events. And that's where it started. I was staying at the Hermitage. Then she left for one of those cruises. I met Ari. Ari knew my father. He was very charming. More than charming! He invited us on the boat and we went on small cruises. Garbo was there. Then I went off to Venice, but we made a date that Tina would maneuver the boat to come to Venice. I was staying at my friend Marina Cicogna's house on the Grand Canal, and one morning I heard this enormous noise outside and there was the boat, right in front of the window. When anyone is in love, you find opportunities. Then I got on the boat in Venice and went back to Monte Carlo. . . . We tacitly understood we were going to be together. We were together so much, people invited us to things as a couple."

Reinaldo's family initially thought the affair with Tina was only "a fling that would pass," but by the end of 1957 "Tina and I wanted to marry, and she told me, 'You've got to talk to my family,' so we went to Stavros Niarchos' apartment in Sutton Square. Eugénie [Tina's sister and Niarchos' wife] was there and so was Mrs. Livanos. I told them I was in love with Tina and wanted to marry her. Surprisingly, there was no Greek chorus. They took it much better than I thought. They were concerned about the children, of course, but they knew we loved each other, which we did. . . . After the meeting in New York, Tina went to Ari and told him, 'I want a divorce. I want to get married to Reinaldo.' He paid no attention: 'You can do what you want, but I'll never give you a divorce.'

"From that moment on I was followed everywhere," Herrera continued. "I remember once I was at Dunhill in New York. Tina had just given me an antique Fabergé picture frame of green enamel and gold, with a photo of the two of us in it. I set it down somewhere to greet Peter Duchin. When I turned around to pick it up, it was gone. I thought someone had stolen it, but later Ari made a scene with Tina and showed it to her."

The affair between Tina and Herrera continued in this uneasy limbo while the couple endured pressure from their increasingly disapproving parents. Tina grudgingly reconciled herself to keeping up appearances as a gracious wife, just as she had been taught to do all her life. Even if she felt more English and American than Greek, she did, after all, have two very Greek parents and she knew that her marriage and her welfare were based on a system of money and ships—and a double standard for wives. She would continue to be the charming chatelaine of her husband's empire.

This was the far-from-idyllic situation in the Onassis marriage when Elsa Maxwell introduced the couple to Maria Callas and cooed to the readers of her gossip column about "Ari's" loving sentiments toward his "baby doll," inquiring coyly: "What more could any girl ask for?"

4

LIFE AT THE TOP

Before the gates of excellence,
the high gods have placed toil,
Long is the road thereto
and rough and steep.

Hesiod, *Works and Days*

On the day in 1957 when they were introduced, Maria Callas, like Onassis, appeared to be at the pinnacle of her life, both professionally and personally. She was the most admired star in her field, known even to those who had never seen an opera. She drew throngs of fans who worshiped her as a near deity and lined up for days to obtain tickets to her performances. Through determination and the help of Elsa Maxwell she had become the darling of international society, and she enjoyed the total devotion of her husband, who seemed to spend every waking moment promoting her and looking after her welfare.

During the two years after she met Onassis, however, every aspect of Callas' life, from her triumphant career to her seemingly idyllic marriage to her friendship with Elsa Maxwell, would unravel, leaving her emotionally vulnerable and questioning everything that had seemed important to her during the first three decades of her life.

In September of 1957, citing doctor's orders, Maria canceled a performance that was to open the San Francisco Opera season, though she promised to honor her appearances scheduled there in October. Furious, the director, Kurt Adler, canceled all her appearances in San Francisco and took her to court.

In November, Maria appeared at a benefit concert in Texas that inaugurated the Dallas Civic Opera Company. Among the socialites in the audience was a tall, striking brunette named Mary Reed. She had been introduced to Callas by mutual friends and would become one of the diva's closest confidantes, so much so that their circle would dub her "Maria Seconda."

Because she was scheduled to attend a meeting of the exclusive Hesitation Club, Mary Reed (now Mary Carter) barely got to the theater in time to hear Maria's final aria, the tower scene from *Anna Bolena,* which Callas sang wearing a stunning black velvet dress. "The concert, which was held at the State Fair Music Hall, was not well attended," she told me. "In fact, Elsa Maxwell bought a bunch of tickets to paper the house but there were still a lot of empty seats. The joke was that no one should try to compete with the meeting of the Hesitation Club, which was then the most prestigious social club in the city."

The two Marias first got to know each other over lunch at the old Dallas airport, Love Field, as Callas was about to leave the city. "Callas' husband, Meneghini, was with her," Mary Carter recalls, "and he was rattling away in Italian, but that didn't stop us from hitting it off immediately. It was as if we had known each other in another lifetime.

"I saw Maria constantly and the more I saw her the more I got to like her," Mary Carter told me when I first interviewed her in 1998 in her Manhattan apartment. "She was the opposite of her image: considerate, unpretentious, and the most totally honest person I had ever known. She would discuss bodily functions openly and graphically and would tell you honestly, but without any meanness at all, if some dress you were wearing did not become you or if your hair was combed in an unflattering way. Once I got a very expensive dress by Dior and she told me, 'Mary, you must never wear that dress again. It makes you look pregnant.' She was, of course, absolutely right. She was a Sagittarian and they're always very blunt."

While Maria Callas and Mary Reed were getting acquainted in the Dallas airport, Elsa Maxwell arrived just as the plane was about to depart. On this flight to New York, the rather one-sided relationship between the seventy-four-year-old gossip columnist and the thirty-four-year-old diva dissolved in a contretemps. Maria refused to speak to Maxwell during the entire journey—a rejection that caught the attention of the cabin crew and was promptly leaked to the newspapers. This falling out took place only two months after Maxwell introduced Maria to Onassis in Venice and less than a year after Maria had first charmed Elsa at the Hellenic Ball in New York.

Although no one has explained the exact catalyst for the dispute, there is strong evidence that it stemmed from Maria's rebuffing Elsa's sexual overtures. The nature of the argument is made clear in a remarkable and emotional "farewell letter" that Maxwell wrote to Maria on December 15, 1957, shortly after the flight from Dallas. In *My Wife Maria Callas,* Meneghini quotes parts of this letter, but his condensed version leaves out several significant details, and having been translated from English into Italian and then back into English, it alters Maxwell's dramatic, helter-skelter style—as well as nearly every word she used. She handwrote the eight pages at frantic speed on Waldorf-Astoria stationery, in a single paragraph, separating sentences with dashes and underlining some words several times for emphasis.

Meneghini, who handled not only his wife's financial affairs but also her correspondence, writes that shortly after the flight from Dallas, Maxwell cabled him from New York saying, "Tell Maria that if *Time* magazine asks if our friendship ended in Dallas, as they asked me, she should deny everything categorically, as I did." Then, shortly before Christmas, Maria received Maxwell's letter, a copy of which I have obtained. It is a fascinating fabric of self-pity, boasting, veiled threats, and the anguished recriminations of a brokenhearted lover.

Maria

As Xmas is just around the corner, when "Peace on earth and good will" should be our guiding thought—I had to write you to thank you for having been the innocent victim of the greatest love one human being could feel for another—Some day perhaps we both shall understand that love and remember it with regret or joy! Who knows—it exists no longer—I had managed to *kill* it—or rather you have helped me to kill it—still born and beautiful as it was it—it brought no happiness to you and after a few wonderful weeks it brought only misery to me. Your role in life (to me) is on the stage—I don't care now if I ever see you again—except on the stage where you—a genius, can portray parts never attempted before by mediocre mortals. You killed my love that day on the plane from Dallas—and that's where this story started because the station master in seating me he said "Your friend Miss Callas will be near you"—"My friend Miss Callas" never spoke to me for five hours and that showed me very plainly where I stood with you— . . . altho I think once or twice I *nearly* touched your heart—but that I could have fallen with such a supreme state of madness and insanity now fills me with self disgust—I don't blame you in the least except that you could have stopped it before it was too late—Now that's completely forgotten and a thing of the past—when we meet we must be amiable and kind to each other or the world will *wonder*—I have kept my promise to you—I have been your greatest champion and will continue to be so—I have fought your enemies (but Maria how many you have and all now with only one thought—to part us completely) but as long as you are that miracle to me on the stage and as long as I can listen and see you—no human being can take you away from me—This had to be said—When I arrived in Dallas, Miss Miller called me up that evening and told me what I already suspected—that your concert was only 50% sold—no tickets were moving at all and it looked as if you would sing to a half empty house—She asked me *despairingly* what could I do? So all the day before I talked Callas, Callas on radio—T.V.—and interviews—that I could easily do for I *loved you*—it is not difficult to speak of one's beloved—it's only hard *not* to—that night nothing had happened so I suggested that I buy $2000 worth of tickets—to be distributed to those who loved opera—students—teachers, music colleges . . . —I claim no credit—I am a free agent and if I choose to buy tickets for *any* artist that is my affair. . . . But *you* were the only one I wished never to hear it (it's really nothing at all) but with your Greek dramatic sense which predominates your entire being you might even resent *any* thing I did in Dallas—even my buying a few seats to fill a huge unsympathetic auditorium—it was my duty to you to do so—and you were so *wonderful* that night—I only tell you this because someone else might— Another thing you might hear. . . . I will be in Rome for your opening in Norma—do not think I am coming just to see you—I am not—The Duchess of Windsor suggested that I fly over and stay with them from Dec. 27th until the 1st— . . . I shall fly to Rome on the 2nd to see Norma (oh you had better be *good*—for I am now in such a state of detachment that no past or present friendship would allow me to lose my integrity as a critic—but somehow I know you will be—. . . . You will never again have your *Elsa* to worry about—I will probably *not* see you while in Rome—you will be busy and so will I—making plans for the end of April when I arrive—if you are singing Anna Bolena—I will come to Milano—if not I won't. But your Traviata will amaze them. . . . Traviata is almost sold out already—I have given several interviews—one especially good to Cosmopolitan Magazine about you—after the editor promised to publish *exactly* what I wrote— Everywhere I *say* and reiterate that we have only known each other a few weeks here and there—and you are *not* for friendships or *any* attachments except your husband—This is now quite clear—it makes it easier for us both—I send you and Battista my best always with Xmas greetings and for the New Year—I think of you always with kindness and tenderness Maria— may you keep well may you sing beautifully and may God always bless you

Elsa

Maria was to welcome the new year by performing at the Rome Opera House on January 2, 1958, in her signature role as the heroine in Bellini's

Norma. This was the performance Maxwell had referred to ominously when she said: "Oh you had better be good—for I am now in such a state of detachment that no past or present friendship would allow me to lose my integrity as a critic." Two nights earlier, on New Year's Eve, Maria had sung *Casta Diva* on Italian television and then stayed up until the early morning hours, drinking champagne in an exclusive Roman nightclub. Many of her fans blamed this partying for the loss of voice that led to her disgrace and the most infamous walkout of her career.

When she woke up on New Year's Day, Maria could only whisper. She asked to be replaced in *Norma.* The artistic director refused—the house was sold out for the gala opening and the president of Italy and everyone else who counted in Roman society was to be there. Surely she could do something to bring her voice back, he insisted.

Despite Elsa Maxwell's protestations that Maria would probably not see her in Rome, she was among the worried supporters backstage who helped Callas spray her throat, put hot compresses on her chest, dose herself with medicines, and pray before the beloved icon of the Virgin Mary that accompanied her everywhere she went.

At curtain time, Maria, in despair, went on stage and forced her voice, shouting her way through the first act. The curtain went down on an astonished audience booing and screaming, "Go back to Milan." The diva collapsed in her dressing room, supported by her husband and entourage, and refused to return for the second act. Everyone pleaded with her. Someone even suggested that she go out and simply declaim her lines, without trying to sing. She had to do something! After all, the audience was beginning to whistle impatiently and the president was waiting in the royal box.

Finally, after an agonizing hour during which the president and his party got up and left, Maria escaped the furious crowd through an underground tunnel to the Hotel Quirinale. The mob shouted curses under her windows late into the night. (Elsa Maxwell scolded the angry crowd, and as usual she only made things worse while pretending to help. "You Romans are still behaving like your barbarian ancestors," she admonished them. "Can't you understand that Mme. Callas is ill? Of course, she had no business staying up late in nightclubs before an important performance.") Ultimately Maria was denounced in the Italian parliament and banned from singing the remaining performances in her Rome contract.

Meneghini filed suit against the Rome Opera for breach of contract. Fourteen years later, the Italian Supreme Court of Appeals found Maria innocent of responsibility and ordered the Rome Opera to pay damages. Maria was vindicated, but too late to repair the damage to her reputation. The episode established a pattern that followed her throughout her career.

On numerous occasions, convinced she had been misused and betrayed, Callas sued directors, institutions, journalists, business associates, managers, agents, and colleagues, only to be vindicated by the courts so many years after the disagreement that it made no impact on her battered public image.

After days of hiding out in her room at the Hotel Quirinale, Maria appeared, looking like Joan Crawford in a somber suit, dark Persian lamb wrap, dramatic makeup, and a heavy veil. After running the gauntlet of reporters and photographers in the lobby, she fled the city.

This crisis—a kind of primal trauma in her career—weighed on Maria's mind for the rest of her life. Her worshipful audience had never before rejected her. "The public can be so cruel," she told her friend and aide, Nadia Stancioff, years later. "They only accept you when you are great. They have no mercy if you are not well and will neither forgive nor forget your failures." Maria had learned a bitter lesson.

After the Rome debacle, Callas traveled to the United States, where she performed to great acclaim in Chicago and at the Metropolitan Opera in New York, singing *Traviata, Lucia,* and *Tosca.* Despite the emotional Christmas letter of farewell, Elsa Maxwell was at her side constantly, leading her through the nightclubs and charity balls of the metropolis. It appeared that, after the drama in Dallas, the women had reached a compromise in their relationship. Though Maxwell might have hoped for more intimacy, she remained the social mentor and frequent companion to one of the world's most glamorous stars, and Maria tolerated Elsa's devotion in exchange for the support she received in Maxwell's influential column and for all the socially exclusive doors her protector opened to her.

Another friend who followed Maria to both cities to see her perform was Mary Carter, who flew in from Dallas. "I was very social then and she wasn't and she was intrigued by me and very interested in finding out about the whole social world," Mary Carter remembers. "In New York, I would go to some of the rehearsals and then we would have lunch. Guess where? At the Automat! She was fascinated by the Automat—how they prepared the food and put it in the little boxes and how they were able to charge so little for it. And she loved Woolworth's. Loved to buy little things: pencil holders and combs, and things like that. She sometimes talked to me about her husband, whom she respected, but was not crazy about: 'You know, Maria Seconda, periodically we have to perform our wifely duties.' She talked about Onassis in a much different way, later."

When Maria returned from the United States to Italy, she was still smarting from the disgrace of the Rome incident. She had become accustomed to being treated as a divinity, especially in Milan, where she and Battista had a villa on Via Buonarroti. "I love La Scala above all other theaters. I consider it my home," Maria often said. Young Milanese fans followed her everywhere, begging to carry out her personal errands. After each performance she would recline on a chaise in her dressing room and receive their homage. Then they would gather in a crowd under the portico to escort her from the theater to Milan's famous arcaded Galleria in the shadow of the Duomo, while her husband waddled along behind, carrying her flowers and collecting the names of fans who wanted autographed photos. When she arrived at Savini's, Milan's finest restaurant, Maria would turn and graciously acknowledge the crowd, who would cheer until she disappeared from sight.

To receive this kind of almost religious veneration every day in the streets of her city was both exhilarating and stressful for the woman who had once been the plump, bespectacled, unpopular Mary Anna Kalogeropoulos at P.S. 189 in Washington Heights. She would later confess to the Dallas music critic John Ardoin, who knew her well: "It's so tiring to be with people, because they all see me as a goddess, so I have to be a goddess for them." Amusing as this statement is, demonstrating Callas' total lack of humility, it also gives an insight into her character few of her biographers have noted: she did not enjoy being surrounded by fans and reporters except while performing. Off the stage, she was acutely shy and insecure, and she found it exhausting to have to perform as La Callas in public. "What you have to understand is that there were two sides to Maria—like two people sharing the same body," Ardoin said. "There was Maria and there was Callas. In fact, she talked about herself in the third person as Callas when she talked about singing. I think Maria was wildly jealous of Callas. Maria was fat, unattractive, unloved by her mother, with all kinds of problems, while Callas was thin, elegant, and adored by the world."

After the Rome scandal, some of the same Milanese who had idolized Maria turned viciously against her. She was scheduled to return to La Scala in *Anna Bolena* on April 9, but when she ran into Antonio Ghiringhelli, the manager of the opera house, outside his office in March, he cut her dead. On the opening night of *Anna Bolena* police officers patrolled the area outside the stage door and were seated throughout the audience to prevent violence. Although Maria sang brilliantly and earned "delirious applause," according to Meneghini, Ghiringhelli canceled a performance that was scheduled for April 12, when the Italian president was to be in town, and replaced *Anna Bolena* with another opera and cast. Nevertheless, each night she sang the role of the tragic queen, Maria challenged her listeners to judge her. In the third scene of the opera, when two guards seize the doomed Anne Boleyn, Callas screamed her defiance directly at the audience, glaring at her listeners and crying out: "Judges! For Anna! Judges!"

During the run of *Anna Bolena* at La Scala, Meneghini says, "At each performance . . . there was always someone who tried to create a disturbance, distracting the public with comments and vulgar expressions. Among the many bunches of flowers thrown on stage, there were radishes, tomatoes and other vegetables; one night there was even an old shoe." (Several witnesses, including the record producer Walter Legge, have said that when this sort of thing happened, Maria, "trading on her well-known myopia, sniffed each bunch as she picked it up; vegetables she threw into the orchestra pit, while flowers were graciously handed to her colleagues.")

Meneghini describes how the harassment in Milan escalated: "One evening, as we were getting into our car to go out to dinner, we found on Maria's seat the remains of a dead dog. Another night we were returning late after a performance of *Bolena*. As she touched the garden gate, Maria emitted a terrible scream. . . . The gate had been smeared with excrement. . . . The telephone rang at all hours with anonymous obscene calls and every day unsigned letters arrived with the most disgusting insults imaginable. We reported all this to Milan's chief of police, but we never received any satisfaction. We had purchased a villa at Sirmione at the end of 1957. Seeing that it was no longer possible to live in Milan, we moved to the villa."

Taking refuge at Sirmione on the tranquil lake, Maria prepared arduously for her next performance at La Scala, in Bellini's *Il Pirata,* opening on May 19, 1958. But the increasingly cold reception she got from Ghiringhelli and the audience eventually convinced her she had to leave La Scala for good. She decided that the May 31 performance in *Il Pirata* would be her last at the opera house she considered her home.

That night she extended her arm in the direction of Ghiringhelli's box as she sang in the mad scene, "There, see the fatal scaffold" (or theater box—the Italian word *palco* can mean either). She continued to sing and point menacingly at the director until he got up and left. At the end of the performance the audience would not let her go and gave her an ovation that lasted nearly half an hour, until Ghiringhelli, cutting off the emotional farewell, ordered the heavy metal fire curtain lowered while Callas was still on stage. According to Meneghini, "He then sent a fireman to tell Maria, 'By order of the theater, the stage must be cleared.' "

Maria later told *Life* magazine, "For my self-defense and dignity, I had no choice but to leave La Scala." Doing so was like pulling up her roots in opera, a kind of professional suicide. Maria had directed all her passion and tremendous self-discipline into her craft, and now she felt her audience had betrayed her. Slowly she was becoming ready to seek love and affirmation elsewhere.

In contrast to the hostility of Milan, nothing but adoration greeted Maria in London on June 10, 1958, when she appeared at the Royal Opera House in a concert gala and stole the spotlight from all the other stars as she sang the mad scene from Bellini's *I Puritani*. A week later she appeared on television, singing arias for the BBC audience. The reviews were ecstatic. But several days later, when her performance in *La Traviata* at the Royal Opera House was broadcast live, many critics mentioned deficiencies in her voice. These would worsen and continue to plague her during the coming year as her voice began to wobble out of control in the upper register.

This was not the first time Maria had lost control of her voice while reaching for high notes. Even at the beginning of her career, critics had noted a shrillness in her upper register, but by nearly superhuman effort she almost always managed to force her voice where it did not go easily. But now, after years of grueling performances, even her talent and will could not make her vocal cords behave.

The reason for the progressive deterioration of Callas' voice is a matter of continuing debate. Many blame it on her dramatic loss of weight. Others are convinced that Aristotle Onassis was the culprit, that his seductions distracted her from devoting herself to hours of practice as she had done every day since childhood. These may have been contributing factors, but it's clear that Maria was beginning to lose control in her upper register before she met Onassis, and she knew it.

The critic John Ardoin, who has devoted much of his professional life to studying Maria's performances and recordings and has written several scholarly books about her career, says: "There were basic physiologic flaws in her voice from the beginning that could never be overcome. She disguised them, she made them look like they were part of the singing and she did this by incredible willpower, by constant studying and work. For example, she had a lot of trouble sustaining a voice above a top C. B, B-flat, was no problem, but above that it was very difficult for her—the physiologic machinery just wasn't there. But she knew this, and she knew as she got older it would get even harder and harder for her to sustain her reputation."

Giulietta Simionato, a mezzo-soprano who was Callas' lifelong colleague and friend, spoke to me in Milan about Callas' voice and career. At one point she broke down in tears. Maria had once asked her with poignant directness why her voice should wobble beyond control. "I've already asked Hidalgo and others," Callas said. "Why does the natural and the flat always dance?" (The Spanish soprano Elvira de Hidalgo was Maria's most influential teacher. Working in Athens to escape the civil war in her homeland, she had recognized Callas' gifts and taken her under her wing when Callas was only fifteen.)

Simionato's answer was that Maria had not conserved her voice in her youth. "I told her, 'You sang strong operas, like *Cavalleria* and *Tosca,* but you needed to sing, not yell.' But the poor girl, inexperienced, yelled. You could see that she had injured the diaphragm to a certain point that she couldn't sustain her breath. The diaphragm is a muscle, like an elastic. Forcing this muscle, she had totally impoverished it. There was no more elasticity. And so that note, the 'natural' and the 'flat,' danced, because the diaphragm could no longer support it. When you lose the elasticity, there is nothing more you can do. Neither rest nor study. Nothing. 'You have sung many operas too strongly,' I told her, 'and not only that, you were too young!' She protested, 'But it was necessary! My mother made me do it and I obeyed.' "

After resting at her country home in Sirmione through the summer of 1958, Maria flew to London for two weeks of recording and then to the United States for a series of concert performances in North American cities, including Birmingham, Atlanta, Montreal, Toronto, Cleveland, Detroit, Washington, D.C., San Francisco, Los Angeles, and St. Louis. She interrupted the concert series to give two performances of *Traviata* at the State Fair Music Hall in Dallas on October 31 and November 2. As she toured, Maria waited to hear what roles the Metropolitan Opera in New York wanted from her in the coming year.

The Met's director, Rudolf Bing, sent her a congratulatory telegram on the opening night of her Dallas performance of *Traviata,* a Franco Zeffirelli production that thrilled an audience of four thousand Texans, including Mary Reed Carter. After *Traviata,* Maria started to rehearse *Medea* in Dallas. The director was Alexis Minotis, a leading actor and director with the Greek National Theater who had played minor roles in several Hollywood films (the butler in *Notorious,* for instance) while in exile in the United States during World War II.

Minotis often told the story of how astonished he was to see Maria, at a critical moment in rehearsal, fall to her knees and pound on the floor in a frenzy. "What are you doing?" he asked her. "Don't you like it?" she asked. Minotis replied, "I was going to tell you to do exactly that, because that is what the ancient Greeks did to call on the gods. How did you know?" Maria responded, "I didn't know, I just did it because it felt right at this moment." John Ardoin, who told me this story, added, "She did just what she felt and, like everything else, she did it all instinctively right. Minotis said he shivered when she told him."

Everyone who has ever worked with Maria, whether friend or enemy, has remarked on her fanatical devotion to her art. "I am a passionate artist and a passionate human being," she told a British interviewer. "I believe in self-discipline and self-control. If you want to live in harmony with yourself, you have to work. Work very hard. I don't agree with Descartes: 'I think therefore I am.' My motto is 'I work therefore I am.' " The record producers Dorle and Dario Soria knew Maria for twenty-five years while they produced her records. Dorle wrote of Maria: "To be involved with her was not always easy, but . . . one could never criticize her as an artist: she was the most professional, conscientious, hard-working artist I have ever known. Her musical morality was beyond reproach." "I'm never satisfied," Maria herself said. "I am personally incapable of enjoying what I have done well because I see so magnified the things I could have done better."

Callas could memorize a score faster than anyone believed possible and had an incredible range. Sopranos usually select the operas most suited to their voices, but Maria became famous for mastering every kind, including operas that had long been neglected because they were so difficult.

This was demonstrated early in her career, in Venice in 1949. She was singing the demanding role of Brünnhilde in *Die Walküre* and another soprano was singing Elvira in *I Puritani*. Suddenly the other singer became ill. Tullio Serafin, the celebrated director of the Teatro la Fenice in Venice, made Maria sight-read one of Elvira's arias, then suddenly informed her, "You are going to sing *Puritani* in a week. I will arrange for you to have time to study." She knew nothing of the part, and the Bellini opera could not have been more different from the Wagner, but Maria did the part and did it brilliantly, which was considered a miracle. This made her famous in Italy. For a hundred years no soprano had been able to conquer such a range of roles. Franco Zeffirelli said of the feat, after her death, "What she did in Venice was really incredible. You need to be familiar with opera to realize the size of her achievement that night. It was as if someone asked Birgit Nilsson, who is famous for her great Wagnerian voice, to substitute overnight for Beverly Sills, who is one of the top coloratura sopranos of our time."

Maria's art was also the core of her marriage to Meneghini; not only had it brought them together but it was also the animating spirit of their life together. They did not go out much or socialize. Callas once told *Time* magazine that her favorite night-time rite was to soak in the bath, drench herself in cologne, put on a slinky silk nightgown, and lie awake late into the night studying opera scores while her husband Meneghini snored beside her: "My best hours are in bed, and my best work too, with my dog cuddling beside me and my husband asleep." "Theirs was a life based on Spartan domestic economy, rigorous self-discipline and hard work," wrote John Dizikes in *Opera in America*. "For a decade, her ambition, will power, passion for self-improvement were focused on her art. Nothing interfered with it."

Those who worked with Maria considered her talent a divine gift, a phenomenon that could not be explained. Zeffirelli once remarked, "For me, Maria is always a miracle [who] can switch from nothing to everything, from earth to heaven." Younger singers like Montserrat Caballé saw Callas as transforming their art: "She opened a door for us, for all the singers in the world, a door that had been closed," Caballé said. "Behind it was sleeping not only great music, but great ideas of interpretation. She has given us the chance, those who follow her, to do things that were hardly possible before her."

For Maria herself, however, her "god-given gift," as Hidalgo called it, was both a curse and a blessing, evoking great pain and almost religious devotion. When Callas was a child, her mother's discovery of her musical talent deprived her of all joy: "Child prodigies never enjoy true childhood," Maria said, looking back. "I can't remember a toy . . . a doll or a favorite game—but only the songs I sang and sang and sang to the point of boredom . . . and, especially, the painful sensation of panic which seized me when, in the middle of a difficult passage, I felt as if I were going to suffocate and thought, terrorized, that no notes would emerge from my dry and arid throat. . . . There ought to be a law forbidding such things. Children treated in such a way become old before their time. It is unfair to deprive children of their childhood. I felt I was loved only when I sang."

Maria first discovered the joy of devoting herself to her art when she went to Greece as a young teenager and met her first great teacher, Elvira de Hidalgo. "As my interest, perhaps my only interest, in life was music, I was before long so fascinated listening to all Hidalgo's pupils, not only the sopranos but also the mezzos and even the tenors . . . that I used to go to the conservatory at ten in the morning and leave with the last pupil in the evening."

Maria began to believe that God had singled her out for an exceptional gift, and she poured her energy into her music as a nun would into her devotions. "I feel privileged to have had a destiny other than the ordinary," she said in 1970. "I am a creature of destiny. Destiny took me, wanted me this way. I am outside myself and witness my own life from the outside." But being a pawn of destiny often left Maria lonely and frustrated, for it seemed that everyone close to her, including her husband, cared only for her voice and her career. In one of her letters to Battista she chided, "I see that you are in love with Callas the artist. You forget my soul. For example, your letter was wonderful, so dear, but I wanted a little more Battista and Maria in it, not Meneghini and Callas. Let's see if I find my Battista in your next letters." Maria had never encountered anyone who loved her for herself apart from her voice, and while she struggled to serve the voice, part of her remained unsatisfied.

Callas worked on the *Medea* production in Dallas with masochistic intensity, says her colleague Jon Vickers, who sang the role of Jason. Then, after toiling until 2 a.m. on the dress rehearsal, she received a telegram from Rudolf Bing on the morning of the opening, saying that she had been dismissed for not agreeing to his proposed schedule quickly enough. With every newspaper in the country running headlines like THE MET FIRES CALLAS, Maria spent the day on the phone fielding questions from the press and complaining of Bing's demands and the Met's impossible rehearsal schedules, while Bing returned the volley with his own sarcastic gibes: "Her reputation for projecting her undisputed histrionic talent into her business affairs is a matter of common knowledge."

That night, after presenting a memorable *Medea* animated as much by her anger as her skill, she arrived at a party at the Dallas home of Mary Carter to find the yard filled with television trucks and reporters. According to "Maria Seconda," the diva was still in good spirits. "She had a wonderful time that evening. She danced and partied until dawn."

Maria completed her scheduled tour of America, which was studded with extravagant dinner parties, including one in New York given by Elsa Maxwell. But when she returned to Milan to celebrate her thirty-fifth birthday on December 3, 1958, there were no more performances to look forward to except one: her Paris debut on December 19 at a charity gala and concert benefiting the Légion d'Honneur. It was to be attended by an impressive array of celebrities; among the expected guests were the duke and duchess of Windsor, the Rothschilds, the Aga Khan, Brigitte Bardot, Charlie Chaplin, and Mr. and Mrs. Aristotle Onassis.

Those who were there describe the gala as the most splendid party Paris had seen since the war. Battista Meneghini took complete credit for organizing the party and groused that others got the glory instead. In the chapter of his book entitled "How Onassis Robbed Me of Maria," he reports: "Since this was to be a benefit recital, it was necessary to take in the largest possible amount. Maria was engaged for five million francs, the highest fee ever paid in the history of opera [approximately $10,000—a phenomenal fee in 1958]. At the end of the concert, my wife generously turned over the entire amount to a member of the Légion d'Honneur, as her

Designer Alain Reynaud with Callas in Paris; the diva's faithful maid, Bruna,
holds the sable-trimmed train of her gown.

contribution to the benefit." Gleefully, Meneghini toted up all the proceeds of the night's festivities: the 2,130 seats in the Paris Opéra were quickly sold out for 35,000 francs each. Boxes went for as much as 300,000 francs. Even the program, which weighed over two pounds, cost 2,000 francs. The recital was followed by a dinner served in the foyer of the theater for 450 guests, who paid 15,000 francs each for the meal. French magazines termed the event "The greatest show on earth: edition 1958."

It is Meneghini's belief that the publicity and splendor of that event fired Onassis' resolve to pursue Maria. "He, with all his money, would never have aroused so much interest or attracted so much attention to himself, even among important men of politics. I believe it was this consideration that put into his head and set in motion the idea for his diabolical project: 'If I take that woman for myself, I will impress everyone.' "

In fact, Onassis may already have decided to pursue Maria long before the Légion d'Honneur gala. On the morning of her Paris debut, a huge bouquet of red roses was delivered to Callas' hotel room; the card bore good wishes in Greek and was signed by Aristotle Onassis, whom she had not seen since Elsa Maxwell's Venice ball. At noon an identical bunch arrived, and in the evening, just before she was to leave for the Opéra, a third bouquet appeared. This time the Greek inscription was unsigned. "How romantic he is!" Maria remarked to her husband.

Callas' lifelong friend and modiste, Madame Biki Bouyeure, recalled that Callas emerged onto the stage of the Paris Opéra in a champagne satin gown with a square train trimmed in sable. She also recalled with amusement Maria's famous frugality: "She looked glorious! Later Maria ruined the gown. She couldn't resist picking off the sable trim. 'It's wasted on the train,' she said. 'I'll do something with it.' Of course it ended up forgotten in a closet. But we all agreed, she looked glorious!" At her ears and around her neck were more than a million dollars' worth of diamonds borrowed from Van Cleef & Arpels.

Maria sang a varied program that included arias from *Norma, Il Trovatore, Il Barbiere di Siviglia,* and the whole second act of *Tosca.* The event was televised live in nine countries, so much of Europe marveled at her voice that night. The performance ended with jubilant ovations, and at the dinner afterward, among the first to congratulate Maria was Aristotle Onassis.

Callas must have been aware by this time that Onassis was interested in more than just her singing. If so, she gave no hint of reciprocating. On April 21, 1959, the tenth anniversary of her marriage to Meneghini, she took the opportunity to tell the press yet again that her husband was the center of her life. They celebrated with a festive dinner at Maxim's in Paris and as they cut their almond anniversary cake, Maria declared, "I could not sing without him present. If I am the voice, he is the soul." Throughout the entire ten years of their marriage Maria had faithfully declared that she would do anything for Meneghini. "I would give my life for him, immediately and joyfully," she stated several years after their wedding. "If Battista had wanted, I would have abandoned my career without regret, because in a woman's life, love is more important than artistic triumphs." To many of her friends, however, Maria's rhapsody about the sublimity of life with the dumpy, awkward, much older man at her side, as mercenary as he was humorless, sounded much like a woman trying to convince herself of something.

A month or so later, at the end of spring, Maria and Onassis came face-to-face again, this time at a ball in Venice given by Countess Wally Toscanini Castelbarco. The party was in Maria's honor, though throughout their lives, Maria and the daughter of Toscanini had a volatile friendship.

On this occasion, both Onassis and Tina insisted that Maria and her husband join them on board the *Christina* for a summer cruise along the Greek and Turkish coasts; it was a reprise of the invitation reported by Elsa Maxwell a year earlier, but this time, significantly, the gossip columnist's name was omitted. Perhaps Onassis was aware that the relationship between Callas and Maxwell had become a difficult one. Maria replied that she had a very busy schedule, but she would consider it and let him know later. Tina probably considered Maria no more than another one of the celebrities her husband enjoyed adding to his collection, like Greta Garbo and Margot Fonteyn. After all, Callas was never far from the side of her adoring husband and seemed completely devoted to him.

At the end of May, Onassis telephoned from Monte Carlo and put Tina on the phone to press the invitation. "Then Onassis spoke, and he was very insistent," Meneghini reported later. "Maria explained that she was leaving for London, where she had an important engagement for Cherubini's *Medea* at Covent Garden, and that she was not in a state of mind to think about a cruise. 'I will come to London for your answer,' Onassis replied."

The impending performance of Callas as Medea became the most sought-after cultural ticket in England. A line began forming outside Covent Garden three days before the box office opened and grew into the biggest anyone had ever seen for an opera. Within three hours, all tickets were snapped up. As the preview approached, £2 seats were being sold for £98 on the black market and £10 boxes were going for £100.

Onassis not only turned up in London for the premiere, he sat through the whole opera, an unprecedented tribute from the shipowner, who much preferred dancing and breaking plates to Greek popular music over sitting through hours of bel canto. He and Tina even organized a party in Maria's honor after the performance; the printed invitations for nearly two hundred guests read: "Mr. and Mrs. Aristotle Onassis request the pleasure of your company at a Supper Party to be held at the Dorchester at 11:15 p.m. on Wednesday 17 June." Onassis also purchased thirty-three tickets to the performance, many secured on the black market through an ad in the *Times,* and arrived early at the theater's bar to distribute the hard-won pasteboards and glasses of champagne to his guests. They included Lady Churchill and Randolph Churchill (but not Sir Winston, who had little taste for opera); the duchess of Kent with her daughter Princess Alexandra; the Queen's cousin Lord Harewood; the actors Douglas Fairbanks, Jr., and Gary Cooper; and the photographer Cecil Beaton.

*The famous photo of Maria being embraced by her once and future lovers
at Onassis' party for her at the Dorchester in London*

Seated next to his wife in the audience, Onassis stared raptly at the woman on the stage. Maria portrayed a Medea as tortured and dangerous as any envisioned by Euripides. One London critic wrote: "From her first appearance, standing between two huge pillars, and wrapped in a huge cape, which exposes nothing but her eyes, heavily rimmed with black and filled with well-composed hatred, to her last, when the temple in which she has murdered her children tumbles to the ground showing her in a snake-entwined chariot with their corpses at her feet, Callas builds her performance into one powerful line of ever-increasing tension. It is the kind of performance which spoils one for anything less from the opera stage."

Such a vision, of the mad priestess flanked by the corpses of her two murdered children, might have challenged a lesser man's resolve to become involved with such a being, but Onassis' enthusiasm for Maria was only enhanced by the performance. She had resurrected Cherubini's opera, based on the ancient Greek tragedy, and Euripides himself could not have imagined a more perfect choice to play the sorceress driven mad by jealousy. As Medea she exuded such power that no one could look away from her. Like a ferocious panther, her tall, feline figure paced the stage, racked with such fury at Jason's treachery that infanticide seemed the only adequate punishment. Even Onassis, no fan of opera, was hypnotized by her performance and became determined to know more about the woman behind the role.

For the dinner afterward, he had spared no expense in decorating the ballroom of the Dorchester Hotel in Callas' honor, with oceans of pink roses and pink champagne. The moment the diva appeared, in her chinchilla coat and parure of emeralds, Onassis bent low to kiss her hand, and thereafter he concentrated all his energy on charming her. When asked her preference for dance music, she replied: a tango. Pressing a fifty-pound note into the hands of the bewildered conductor of the Hungarian orchestra, Onassis insisted that they play nothing but tangos all night.

Among the guests was Mary Carter, who had traveled from Texas for the performance. "It was a very glitzy crowd," she recalled. "When Gary Cooper arrived, he was so beautifully tailored, in white tie, that I almost fainted. I couldn't keep my eyes off him! Elsa Maxwell was there, of course, with Douglas Fairbanks and many others. Onassis was very gracious to everyone, as was Tina, his wife. As Maria and Meneghini left, Onassis escorted them out with his arm around Maria and I felt a premonition."

When Maria, pleading exhaustion, said farewell and headed for the door at 3 a.m., a photographer caught perhaps the most famous image of the soon-to-be notorious triangle: Onassis (in dark glasses and tuxedo) and Meneghini clasping each other's hands, while Maria, who towered over them both, looked surprised, caught between the arms of her husband and her host like the victim in a game of "London Bridge Is Falling Down."

Some biographers of Onassis claim that he and Maria first became intimate in London at this time. Peter Evans writes: "Maria and Ari had settled the matter . . . in several secret rendezvouses [sic] during her London engagement, when they had become lovers." He refers to "illicit trysts in a London mews cottage."

When I called to ask Evans what his sources were for the assertion, he named the longtime Onassis aides Costa Gratsos and Johnny Meyer (now both dead), who told him they had been given the information by Onassis himself. If he did tell them this, Onassis was probably boasting, as he tended to do when it came to tales of his sexual prowess (for example, there was his often-published claim that he had sex five times in one night with Jacqueline Kennedy Onassis on their honeymoon, when he was sixty-four years old).

Those who knew Maria best, however, insist that she was not physically involved with Onassis before they set sail on the *Christina*. Mary Carter says, "Maria told me that the first time she ever slept with Onassis was on the cruise. I have no reason to doubt her. She was always very straight with me."

Maria was still vacillating about accepting the invitation to the cruise when she finished her London engagement of *Medea* and traveled with Meneghini to Amsterdam for the Holland Festival. She was to perform concerts in Amsterdam and Brussels on July 11 and 14. The director of the festival was Peter Diamand, and, according to the Callas biographer Arianna Stassinopoulos, on the day before the Amsterdam performance Maria told Diamand she wanted to speak to him in private, "without Battista." On the day after the performance, as they walked among the gardens of a park near Leiden, she told the director not to pay her fee into the joint Callas-Meneghini account: "Keep the money until you hear from me. There will be many changes in my life in the next few months. . . . You'll hear many things. . . . Please stay my friend."

The natural inference to be drawn from this account is that Maria had already made up her mind to leave her husband for Onassis, but many of her friends say this is not true; they insist that her statement to Diamand was the result of a fight between her and Battista over his handling of her money.

"Even before Onassis came into her life she was having problems with Meneghini," recalls Mary Carter. "Before the cruise she told her husband she wanted to slow down, and on the cruise she told him she wanted to retire from performing altogether. She said she was mentally exhausted and needed to rest. She was very sensitive to critics and they always harped on how her top notes were wobbly. But Meneghini told her she couldn't afford to retire because the money she had earned up to then was gone; he had used it to finance the buildup of her career and to repay loans to himself and others that he had taken out to pay for their expenses when she wasn't earning big money. Maria was furious, of course, and even before she went on the cruise she took actions to be sure all her earnings after that went to an account in her name, not to Meneghini."

Maria's disenchantment with her husband as a manager was also confirmed by Giovanna Lomazzi, a Milanese woman ten years Callas' junior who became friends with her because her own father was close to Meneghini. After the early 1950s Lomazzi often traveled with the couple, and she said of the marriage, "By the time we went to New York in 1956, the cracks were beginning to show. He was much older, and tired early. Maria was thin and elegant by then and wanted to go out and enjoy a little her success. And she had problems with him as a manager. He couldn't speak any languages and kept shouting at everyone in Italian. She became frustrated with him. 'If you can't be my manager, don't do it,' she would shout at him. He was a wonderful husband-manager for a good singer but not for a great star, which Maria now was."

Callas herself seems to substantiate the view that the first fissure in her marriage was caused by money matters, not alienation of affections. In an interview that appeared in a London newspaper on November 8, 1964, five years after she had divorced Meneghini, she said, "The world has condemned me for leaving my husband. But I didn't leave him—the rift came because I would not let him take care of my business affairs any more. Battista himself said it was pointless, our living together, if he had not complete control over me—that's all he wanted, I believe."

Though it is highly unlikely that as of July 11, 1959, in Amsterdam, Maria had any intention of leaving her husband for Onassis, her anger and disillusionment with the man who had been her mentor and companion for so long undoubtedly made her more susceptible to the shipowner's attentions and his entreaties to join the cruise.

Maria and Battista returned from Belgium to their home in Sirmione on July 15, and the next day, according to Meneghini, at around eleven in the morning, their housekeeper Emma announced that Mr. Onassis wished to speak with Maria. " 'We are absolutely not here,' replied my wife. 'Tell him we're in Milan,' I added." A half hour later, writes Meneghini, the telephone rang again—Onassis had tried the Milan house and learned they were not there. He insisted on speaking with Mme. Callas, who refused to accept the call. This evasion continued, until, by the afternoon, Maria told her husband to take the phone. He heard himself addressed in Italian by the shipowner, using Maria's nickname for him, Titta, and the familiar form of "you": "I want you on the *Christina*. We'll have a good time. Persuade your wife." Then Onassis put Tina on the phone to implore Maria to join them. In the end, she agreed reluctantly, according to Meneghini. He reassured her: "This invitation comes at just the right time. The doctor recommended sea air. . . . If you don't like it, at the first port we can return home."

While that is the way Meneghini remembered the pivotal decision to go on the cruise, there is a published indication that Maria had actually accepted Onassis' invitation, without telling her husband, while she was still performing in Amsterdam on July 11. The source of the information is Elsa Maxwell, who was with Maria in Amsterdam. Whether Maxwell was telling the truth or just trying to get Maria in trouble with her husband, she wrote in her column of July 22, after noting that Callas and Meneghini had just set sail on the Onassis yacht: "One little incident concerning Callas and this cruise amused me a great deal. Maria, who had first met the Onassises with me in Venice two years ago, called up Mrs. Onassis from Amsterdam, where she was singing, to ask what clothes she should take along for this glorious cruise. She got 'Ari' Onassis on the phone instead. Naturally, he knew nothing about clothes and, just like a man, advised her to 'bring along anything you want—sweaters and something for the water.' Maria must have been dismayed, for she wanted to look her best."

In the same column Maxwell wrote prophetically, "This cruise will make a great difference in her life. Madame Callas has been untouched by the technique of the fashionable world. But she will learn fast."

With only a week to get ready, according to Meneghini, Maria called her friend and dress designer, Madame Biki Bouyeure, and persuaded her to create an appropriate wardrobe in record time. (Biki, who was a granddaughter of Puccini, headed the atelier and oversaw the designs of the gowns, but it was actually Alain Reynaud, Biki's associate and son-in-law, who had become Maria's personal dresser and fashion Svengali. Madame Bouyeure described to me, when we met in her palazzo in Milan shortly before her death in 1999, how the late Reynaud influenced Maria's transformation from ugly duckling to swan, teaching her how to dress and walk and how to choose accessories for each outfit after her transforming weight loss.)

Madame Biki and her staff managed to turn out the necessary trunks full of cruise wear on time. But Maria still felt insecure about her wardrobe. Meneghini describes her odd behavior when they left Sirmione and went to Milan two days before setting out on the cruise. "I said to Emma just as we were stepping into the car: 'Keep everything ready. We may be gone a week, we may come back in a day. It depends on the people we find on board.' Maria went shopping in Milan and made some absurd purchases. I think she was afraid of looking out-of-place among the other guests. She spent millions of lire on bathing suits, ensembles and lingerie. It all seemed rather excessive to me, but I didn't say anything. I had never seen her so intensely concerned."

On July 21, Meneghini writes, he and Maria left Milan and flew to Nice. From there they took a taxi to Monte Carlo, then Onassis' personal kingdom. (He was still a majority stockholder in the Société des Bains de Mer and still on good terms with Prince Rainier and Princess Grace.) The Belle Epoque city, composed of gilded and arcaded buildings of pale stone and marble, is perched on a rock curved like a theater. The arched and balconied windows of the palatial hotels and the famous Casino, frosted like a wedding cake and adorned with statues of nymphs and goddesses, overlook the blue Mediterranean. In the summer of 1959 the harbor was dominated by the white, streamlined form of the *Christina* in the berth of honor to the left of the entrance—at that time the only one that could accommodate a vessel that large. At night, the strings of lights suspended from the ship's masts glittered like diamond necklaces.

From distant points in England and Europe, the illustrious guests were assembling in Monte Carlo for the pleasure cruise that had yet to begin but was already being watched with fascination.

Winston Churchill, eighty-five, long retired from politics but still revered for his defiance of both fascism and communism, was the focus of interest as the guests came on board. But it was the other guest of honor— the notorious soprano—and the equally controversial host who would soon draw the world's attention as the *Christina* sailed toward the former empire of Byzantium, whose warships were famous for bombarding enemy vessels with "Greek fire"—an incendiary mixture of mysterious composition that engulfed and destroyed everything it touched.

5

WEIGHING ANCHOR

When you set out on the voyage to Ithaca
you must pray that the journey is long,
full of adventures, full of knowledge.

C. P. Cavafy, "Ithaca"

On their arrival in Monte Carlo on Tuesday, July 21, 1959, Maria Callas and her husband checked into a suite at the Hermitage Hotel, which is joined by an underground passage to the even more luxurious Hôtel de Paris. In the days when royal high-rollers and Arab sheiks would win and lose fortunes at the Casino de Monte Carlo, they would stay with their wives at the Hôtel de Paris across the park and reserve rooms for their mistresses in the adjacent Hermitage Hotel. The passageway between the two establishments opens on a large, shared indoor swimming pool, flanked by Turkish baths. Between dips, guests, clad only in the hotel's terry-cloth robes, can stroll onto the outdoor terrace to sip an aperitif and admire the stunning view of the harbor below. (It was at this pool that Christina Onassis later met the Los Angeles real estate broker Joseph Bolker, which led to a marriage that enraged her father and ended with her failed attempt at suicide.)

On the morning that Callas and Meneghini and their many trunks and valises arrived at the Hermitage, Maria was handed an unsettling letter from Elsa Maxwell, who was staying next door at the Hôtel de Paris. As Meneghini rather inelegantly put it in his memoirs, "That gossip already knew everything and was meddling with the slobbering advice of a bird of ill omen." Maxwell clearly was feeling jealous, angry, and vengeful at not being included on the cruise, after she had introduced Ari and Maria two years earlier and had originally been invited on the *Christina* by Onassis. This is how Meneghini quoted her letter:

> Dear Maria, I am only writing to wish you and Battista a splendid voyage on board that marvelous yacht, with that marvelous and intelligent "master of the house" Ari, and the ex-man-of-state (now perhaps a little in decline) who saved the world in 1940. In fact, you are taking the place of Garbo, now too old, on board the *Christina*. Good luck, I never cared for Garbo, and I loved you. From this moment on enjoy every moment of your life. *Take* (and this is a delicate art) everything. *Give* (that's not a delicate art, but an important one) all that you can bring yourself to give: this is the way to true happiness which you must discover in the wilderness. I no longer even wish to see you. The world will say—in fact they are already saying—that you only wanted to use me. This I deny categorically. The little I have done, I did with my eyes wide open, and with my heart and soul. You are already one of the great, and you will become even greater. . . . (P.S. Yesterday Ari and Tina invited me to dinner with you. I couldn't say no.)

That day Callas and Meneghini lunched with an old acquaintance: Onassis' half sister Merope; she maintained a residence in Monte Carlo, where her husband, Nikos Konialidis, ran the Onassis shipping empire. Merope Onassis Konialidis is one of Onassis' two half sisters, born to his father's second wife, Eleni, whom Socrates Onassis married in 1912. In 1938 Merope married her first cousin Nikos Konialidis—Nikos was the child of Aristotle and Merope's aunt—after getting a special dispensation from the Greek Orthodox church. Nikos had followed Onassis to Buenos Aires to help him operate his growing business enterprises there. When he began to prosper, he made a trip back to Greece to find a bride, and his eye fell on the daughter of his late mother's brother, Socrates Aristotle Onassis.

When I interviewed Merope, a tiny, spry, bright-eyed woman in her mid-eighties, on the outdoor terrace of a Greek restaurant in the shadow of the Acropolis, she told me how she had known Maria Callas a decade before that luncheon in Monte Carlo.

"We were prominent in the Greek community in Buenos Aires," she said, "and in 1949 the Greek consul asked me to host a reception for a Greek singer who had come to B.A. with an Italian opera company. The two things I remember about her are that she was so fat she could barely get through the door and her legs were covered with long, thick black hair because she had recently married an Italian, and Italian women didn't shave their legs then. Her name was Maria Callas, of course. When I saw her again in 1959, so thin and elegant, I could hardly believe it was the same woman."

That evening, Maria and Battista dined at the Hôtel de Paris with Ari and Tina Onassis and Elsa Maxwell. It was an uncomfortable meal, filled with tension all around. Meneghini could barely follow the conversation in French and English and certainly could not catch the double entendres issuing from the jealous gossip columnist, but he did understand that she was up to no good. Later he wrote of the "Hollywood witch": "It was she who introduced my wife to a certain circle of people who were rich but deceitful, without purpose in life, and involved in questionable business pursuits. . . . The change in Maria which caused her to leave me in 1959 probably started after her introduction to that witch, who was even then an extremely intelligent woman, and, for that reason, fascinating."

Maxwell was undeniably an intelligent woman and perhaps more aware than anyone else at the table that night of what could unfold on the cruise. She made sexual innuendos as she turned her gaze from Tina to Ari to Maria. In her memoirs, and to her intimates, Maxwell had often bragged that she was a virgin. Onassis' biographer Peter Evans speculates that her repressed sexuality engendered an obsession with observing and reporting the sexual pecadillos of friends and acquaintances. Perhaps in this case she was also hoping to provoke a misadventure.

At the dinner under the gilded, arched ceilings of La Salle Empire, Elsa coyly told Tina how lucky she was to be married to such a rich and brilliant man. Such men are powerful, she said, and their power makes them exciting and dangerous. But, she warned, they invariably try to roam, and so must be watched carefully. Tina understood perfectly what Maxwell was getting at and sensed the old woman's fascination with Maria and her resentment at being excluded from the cruise. At the end of the evening Tina kissed Maxwell's crepey cheek and said, "You know, my dear, there really isn't a lot of difference between being married to a moderately rich man and a very rich man. . . . If only you could understand that, you'd be a much smarter person."

It's difficult to be certain what she meant by this cryptic statement, but Tina may have been reflecting that she was not as happy in her marriage to her fabulously wealthy husband as she might have been married to some other, less affluent man, and that she did not feel it necessary to follow Maxwell's warning and police the behavior of her husband on the cruise.

The next afternoon, July 22, Onassis escorted Sir Winston Churchill aboard the *Christina* around 2 p.m. While the staff carried the luggage below to his staterooms, Sir Winston and the other guests settled themselves on the rear deck under the shade of the green canopy. Sir Winston

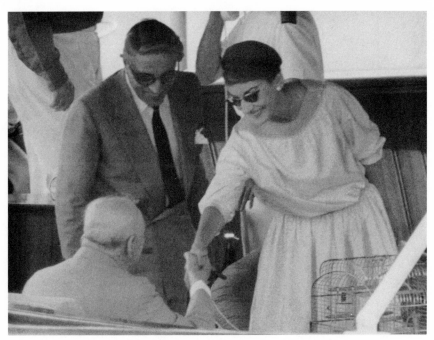

Summit on the Christina: *Callas and Churchill brought together by Onassis*

insisted that the cage of his parakeet, Toby, be kept by his side. As Tina and Ari hovered, making sure he was comfortable, and a crowd of reporters watched from the shore, Maria and Meneghini were nowhere to be seen. It was later reported that the singer was enjoying herself swimming at Monte Carlo Beach.

An hour after Sir Winston's arrival, Callas finally made her appearance, escorted up the gangplank by Onassis with her husband trailing behind. She was wearing flat sandals and a blousy beige top with a crocheted cowl neck and full skirt, and her nervousness was evident as she leaned over deferentially and extended her hand to the seated Churchill during the introductions. The next day a newspaper, *L'Espoir de Nice et du Süd-Est,* reported a droll story of the meeting—which may be apocryphal, because the reporters were too far away to hear what was said:

> *The singer, dressed in beige, approached Churchill. Was the "old Lion" weary? Was he annoyed by the tardiness of the diva? In any case, it was without getting up that he took the hand of Maria Callas, who bowed before him. Toby, on his perch, observed the scene. . . . And as the singer stood there speechless, he spoke: "Kiss!" Then one saw Churchill and Callas look at each other and laugh. . . . The ice was broken.*

*Before the fateful cruise, Onassis and Maria are deep in conversation,
oblivious to Tina and Sir Winston across the table.*

Photos record that the parakeet's cage was indeed at Sir Winston's side
at this moment, but Anthony Montague Browne insists that the bird's
vocabulary did not include this command: "His only phrase was: 'Toby,
Toby, my name is Toby.' "

Later that evening, Onassis' guests descended the gangplank in full
evening dress to dine under the stars on the terrace of the Hôtel de Paris.
Paris Match reported that crayfish and cigars were on the menu of this first
repast. A photograph shows Maria, in a beaded black lace gown, intently
conversing with Onassis on her right. Directly across the table from them,
Tina was telling Sir Winston a story. On Maria's left, ignored by her and
chatting with the rest of the table, was none other than Onassis' rival Stavros
Niarchos. It may seem odd that his despised brother-in-law was invited to
the dinner that launched the great journey, but when Onassis had such
illustrious guests as Churchill and Callas among his flock, he probably
could not resist flaunting them.

Onassis had first met the former prime minister in 1956, when Churchill's
son, Randolph, a journalist grateful for having been granted an interview
with the shipowner, brought him to dinner at La Pausa, the art-filled villa of
Sir Winston's literary agent, Emery Reves, and his wife, Wendy, six miles
east of Monte Carlo, while Churchill was staying there as a guest. The day
before the dinner, Onassis, as nervous at the prospect of such an encounter

as Maria would be three years later, called Anthony Montague Browne, Churchill's personal secretary, and asked to meet with him "as a matter of urgency." The urgent matter turned out to be a plea for advice about what he should or should not say to the grand old man. Montague Browne recalls telling him to say anything he wanted—"After all, he [Onassis] had a brilliant and original mind"—but to avoid any mention of Cyprus, which was then a sore subject because British soldiers occupying the island were being attacked by Greeks desperate for *enosis*—union with mainland Greece.

The dinner conversation was convivial until Churchill turned and said, "Mr. Onassis, what is your comment on your country's monstrous conduct on the Cyprus issue?" The table fell silent as everyone waited to hear Ari's reply. According to Montague Browne, the shipowner fumbled in his pocket and pulled out a letter with a Greek stamp on it showing the island of Cyprus and an inscription in Greek. Churchill asked what the postage stamp had to do with the subject at hand. "It quotes what you said when you were under-secretary for the colonies, Sir Winston," Onassis replied. (Sir Winston held that ministerial position, his first, from 1905 to 1908.) "And what was that?" the old man rumbled. Ari answered, "You said that Cyprus should belong to Greece."

This led to an explosion of Churchill's notorious temper, after which Onassis departed glumly, convinced that he had botched any chance at friendship with the man he idolized. But that night, as Churchill was preparing for bed, he said of Onassis, "That is a man of mark. I would like to see him again."

Soon Churchill was invited for a day trip on the *Christina,* accompanied by the entire band from the Hôtel de Paris, which Onassis borrowed for the occasion. Onassis still owned a majority interest in the hotel and always made sure that Sir Winston was installed in the penthouse suite there when he was in town. This excursion was followed by invitations to cruises aboard the *Christina,* eight in all from 1958 to 1963, which Churchill accepted. He was always accompanied by Anthony Montague Browne and Browne's wife, Noel, who was known as Nonie.

The July 1959 voyage was Sir Winston's third aboard the *Christina.* On this one, he was accompanied by his wife, Lady Clementine, his daughter Diana Sandys (who was separated from her husband, Britain's minister of defense, Duncan Sandys), and Diana's sixteen-year-old daughter, Celia. Also present were his bodyguard, Edmund Murray (a Scotland Yard detective), his nurse, and, as usual, the Montague Brownes. This pair—attractive, young, and fluent in French as well as English—were well liked by Tina and Ari, who found them good-natured, ready for adventure, and on the whole more congenial than some of the older guests.

The Onassis children, Alexander, eleven, and Christina, eight, were lodged in the stateroom closest to the stern and the crew's quarters. They also had their own combination playroom and dining room, brightly painted with wall murals by the Austrian artist Ludwig Bemelmans, depicting Madeline's adventures in Paris. (Bemelmans had been one of Ari's friends ever since they met in Hollywood's film colony during the war years, when Onassis often visited the West Coast.) By now, however, Alexander and Christina felt themselves too grown up for the miniature chairs and tables of the children's room and often preferred to eat in the staff dining room with the crew.

Christina was accompanied on this cruise by a rather stern English governess in her early fifties named Miss Kathleen Lehane, and Alexander came on board with a Greek "tutor" named Kostas Koutsouvelis, who was quite a different type. The handsome thirty-year-old was a famous ladies' man. According to Captain Kostas Anastasiades, Onassis was concerned about his eleven-year-old son's indifference to girls, and had hired Koutsouvelis as a companion for Alexander in the hope that his skills with women might rub off on the boy. "He was deathly afraid that Alexander might turn out homosexual," Captain Kostas told me. "He need not have worried on that score. Alexander wound up liking women fine, but not in the voracious way of his father."

By the late evening of Wednesday, July 22, 1959, all the guests had reboarded the yacht and the crew of forty-two were in place. There were two chefs, according to Captain Kostas—one French and one Greek—a woman engaged solely to handle dry cleaning, an array of seamstresses, valets, masseurs, stewards, bartenders, maids, engineers, and communications experts, in addition to the sailing crew. Onassis always insisted that his crew be able to speak at least one language besides Greek and to perform expertly on the dance floor, in case any unaccompanied female guest (Greta Garbo, say, or Ava Gardner) required a dance partner.

At the last minute Meneghini complained that he really shouldn't leave, because his aged mother was gravely ill in Italy. Onassis retorted that he'd have no trouble checking on her condition: "There are forty-two radio telephones on the *Christina*." Ari liked to brag to his guests that he could be connected to any spot in the world in minutes, and if he had to go anywhere in a hurry, there was the twin-engined Piaggio amphibious seaplane on the top deck, the white Fiat automobile in the hold, four Chris-Crafts, a hydrofoil speedboat, two smaller speedboats, and various lifeboats, kayaks, and water sports toys. Such a variety of conveyances gratified the restless Alexander, whose passion, even at eleven, was racing about in anything with an engine. The previous summer he had destroyed the first of many ill-fated speedboats, driving it at the full speed of 45 knots "just to see what happened."

The *Christina* also boasted a hospital fully equipped with an operating theater, an X-ray machine, and an emergency generator; an air-conditioning plant; and a temperature-controlled swimming pool with a mosaic floor copied from one in the Palace of Knossos that showed Cretan athletes vaulting over the back of a bull. A system of water fountains with colored lights danced at the rim of the pool, and the floor could be raised hydraulically to become a dance floor. Montague Browne said, "One of Ari's entertainments was to set it [the dance floor] descending gently . . . when dancing was proceeding, with brightly illuminated jets coming in from the sides."

The famous yacht that was the cornerstone of Onassis' reputation for decadent wealth was by no means the swiftest or most stable vessel plying the seas along the Riviera. Formerly a war-surplus Canadian frigate called the *Stormont,* she had been bought by Onassis in 1953. He spent over four million dollars to have her gutted and converted into a pleasure craft in Kiel, Germany, under the direction of Caesar Pinnau, a German professor of architecture who had also designed Hitler's mountaintop hideaway near Berchtesgaden. Onassis was warned that adding the third deck, the hydroplane, and the crane made the *Christina* top-heavy and risky to pilot in a storm. The fastest she could go was a mere 18 knots, but according to Captain Kostas, "We rarely approached that speed because great vibration resulted when we tried. Our maximum speed with guests aboard was fourteen knots." The yacht's design included stabilizers that were extended to keep her steady in rough seas.

The *Christina* made her maiden voyage in June of 1954, sleek and streamlined, pristinely white with a bright yellow funnel, 325 feet long and with a displacement of three thousand tons. A long green canopy protected the rear sitting area on the deck around the mosaic pool–cum–dance floor. Here guests would gather all day long and take casual meals in good weather.

The yacht's interior was described as "the last word in opulence" by Egypt's King Farouk, a man who knew something about conspicuous consumption. Onassis had personally overseen every detail. His own four-room master suite atop the boat on the bridge deck continued the theme of the Palace of Knossos. The bathroom, in Siennese marble, was a copy of King Minos' bath in ancient Crete, complete with a sunken bathtub lined with mosaic and featuring a flying-fish motif. The gold-plated dolphin fixtures used in the bathrooms throughout the vessel spewed hot and cold

The most luxurious yacht in the world, Onassis' pride and joy

fresh water. One-way mirrors ensured the privacy of the shower and toilet stalls while allowing the occupant to observe anyone who entered the bathroom area.

In Tina and Ari's bedroom with its king-sized bed, seafoam-green walls were lined with beveled Venetian mirrors built into arched ivory frames carved with scallop-shell designs. The furniture was also Venetian, lacquered and painted with floral motifs. Many precious Byzantine icons glimmered from the walls. From the dressing room adjoining the master bath was a secret door to the radio room and chart room so that Onassis could evade unwanted visitors by vanishing from his suite or could easily slip out in the middle of the night to place international phone calls, as he was wont to do.

On the other side of the master bedroom was Ari's personal study, where he kept his most valuable treasures, including his favorite El Greco, *Madonna with an Angel* (which experts consider to be the school of El Greco, not an original). The serene image of the Madonna was incongruously flanked by mounted weapons, including a pair of solid gold sabers—a gift of King Saud—and Turkish dueling pistols hanging on the teak-paneled walls, over a Louis XIV desk. A green jade statue of Buddha studded with rubies was perhaps the most precious object on board, certainly the most

The Christina*'s bar, with stools covered with the foreskins of whales*

ornate. In this study Onassis would often sit up all night, talking on several phone lines at once, monitoring his holdings around the world.

On the deck level below Onassis' suite, guests driven from poolside by chilly weather took refuge in the large oak-paneled game room. It was lined with bookshelves full of gilded, leather-bound books in several languages—mostly Greek history and mythology, art books or detective novels, and, of course, the complete works of Sir Winston Churchill, all personally signed to his friend Aristotle. (Onassis was fascinated by history, which seemed to him to be personified by Sir Winston, and he was well versed in mythology and art, but he had less esteem for literature and poetry.) The focal point of this room was a fireplace of brilliant lapis lazuli; on either side of it stood two cloisonné and bronze temple lions from China's Yuan dynasty, whose open mouths Onassis liked to use as ashtrays. The rugs were the finest produced in his native Smyrna. A grand piano stood in the corner. In this cozy, book-lined room with the atmosphere of an elegant gentleman's club, Onassis and Maria Callas would sit up late at night, staring into the fire and talking.

Just off the game room was a bar room, where the Onassis taste in decor reached the very heights of whimsy. If the decor of the bedroom suite implied that Aristotle identified with King Minos, the bar suggested that he saw himself as an adventurer of the seas, especially the mythic Greek hero Odysseus. Barrels of Barbados rum and sea chests hinted of pirate treasure. Large illustrated wall maps of the world and whaling harpoons were mounted nearby, and the circular bar itself was wound with heavy hawser rope. Beneath its glass top was a diorama with miniature ships that could be moved with magnets around a painted blue sea. They illustrated the development of sailing vessels from ancient to modern times, starting with a tiny antique vessel bearing a flag reading JONAH—THE FIRST SHIPOWNER.

Whale's teeth were used for footrests on the bar stools and for handles along the bar, ready in case the sea got so rough or a guest's blood alcohol level rose so high that he was in danger of falling off his stool. When I visited the *Christina* in June of 1999 at a shipyard on Salamis, an island opposite Piraeus, where it was being restored by its present owner, I noticed that the handles on the bar are scrimshaw, delicately carved with scenes illustrating the adventures of Odysseus. But the most notorious Onassis decorating touch was the cushions of the bar stools, which were covered with the foreskins of whales killed by his whaling fleet. They permitted Ari frequent opportunities for his favorite bon mot: "Madame, you are sitting on the largest penis in the world."

On the same deck level were the hospital, all the way forward, and the guest staterooms—nine in all. Most had pale sea-green walls and bathrooms of either golden- or pink-and-gray striated marble. Each stateroom was named for a Greek island and was identified by an oval white-and-gold plaque on the door that bore a silhouette of the island and its name in both English and Greek. Entering from the hallway one first saw the smaller staterooms "Andros" and "Lesbos" opposite each other. "Andros" was the captain's room, situated so that he could quickly run up to the bridge when needed. "Lesbos" was the children's stateroom, unless it was required for extra guests.

On the July 1959 cruise, the four staterooms on the port side of the vessel aft of the captain's room were all put at the disposal of the Churchills. Sir Winston and his parakeet had the large, elegant stateroom called "Chios," which had a double bed; "Crete" served as a sitting room for Sir Winston and Lady Clementine; and she slept in the next room, "Santorini." Last on that side was the smaller room "Corfu," occupied by Sir Winston's valet-bodyguard Edmund Murray, who helped him dress. (Sir Winston was not yet senile, as Elsa Maxwell had snidely hinted in her letter, but he had a problem with incontinence. Onassis made it clear that such weaknesses were never to be mentioned and he paid a laundress extravagant wages to change and wash Sir Winston's linens several times a day.)

On the starboard side, Maria Callas and her husband, Battista, were given the premiere suite of honor, "Ithaki," previously occupied by Greta Garbo and later by Jacqueline Kennedy. Next to the Meneghinis were Diana Sandys and her daughter, in "Mykonos," with two single beds. Beyond them, the Montague Brownes occupied "Rhodos," just beside the hospital.

An extravagant spiral staircase of bronze banisters and onyx balusters connected the three levels of the ship's public rooms. At the lowest level was an oval dining room where as many as twenty guests could be seated for a formal dinner. The walls of this room had been painted by the French artist Marcel Vertes with scenes of Tina and the children frolicking through the four seasons—skating in winter, riding donkeys in autumn, sunbathing topless in summer, riding on a flower-strewn gondola through the canals of Venice in spring. If more than twenty people were expected, there was a reception hall on this level that had room for two hundred guests and an orchestra. Nearby was a movie theater. Throughout the yacht a nautical theme prevailed, and there were dozens of ship models on display, including antique sailing vessels carved out of bone by French sailors taken prisoner during the Napoleonic Wars.

Onassis often said that the *Christina* was his preferred residence, and he was obsessive about it, ready to fly into a fit of temper if a single brass knob was not properly polished. Tina once said that to Ari the *Christina* "was not a fantastic plaything but a real passion. He is almost like a housewife fussing over it."

(Understandably, some visitors found the interior decor of the yacht a bit *de trop,* among them Jacqueline Kennedy Onassis, who was eager to revamp it with her famous decorating skills. Ari would tell his bride that she could change nothing on the *Christina,* his floating sanctuary. She finally talked him into letting her replace the upholstery on some of the banquettes, but he agreed only to temporary covers that could be whisked off as soon as she left the ship.)

Late at night on July 22, 1959, after the passengers had gone to sleep, lulled by the fine wines served at dinner and the gentle swell of the sea, Captain Anastasiades made an entry in his log noting the date and time of departure: July 23, 1959, at 12:08 a.m. He gave a signal to the ship's first mate and eased the *Christina* out of its berth and into the harbor. Onassis walked to his favorite spot on the stern of the ship to watch the lights of Monte Carlo slip away.

Aristotle Onassis often told friends how, as a young, penniless refugee in 1923, sailing in steerage class on the *Tomaso di Savoya* from Naples to a new life in Argentina, he had first seen from afar those sparkling lights of Monte Carlo reflected in the sea, and how he had vowed to visit the country in better circumstances. Now Onassis, dubbed by the press the "King of Monte Carlo" (to the annoyance of Prince Rainier), had more than fulfilled his youthful vow. The lights radiating from the turrets, towers, and arched windows of the Casino and the Hôtel de Paris were illuminating his own personal kingdom as his luxurious yacht sailed out of the harbor toward the open sea.

Traveling as his guests were Winston Churchill, the world's most revered statesman, and Maria Callas, opera's greatest prima donna. Onassis had asked Churchill himself to choose the itinerary for the voyage and the old man had replied that it would give him great pleasure to visit the home-lands of his hosts. They planned to stop at Chios, the rugged island near Turkey where Tina Onassis' father, Stavros Livanos, began his career as a cabin boy and where he now had an opulent seaside villa. They would call in at Smyrna, in Turkey, where Onassis himself was born, grew up, and watched as the whole Greek community was burned to the ground. Ari took pleasure in anticipating their stops at ancient historic sites on the Greek mainland, where Maria Callas had endured the dangers and priva-tions of the war and her early struggles to establish a career. She had left Greece an unknown, and he was bringing her back as one of the world's greatest celebrities.

Onassis had personally planned every detail of the cruise to maximize the enjoyment of his guests, from the films and music provided for their entertainment to the dignitaries and entertainers who would come aboard at each stop. Seven hours after clearing the harbor of Monte Carlo the *Christina* would reach its first destination, Portofino, Italy. As the others slept, Onassis paced the deck, a cigar in hand and a glass of scotch nearby. Throughout his life, he had never slept more than a few hours a night, and as he enjoyed the beauty of the stars reflected in the water below and the rush of the sea breezes on his face, he was filled with anticipation and excitement.

Later, a journalist would describe this cruise as the "voyage of the damned," and Meneghini, in his memoir, would recall the embarkation in equally heated prose: "Thus began the tragic adventure." But to Onassis it seemed an auspicious beginning.

6

CITIES ON A HILL

May there be many a summer morning,
when full of gratitude, full of joy,
you enter harbors seen for the first time.

C. P. Cavafy, "Ithaca"

Southeast of Genoa in the wide gulf of the Ligurian Sea a tongue of land juts out into the sapphire water and rises to the peak of Monte de Portofino—an ecological paradise clothed in the burnt colors of wildflowers and Mediterranean maquis thickets. Erosion of the coastal rocks has exposed horizontal layers of reds and ochers, pinks, yellows and browns. In the towns, brightly painted houses, churches, and monasteries echo the earth's colors: apricot and peach, pale stone, and verdant green. Once a sleepy fishing village at the foot of the mountain, innocent of traffic and threaded by paths of steps, Portofino had become a playground for the international set, frequented by wealthy foreigners in their yachts ever since Guy de Maupassant arrived on his boat, the *Bel-Ami,* in 1889.

The harbor was crowded with pleasure craft on the morning of July 23, 1959, when the passengers aboard the *Christina* awoke and rang for breakfast to be brought to them in their staterooms. First to be served—even before the arrival in port—was Sir Winston, following a pattern established on his two cruises on the *Christina* during the previous year. He was awakened at exactly 9 a.m. by his valet with a glass of orange juice and a pot of coffee. Shortly after came a second tray with various cereals. When that was finished, a third tray appeared with a single glass of whiskey. After breakfast, he usually spent the morning in bed reading books selected from the Onassis library, and rose to dress only when it was time for lunch.

Maria arose earlier than was her custom to have ample time to dress for an excursion on shore. She had taken pains to be appropriately attired for this trip, but her judgment was not infallible. The outfit she chose on her first morning was "cruise pajamas" brightly printed with cabbage roses, and when she got on deck, she discovered that she looked a bit conspicuous next to Tina in her more conservative dark slacks and light T-shirt, and Nonie Montague Browne in a full-skirted, belted cotton sundress.

Before she lost her excess weight, Maria's careless clothes sense often led to disastrous missteps, but since becoming slim, she had made a great effort to learn to be stylish. In this she was aided by Madame Biki, the premiere fashion designer of Milan, and Biki's son-in-law and partner, Alain Reynaud. According to Madame Biki, the first time Maria and her husband came to her Milan boutique, Maria weighed more than two hundred pounds, and it was an awkward occasion for all. Meneghini, horrified by the prices, said in his heavy Veronese dialect, "Maria, we'd better go; this is not for us. There's nothing here that's our style." Meanwhile, Madame Biki, eyeing the overweight customer in her shapeless suit, flat shoes, and plastic earrings, muttered to the director of the boutique: "A peasant on her Sunday outing." Maria, however, left the store that day with a comment worthy of her theatrical temperament: "I'll be back." When she fulfilled her promise a year later and sixty-five pounds lighter, the designer didn't recognize her. "She had the radiance that comes from the knowledge of beauty from within," Biki recalled. "The revelation of her beauty as a woman was as important as her artistic success, if not more so."

Biki entrusted Maria to Reynaud, a Frenchman who had previously worked for the couturier Jacques Fath. He became Maria's Pygmalion, teaching her how to walk in high heels, how to emphasize her best features—her eyes, her neck, her breasts, and her tiny waist—and to camouflage her worst ones—the wide hips and the swollen legs and ankles that no regimen could alter. (Her legs particularly were a cause of great anguish. In a review of one of her early performances as Aida, a critic wrote snidely, "It was impossible to tell the difference between the legs of the elephants on the stage and those of Aida sung by Maria Callas." Until the last days of her life Maria would recall how she wept over these words.) When she went on tour, Reynaud would give her plans for the shoes, jewelry, and accessories to wear with each outfit, and when she lived in Paris they would design her gowns together over the telephone.

Maria was ever after obsessed with self-adornment. A *Time* cover story about her in 1956 breathlessly reported that she owned "25 fur coats, 40 suits, 150 pairs of shoes, 300 hats and 200 dresses." When I interviewed Madame Biki in her home in Milan she told me, "Maria had marvelous eyes, so Alain told her, 'You need to wear veils to make your eyes more gorgeous, more mysterious.' These were the small secrets that he taught her. I am certain that if he hadn't made her secure in her beauty, taught her how to be so elegant, she wouldn't have become Callas.'"

Maria Callas' sudden weight loss in 1953 and 1954, when she was thirty, is a keystone of her legend. Many who can't name a single opera she sang are aware that she transformed herself almost overnight from an obese soprano into a slender fashion plate.

As her fame increased, Callas, the consummate actress, resolved to lose weight to portray more credibly some of the fragile heroines of her repertoire. She would later comment, "I felt—as the woman of the theater that I was and am—that I needed these necklines and the chinlines to be very thin and very pronounced." She knew, as an artist and a perfectionist, that no matter how good an actress she was she could hardly be convincing portraying such delicate creatures as the frail Madame Butterfly and the consumptive Violetta while weighing over 220 pounds.

All her life Callas had tried without success to lose her excess weight. In Mexico, with Giulietta Simionato, she consulted a plastic surgeon to see whether an operation could improve her swollen, heavy legs, but he said no. In her king-sized bathroom in Milan she endured countless hot-wax treatments and electric massage. Together with Meneghini, she consulted noted European doctors about medications for weight loss, but "none of the specialists wished to experiment on such a famous singer," he wrote in his memoir.

Maria's desperate campaign embraced all the popular weight-loss stratagems of the day; she ate only salads and nearly raw meat, and had constant massages, striving to look like her idol, the wraithlike Audrey Hepburn. Nothing seemed to work. Then, starting in 1953, a remarkable transformation began, which her husband carefully charted in kilos as she sang each role. She lost 66 pounds (30 kilos) between her performances in *La Gioconda* in December 1952, when she weighed 210 pounds, and in *Don Carlos* in April 1954, at La Scala, when she was 144. Eventually she was down to a sylphic 117 pounds on her five-foot-nine-inch frame. Now, Callas believed, she could be convincing as the gaunt Medea or the ghostly, sleepwalking Anina in *Sonnambula*. When she performed at La Scala in June of 1954 as Queen Alcestis, she was lifted over the heads of three bearers, who carried her on high into the temple at the end of the second act. The conductor, Carlo Maria Giulini, said, "She had become another woman and another world of expression opened to her." She had transformed herself before the astonished eyes of her fans, and everybody wanted to know how she had done it.

Typically, throughout her life Maria gave a variety of contradictory explanations for this transformation, often emphasizing her spartan diet and her great self-discipline. But the story she told friends and the one confirmed by Meneghini in his memoir is bizarre: it all started with a tape worm. Maria said that she had contracted the parasite accidentally from eating salads and uncooked meat. In fact she told a horrified Nadia Stancioff, Maria's assistant and friend, that she had done so *twice,* saying, "You don't have to make such a face. It's a perfectly harmless, clean animal. In my case, instead of making me lose weight, it made me gain weight. As soon as I got rid of it, I started to lose weight. What happened to my body after that was nothing short of a miracle." (As Nadia points out, medical authorities find it hard to account for this.)

Meneghini tells how one day, while bathing, Maria was startled to find the head of a tapeworm emerging from her body. In hysterics, she had him called out of a performance he was attending at La Scala. When he phoned to find out what was wrong, she shocked him with the cryptic exclamation: "Battista, please come immediately. I've killed it!" He rushed back to their suite at the Grand Hotel in horrified apprehension. "In a moment of rage she was capable of irreparable actions," he wrote, recalling an incident in Brazil when a room service waiter "tried to touch her breasts" and Maria flung him out of the room with such force that he had to be hospitalized. After learning the truth, Meneghini called Callas' doctor, who prescribed some medicine to eliminate the problem; nevertheless, he reports, in the next week she lost six pounds. "With the help of the doctor we arrived at the conclusion that the change was due to the expelling of the tapeworm," Meneghini wrote. "While in the majority of people this parasite causes a drop in body weight, in Maria it was having the opposite effect. Once she was free of it, the pounds began to melt away."

Close friends of Maria's from this time, however, dispute Meneghini's account and argue that Callas swallowed the tapeworm on purpose. Giulietta Simionato told me that Maria confessed to her: "I know what happened because she told me, 'Look, there have been many stories about this, but it's true that I ingested a tapeworm. I took it voluntarily and that's how I lost thirty kilos.' "

Whatever the truth about its cause, Maria's weight loss inspired vast popular interest in Italy. While the newspapers were speculating about her diet regimen, a pasta company executive who was a friend of Meneghini's brother-in-law, Dr. Giovanni Cazzarolli, convinced him to write a testimonial saying that he, Cazzarolli, had treated Callas and that she had lost

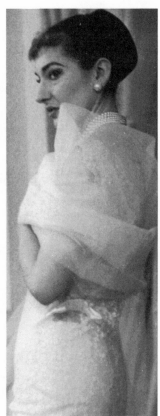

*Callas transformed herself from hefty prima donna to
sylphlike fashion plate in less than eighteen months.*

weight by eating "pasta from the Pantanella Mills," which he praised as
"physiological pasta—dietetic foods from the great Roman industries of
nourishment." Callas immediately filed suit against the doctor and the pasta
maker.

As it happened, the president of the pasta firm was a prince, a lawyer,
and the nephew of Pope Pius XII. When the Meneghinis accepted an invitation to meet the pope in 1954, Maria and the pontiff found themselves in
an animated argument provoked by his suggestion that she sing Wagner in
the original German rather than Italian, a notion to which she took exception. Then he addressed Meneghini on behalf of the pasta company. "Our
nephew is president of that organization and . . . we would be grateful if
you could arrive quickly at an agreement, in a manner in which the pope
could be left in peace." Whenever Maria felt she had been betrayed or
misused—as when she was exploited by the pasta company for advertising
purposes—she would insist on taking the matter to court, no matter how

great the authority of anyone who tried to dissuade her. Despite the pope's request, Callas insisted on pursuing her claim in the courts, even after he died in 1958. Once again she ultimately prevailed, but the final decision arrived in July of 1959, as Callas was aboard the *Christina*. She only learned of it upon her return to Milan. Meneghini wrote, "Now it no longer mattered. Maria was totally absorbed in other matters."

On the deck of the *Christina* on July 23, 1959, as Onassis' guests admired the bright tableau of Portofino's harbor, Maria hoped her flowered outfit would go unnoticed or at least unremarked. Tina proposed to lead the ladies on a shopping excursion through the town, and all eagerly agreed, except for Lady Churchill.

They were somewhat dismayed when they disembarked to find press and photographers waiting on shore. No one was supposed to know their itinerary ahead of time. Undaunted, Tina gamely led them on a round of the tourist shops, where hand-made lace and embroidered shawls caught Maria's attention. Even as photographers trotted along behind them snapping away to the party's annoyance, she chatted amiably with her hostess, who looked tiny walking beside her. They were joined by Antonella Agnelli, the wife of the Fiat executive Umberto Agnelli, whose yacht was also anchored at Portofino. When they finished shopping and were headed back to the *Christina*, Maria ran into Countess Consuelo Crespi, a prominent Milanese socialite who was a guest of the Italian industrialist Giorgio Vavaro on his yacht, the *Taitu*. A month later, in Milan, Countess Crespi was one of the first to whisper of a separation between Maria and Meneghini, although no one else in Maria's circle believed her. "Maria was so distant toward Battista after the cruise, it was obvious something had happened," she told friends.

When the women returned to the yacht, there was a light lunch under a green canopy at tables arranged around the pool near the stern, after which Maria went below to show Meneghini her purchases and to rest. By late afternoon everyone would collect in the game room for cocktails before the formal dinner.

At the beginning of the cruise, according to both Nonie and Anthony Montague Browne, Maria and her husband were almost cloyingly affectionate with each other, to the amusement of the other guests. "When they got on the boat, they were literally sort of turtledoves," Nonie recalled. "It was very remarkable, all sort of cooing and whistling to each other, kiss, kiss, glowing. She couldn't go anywhere without him and she said to Anthony that Meneghini had entirely helped her through her life, he had discovered

Maria, in a floral print, touring Portofino with
Tina and Nonie Montague Browne

her and her lovely voice, that she wouldn't be anywhere without his dedication. It was rather sweet, actually." This is hardly behavior one would expect of a woman who was angry at her husband over money matters, but Maria's demonstration of affection toward Battista may have been an effort to convince the others, and perhaps herself as well, of her attachment to him.

On those first sunny days sailing down the Italian Riviera, Meneghini saw no signs that his rapturous marriage was in trouble. "Even on Onassis' yacht, everyone was aware of how much we were in love," he wrote in his memoirs, in his rather mannered prose. "Our reserve and our romantic comportment made them smile. They said that, because of our presence, it was a love cruise. It was Maria's wish that we were always elegant, at every hour. Together we decided what suits and outfits to wear. . . . Comparing our life style with that of the millionaires, Maria said, 'They have what they have, yes, but I have you, always, always.' . . . She saw only me and still behaved like a young girl on a honeymoon. . . . This was our relationship until August 7. Before that date, I noticed absolutely nothing that could have foreshadowed the tragedy."

Shortly after the cocktail hour began in Portofino, two distinguished-looking men paid a call on the *Christina* to greet Sir Winston. They were Don Juan, the son of King Alfonso XIII of Spain, who had been deposed by the dictator Francisco Franco in 1939, and Juan Carlos, his handsome son, who had been chosen by Franco to restore the monarchy and take over as king upon the dictator's own death. In 1947 Franco had brought the nine-year-old Juan Carlos back to Spain to supervise his education at the country's various military academies. Now, as the twenty-one-year-old prince was introduced to the guests on the *Christina*, clicking his heels and bowing low to kiss the hand of each woman, no one could help thinking that this tall, fair, wavy-haired young man was one of the most eligible bachelors in the world.

When the Spaniards left, Onassis guided everyone into the dining room, where the Vertes murals of the four seasons decorated the walls. It was Ari who planned the placement every night, seating Lady Churchill on his right, of course, and Maria on his left. Maria was delighted to find Sir Winston seated on her other side and concentrated on charming him throughout the meal, even feeding him tidbits from her plate. She didn't notice the effect of this behavior on the other guests. "Maria always wanted to sit next to my grandfather," Celia Sandys recalls. "I don't suppose she got terribly good vibes from the rest of us. We all hated her. We were all sort of revolted by her trying to feed him ice cream from her plate, but he was enchanted by her. He loved glamorous women. Every time we sat down to dinner she would do something to aggravate everyone else."

Nonie said that she usually got stuck next to Meneghini, but was often compensated by having Sir Winston on the other side. "I usually sat on Sir Winston's left, because he was polite to the person on his right, and after he had done his stuff, he knew we could have a cozy chat," she recalls. "I think Diana [Sandys] didn't like me because she thought I was in a way closer to her father than she was. I wasn't really, but I could talk to him and she was quite nervous with him."

Diana Churchill Sandys, then forty-nine, was in a fragile emotional state during the summer of 1959. She was separated from her husband, who would divorce her the following year, and she had been battling mental illness for more than a decade. Sir Winston and Lady Clementine thought that a relaxing cruise aboard the Onassis yacht would take Diana's mind off the breakup of her marriage to Duncan and give her an opportunity to relax and calm her nerves in the company of her sixteen-year-old daughter. She seemed in fine control of herself as the cruise began, but was somewhat reserved, even in the company of her parents, and Onassis made a concentrated effort to include her in the dinner table conversation.

When the meal ended and the guests went out on deck to admire the beauty of Portofino's harbor, which looked like a set for a Verdi opera as the lights from the cafés reflected on the cobblestones of the main square, Onassis proposed to take his guests to a nightclub he knew in the hills above the town, after the Churchills retired. Celia Sandys, at sixteen, at first was pleased to be included as one of the adults.

Onassis had at least one favorite *boîte*, or taverna, in every port city in Europe and the Middle East. His arrival in any one of them typically created a furor comparable to that surrounding an international film or sports star. Once he was seated, a continuous stream of women would come up to him, ignoring any females in his party, and whisper in his ear, inviting him to visit, chiding him for neglecting to call, dropping the names of mutual friends. It is difficult to understand how a squat, swarthy man with an oversized nose, wearing dark sunglasses and baggy clothes, could cause such excitement wherever he went (although someone once remarked, "He looked a lot taller when he stood on his money"). Nadia Stancioff described her first sight of Onassis like this: "He was the opposite of the word 'handsome,' yet his magnetism and enveloping smile would have brought a number of movie stars down a peg or two. . . . Even in casual company he gave the impression that his strength lay in the fact that he had never bent to rules and conventions as he reached for the top. His rough ways and egocentric interest in captivating those around him were riveting."

Maria Callas herself described what first attracted her to Onassis on the cruise in a conversation with Stelios Galatopoulos, a music critic and author who interviewed her near the end of her life. "In Monte Carlo, where the cruise began," she told him, "I was very impressed by his charm but above all by his powerful personality and the way he would hold everybody's attention. Not only was he full of life, he was a source of life. Even before I had the chance to talk to him alone for any length of time . . . I began to feel strangely relaxed. I had found a friend, the kind that I'd never had before and so urgently needed at the time."

On this first evening of the journey, as Onassis held court in the dark, noisy cabaret overlooking the lights of Portofino, his guests found themselves enveloped by his charm and hospitality. But young Celia Sandys wanted only to go back to the ship. "It was very dark indeed and we all sat there for an interminable time," Celia recalled. I interviewed her in London's underground War Rooms, from which her grandfather had directed England's defiance of Hitler during World War II. (She was preparing to address a meeting at the museum that has been established there.)

"I mean it was dark, dark, dark! I'm sure it's a lovely nightclub but I felt terribly bored. Finally everyone got up, all ready to go, and I thought 'Thank God for that,' and then this man came over and asked me to dance. So I said, 'Oh, so kind, thanks very much but we're just leaving.' At that moment I felt two pairs of hands on my back, one was my mother's, and I was *propelled* onto the dance floor. I didn't have a clue who he was and I thought it most odd that I'd been pushed into the arms of some unknown man, so I said, 'What do you do?' and he said, 'Don't you remember me? We met today on the yacht.' Of course it was Prince Juan Carlos. I was totally overcome with embarrassment at that point. I thought someone might have told me who I was made to dance with! In the morning we set off for Capri."

When the *Christina* steamed out of Portofino at 2 a.m. and headed down the Tuscan archipelago, pausing on the morning of Friday, July 24, near the coast of Elba, Meneghini, still bothered by the rocking of the boat, was in no mood to join the others at the rail to gaze at the island where Victor Hugo spent his boyhood and Napoleon passed his year of exile in 1814.

That night was spent at sea, with an after-dinner movie in the ship's theater. Before every cruise with Churchill, Onassis would request a list of films that the old man might enjoy, according to Montague Browne. "One of the secretaries always prepared the list," he told me. "They always had the same sort of theme: a Western, a spy film, a military one. That one about Lady Hamilton was one of his favorites [*That Hamilton Woman*, with Vivien Leigh and Laurence Olivier]. As long as it had lots of action, was simple, and good triumphed over evil in the end—'That's excellent—woo, woo, woo!' "

The nightly film was only one of the routines that agreeably organized the days and nights aboard the *Christina* around the presence of Sir Winston. After arriving on deck around noon, Churchill would remain there with the others for the rest of the day, either dozing in his chair or watching the sea with Onassis by his side. Often, a game of cards or bezique would help the time pass. Before the cocktail hour, he would return to his cabin to don his dinner jacket and black tie.

Although cocktails were usually served around the pool area on deck, dinner itself was always in the formal dining room when Churchill or other dignitaries were on board. The waiters wore their dress uniforms, white jackets and dark pants, and the ship's officers wore white uniforms in summer and blue in winter.

It was at dinner that Sir Winston would most often astonish and delight the others with his legendary eloquence, re-creating scenes from his wartime exploits with an uncanny memory for dates and details, debating issues of history, citing philosophers, and reciting long sections of poetry without faltering. Nonie insists that Sir Winston was not at all "gaga" on this cruise, as some have reported. "He was actually always deaf and would get tired with too much talking. But if you asked him any questions, he'd think and then give you a perfectly bright and sometimes very amusing answer or an observation with great depth. I remember Anthony said to him one day, 'What did you really think of Lawrence of Arabia?' He thought for a little while and said: 'A very remarkable character and very careful of that fact.' Now that came from an old man nearly ninety."

Onassis liked to sit with Churchill after lunch or dinner and engage him in discussions of history or philosophy. The two could finish off a bottle of Dom Perignon each at dinner, and afterward, Churchill never missed his brandy and cigar. "[Onassis'] conversation was very interesting," Anthony Montague Browne recalled. "He was full of questions [for Churchill]. He was deeply interested in history—one reason [Onassis] got on so well with the Boss. He liked to talk. Funny thing, Ari liked historians, but he loathed poets. 'Poets are seducers,' he used to say." Recalling one such conversation when Onassis was denigrating poets, Anthony writes in his memoir, "I managed to dredge up from the rag-bag of memory a quotation from Aristotle and presented it to his modern homonym at dinner. It ran approximately: 'Poetry is a much deeper and more significant matter than either philosophy or history.' The quote provoked indignant incredulity. Cables were despatched to Athens University and great was the consternation when the quotation was verified."

Onassis' concern for Churchill was entirely sincere, according to all the surviving guests from that cruise, and not merely another form of self-promotion, as some of them had suspected at the start. Before the "Old Naval Party" (Churchill's World War II code name) retired for the night, if the ship was moving, Onassis and Captain Kostas would go into Churchill's stateroom, sit on his bed, and, talking to the bridge by telephone, regulate the engines to just the right pitch to guarantee the least vibrations for the old man. "He really cared [about Churchill]," Nonie Montague Browne told me. "He really loved that man. It was very sweet. I was wrong when I thought originally that he was collecting him like Greta Garbo and the rest. I got a very wrong impression on first meeting him. I must admit, when I first met Ari he was always in nightclubs. He hadn't much to say to me. But as I got to know him I came to consider him a real friend."

About Maria Callas she added, "I don't think that Sir Winston ever quite cottoned on to what it was that she did. He must have heard of Maria Callas, but he didn't particularly know that much about her. He liked music hall things. She never sang for him [on the cruise]. He loved music but he couldn't quite make out who this woman was. There was Ari and Tina and this odd woman and then there was his eldest daughter, who was a little bit unhappy—broken-up marriage and so forth—and a nice daughter who's about fifteen. It makes one's mind boggle to think how we could all get on!'"

If Onassis observed his customary reverential solicitude toward Churchill, he paid more discreet though no less intense attention to his other guest of honor. On that evening of the cruise another pattern emerged. Maria and Onassis would sit up and talk after their respective spouses had gone to bed. Each had a lifelong habit of wakefulness through most of the night. Maria would sleep until nearly noon. Onassis got by on only a few hours' sleep every day. (He once bragged to the society columnist Doris Lilly, while they were sitting in a nightclub at 4 a.m., "I can go for three days at a time without sleep at all. At the most I need about three or four hours a night. If I stay up for three days, I can sleep twenty-four hours without waking up once.")

At first these long private conversations, mostly in Greek, were not deeply personal, Maria later told friends, but involved sharing stories of their lives and discussing Callas' problematic financial situation. Having been so poor during the war in Greece that she was reduced to scavenging for food, Maria had a chronic fear of being left penniless in her old age. She complained to Onassis about her husband's handling of her funds and his disclosure that she couldn't afford to retire, because they had nothing in the bank. The pressures of her grueling schedule of performances, her uncertain health, her growing difficulty controlling her voice, and the fickleness of her fans were all beginning to tell on her, but she could ill afford her fantasy of giving up the exhausting routine she had followed for the past twenty years.

Whether out of his sense of personal honor (*philotimo*) or an awareness of the seductive power of paternal benevolence, Onassis told Maria to let him take care of everything. He already managed the finances of many members of his extended family and he would be honored to advise someone like her. Aristo (as she came to call him) said that he and Prince Rainier had long lamented the lack of an opera company in Monte Carlo. He would create for Callas her own company there and she could perform whenever and whatever she wished. This sounded like the fulfillment of her fondest dreams: she always chafed at the inadequate staging and production and rehearsal schedules of old established institutions like the Met in New York, but with her own opera company, she could control every detail of the productions, including the cast who would perform with her.

These conversations stretching far into the night around the colored fountains of the swimming pool were at first quite innocent, and Onassis always took pains to secure the company of a third person to stay up with them for appearance' sake. Churchill was, after all, a paragon of dignity who would hardly condone any irregular behavior on board, and Lady Clementine was notoriously prudish. And so the inauguration of yet another evening ritual created special shipboard duties, these usually falling to the good-natured Montague Brownes.

"Maria and Ari would just sit out there, talking and drinking, and they terribly wanted somebody to be there too," Nonie explains. "He would say, 'Oh, don't go to bed, Nonie, have a little swim.' So I'd have a midnight swim. It was my night on. And Anthony would do it the next night. We had to stay up, to keep things proper. Mind you, I had plenty of champagne. I didn't mind at all. I made a note in my diary occasionally. If I wrote 'danced and star-gazed until two thirty,' you'll know that they're sitting up till two-thirty and I'm having to swim, dance, and drink champagne. It wasn't too hard a life if one doesn't have to get up too early in the morning. I had a very nice time. It wasn't every night, obviously. When you go on a lovely cruise it's a very small thing to do for Ari to stay around. I was quite fond of him. He liked to trail his fingers in the water and look at the stars. He had a great sentimental side, philosophical and sweet."

Anthony Montague Browne, whom I interviewed at Claridge's, separately from his former wife, describes things much the same, although he recalls the late nights à deux as not beginning until later in the cruise. "They used to sit up very late, not holding hands or anything, and eat what he called saletés grecs [Greek filth]. He was a night bird. He was a terrifically nocturnal man. When he was on shore he used to go for walks at night, many kilometers. On deck we used to take it in turns to stay up with him. Actually it was no chore. I enjoyed it."

Perhaps because of their special duties as night watchmen, Anthony and Nonie were the first to notice Maria's attitude toward Battista slowly and inexorably changing. Meneghini himself apparently sensed nothing. "Maria would say, 'Oh, you go to bed, Battista. Don't put open the air conditioning dear, you know it upsets my throat.' And off he'd trot like a good little dog. It was rather sad," Nonie remembers. Anthony noted in his memoir Maria's "rather engaging explanation" of why she insisted that Meneghini swelter in the cabin below decks, no matter what the temperature: "Sopranos hate air conditioning even more than they hate other sopranos."

On the morning of Saturday, July 25, the *Christina* entered the Bay of Naples. No sooner was the yacht moored at 10:40 a.m. off the Isle of Capri, in the Marina Piccola, than Meneghini made a declaration; he told his wife that he was not enjoying himself and he wanted to disembark at once and head home to Sirmione. Maria was appalled and vetoed the notion. To leave so early would be ungracious and an insult to their hosts, she pointed out, and besides, she was having a lovely time.

Onassis organized transportation to take the group by water to the Grotta Azzurra. Already known to the Romans, the Blue Grotto is the most famous tourist destination on the island; today visitors to Capri pay a steep fare to sail in a tiny boat through a four-foot-high opening to see the famous cave, which has slowly sunk to over fifty feet below sea level. This causes the refraction of sunlight through the water, creating an otherworldly blue color inside the grotto, while light reflected off the white sand bottom gives objects below the water's surface a silvery glow. Nonie recalls with amusement that when Clementine Churchill was being conveyed through the small portal into the cave, a bystander shouted in English, "Now granny, keep your head down!" The stately Lady Churchill stiffened in dismay at such familiarity.

Anthony Montague Browne did not go along to see the Blue Grotto. He was plagued with a painful abscessed tooth and managed to find the only dentist on the island, who sat him down in a kitchen chair and treated him with a pedal drill. While Anthony was undergoing this torture, the other guests (not including the Churchills) had time to take in Capri and do a little shopping. The same photographers who had accosted them in Portofino were once again on their trail, snapping Maria and Tina as they debated the qualities of a knitted shawl in an outdoor shop.

By this time the British passengers on board were beginning to suspect Maria of tipping off the press. As Celia Sandys expressed it to me: "The first thing we noticed was that this group of reporters would turn up, the same ones each time, and it was quite clear that she'd rung them up and told them to come. And everyone was feeling very aggravated with her. The tension was building. Not necessarily because anyone was aware of the relationship between Ari and Maria Callas, but I think because she was such a prima donna. Everyone else on the ship considered that the star of the show was my grandfather. But she was ruining everyone's holiday by having her group of what we now call paparazzi following her around."

In fact, it's much more likely that Onassis himself was alerting the press to the whereabouts of the *Christina* and her guests. The first time Churchill ever set foot on the yacht, in 1956, when Onassis had just met him and invited him on a day trip out of Monte Carlo, Churchill, together with Emery and Wendy Reves, his hosts on the Riviera, agreed to come on the condition that there would be no press. But when they arrived at the gangplank and Ari came forward to meet them, a swarm of photographers and reporters was waiting to commemorate the beginning of the friendship between the controversial shipowner and Britain's greatest living statesman. (The Reveses were furious, but Churchill got over his dismay and the trip proceeded as soon as he saw the bottles of Dom Perignon and bowls of caviar awaiting him on board.) Onassis typically liked to use reporters to record his exploits, whereas Maria despised them, sometimes becoming hysterical when they mobbed her. Once in New York, when she was particularly annoyed, she used the voice projection she had learned as a singer to indicate her displeasure in a sharp New York accent as she screamed, "Lay off me, will you?" "She had a very ugly American voice," Nonie told me. "She had a very nice voice in Italian and in Greek, but in English she had sort of a Bronx accent."

Although Maria was not in fact responsible for the press attacks in Italy, the rest of the passengers, who increasingly cooled to her, quickly blamed the paparazzi on her, just as they would other problems during the cruise. Maria's lack of humor was partly to blame. Most of the others had traveled together before and enjoyed a kind of Anglo-Saxon prankishness that was completely alien to Callas, who had never been to boarding school or camp or anywhere that might have accustomed her to the good-natured hazing that enlivened the days on the *Christina* (as, for example, when Nonie and Tina decided to short-sheet all the beds—making "apple pie beds," as it was termed in England. "It was not very well received," Nonie recalled dryly).

Such frivolity was utterly incompatible with Maria's sense of self-importance—especially her position as "La Callas"—which endeared her to no one on board but did furnish some amusement. In his memoir, Anthony Montague Browne remarked that Maria "seemed almost to be trying to parody the stereotypical prima donna in her behavior." He recorded her comment to him early in the cruise: "I like travelling with Winston Churchill. It relieves me of some of the burden of my popularity."

By the time the shadows were lengthening over Capri, most of the passengers were back on board waiting for the cocktail hour to begin. Anthony Montague Browne had returned from the dentist, taken a strong drink to calm his nerves, and decided to relax with a swim off the boat in the mirror-like waters near Marina Piccola. "I swam off into the warm and silk-smooth sea," he recalled. "The combined effect of the anesthetic, alcohol and the sea was soothing, and I drowsily watched the setting sun. The *Christina* appeared to be an awful long way off, and receding further. The peaceful water concealed a strong southward current. The next stop appeared to be Sicily or North Africa. Fortunately, *Christina* had an almost naval watch system, and the officer on the bridge had been following me. Within ten minutes a launch picked me up." Montague Browne was saved by the watchfulness of Captain Kostas and his crew, but this was not the last time one of the passengers on the voyage would narrowly escape a fatal misadventure.

That evening, the chanteuse Gracie Fields and her Yugoslav husband, Boris, who owned a restaurant on Capri, were invited on board. Between the two wars, Fields, a Lancashire music hall star, had been wildly acclaimed in England, and her ditties were just the kind of slightly naughty popular music that Sir Winston liked best. "I think Maria was rather cross when Gracie Fields came on board," Celia Sandys told me.

After dinner, Fields favored Churchill with a special performance, singing with the "very powerful North Country voice that had earned her fame and great affection," as Montague Browne put it. To the tune of "Volare," a song that was blasting endlessly from every radio in the Western world that summer, she improvised a song that began, "We love you Sir Winston, We love you, we doooooo." Everyone supposed that the old man would be delighted by the show, as Fields performed all the songs that had heartened his soldiers during the dark days of the war, but Montague Browne recalls Churchill muttering to him, "God's teeth! How long is this going on for?" Nonie also recalls the performance to have been excruciating. "Our toes were curling slowly. But he loved seeing her. He remembered all her songs."

During the cruise, Maria never sang on her own, according to the Montague Brownes. Several accounts, including Meneghini's, say that Churchill asked her to sing and she turned him down cold, but the surviving passengers insist that that never happened. What they do recall is Sir Winston and Onassis and the other guests, including Maria, gathered around the piano belting out old popular songs like "Daisy, Daisy, give me your answer do."

After the musical entertainment was over and Gracie Fields and her husband had gone ashore, the passengers on the *Christina* went to bed, except for Aristotle and Maria. They sat up on the stern sipping brandy. At 5:10 a.m. the next morning the captain steered the yacht away from Capri toward the toe of Italy's boot.

Sunday, July 26, was spent at sea, but the *Christina* paused to circle the easternmost of the seven Aeolian Islands, just as Odysseus had done in his journey home toward Ithaca. Stromboli is a volcano rising out of the sea, and it is one of the most active in Europe. When it erupts, which it does unpredictably, lava flows down the *Sciara del Fuoco,* or Trail of Fire, on the volcano's northwestern flank, so that the inhabitants of the villages on the east and south remain safe.

When the *Christina* came around the smoking volcano, Onassis called his guests to come see it, but Meneghini was too seasick and insisted on staying in his stateroom. As the others gathered at the rail, Onassis told ancient tales about the volcano. "He wanted it to erupt in the dusk," Montague Browne said. "It was constantly erupting, but now it was silent. He shouted, 'Come on, show us your face.' Then he pressed the siren on the boat and at that moment it went off. It erupted, startling Ari, who was merely posturing when he challenged it. Lava started rolling down, red hot, as if down a staircase. Ari said, 'I don't like that.' He felt it was a bad sign."

Like her host, Maria was just as superstitious as most Greeks, and she quickly crossed herself to ward off evil.

As the sun faded into darkness, leaving only the ominous Trail of Fire on the horizon, Onassis instructed the captain to head south. They had another day of sailing before they reached the Ionian Sea. Before they entered Greek waters, they would have to cross the Straits of Messina, where sailors in ancient times refused to go because of the strong currents and jagged rocks, and where Onassis' hero, Odysseus, found himself caught between two horrific monsters—Scylla, whose six heads were armed with triple rows of sharklike teeth, and Charybdis, the whirlpool, which drank down and spewed forth ships as they passed between Sicily and the Italian mainland.

7

PASSAGE TO DELPHI

The Lastrygonians and the Cyclops,
angry Poseidon, you won't encounter them
unless you carry them inside your soul.

C. P. Cavafy, "Ithaca"

The nightly talks between Onassis and Callas intensified as the *Christina* sailed toward Greece, the country they felt to be their cultural and spiritual home although neither had been born there. As they watched the phosphorescent trail of the ship's wake trace their journey toward the Ionian Sea, Maria worried about how she would be received by her compatriots and how she would feel upon returning to the place where she had lived between the ages of thirteen and twenty-one. Those had been the most painful years of her life, and she was dreading the unpleasant memories that would be stirred up by seeing Athens again.

Maria told Aristo about her conflicting emotions as a thirteen-year-old girl on the day in February 1937 when she and her mother sailed aboard the liner *Saturnia* from New York City, leaving her father behind. Jackie, her pretty nineteen-year-old sister, had been sent ahead several months earlier to stay with their grandmother and charm the relatives while Maria remained in Manhattan with her mother until her graduation from eighth grade in January 1937.

Evangelia "Litsa" Dimitriadis Kalogeropoulos was a bitter and disillusioned woman even before Maria was born. She felt that she had married below herself when she agreed to wed George Kalogeropoulos, from Meligala, a town in the Peloponnesus, in 1916. "My father was a general and my great-uncle was physician to the king," she would complain to her friends and to her children. "And I married a pharmacist." In 1917 the couple had a daughter, Yacinthy (Hyacinth), nicknamed Jackie in America. Three years later a boy, fair and blue-eyed like his mother, was born and christened Vassili. He quickly became the center of his mother's life, the usual position for an only son in a Greek family.

Everything began to fall apart for Evangelia when Vassili died at the age of three in 1923 from meningitis. Not long after the tragedy, George Kalogeropoulos sold his house and business without consulting his wife and announced that they were moving to America. Evangelia, who was pregnant and sure she was carrying another son, opposed the move from the moment she learned of it. George's pharmacy, the only one in thirteen counties, had brought them social prestige, servants, and the finest house in their small town, and he was sacrificing it all to move to a country where neither of them could speak the language. Evangelia's tears could not persuade her husband to change his mind, and the unhappy family arrived in New York Harbor on August 2, 1923.

Four months later, on December 2, at Flower Fifth Avenue Hospital in Manhattan, Evangelia was delivered of a twelve-pound baby girl who had the dark features of her father. Litsa was so disappointed it wasn't another boy that she refused to hold her child for four days. She also refused to give the infant a name until her husband proposed Cecilia, whereupon she insisted on Sophia. On the birth certificate, the little girl was finally called Sophia Cecilia; "Anna Maria" was added when she was baptized three years later. (Maria didn't know her actual birth date until she managed to track down the certificate late in life. The document was filed not under "Callas" or "Kalogeropoulos" but "Kalos," a short version of the family name that her father had used briefly after his arrival in New York before settling on "Callas." The second sentence of Evangelia's book, *My Daughter Maria Callas,* reads: "The day she was born, the fourth of December, 1923, there was a snow storm such as I had never seen before." Both the birth date and the weather report are wrong.)

In the ensuing years in Manhattan, Evangelia's life did not improve. She suffered mood swings and hysteria. When the stock market crash of 1929 and the subsequent Depression forced her husband to sell the family's pharmacy in what was called Hell's Kitchen, her bitterness over her misalliance was inflamed once more. Before the sale, she flew into a rage following a fight with George and swallowed poisons she found in the back of the store. Her husband rushed her to the hospital, where her stomach was pumped. Although she was eventually allowed to return home, Maria's godfather, Dr. Leonidas Lantzounis, later told a friend of Maria's that Evan-

*Evangelia, Maria, Jackie, and George Kalogeropoulos in New York,
mid-1920s, before they changed their name to Callas*

gelia was confined for a period to a mental hospital. "After George lost the
drugstore, her mind turned," he said. "She was an ambitious, neurotic
woman who never had a friend. She was in Bellevue for a month."

George Kalogeropoulos was a handsome and charming but rather
ineffectual man. He did not share his wife's passion for opera, theater, and
the arts in general, but enjoyed Greek popular music. There were constant
arguments about what the family would listen to on the large console radio.
When Maria was only five, Evangelia heard her singing along to the broadcast and realized that the pudgy, myopic child had an extraordinary voice.
She was convinced that "Mary," as they called her, had inherited the great
natural musical talent that was evident in Litsa's uncle, Colonel Petros Dimitriadis, who was called the "Singing Commander" during the Balkan Wars
of 1912–1913.

Evangelia bought a pianola, a piano that would also play music rolls
when the pedals were pumped, and nagged George to pay for voice lessons.
Without telling him, she arranged for the child to enter radio contests like
Major Bowes Amateur Hour and hid Maria's identity under assumed names.
Looking back, Callas wasn't sure exactly which talent competitions she'd
entered, but she did remember winning second prize—a watch—in an amateur contest hosted by Jack Benny.

Maria performed in school musicales, and when she practiced at home
with the windows open, according to her mother, passersby would gather

Maria, Evangelia, and Jackie Callas in Athens

in the street below their Washington Heights apartment and applaud. Evangelia was also encouraging Jackie to become a pianist, and soon she began to contemplate taking both her daughters to Greece to promote their musical careers. At the same time, the marriage she had always regretted was disintegrating. George Kalogeropoulos, now a traveling salesman of pharmaceutical products, had found his way into a number of extramarital liaisons, including one with an old family friend, Alexandra Papajohn. Evangelia vowed that as soon as Maria finished eighth grade she and the girls would move to Greece, leaving her husband and their middle-class life in America behind for good. She would find teachers for Maria and enroll her in the national music conservatory. Litsa believed, perhaps naively, that her extended family in Greece would be willing to help finance her daughters' careers. Her marriage was so shattered by then that when she told her husband she was leaving him, according to her daughter Jackie, "He knelt down, crossed himself, and said, 'At last, my God, you have pitied me!' "

In December of 1936, Jackie, who had finished high school, was sent on ahead to Greece, and Litsa would follow with Maria after the girl's graduation from eighth grade at the end of January. They set sail on the *Saturnia* on February 20, 1937, and Litsa soon brought her daughter's singing talents to the attention of the ship's captain, who asked her to perform at a party for the officers and some first-class passengers. The awkward thirteen-year-old was transformed as she performed a spirited version of the Habañera from

*A Callas cousin, Evangelia, Maria, Miltos Embiricos, and Jackie
on the beach in Vouliagmeni, Greece*

Carmen, accompanying herself on the piano. She had removed her thick glasses, and at the end of the performance she plucked a red carnation from a nearby vase and tossed it coquettishly to the captain. It was an early instance of the magic that would grace every ensuing performance of her life; her talent for becoming the character she was portraying would introduce a level of dramatic acting that had never before been seen on the operatic stage.

Evangelia had not anticipated the problems that would await them in Greece. After a round of free meals and offers of temporary lodging, her kin, including Litsa's mother, made it clear that they had no intention of funding the social and musical aspirations of their young American relatives, who could barely speak Greek. To make matters worse, Evangelia discovered that at thirteen Maria was too young to be enrolled in the Conservatory of Athens, the best in Greece, so she applied to the second-best, the National Conservatory. She told them that Maria was sixteen, a claim that aroused no suspicion, given the girl's height and imposing size.

Maria won a scholarship to the National Conservatory, beginning in September 1937. She was taught by Maria Trivella (who gave her French lessons as well), and her first appearance on the stage came in April 1939, four months after her fifteenth birthday: she sang Santuzza in Mascagni's *Cavalleria Rusticana* and won the school's first prize in opera. In December of 1939, Maria managed to win a place at the more prestigious Conservatory of Athens, after performing an audition before the famous Spanish soprano Elvira de Hidalgo, who was trapped in Greece by the civil war in her homeland and had taken a position both at the school and with the Greek National Opera.

Hidalgo's first sighting of Maria has become a staple of the Callas legend. A former member of the Metropolitan Opera who had sung leading roles with Enrico Caruso, Hidalgo looked at the unhappy child—fat, pimply, nervously biting her fingernails, staring shyly down at her worn sandals—and dismissed her as having no presence whatsoever. "The very idea of that girl wanting to become a singer was laughable," Hidalgo recalled. Then Maria opened her mouth and out came "Ocean! Thou Mighty Monster," from Weber's *Oberon*. Hidalgo closed her eyes and was overcome by the "violent cascades of sound, full of drama and emotion." She instantly understood all that Maria could become. From that moment, Hidalgo became Maria's teacher, mentor, and substitute mother. (Hidalgo would remain one of the few people never to have a falling out with the diva, and her photograph was in Maria's apartment on the day she died.) "I owe all my artistic, stage and musical preparation and training to this illustrious Spanish artist," Callas later wrote.

When the conservatory balked at giving Maria a scholarship, Hidalgo simply taught her as her private student for free. Thus began a period of intense training, from ten in the morning until eight at night, as Maria, in addition to having her own lessons, sat in on all the other students' lessons as well. She pored over opera scores on the bus to and from school. There was nothing in her life but music. She had no desire to hurry home at night to spend time with her socially ambitious mother and popular, blond twenty-two-year-old sister.

Jackie, meanwhile, had landed an extremely eligible young man, Miltos Embiricos, the son of a wealthy Greek shipping family, and the couple became engaged in the summer of 1939. It was thanks to the protection of Miltos, who moved them to a spacious apartment on the top floor of 61 Patission Street, that the family would manage to avoid starvation during the worst years of the war. Evangelia was thrilled that her beautiful elder daughter had made such a prestigious match, but Miltos' family considered the girl unworthy of their son. Their disapproval would ultimately prevail, for although Jackie stayed with Miltos and cared for him until he died of a slow and grotesque cancer of the jaw twenty-eight years later, he never got around to marrying her.

On October 28, 1940, a day that is still celebrated throughout Greece, Mussolini's demand that his army be allowed to enter the country was met with the response of Prime Minister Ioannis Metaxas: a resounding and famous "No!" As Italian troops poured over the country's northern border, they were engaged by the much smaller Greek forces, who managed to repel them far into Albania. This astounding triumph was still being celebrated four months later, when Maria made her professional debut at the National Lyric Theater, in the small role of Beatrice in the operetta *Boccaccio*. It was hardly an elegant beginning, but she was well received, and enjoyed her first intoxicating taste of applause and love streaming across the footlights from an audience.

By spring of 1941, German troops replaced the humiliated Italian army, and on April 27 they marched into Athens and raised the swastika over the sacred hill of the Acropolis. Amidst the occupying forces, Maria continued walking to Hidalgo's home every morning and defied the Nazis' six o'clock curfew every night, returning after a long day of practicing her arias, trills, and scales. By the time the Germans, confidently in power, relaxed their rule a few months later and extended the curfew to midnight, Maria learned that Hidalgo had found her a place in the Athens Opera. As she was only seventeen, this success naturally inflamed the jealousy of the other sopranos in the company, who mercilessly criticized her voice's harsh and unruly upper register. Soon, however, they would become even more unforgiving of Maria's growing popularity with the occupying troops.

Like everyone in Athens, the Callas family spent most of their waking hours scrounging for nonexistent food. The occupation and an Allied blockade of Greek ports had choked off all imports, and Athenians were forced to walk to the mountains where food was sold or bartered on the black market—a day-long journey on foot, since there was no gasoline to be had, either. Maria later recalled the winter of 1941: "For the entire summer I had only eaten tomatoes and boiled cabbage, which I was able to find only by walking for miles and miles into the country to persuade the people there to give me something to eat."

Even allowing for Maria's tendency to exaggerate her own miseries, this was a period during which every Athenian knew hunger—indeed, most of the thirty thousand who died starved to death. To avoid surrendering the ration cards of deceased loved ones, families did not report deaths but threw the corpses over the walls of cemeteries. Maria's mother took her own desperate measures: she indiscriminately invited Italian and German officers to her house and encouraged her daughter to sing for them. This of course secured not only food and money for the family, but the deep hostility of other Greeks, including their neighbors on Patission Street and Maria's colleagues at the opera company.

During this period, Maria's mother also embarked on an affair with an Italian officer, but she was at least not partisan in her associations and was willing to welcome officers of any nationality in her house. In the fall of 1941, she agreed to shelter two British officers who had escaped from prison and would have been killed if they were discovered. A Greek friend, knowing that the family spoke fluent English, asked her to hide the men until an escape from Athens could be arranged. Six weeks later the Britons were spirited away, but the next day Italian troops, called by an informer, broke in to search for signs of the men. They would have discovered incriminating possessions left behind, but Maria immediately went to the piano and began singing an aria from *Tosca.* The opera-loving Italians were soon sitting at her feet, enthralled, their search forgotten. They came back the next night for an encore, bringing precious bread, salami, and macaroni.

She would continue to sing for the enemy. *Tosca* was the opera that in 1942 gave the eighteen-year-old Maria her breakthrough opportunity, when she performed the title role for the Athens Opera—the first time, on August 27, in Greek, then the following month in Italian. This major success made the young soprano famous in war-torn Greece, especially for *Tosca,* which she reprised in the summer of 1943. The Italian soldiers made up a good portion of her audience, and the commander of the Italian army of occupation took Maria and five colleagues from the Athens Opera to sing for the Italian troops in Salonika. In the spring of 1944, she performed the lead in Eugen d'Albert's *Tiefland.* Produced to appease the German troops in Athens, who were complaining about hearing so many Italian operas, it brought Maria, on April 22, 1944, her first standing ovation.

By June 6, the Allies had landed in Normandy and it became clear that the war was ending. The Germans marched out of Athens in October, inaugurating a period of euphoria as the emaciated populace danced in the streets. "For three days and nights," wrote an observer, "hungry, sick people spitting blood marched without sleeping, kept going by a collective delirium, the joy of new-found freedom." But jubilation would prove short-lived. As Maria continued to perform for her countrymen, tensions were growing between Communist resistance groups and Greek army forces returning from the Middle East. By November there erupted a full-scale civil war that would exact an even more horrific toll on the country than the World War that had just ended. (In Meligala alone, the hometown of Maria's father, 816 civilians were systematically executed by Communist forces and many of the corpses were tossed into the town well.)

On December 3, 1944, the day after Maria's twenty-first birthday, the Communists staged a coup. At the height of the battle, the Communist military force, ELAS, had the Nationalist troops pinned into a few pockets near the center of Athens. Its secret police came in the night, executing thousands of real and imaginary enemies of the party. In the terrible slaughter that December, almost all of Athens fell into Communist guerrilla hands, except for two small islands of Nationalist strength, one around Constitution Square that included the Grande Bretagne Hotel and the British embassy, and the other centered on the police headquarters just below the Acropolis.

At this time Jackie Callas was barricaded in a hotel near Constitution Square with her fiancé, Miltos Embiricos, and Maria and her mother were trapped in their apartment in a Communist-held area. The mother and daughter had no food other than a bag of dried beans. A cacophony of bombs, machine-gun fire, and the screams of the dying filled the street. At one point Maria and her mother tried to peer out the door of their building but found it blocked by the body of a dead soldier. One night, as their shadows inadvertently fell on a window shade, the windows were shattered by a barrage of machine-gun fire; the sniper missed the two women but slaughtered three pet canaries that they had brought with them from New York.

After twenty days there was a knock at the door, and Maria and her mother opened it to find a small boy who said that he had been sent to lead them out of the Communist sector to the safety of the British embassy on Constitution Square. They refused to go, suspecting a trap, but the next day he came back with a letter from a British officer, and Maria and her mother decided to take the chance of dying in the crossfire. Jackie Callas says that she and her fiancé sent the boy to lead Maria and Evangelia to safety, but Maria always maintained that it was the British embassy, concerned about her welfare because she had been employed as a clerk there after the Athens Opera was closed due to the fighting. "I was assigned to sorting the secret messages," she wrote later. "I carried on like that [walking to work at 6:30 a.m.] until winter, but I still suffer from the strain of those times, which have left me the melancholy heritage of liver problems and [systolic] blood pressure of about ninety when I'm well. . . . [After the seige began] the British advised me not to leave the headquarters; had my delicate task of sorting secret messages for them been discovered, I would have inevitably suffered at the hands of the Communists. But my home was located in an area controlled by the Reds and I didn't want to leave my mother on her own."

On the day before Christmas, 1944, Maria and her mother left their home with only the clothes on their backs and took shelter in the British embassy, where they were reunited with Jackie and Miltos. The next day, the disheartened Athenians were inspired by a surprise Christmas visit from Winston Churchill, who had come with his foreign minister, Anthony Eden, to promise British aid to the beleaguered government troops and to negotiate with the Communist commanders. As a crowd of joyful Athenians formed outside the Grande Bretagne Hotel, Maria, hearing the commotion from the family's quarters nearby, ran to Constitution Square just in time to

Maria with her friend and colleague Giulietta Simionato

see the great man entering his car. He raised his hand in the famous "V" for victory gesture, which the exultant crowd of Athenians returned in salute. It was the first hopeful sign of this desperate winter.

Churchill's intervention turned the tide of war, and in the end the Communists were defeated. With British troops and tanks arriving at the port of Piraeus and streaming into Athens, a truce was negotiated on January 13, 1945, and a semblance of peace returned to the capital. Maria and her mother and sister were able to return to their apartment on Patission Street, but their lives, like those of everyone else, were severely scarred by the months of starvation and internecine brutality.

When she returned to the Athens Opera, Maria found it was now in the control of leftists, and Greece's youngest, most celebrated soprano was informed that her contract was not to be renewed because she had "played too active a part in the last months of the occupation." Envy and fear of her talent were probably the motivating factors, but in any case, her career in Greece was over.

In the brief period between the end of the occupation by Axis forces and the beginning of the Greek Civil War, Maria had received a letter from her father—the first in six years—and in it was enclosed one hundred dollars. She decided, without consulting her mother or sister, that she would return to America. There, she was sure, she would achieve the professional opportunities that she deserved. She gave some private concerts to raise additional funds. Just before her departure, she told her family that she did not want them to accompany her to the port of Piraeus to say good-bye. (By this point her resentment of her mother and her sister had grown so strong that she felt she could oppose them; it would continue to grow, until she would eventually break with them completely.) On September 14, 1945, Callas sailed on the S.S. *Stockholm,* bound for America with little more than hope and a high opinion of her own talents.

While the *Christina* churned toward Greece, Maria recounted her travails in Athens during the war to Onassis. Among the terrible memories of those years, perhaps none was more touching than that of the calculating use her mother made of Maria's singing talent to preserve the family. In fact, it's likely that Maria told Aristo the same story of maternal abuse that she later repeated to her lifelong friend and fellow soprano, Giulietta Simionato.

Still glamorous, slim, and charming at eighty-six when I spoke with her in the fall of 1998, Madame Simionato revealed to me what Maria had whispered to her long after the war. She told Giulietta that her mother had sent her out to prostitute herself among the enemy soldiers.

"She confessed to me in Rome, and I believe she was sincere, because she was always genuine with me—that these men that her mother forced her to go with, she was able to go with them without being touched. Weeping, she told me her story—that those people gave her money, without taking her, you understand. Without taking her! And she brought the money home and her mother thought she gave for it—she nearly brought her to prostitution." Simionato sighed and shook her head in dismay. "These were the delicate things that I didn't dare say until now, twenty years after her death."

A young girl being sent out by her mother and somehow managing with her singing to charm her would-be deflowerers into paying without touching her is worthy of an operatic plot. Even given Maria's history of exaggeration, the tale may be true, as Simionato believed. But Jackie denies that their mother ever put such cruel and abusive pressure on Maria.

Whatever the facts, the stories that Maria told Onassis on those long sea-bound nights early in the cruise moved him deeply. He, too, in youth had suffered a terrifying cataclysm in Smyrna, and he could well imagine every awful detail of her ordeal. Later, speaking to the press about Callas after their names had been linked romantically, Onassis would say, "More than her artistic talent, even more than her success as a great singer, what always impressed me was the story of her early struggles as a poor girl in her teens when she sailed through unusually rough and merciless waters."

What Maria probably did not mention to Onassis, however, were the intimate details of her earliest romances. The young Maria Kalogeropoulos, despite being far less attractive than her sister and nearly as dedicated to her calling as a nun, nevertheless managed to find romance with a number of male admirers. "Maria had several close relationships and intimate friendships for the first time, including two with well-off older men (a pattern maintained right through her life), one of them a doctor and neighbor who may have been her first lover," says Nicholas Petsalis-Diomidis, who has written a detailed account of Maria's formative years in Athens.

Petsalis explains in his book that these "intimate friendships" did not necessarily include sexual relations, but "it seems almost certain that some Italian soldier or soldiers played some part in her sexual enlightenment. And the same applies, at around the same time . . . to her neighbor, Dr. Ilias Papatestas."

Dr. Papatestas, a lung specialist, had his offices—a waiting room, an examination room, a study, and a bedroom—on the ground floor of 61 Patission Street, where Maria occupied the top floor with her mother and Jackie. Her sister told me that Dr. Papatestas, who was thirty-six when he met Callas, then nineteen, was Maria's "first lover," a view held by half a dozen friends and neighbors of the singer's interviewed by Petsalis.

In 1957, twelve years after her departure from Athens for New York, where she had been reunited with her father but had failed to find employment as a singer, Maria returned to Greece from Italy for a concert at Herodes Atticus Theater at the foot of the Acropolis. A huge scandal erupted when the performance was canceled at the last minute because of Maria's poor health and the tumultuous political uproar over her fees and poor reputation in Greece. Although she finally did sing in Athens a week later, according to Petsalis, "On that occasion she also received a lot of obscene, offensive, and unbelievably venomous anonymous messages that brought back memories of the worst moments of her past life in Greece."

No wonder Maria was filled with trepidation in 1959 as the *Christina* sailed into the Ionian Sea, toward Athens. This time, however, she was arriving on the pleasure boat of Aristotle Onassis and in the illustrious company of Sir Winston Churchill, whom many Greeks viewed as a savior of their country.

. . .

On Monday, July 27, the second day spent entirely at sea, the *Christina* passed through the Straits of Messina. Even without the jagged rocks of Scylla and the whirlpools of Charybdis, the passage was a bit rough. Meneghini miserably continued to suffer the vagaries of the currents in his stateroom.

At dinner that night, according to Anthony Montague Browne, Sir Winston was inspired to recount how the German battle cruiser *Goeben* evaded the British ships in those same waters in 1914 and sailed to Constantinople, where its arrival reinforced the wavering will of the Turks to fight against the Allies. Onassis thrilled to Churchill's eloquent recollections. It was as if one of the leather-bound books in the library had suddenly come alive, and there was nothing that Ari enjoyed more than learning about history from those who participated in it.

When, on the cruise, Maria remarked to Onassis about his great devotion to Churchill, he gave what she called "a marvelous answer," which she later repeated to friends: "We must remember that it was he, the man of our century, who saved the world in 1940. Where would we all be today and in what state without this man!" It was hardly a view of which she needed to be convinced. Maria, for her part, took the opportunity at dinner that night to tell Sir Winston how much it had meant to her and her family and all the dispirited and starving Greeks to see him arrive in Athens on the terrible Christmas Day in 1944. As she described in detail the suffering of her family, she spoke intently, with tears in her eyes and her hand resting on that of the grizzled statesman, while the others at the table stared at her with surprise, discomfort, and not a little annoyance.

Without waking the passengers, the *Christina* made its first landfall in Greece at 1:30 a.m. on Tuesday, July 28, when the ship stopped at Katakolo, a small port on the westernmost bulge of the Peloponnesus, to pick up Onassis' sister, Artemis, and her husband, Dr. Theodore Garofalidis. The area was one of Theodore's favorite places to hunt and vacation. Having sailed with Sir Winston on his two previous cruises, the couple were old friends of the Churchills' and the Montague Brownes'. The tall, debonair, and good-natured Garofalidis was an orthopedic surgeon. Charming and adept on the dance floor, he was always a hit with the ladies, even though he spoke no English, only French and Greek. And being an opera lover, he was already a great fan of Maria's. (According to Marilena Patronikola, Onassis' niece, Theodore was introduced to Maria when she first sang at the Herodes Atticus Theater in 1957, by his colleague and friend, Dr. Leonidas Lantzounis, Maria's godfather.) His wife, Artemis, was a different matter however. The tiny, intense woman, in her couture clothes and ever-present jewels, would prove more difficult for Maria to win over.

Artemis' life had been a painful one. As a young woman in Smyrna she had met and married a Greek naval officer who was a teacher by profession, and they had a daughter, Popi (short for Penelope, after her grandmother). She told Anthony Montague Browne a dramatic tale of her travails, which he recounted in his memoir: "Artemis had been severely burnt by an exploding paraffin lamp and could never wear a swimsuit or a décolleté dress. She was pregnant at the time, and told me that while in the hospital she heard her husband, who thought her unconscious, telling the doctors that he did not care about his wife's survival as long as the baby was saved. Both in fact did survive, but the baby was born severely mentally handicapped. Artemis was later divorced and married happily a truly engaging and honourable orthopaidic surgeon, Theodore Garafalides [sic] . . . who came on nearly all our cruises to watch over WSC [Winston Spencer Churchill]."

I have learned that Artemis—much like her brother—rewrote her own history to cast herself in a better light. According to her niece Marilena Patronikola, whose mother, Kalliroe, was present when the accident happened, it was in 1930. Artemis had invited her two half sisters, Kalliroe and Merope, for a meal at her home in Kifissia. While she was cooking chops, "she saw the coals weren't burning well, and she took some alcohol and threw it on the coals, which exploded and severely burned Artemis and the little girl, who was three," Marilena told me. "Much later the girl developed signs of schizophrenia and at some point, around twenty-four to twenty-five [actually twenty-seven] years of age, Popi commited suicide while she was at a clinic in Switzerland.

"Artemis was very smart, very sweet, and very determined—cunning— what we called 'Smyrnaiki,' " Marilena continued, using an adjective that implies that people from Smyrna are particularly clever and devious. "She met Theodore while she was at the clinic recovering from her burns, which she suffered on both legs. She was looked after at the hospital by Dr. Garofalidis, who got her the best attention and care. She had a lot of plastic surgery to cover the burns. She fell in love with Theodore and asked for a divorce to marry him. Her father was furious but she wouldn't change her mind." (However, she waited until her father died in 1932 to marry Theodore.) Artemis' story of the cruel husband who said he cared only that his unborn baby be saved is a creative variation on the truth—one that provides justification for asking for a divorce. In those days in Greece, divorce was such a scandal that Artemis' first husband refused to give her custody of the little girl, and Popi did not see her mother for ten years, between the ages of three and thirteen, until her father had to find a home for the child because he was recalled into the Greek army at the outbreak of World War II, and sent her to her mother.

Four hours after Artemis and Theodore came aboard, the *Christina* sailed back up north and turned east into the Gulf of Corinth, between the "hand" of the Peloponnesus and the mainland of Greece. There, at 3:55 in the afternoon, the yacht dropped anchor at Itea, which since ancient times has served as the harbor for the shrine of Delphi, the holiest site in pre-Christian Greece. The small port in the Bay of Itea lies on the margin separating the Ionian Sea's aquamarine waters from the dusty green waves of the Sacred Plain, an unbroken stretch of olive groves that wash up against the mountain bearing the ruins of Delphi on its flank and, on its summit, the peaks of Mt. Parnassus. As the setting sun dyes the cliffs red and the terraced vineyards and ravines are filled with a deep purple light, the shadows of the marble columns stretch up the hill like fingers and eagles wheel overhead.

The disembarkation of the Onassis party was like a feast day in the sleepy port. As the winches on the *Christina* were employed to lower the specially made jeep given to Onassis by a friend, Fiat chairman Gianni Agnelli, Churchill was helped by his bodyguard across the gangplank, which was gingerly suspended by ropes to remain level with the ship's deck. After he was slowly lowered to the dock, Churchill, in naval garb, saluted the cheering crowd, and to the residents of Itea it was almost as if the British forces were returning fifteen years later to save the country yet again.

Filled with pride at his guest of honor's reception, Ari drove the open Fiat himself, with Sir Winston at his side and Tina and Diana Sandys in the back seat, at the head of the *Christina*'s motorcade on this first land excursion in Greece. Meneghini was among the shore party, and though doubtless relieved at the respite from his seasickness, he still found cause to complain: "It was extremely hot and those excursions were, for me, damned exhausting." Perhaps having learned the awkward lesson of her first appearance on deck in cabbage roses, Maria had chosen to wear sandals and a dark, almost somber shirtwaist dress with long sleeves and a five-inch-wide belt, and a white headband binding her upswept hair. Still, it can't have pleased her to see Tina's sexy décolleté checked sundress, its shirred bodice cut like a bra.

The small parade of vehicles wound its way across the Sacred Plain and up the winding mountain road to the site of the shrine, which the ancient

Celia Sandys, Lady Churchill, Maria, Tina, Anthony Montague Browne,
and Nonie Montague Browne at Delphi

Greeks considered the center of the world. (It was believed that Gaia, the earth mother, sent two eagles flying from opposite ends of the earth and that they met over this spot.) Eight centuries before Christ, the legend goes, a shepherd on the steep slopes of Mt. Parnassus felt a rush of cold air coming from a crevice in the earth and fell into a divine, babbling frenzy. From that time until four centuries after the birth of Christ, Delphi was the seat of a divine oracle. About 1000 B.C. the site became sacred to Apollo. Sitting on a high chair perched over the same crevice, where the sacred breeze washed over her, the priestess, or *pythia,* would enter an ecstatic trance to answer the questions of pilgrims seeking to know the future.

Remaining on the main road below the ruins, Onassis and Churchill stepped into the Hotel Vouzas to have a drink on the terrace and enjoy its vertiginous view, while the rest of the group clambered up the steep slope. The modern pilgrims were led by a guide along the Sacred Way to the great temple itself, the Sanctuary of Apollo, with its ruined temples, treasuries, and foundations of monuments. When they reached the podium and peristyle of the temple, where the oracle once sat, they perched on parts of fallen columns and listened to the story of how Apollo slew the python at this spot and established the worship of his cult. They were told how the priestess— always a woman over fifty years old, to guarantee celibacy—would purify herself with water and chew poisonous laurel leaves before seating herself to receive her magical visions. In photographs of the trip, the group, *sans* Onassis and Churchill, are seated on the ancient rocks beneath the fluted marble columns, listening in fascination to the story of the oracle. Lady Churchill, in her sensible rubber-soled shoes and double-strand pearl necklace, is beaming. Meneghini is scowling. When asked why they were all staring with such anticipation, Nonie smiled. "We were waiting for the oracle." The priestess did not advise the pilgrims from the *Christina* that day, but some of them might have done well to study the most famous of Greek maxims, which was inscribed on the Temple of Apollo: KNOW THYSELF.

Back on board, most of the passengers rested from the exertions of the trip to Delphi while the more energetic ones jumped overboard to swim in the tranquil bay. Kostas Koutsouvelis, Alexander's handsome young tutor, volunteered to give waterskiing lessons and acquired as pupils Nonie Montague Browne and Celia Sandys, who was somewhat smitten with the young man. "I wasn't very successful at attracting his attention," she told me forty years later. "I'd led a very sheltered life and was very immature." Maria, in a fetching black bathing suit, was lounging in a deck chair and listening intently to Onassis, also in bathing costume, as he held forth in rapid-fire Greek. Tina, eager as always to flaunt her perfect body, was nearby, lounging in a minuscule bikini.

Meneghini, still perpetually nauseated, watched the activities around him with a baleful eye, and in his recollected version of them, his imagination gets the better of him: "For most of these people, life on board was light and carefree. Their manner of comporting themselves was very different from that to which Maria and I were accustomed. We had the impression of being among people a little crazy. Many of the couples split up and found other partners." This was one of the passages in *My Wife Maria Callas* (including Meneghini's report of nude sunbathing) that drove Montague Browne to bring his libel suit against Meneghini, which he won (after the author had died). There was, of course, no nudity on board, and as for couples "splitting up and finding other partners," it was hard to imagine who, aside from Onassis and Maria, these couples might be. As Nonie said with a laugh, "Who was there for me to fool around with?" In truth, both Onassis and Tina, though playful by nature, were on their guard against even the slightest hint of impropriety, lest any older guests, particularly the strait-laced Lady Churchill, take offense.

The next morning, July 29, the *Christina* sailed through the narrow gash in the rocks that is the Corinth Canal, bound for Athens. That evening there was to be a formal dinner on board. Invited to dine with Sir Winston were the Greek prime minister, Konstantine Karamanlis, and his wife, Amalia, as well as the British ambassador to Greece, Sir Roger Alan, and his wife. The crowd of hovering press and paparazzi would certainly be worse in Greece, so a plan was made to evade them by sailing past Athens down the coast and picking up the prominent dinner guests off the small town of Anavisos, thirty-five miles southeast of Athens. It was hoped the yacht could then sail unmolested out into the Saronic Gulf for a peaceful dinner somewhere beneath the peak of Cape Sounion, which marks the southernmost tip of Attica.

As soon as the guests were safely on board, the *Christina* glided out into the bay and dropped anchor within sight of the cliff at Cape Sounion, which is crowned by a temple.

Along with Delphi, Sounion is one of the most famous sites in Greece, renowned since antiquity for its dramatic setting and stark beauty. Atop the rocky promontory was perched, in the fifth century B.C., a temple to Poseidon, of which twelve Doric columns still stand. These remain a beacon to ships at sea, where Greek sailors have always looked and whispered prayers for a safe passage as they commit themselves to their journeys.

The dinner began with drinks and introductions on deck. Then the guests were escorted down the spiral onyx-railed staircase to the long table, set with Baccarat crystal, gold vermeil flatware, and Sèvres china, and with an arrangement of fresh roses in colors chosen to complement the decor. The chairs were positioned to take advantage of the spectacular view.

The Greek prime minister was of peasant stock from Seres, in Macedonia. Tall, handsome, and stern with his trademark bushy eyebrows, he resembled Charles de Gaulle, and he would come to inhabit a place in his country's history similar to de Gaulle's in France, for Karamanlis led Greece back to democracy after the fall of the junta in 1974 and, later, into the European Union. That evening Karamanlis was accompanied by his beautiful, well-born wife, Amalia. She, too, had attended Maria's controversial performance at Herodes Atticus Theater in 1957, and later had dined with her in Paris and seen her perform there. Amalia was a great admirer and friend of the diva's.

When I spoke to the former first lady of Greece in the fall of 1997 at her home in Athens, she remarked that Maria was very insecure about herself off the stage until she fell in love with Onassis. "I remember a dinner at the home of Louis Aragon, the French historian, in honor of Rostropovich. I was chatting with Princess Irene of Greece. Rostropovich had drunk a bit too much and he was showering Maria with compliments. When he said how beautiful she was, she replied, 'Ach, but you haven't seen my Norma, my Traviata!' She felt she was only beautiful on the stage! And the *kerasi*

Era of good feelings: Onassis, Theodore Garofalidis, Callas, Meneghini,
and Nonie enjoy life on board the Christina.

stin tourta [the cherry on the cake] was that after the dinner, he took a rose from a vase and fell to his knees and offered it to her with a grand gesture, and she didn't know what to do. A great diva and she didn't know how to take a rose from a man! Until Onassis. He made her feel like a woman for the first time."

The former Mrs. Karamanlis shook her head at the memory. "That night in 1959, when we came on board the Onassis yacht," she continued, "Churchill was the true star. She was just there, on board. Maria hadn't changed then. She changed the moment she was free to be with him. Afterward—after she met Onassis—she became a glamorous woman. She took on the air of a loved woman. The only person who existed for her, besides her art, was Onassis."

The British ambassador, Sir Roger Alan, and his wife were the other special guests of honor at the table that night. Churchill's daughter Diana, seated beside Sir Roger, had evidently been indulging in the excellent 1953 Château Lafitte when Onassis bragged that his fine Baccarat crystal was so thin and delicate that it was actually flexible and would change shape slightly under pressure. Diana attempted to test this claim; her glass exploded, spraying the red wine all over the white dinner jacket of the startled ambassador. As everyone gasped, Onassis quickly moved to remedy the embarrassing situation, ordering the stained jacket whisked away to the on-board dry cleaner. Lady Clementine insisted that Sir Roger wear her fur evening wrap against the chill of the air conditioning. And Onassis remarked, "That's strange. I've never seen that happen before!" Then he squeezed his own water goblet until it shattered. Diane's gaffe was quickly forgotten.

The rest of the dinner went swimmingly despite the Babel of the guests' backgrounds and linguistic skills. Inspired by the view, Sir Winston quoted Lord Byron, who, like many other nineteenth-century travelers, had hiked up to the Temple of Poseidon on Sounion and carved his name into one of the marble columns. Churchill's distinctive orotund voice intoned the famous lines from *Don Juan* in which Byron laments the Turkish subjugation of the Greeks and proclaims the determination of the Philhellenes that those chains will one day be broken:

> *"Place me on Suniun's marbled steep,*
> *Where nothing, save the waves and I,*
> *May hear our mutual murmurs sweep;*
> *There, swan-like, let me sing and die.*
> *A land of slaves shall ne'er be mine—*
> *Dash down yon cup of Samian wine!"*

Even the aloof and undemonstrative Karamanlis found himself moved by this recitation. The prime minister, like all Greeks, revered Byron, who died at Missolonghi of a fever during the struggle for Greek independence.

Maria and Onassis, too, were filled with emotion at hearing the world's greatest living statesman quote words of tribute written by their country's most beloved Philhellene on the very spot that had inspired them. It was a perfect moment in a perfect setting, and when the dignitaries were ferried back in the moonlight to the dock at Anavisos (Sir Roger now wearing a pristine white dinner jacket), those left on board agreed that their first evening in Greece had exceeded all their expectations.

After the dignitaries departed, around midnight, Captain Kostas set out at 1:12 a.m., steering the yacht back up the coast and pausing an hour and forty minutes later so that Theodore Garofalidis could disembark in the town of Glyfada, where he and Onassis had villas on adjoining properties. His wife, Artemis, would stay on board for the rest of the cruise, and the busy doctor would fly to rejoin her in Rhodes.

Ari and Maria lingered on deck, mesmerized by the view and the moonlight reflected in the sparkling water all around them as the lights of the Saronic coast slipped by. As was becoming routine, Onassis asked Nonie to stay up and have a nightcap with them. Celia Sandys also wanted to remain a while longer, hoping perhaps to take a walk around the deck and run into Kostas Koutsouvelis, who had patiently coaxed her through her first water-skiing lesson the day before, but her mother insisted that Celia should retire with her: the next day would be a busy one. A disappointed Celia followed her below to their stateroom, where Lady Clementine was waiting to analyze the dinner party with them.

Feeling sorry for the sixteen-year-old, Nonie remarked that it was a shame there was no one on board her age. That inspired Onassis to tell one of his most well-worn anecdotes. During his earliest days in shipping, he found himself a guest at the home of a wealthy business associate in Sweden, where he had gone to order his first two tankers. After the meal, the hostess asked to be excused because she had to take their fourteen-year-old daughter to see a gynecologist. When Onassis expressed surprise that a girl so young should need one, the mother reassured him: "Oh, there's no problem whatsoever. I'm just taking her so that he will cut her hymen and she won't have any difficulties when she has intercourse."

Though he confessed to being taken aback at first by the woman's attitude toward her young daughter's sexuality, after consideration Ari decided it was a very enlightened one. "In a lot of countries, including Greece, many crimes of honor are committed over that piece of skin," he concluded. "I say, 'Bravo to Sweden!' "

Nonie greeted this story with a weak smile and got up to find more champagne, but Maria engaged Onassis in Greek with her characteristic bluntness. What she told him, and later repeated to friends, was that, though Greek men may pretend to be worldly and open-minded when talking to Europeans, they were all Anatolians at heart, especially when it came to their own women. ("Don't ever believe what you see in Greece," she later told John Ardoin. "It looks European, but believe me, it is totally Eastern. The man is the pasha.") She challenged him: Would Onassis tell his daughter, when she became a teenager, that it was all right to have premarital sex? Would he be able to shrug off a sexual adventure by his wife the way many European men do?

"You're right about my daughter," he replied, "but not about my wife." He then told her, and she later repeated, the story about Tina's affair with young Reinaldo Herrera and Aristo's decision not to give her a divorce, because of the children. Seven months after the cruise, when every newspaper in the world was accusing the diva of breaking up the Onassis marriage, Callas would defend herself indignantly to a reporter for *France-Soir:* "It's not because of [me] that Tina Onassis asked for a divorce. She's been thinking about it for two years. She wanted to marry Mr. X. . . . No, I will not say his name. I am a lady. But there is no 'woman of the world' who wasn't aware of this. Ask them!"

As Poseidon's temple faded into the velvet darkness, Onassis told Maria that he had been trying to rationalize Tina's affair because he had

*Onassis leads Maria through the ancient theater of Epidaurus,
where she would later triumph as Norma.*

been unfaithful to her often during their marriage, but it hurt him to think of
his young wife, the mother of Christina and Alexander, with another man.
"So I suppose I have to admit you're right about Greek men," he said. "I
may talk as if I'm open-minded, but at heart, I'm just a *Romios*"—he used
the name Greeks call themselves when they are feeling chauvinistic. Maria
replied that she liked Tina, who had been very kind to her on the cruise, but
she couldn't comprehend her behavior. "I don't understand," she said,
"how a Greek woman could pretend to love one man and sleep with
another."

After dropping off Theodore Garofalidis in Glyfada, the captain sailed
southwest past the islands of Hydra and Spetse and into the Gulf of Argolis.
That afternoon, at 2:32 p.m., July 30, Onassis' guests found themselves
in the harbor of Nauplion. The picturesque town of winding streets and
pastel-painted stucco houses, which for a brief time was the capital of
Greece after the War of Independence, is dominated by a grim Venetian fort
high above and a tiny prison on a rocky islet in the bay. Onassis had
arranged for his guests to take an excursion inland from here to Epidaurus,
the site of an ancient shrine to the god of healing, Asclepius. The drive from
Nauplion took them through some of the most lush vegetation in Greece,
until they entered the gates and walked on foot through the pines to see the

museum and the shrines. A kind of pre-Christian Lourdes, Epidaurus drew invalids from all over the ancient world, who built temples and brought offerings in hopes of finding a cure for their ailments. There was even a round building, the Tholos, containing a labyrinth where the insane were given a kind of "shock" treatment in which they were forced to walk down a spiral ramp in darkness past hundreds of hissing snakes, an experience that was supposed to dispel the evil spirits that had invaded their minds.

The highlight of Epidaurus is the ancient theater, so well preserved that classical tragedies are still performed there every summer. Owing to its famously perfect acoustics, a person sitting on the topmost tier can clearly hear the sound of a match being struck in the center of the proscenium. Inside the theater, the group was surprised to see that the Greeks had erected on the ancient stage a large V made of flowers, as a tribute to Sir Winston. But Callas leapt to divalike conclusions. With amusement, Montague Browne related the incident: "Maria exclaimed, 'Flowers for me! How kind! But why is it a V, Anthony?' I replied that it was undoubtedly meant to be an M for Maria but that they had not had time to finish it. 'How dreadful for them!' " For a moment Callas believed him, then she realized he was teasing her. "Maria's reactive smile was rapidly replaced by the sort of glance she should have remembered when she sang 'Medea,' " he recalled.

It would be here in the theater of Epidaurus a year later that Maria Callas would achieve her greatest triumph on Greek soil: two performances of *Norma* that would become legend to the thirty thousand spectators who beheld them. In July of 1959, however, as she discovered to her mortification, Sir Winston was the star of the show.

Photographs from that day show Onassis holding Maria's hand as he leads her up the steps of the ancient theater, both of them smiling. It was a solicitous gesture, not out of bounds for a concerned host, but it was also testimony to the intimacy that was developing between them. If the others in the group noticed, they kept their opinions to themselves.

8

DINNER FOR TWO

May you stop at Phoenician trading stations
to buy many fine things,
mother of pearl and coral, amber and ebony,
sensual perfumes of every kind.

C. P. Cavafy, "Ithaca"

Before the *Christina* set sail from the Greek mainland toward the island of Santorini, Maria posted a letter to her maid, Bruna Lupoli. Bruna, just two years older than her mistress, was not only Maria's servant from the time she married Meneghini, but also her best friend and confidante. Years later, feeling abandoned by everyone else, Maria told John Ardoin, "If you can't trust your husband or your mother, to whom do you turn? When I go back to Paris, you know who takes care of me and who I know will always be there? My maid Bruna, who adores me and who has been a nurse, sister and mother to me."

Generally, Maria consulted Bruna about everything—even which professional commitments to accept and how her voice sounded at each performance—but in the letter she mailed to her from Piraeus on July 29, 1959, she gave no hint of the increasing tension on board the yacht; it contained only pleasantries: "A brief hello from this *small* boat. . . . Here I finally have a real rest—no telephone, etc. Fresh air, sun and sea." Bruna had arranged for her own vacation in her home village of Travagola Pedavena, north of Venice, to coincide with the cruise. "I plan on returning around when you come back," Maria continued. "Earlier, I don't think so, because even if I am better off at home, it's a shame to lose such a beautiful cruise. They continue on until the thirteenth of August. I don't think that I'll manage to stay that long on board. . . . I plan on being back around the fifth—more or less—we'll see. You in any case have all your days. Enjoy it there and return rested and fresh for our ups and downs, which basically we enjoy." This lighthearted letter notwithstanding, Maria would in fact stay for the entire cruise, until August 13, and would encounter more "ups and downs" on board than she could have imagined.

The *Christina* left Nauplion just after midnight on July 31, while the guests slept, worn out from the excursion to Epidaurus and another round of waterskiing lessons. Nonie Montague Browne was proud about mastering the sport after an initial spill in which she found herself floating next to a "vast jellyfish with legs hanging down. I screamed, 'Quick! quick!' and they pulled me in. I can tell you, I never fell again." But as a result of her exertions in the water, she came down with a throat infection and soon developed a fever.

After passing a number of islands in the night and morning, the *Christina* dropped anchor at 1 p.m. on July 31 in the curved bay of Santorini, with its black sand beaches at the base of steep volcanic cliffs of black, red, and white stone. The southernmost of the Cyclades Islands, Santorini (called by its ancient name, Thira, in Greece) is a volcano like Stromboli and reputedly the site of the fabled Atlantis, the great civilization that was destroyed by a catastrophe in a day and a night and collapsed to the bottom of the sea. The central part of Santorini was wiped out by a volcanic eruption in 1450 B.C. that caused tidal waves and aftershocks which destroyed the entire Minoan civilization and left only the present crescent-shaped island—its outer shell. Because of their situation high atop the volcanic cliffs, the towns of Santorini are among the most picturesque in Greece, but it's no easy job to reach them. Visitors ride up the steep, terraced slopes either on donkey trains or on cable cars to reach the capital of Fira.

The sea was a bit rough on the afternoon of Friday, July 31, and Nonie convalesced in bed, but Anthony Montague Browne was among the more adventurous passengers of the *Christina* who elected to climb to Fira on a donkey. On the way up the steep zigzagging track, which the plodding animals traverse many times a day, he collected local folklore. Santorini is the only island where the beasts of burden are well treated, he was told, because the islanders fear they will be punished for their sins by being reincarnated as donkeys. There is also a custom of never opening a door to only one knock for fear that a vampire may be calling. A visitor must knock three times, which vampires are unable to do (though, as Anthony Montague Browne pointed out, an enterprising trio of them could well conspire to knock one time each).

At the top of the climb, in the pretty capital of the island, which clings to the edge of the cliffs, the travelers from the *Christina* stopped at the first taverna to enjoy a stiff drink of ouzo and the breathtaking prospect below, in which the *Christina* floated like a tiny toy on the sapphire bay. When they tried to pay the check, the owner refused to take money from Onassis or any of his friends. Only three years earlier, in 1956, when Santorini was devastated by an earthquake, Onassis learned that all the wells had collapsed. He filled the swimming pool of the *Christina* with fresh water and sailed at once for the island, "along with hoses and mobile pumps to deliver it, together with the ship's own output of thirty tons of water a day," according to Montague Browne. The islanders remained profoundly grateful to their Good Samaritan.

The *Christina* sailed out of the deep bay at 9:20 p.m. This may have been the night of a pivotal incident that heightened the general animosity toward Maria and brought her developing relationship with Onassis to the attention of the other guests. Both Celia Sandys and Nonie Montague Browne told me about the critical dinner, but neither could recall exactly on which night it came to pass.

The scandalous event, although it hardly seems equal to Meneghini's fantasies, unfolded as the passengers arrived in the formal dining room dressed for dinner, to discover that Ari and Maria were missing. When her guests inquired where the two were, Tina replied, "Oh, they've already eaten. Maria ordered a special Greek meal, just for them."

Everyone pretended not to feel the awkwardness of the situation, but later that night Celia heard her mother and Lady Churchill in their stateroom, whispering in horrified tones about Maria's shameless behavior. Celia recalled, "Although my grandmother wouldn't have discussed it with me, she certainly talked to my mother about it. . . . The grown-ups noticed it [the affair] before I did. It was quite a drama. . . . There was Tina sitting there, and the poor husband—Meneghini. There was a lot of talking and everyone was feeling sorry for Tina, who was too lovely and too charming, and she was trying to make everything beautiful and wonderful. She was the perfect host on the surface. Perfect! There was a lot of discussion afterward."

Following the dinner, all the guests on the boat cooled dramatically toward Callas, which bewildered the diva, who finally came to Nonie to find out the reason. Maria was most comfortable with the young and affable Mrs. Montague Browne, and they had exchanged a good deal of "girl talk" as Nonie put it. "She was very easy and friendly to talk to. She used to tell me how she'd plucked her legs in the morning, that sort of thing," she said. "Nothing about her love life. Except that I could see the way she totally dropped Meneghini." They often chatted about clothes and makeup (which Maria wore in an exaggerated, stagey manner). "Maria asked me to brush her long brown hair for her, and in exchange she would paint my toenails," Nonie recalled. "I rather enjoyed it. I think that was Battista's job before, but I suspect he was on strike by then." (A comment that Celia Sandys made to me is indicative of the general attitude toward Maria, especially among the British guests: "I studied her for three weeks, and what stuck me greatly . . . what I found repulsive . . . was that she didn't wash her hair the whole time. She had ghastly hygiene." In fact, Nonie, who regularly brushed Maria's hair, said it was "obviously washed often. . . . She did wear a wig at night after a swim. She had a lovely wig that I envied because she could come to dinner looking perfectly coiffed after a swim while I looked like a wet chicken.")

When Maria asked her friend about the *froideur* of their shipmates, Nonie tried to stay out of it. "My intent was to keep my mouth shut. There was a sort of competition going on between Tina and Maria in their own Greek way, and for some reason I'm always sort of the pig in the middle. But I said to Maria, 'I gather that you arranged for a special Greek dinner last night?' and she said, 'Me? I did it? It was Tina!' And of course Tina had done it! I decided not to say anything anymore, because you only put your foot in it. Tina had done it to Maria. There was never an awful quarrel between them, but just snide little remarks. It wasn't about Ari, I don't think. Sort of one-upmanship. They just irritated each other."

It's highly unlikely that this indiscreet dinner *à deux* was something that Tina plotted to sully Maria's reputation among the other passengers. It's more likely that the hostess, annoyed at the way Callas was dominating both her husband's attention and the general spotlight, saw an unexpected opportunity to make the singer seem rude and seized on it. The scenario probably unrolled as Nonie imagined it: Ari and Maria were sitting in the stern near the pool, chatting as usual, and Tina showed up, only to be greeted by her husband saying: "I'm hungry and dinner's not for hours. I feel like eating Greek food tonight." Maria may have chimed in, "I'd like Greek food too. We're always eating French." Tina, by then thoroughly annoyed at both of them, replied sweetly, "I'll just ask the chef to prepare you both a nice Greek meal and have it served right here." When the Churchills and the rest arrived in the dining room and began asking about the missing pair, Tina was able to cast Maria as the villain.

As a result of this event, everyone on board, with the possible exception of Sir Winston, became aware that something was brewing between Ari and Maria. Though Tina may not have objected to her husband's extramarital adventures any more than he did hers, she intended, as long as she was the hostess and the mistress of the ship, to remain the most admired woman on board for her beauty and her perfect congeniality, and she did not want this newest celebrity in Ari's collection to outshine her.

Nonie also believes that Tina was not so much protective of her husband as annoyed that Maria was usurping her place in the spotlight. "I think that Tina was no longer very jealous of Ari," Nonie told me. "I think he loved her rather more than she loved him, really. She had given him his children and now she had other interests. He was often away on business. I don't know about her lovers, but there seemed a one-upmanship in their subsequent marriages. Ari gave her everything she wanted. She dressed extravagantly and was extravagant. I don't suppose Ari was all that faithful."

It was undoubtedly part of Tina's strategy to bring the growing friendship between her husband and Callas to the attention of Ari's older sister, Artemis. She knew that in any potential competition between Maria and herself, Artemis would be her most powerful ally, for she had more influence over Onassis than anyone else.

Just two years older than Aristotle, Artemis was his only full sibling. When their mother, Penelope, died after a kidney operation in 1912 and their father took a second wife, they resented her and found a substitute mother in their aged grandmother. But as the pair grew up and were joined by two younger half sisters, Artemis slowly took over as maternal protector of her brother. Throughout their lives, Artemis could nag and tease Aristo as could no one else, but she adored him and he returned an equal devotion. Artemis' niece, Marilena Patronikola, told me, "She would say, even in front of her husband, that she loved her brother above everyone and everything in life."

In principle, there should have been an essential affinity between Maria and Artemis, for they shared a common class background that was different from that of everyone else on board the *Christina* apart from Ari. Although Socrates Onassis had been a wealthy merchant in Smyrna, his children both thought and spoke like bourgeois Greeks, often crudely, and so did Maria. Artemis had many traits of the nouveau riche. Day or night she wore diamonds, and an Onassis secretary described how Artemis, in her art-filled Glyfada boudoir, liked to have the maid spread her collection of precious jewels over her king-sized pink satin bedspread every morning so that she could admire them. In fact, Artemis was not so different from Callas' mother: socially ambitious, eager to appear wealthy and refined, yet easily slipping into the language, behavior, and prejudices of a middle-class Greek. It was perhaps for this very reason that Maria's exertions to charm

Ari's older sister would never succeed—not only was Artemis in flight from her origins, but she wanted better for her brother.

Maria and Ari's nonappearance at dinner was still the main topic of conversation when the *Christina* arrived at Rhodes on the morning of Saturday, August 1, and tied up at 9:20 a.m. in the small port of Mandraki. The entrance to the harbor was once marked by the huge bronze statue of Helios, the sun god, known as the Colossus of Rhodes, which was one of the seven wonders of the ancient world until an earthquake brought it down in 224 B.C. Beginning in 1306, crusader knights of the Order of the Hospital of St. John of Jerusalem owned and occupied Rhodes for two centuries, and today it looks more like a medieval Gothic town than a Greek one. The walled city was so well fortified that the crusaders were able to hold off an army of 70,000 Turks until 1522, when they were forced to surrender to the 200,000 men of Suleiman the Magnificent after a six-month siege. The Knights' fortifications are still there, with arcaded streets and cloisters, mosaic floors, statues, and ancient cannons.

The group planned to spend two days on the large island, where Onassis' brother-in-law, Dr. Gerasimos Patronikolas, had opened the luxurious Miramar Hotel only a year before. He and his wife, Kalliroe, the younger of Onassis' half sisters, were planning a reception and dinner dance for the guests, which would serve not only to honor Sir Winston but also bring the new hotel to the attention of the world.

When Dr. Patronikolas came to collect the *Christina* party, Nonie was too sick with her throat infection to get out of bed. Artemis' husband, Theodore, had flown in to rejoin the group, and he came aboard with Patronikolas, who was a pulmonologist. They were accompanied by a local general practitioner. When she awoke, Nonie was alarmed to find herself surrounded by three Greek doctors, including one who wanted to look down her throat with a light that was powered by old-fashioned batteries hanging from his belt. The joint examination concluded with a consultation in Greek that quickly escalated to a shouting match. When it seemed that the two brothers-in-law were about to come to blows, Nonie's worried husband inquired what was wrong. Theodore informed him (in French), "I simply told him [Gerasimos] that he might be a good hotelier, but when it came to medicine, he would do better to remain as silent as a sea urchin."

Leaving Nonie aboard ship to swallow the foul-tasting potions prescribed for her, the group followed Gerasimos Patronikolas to the Miramar. By this time the army of paparazzi waiting for them on shore came as no surprise. Eleven-year-old Alexander had snuck away from the crush to page through magazines at a nearby kiosk, when a fifteen-year-old friend of his, who was also on Rhodes at the time, remarked to him how awful it must be for his father to face such mobs of press. Alexander replied crossly, "He loves it. He can't get going in the morning unless four flash bulbs go off in his face."

Once the group reached the Miramar Hotel, the guests were each given a suite where they could rest, swim, and change for the dinner dance later. Photos show Tina, in her checked bikini and feathered bathing cap, dangling her feet in the hotel's outdoor pool while chatting with a smiling Celia Sandys (demure in a modest one-piece suit), while eight-year-old Christina Onassis and twelve-year-old Marilena Patronikola, her cousin, hover nearby.

The dinner that night was held outside in the dusk, perfumed with the heavy scent of star jasmine and night-blooming vines. Maria in diamond earrings and a short dark sequined gown smiled dreamily as she danced with Dr. Patronikolas, who was exactly her height, in his white dinner jacket.

There was no sign on that warm August evening in 1959 that all the married couples on the dance floor except for the Churchills and Garofalidises would soon separate. It was after midnight when the entire party was ferried back to the yacht. Nonie, sound asleep, was unable to serve as a chaperone that night.

The next day, August 2, Onassis had arranged for sight-seeing. The first stop was the famous Valley of the Butterflies (populated, in fact, by Jersey tiger moths) for a walk through woods, over footbridges, and past waterfalls. In the summer the countless insects settle thickly on the leaves and trunks of the *Liquidambar orientalis* trees, and when they are disturbed and take wing they fill the air with clouds of reddish gold. From there the group was driven to the town of Lindos, a palimpsest of Greek history. On donkeys, they climbed to the top of the high headland, where there stands a white acropolis that is one of the best-restored in Greece. Just below it on the hillside is a picturesque village of white stone houses, winding, narrow streets, and courtyards lined with black and white pebble mosaics. At the foot of the cliff is a curve of a white sand beach lined with fish restaurants. Here the Apostle Paul landed to bring Christianity to a population that worshiped Athena Lindia.

Concluding the second day's excursion, the group returned to the *Christina* to find Onassis in swimming trunks, amusing the children around the pool with comic dives. As he clowned for his appreciative audience, which included Christina and Alexander Onassis as well as assorted visiting nieces, nephews, and friends, "Ari did a dead man's dive into the

Tina Onassis (right) and Celia Sandys cool their feet in a Rhodes pool while Christina and Marilena Patronikola play in the background.

shallow end," Montague Browne recalled, "and he hit the bottom with a tremendous sound and floated to the surface semiconscious. Theodore Garofalidis, members of the crew, and I jumped in and pulled him out, whereupon he lost consciousness for a few minutes. When he recovered, he angrily refused suggestions of an X ray but allowed Theodore to examine his head and neck, which seemed, as far as he could tell, intact."

Montague Browne has a theory that it was this blow to the head that precipitated Ari's obsession with Maria. "Thereafter, Ari's demeanor changed substantially. His equable temper became aggressive, though never to his guests. He drank more than before and fell into abstracted silences. Above all, he began to pay marked attention to Maria Callas."

Whether Montague Browne is right or not, the incident did provoke coverage in the European press. Dinner on board the *Christina* that night was indeed, to use his words, "a bibulous affair." Much wine flowed, as Ari drank in silence, staring rather fixedly at Maria while her husband fretted.

The mayor of Rhodes had been invited aboard for dinner, and when he learned that Anthony Montague Browne had not seen the old fortifications of the crusader knights with the rest of the group, he insisted on taking him on shore for an after-dinner tour. Even though it was past midnight, the two slightly tipsy men set off into the darkness. "Soon his car stuck in the soft sand and we continued on foot through remote groves of oleander, with the battlement looming close or far," Montague Browne recalled. "In the distance we heard *Christina*'s horn, indicating her departure. We looked at each other in consternation and raced back, slipping in the sand and sweating in our dinner jackets. Soon we were pursued by a large and hostile pack of feral stray dogs. . . . I love dogs, on the whole more than people, but these were not the sort with whom you could discuss friendship. At last a police jeep met us and I reached *Christina* just as she was casting off."

With Nonie sick, Ari nursing his aching head, and Anthony exhausted from chasing the ship, the *Christina* sailed out of sight of Rhodes on August 3 at 2:55 a.m. The captain had to leave promptly, for there was a long stretch of water ahead and they had an appointment the next day at the island of Chios, where Tina Onassis' parents were waiting to receive them at her ancestral home.

Chios is an isolated and repeatedly subjugated island only seven miles off the coast of Turkey that, together with Oinoussai, the small barren rock just beside it, has managed to produce most of the century's great Greek shipping dynasties, including the Lemos, Carras, Chandris, Fafalios, and Pateras clans and, foremost among them, the Livanos family. Notoriously intermarried, patriotic, conservative, and publicity-shy, these families are descended from hardscrabble sailing captains who fought the invading Turks for centuries. (The massacre by the Turks of 30,000 Chiots in 1822 is the subject of Delacroix's famous painting *Le Massacre de Chios*, and of Victor Hugo's poem "L'Enfant de Chios." The crypt of a famous monastery on the island is lined with the skulls of the victims.)

Stavros Livanos, the father-in-law of both Onassis and his rival, Niarchos, was named for his grandfather, who was born and died on Chios. The original Stavros Livanos was a humble sailor in the eastern Mediterranean in the early 1800s. Having survived the Greek War of Independence, he taught his son George the ways of the sea but never managed to achieve his dream of becoming a shipowner. It was left to George Livanos, Tina's grandfather, to become one of the first Chiots to own a steamship. He would also sire four sons, of which Stavros, born in 1891, was the third. Stavros, too, spent his early years on the sea, rising from deckhand to become, at nineteen, the youngest chief engineer in Greece and then, at twenty-one, the youngest captain.

"I remember liking Tina's father very much," Montague Browne told me when I interviewed him in the summer of 1998 at Claridge's in London. "He was a real pro sailor. He had a master's certificate, he had a chief

Meneghini, Maria, Onassis (in background), and Lady Churchill on Rhodes

engineer's certificate. Tina said, 'That's the difference between my father and Ari. Ari's ships are all beautiful and white outside, but inside they're crap.' But it wasn't so. Ari's ships were beautifully kept up as well."

Having earned his master mariner's certificate, Stavros Livanos was sent to London to open an office there following the outbreak of World War I. Before long his diligence and shrewd eye for emerging economic trends would move the Livanos family to the forefront of London's Greek shipping community. For instance, in expanding his father's small fleet, Stavros insisted on buying with cash rather than on credit, and when the postwar shipping boom collapsed in the 1920s, dragging many debt-laden shipowners under, the Livanos empire only became stronger.

His extraordinary business acumen may have owed something to a near-pathological tightfistedness. Livanos was known to walk miles in London to avoid a taxi fare, and once when a Greek sailor complained about his low wages of a pound a month, Livanos retorted, "In a thousand months that would be a thousand pounds. If you saved your money, think what you could do with a thousand pounds!"

In 1924, when he was thirty-three years old, Stavros returned to his native island to marry; he chose Arietta Zafirakis, the daughter of a wealthy Greek merchant, who was only fifteen years old. He brought the girl back to England, where she bore him three children: Eugenia in 1926, Tina in 1929, and George in 1934. The marriage would prove long and happy, and the children, especially the girls, were brought up strictly. They were sent to church every Sunday and attended the best boarding schools in England, Canada, and the United States.

All the shipping Greeks spent most of the year abroad, running their empires from New York, London, or Paris, but August was the month in which they brought their large families home to the ancestral mansions on their native islands. The beachfront of Chios is lined with these old Turkish-style estates, fortified with stone walls that hide lavish gardens shaded by orange, lemon, and kumquat trees. Kumquats are a speciality of the island, along with mastic, which is the sticky resin of the mastic tree. (Mastic was much prized by the women of the Turkish seraglios and is still savored by Greeks as a white sticky jam.) The most imposing of the villas was Bella Vista, the Livanos home.

Though Stavros Livanos eschewed publicity and considered Onassis a nouveau riche upstart, the arrival of the *Christina* bearing Sir Winston to their island was a different matter altogether. The prospect of entertaining Churchill and the guests from the *Christina* had driven the patriarch of the shipping Greeks into a frenzy of activity. Livanos had brought his butler and his chef from his home in Paris and had personally supervised the preparation of the gardens, making sure that all the rose bushes would be in bloom on the day of the yacht's arrival. He ordered a special pier built in front of his villa to accommodate the small boat that would bring Sir Winston from the main ship. Meanwhile, all Livanos' neighbors on Chios, having also returned from abroad for the annual reunion, were waiting in their mansions for the favor of a summons to meet the great man. Stavros Livanos may have abhorred seeing his name in the newspapers, but he was very keen on parading the illustrious guests of his daughter and son-in-law before the noses of his rivals.

As the guests of the *Christina* gathered at the rail for the ship's entry into the town of Chios on Monday, August 3, church bells all over the island exploded into a chorus of welcome for Sir Winston—although, according to Montague Browne, Maria once again mistook the outburst for her own tribute. "It did not in the least matter, and I don't think WSC was even aware of it," he commented wryly. Livanos sailed out to the yacht in his Chris-Craft, according to Captain Kostas. He embraced his daughter, was introduced to the distinguished guests, and escorted them back to the new pier and through the wrought-iron gates of his mansion.

That night after dinner, Tina's parents were entertained aboard the *Christina* with champagne and dancing on deck. Radiant in a strapless gown, Tina presided over the festivities with the poise she could summon without fail on such occasions. But during a private moment with her father, she probably confided her frustration at her husband's new infatuation and Maria's insufferable behavior during the cruise, for, as the evening ended, Livanos was seen having an animated conversation with his son-in-law, and when he left the ship he didn't bother to say good-bye to Callas.

At 3:25 a.m. on August 4, the *Christina* set sail for the nearby coast of Turkey. The next stop on the journey would be Smyrna, on the Turkish mainland, where Aristotle had been born and educated and where several of his relatives had been tortured and hanged during the Turkish atrocities of 1922.

9

VISIONS OF SMYRNA

Ithaca gave you the marvelous journey.
Without her you would not have set out
She has nothing left to give you now.

C. P. Cavafy, "Ithaca"

History would not record a more brutal destruction of an ethnic minority than what happened to the Greek and Armenian communities in Smyrna in the fall of 1922 until the Nazis began their extermination of European Jews two decades later. As Turkish soldiers torched the Armenian and Greek sections of the city, executing civilians with knives to conserve ammunition, the survivors crowded onto the harborside, doggedly hoping for salvation to come from the sea.

Foreign battleships—English, American, Italian, and French—were anchored in the harbor, sent by the major powers initially in support of Greek forces but later told to maintain neutrality. They would or could do nothing for the 200,000 refugees on the quai. The pitiful throng—huddled together, sometimes screaming for help but mostly waiting in a silent panic beyond hope—didn't budge for days. Typhoid reduced their numbers, and there was no way to dispose of the dead.

Occasionally a person would swim from the dock to one of the anchored ships and try to climb the ropes and chains, only to be driven off. On the American battleships the musicians on board were ordered to play as loudly as they could to drown out the screams of the pleading swimmers. The English poured boiling water down on the unfortunates who reached their vessels. The harbor was so clogged with corpses that the officers of the foreign battleships were often late to their dinner appointments because bodies would get tangled in the propellers of their launches.

Among the foreign press who covered these events in Smyrna was a young reporter named Ernest Hemingway, then a correspondent for the *Toronto Daily Star*. He later incorporated his impressions of the scene at the harbor into his fiction. Here is how he described the scene in "On the Quai at Smyrna," from an early collection of his stories:

> *The strange thing was, he said, how they screamed every night at midnight. I do not know why they screamed at that time. We were in the harbor and they were all on the pier and at midnight they started screaming. We used to turn the searchlight on them to quiet them. That always did the trick. . . . The worst, he said, were the women with dead babies. You couldn't get the women to give up their dead babies. They'd have babies dead for six days. . . . You remember the harbor. There were plenty of nice things floating around in it. That was the only time in my life I got so I dreamed about things. You didn't mind the women who were having babies as you did those with the dead ones. They had them all right. Surprising how few of them died. . . . Not one of them minded anything once they got off the pier. The Greeks [the retreating soldiers] were nice chaps too. When they evacuated they had all their baggage animals they couldn't take off with them so they just broke their forelegs and dumped them into the shallow water. All those mules with their forelegs broken pushed over into the shallow water. It was all a pleasant business. My word yes, a most pleasant business.*

The Turkish army had marched into Smyrna on September 9, 1922, in pursuit of the retreating Greek soldiers, who had already escaped via the harbor. The Greek army had occupied the city three years earlier with the encouragement of the major powers, then moved on to the interior in an effort to recover the lands in Asia Minor lost to the Turks five hundred years earlier. Now the civilian population had been abandoned and could only hope that they would not be made to pay for the mistakes of the Greek leaders.

In 1922, the approximately 700,000 citizens of this bustling port on the southwest coast of Turkey included 400,000 Greeks, 50,000 Armenians, and only 200,000 Turks, along with a mixture of French, Italians, English, Germans, and Sephardic Jews. Six days after the Turkish army entered Smyrna, 120,000 of the non-Turks would be dead.

Socrates Haralambos Onassis, one of the richest merchants in the city, had come from the provincial village of Moutalasski, near Cappadocia, deep in the interior of Asia Minor, in 1892 and had made a fortune in the import-export business, specializing in cotton, tobacco, and the legal traffic in opium. His first wife, Penelope Dologlou, died in 1912 after a kidney operation; later the same year he married Eleni Tzortzoglou, and brought his mother, Gethsemane, from the village to help raise his children, Artemis and Aristotle. In 1913 Eleni gave Socrates a second daughter, Merope, and, five years later, a third, Kalliroe. By then he was treasurer of the Smyrna Stock Exchange and president of the tobacco exporters association, according to documents I found in 1997 in the city, now called Izmir.

The Onassis clan (known as Onassoglou in Moutalasski), had lived in Turkey for so many generations that Gethsemane, though an ethnic Greek and a devout Orthodox Christian, spoke only Turkish. She had taught herself to read and write (illegal for women of her generation) so that she could study her bizarre Bible, which was written in Turkish with Greek letters. Every year at Easter she insisted on making the *hadj,* a journey to Jerusalem, which allowed her to add the honorific *hadji* to her name. Aristotle and his sisters called her Hadji-néné (*néné* is Turkish for "Grandma").

The Onassis family lived in a villa on a steep slope above the southern edge of the harbor in a quarter called Karatas, a cosmopolitan, ethnically mixed community connected to the center of Smyrna by a short ferry ride. Socrates was well connected with the Turkish community and was also a good friend of the American consul, George Horton, and Horton had warned him that the Turks would soon take vengeance on the city's Greeks for the incursion of the Greek army into the interior. According to Merope, their father took these warnings to heart and by way of insurance sent two ships filled with tobacco, cotton, and dried goods to companies he supplied in England, so that the profits could be deposited in his English bank.

When word of the Greek army's defeat on August 26, 1922, at Afyon-Karahisar, two hundred miles to the east, first reached two of Socrates' brothers, Vasilis and Alexander, they quickly left for the provinces. The youngest brother, Omeros, had already fled to Athens. They were members of a separatist movement seeking an autonomous Greek enclave inside Turkey, and all the family members were at risk, even though Socrates had carefully avoided politics and done everything he could to protect his family. He had spent a fortune to secure passage for his three young daughters and Eleni on one of the first boats taking refugees to the nearby Greek island of Mytilene (Lesbos). "He and my grandmother stayed behind along with two of my uncles and my brother," Merope told me. "The feeling was that the Turks wouldn't hurt old women, and that only young women and men who could fight against them were at risk."

Once the women had been sent away, with gold sovereigns carefully sewn into their several layers of clothing, Socrates and Aristotle went to his office in the business district on the afternoon of Friday, September 8, and burned any papers that might incriminate them as supporters of Greek nationalist organizations. At the elite Greek Evangheliki Scholi the boy had attended, he and his fellow students had long ago been forced to give up their English school caps for the red Turkish fez and to wear armbands emblazoned with the star and crescent. Socrates elected to keep his son with him because he needed help in protecting the business, and in any event, the boy looked too young to be drafted into the army.

On Saturday, the ninth of September, 1922, the Fourth Turkish Cavalry, brandishing scimitars, occupied the city of Smyrna without opposition. Sunday was silent, as all non-Turks stayed home, waiting to see what would happen. On Monday, September 11, it began.

Men were herded into the central squares and made to kneel, and then their throats were slit. Women were raped and killed and their bodies were mutilated. A priest from the church in which Socrates and Eleni had been married was crucified with horseshoe nails through his hands and feet.

The Greek Metropolitan Chrysostomos was literally torn apart by a Muslim mob, who gouged out his eyes and cut off his nose, hands, and ears with a barber's razor. Three days earlier he had gone to the American consulate to ask his good friend George Horton whether something could be done to protect his people. Looking "infinitely sad," he had refused the offer of a marine escort to safety on one of the American battleships. "As he sat there in the consular office, the shadow of his approaching death lay upon his features," Horton said later.

By Wednesday, September 13, the Turkish soldiers lit kerosene fires to destroy the evidence of the atrocities. They had been waiting for the winds to turn so that the flames would be carried through the Armenian and Greek sections and spare the Turkish neighborhoods. A Greek policeman, Sergeant Tchorbadjis, described to the historian and novelist Marjorie Housepian Dobkin what he saw while working with the Smyrna fire brigade in a futile effort to quench the fires. "In all the houses I went into I saw dead bodies. In one house I followed a trail of blood that led me to a cupboard. My curiosity forced me to open this cupboard—and my hair stood on end. Inside was the naked body of a girl, with her breasts cut off. . . . On one of the roads I saw a man about forty-five or fifty years old. The Turks had blinded him and cut off his nose and left him on the streets. He was crying out, in Turkish, "Isn't there anyone here Christian enough to shoot me so that I will not get burnt in the fire?""

Fearing for his mother's life, Socrates entrusted Gethsemane to the care of a neighboring family, who said they had secured passage on a Turkish caïque that would take them to a nearby Greek island. The old woman protested loudly, unwilling to leave behind her son and adored grandson, but in the end she was led away, tearfully repeating pleas to Aristotle to light candles on the family altar (which every Greek household maintained in the eastern corner of the parlor) and to put his fate in the hands of Jesus Christ. She, too, was carrying a large cache of British gold sovereigns knotted in a handkerchief concealed under her voluminous black skirt.

From his balcony, Socrates could see that the entire market section, including his warehouse, was ablaze. All night the city burned, the sky a hellish crimson that was visible 150 miles away. The minarets of the mosques and the domes of the churches were dark silhouettes against the curtain of flame. Exploding ammunition caches rumbled like distant thunder until dawn. The next day a Turkish lieutenant came to the house asking for the tobacco merchant named Socrates Onassis.

As Aristotle watched, the officer's initially polite tones gave way to angry accusations that the merchant had connections with enemies of the state. Socrates was taken away in shackles to a prison deep in the Turkish section near the *cunak*—prefecture—leaving his son alone in the house.

Soon the boy would learn that his favorite uncle, Alexander, had been hanged in the public square in Kasaba, forty miles east of Smyrna, and two more of his uncles, Yannis and Vasilis, were imprisoned in *sevkiats*, deportation camps, in the interior. The three uncles had lived in market towns east of Smyrna, where they acquired goods for Socrates to export to Europe. Set at hard labor and tortured for nearly two years, they were finally released and found their way to Greece. A fifth uncle, Kyriakos, who has never been mentioned in any Onassis biography, had been killed by a stray bullet on an Athens corner in 1916 during a street demonstration.

The bewildered and abandoned Aristotle walked through the city to find his father's warehouse at Daragaz Point burned to the ground, though the office on the Grand Vizier Hane still stood, despite the fires, guarded by Turkish soldiers. Mutilated corpses were everywhere. A cluster of women's heads bound together like coconuts by their long hair floated down a river toward the harbor.

Within a few days, a Turkish general decided to take the Onassis villa as his residence, and his aide-de-camp, a young lieutenant, ordered Aristotle to move out. To prevent their joining the rebel forces, all male Christians between seventeen and fifty were to be deported to the interior to work in labor gangs, he told the boy.

At this critical juncture, young Aristo demonstrated a cunning that would serve him well throughout his life. He not only convinced the young lieutenant that he was only sixteen, but also won permission to stay in the family home as a sort of major domo. He would maintain the temperamental heating and plumbing systems as well as obtain the latest cylinders for the gramophone and scrounge up the best cigars. ("You usually find that if you make things comfortable for people they like you," Onassis told Maria, as he recounted this story.) In exchange, the Turks agreed to let Aristotle stay in his own room. (According to at least one Onassis biographer, Peter Evans, the boy's services to the young lieutenant included a sexual liaison, but this claim cannot be proved and it is one that Onassis, doggedly homophobic in later life, would certainly deny.)

Aristotle's tallest order was finding contraband alcohol for the general's table. Fortunately, a few days after receiving his assignment the young man encountered the American vice consul in Turkey, James Loder Park, who had been a friend of his uncle Alexander's. Park, too, was desperately searching for liquor—in this case for the officers of the American battleships in the harbor. Though he tried to use his family connections, Aristotle had had little success when riding around town with a Turkish officer; but when he approached the same contacts in the company of the American vice consul, bottles of gin and whiskey and a keg of raki were miraculously forthcoming.

Soon the boy had obtained enough alcohol to satisfy both the Americans and the Turks. The latter rewarded him with a passe-partout, guaranteeing him free passage throughout the city, while the former gave him an identity card that admitted him to the mile-square U.S. military zone in Smyrna centered on the partially burned American consulate. These credentials would prove to be life-savers for the Onassis family.

The young Aristotle who roamed around the city, making shrewd deals and passing for a sixteen-year-old boy, was in fact eighteen. His actual birth date was a matter of some mystery, a mystery carefully fostered by the tycoon himself throughout his lifetime. (When he died in 1975, the *New York Times* obituary did not state his age but reported that he was twenty-nine or twenty-three years older than his wife, Jacqueline Kennedy Onassis, "depending on which of his birthdates he gave at various times.")

Onassis' Argentinian passport, issued in 1927, and most of the official documents he signed, including World War II draft declarations and the birth certificates of his children, give his birth date as September 21, 1900. He always insisted, however, that he was born on January 20, 1906, and that he had been saddled with the earlier date from the time he went to Argentina to make his fortune in 1923. He explained that he was unable to find work as a seventeen-year old, so he gave himself more years of maturity and experience, which stuck for life.

To try to establish his real date of birth, I first approached his closest living relatives. When I asked his half sister Merope what year her brother was born, she dutifully said it was 1906, but later, when I inquired how many years younger she was than her oldest sister, Artemis, she said twelve. Merope admitted to being born in 1913, which would put the birth of Artemis in 1901, a contradiction of her own claim that she had been born in 1904. Her apparent misrepresentation may have been calculated to corroborate her brother's, since Onassis was known to be two years her junior. But if we assume Merope is correct, that would put his birth date in either 1903 or early 1904.

Since any documents that might confirm my suspicions had been destroyed in the Smyrna fire, I tried to track down several of Onassis' schoolmates to find out when they were born. By his own account, one of his closest friends was Yianni Voulgarides, whom he called Yanko and who was in the same class as Onassis at Evangheliki Scholi. Voulgarides had died in 1995, but I located his son, who told me that his father was ninety-two at the time of his death, which means he was born in 1903. A second classmate, Nikos Ekmekzoglou, I would discover, had died in 1981, but I learned from his family that he was born in 1904.

A third classmate, George Katramopoulos, turned out to be still alive and, being the father of a widely known and respected Greek journalist, Eleni Bistika, was rather easy to find. With her help I arranged to interview him at the jewelry store he still operated in downtown Athens. Frail and nearly blind, he told me he met Onassis when he transferred in the third grade to the Aroni School. He stayed in the same class with Aristotle for the next four years and moved on to the Evangheliki Scholi with him. "I was in the liberal arts division, which was six years, and Onassis was in the commercial division, which was five," he remembered. "I had one year to go when the great catastrophe came in 1922."

When I asked him when he was born, Katramopoulos said that it was on August 15, 1904. "Onassis was a few months older, but not a full year," he added. Since Onassis always celebrated his birthday on January 20, he had to have been born on that date in 1904.

Onassis opportunistically added winters to his back in Argentina in 1927, but five years earlier, in Smyrna, he had realized that maturity was a "virtual death sentence," as he later described it. Hoping to rescue as much of his father's liquid wealth as possible and perhaps even win the old man's freedom, he made himself sixteen, and his beardless face and small size allowed him to get away with it.

· · ·

With his Turkish pass, Aristotle had free access to the prison that held his father. He carried letters to and from families of the Greeks and Armenians and other foreigners detained for political crimes. He learned that the prisoners were being taken away every night, in tens and twenties, sentenced by kangaroo courts, and summarily hanged.

Socrates instructed his son to contact his Turkish friends in the city, especially one named Sadiq Topal, who owed him money, and to rally them to his defense. Soon the boy had three hundred Turkish signatures on a petition to the governor asking clemency for his father. Finally Socrates was moved out of death row and unmanacled. His life would apparently be spared, but he was not released from the prison.

At the family's offices on the Grand Vizier Hane, Socrates kept deeds and jewelry that Sadiq Topal had put up as collateral on loans. When Aristo, accompanied by the Turkish merchant, was allowed into the burned building, he found two of his father's safes intact, still containing thousands of Turkish pounds. When he told James Park about the windfall, the vice consul advised him to take the money and leave Turkey. He arranged for the boy to have passage on the U.S. destroyer *Edsall*, which was sailing the following morning, October 15.

That night Aristotle went to see his father for the last time. In a public cell filled with two dozen other prisoners the boy managed to slip 500 Turkish pounds into Socrates' shirt while embracing him. The elder Onassis was suffering from dysentery and exhaustion, and with this money he could at least buy better food and treatment from his jailers. Aristo assured his father that once out of Turkey, he would find his sisters, stepmother, and grandmother and that their Turkish friends in the community would soon manage to get Socrates freed.

On the way out of the prison, Aristotle was stopped at the gate. He had been seen passing the money to his father and was summoned to the camp commandant's office. Terrified because he was carrying the rest of his money bandaged to his body and several incriminating letters from prisoners hidden in his clothing, the boy was led to the warden's office. In the middle of the interrogation, the commandant was called away to an urgent meeting. He entrusted his captive to two guards until he got back.

With his frequent comings and goings and passe-partout, Aristo was well known to the prison guards by now, and they paid little attention to him as they patrolled the grounds. Casually, he slipped out of the room and drifted closer to the gate. He waved at the gatekeeper as he had done many times before and, once out of sight, bolted across the three miles to the sanctuary of the U.S. military zone.

There Aristo found James Park, who agreed to harbor him in his office in the Hotel Majestic until morning, though the boy was now a fugitive. That night the Turkish police did come, looking for a young Greek who had been seen entering the U.S. zone after, they said, stealing money and raping an Armenian girl. Park had hidden the fugitive in his rolltop desk, and from there the boy listened as his friend declared that he had no idea where the thief could be found. After the police left, Park outfitted Aristo in an American sailor's uniform and drove him to the harbor, where he saw him safely aboard the *Edsall*. The next day the ship sailed, and within hours Ari was rowed ashore to the island of Mytilene, the nearest encampment for the thousands of homeless refugees of the Anatolian catastrophe. There he would eventually find his sisters and his stepmother, but he would learn that his grandmother, whom he loved more than anyone in the world, had disappeared.

As harrowing as the actual events of the Smyrna massacre were, the version that Onassis recounted to Maria Callas on August 4, 1959, and to many others over the years, grew more terrible with each rendition. When Metropolitan Chrysostomos was hacked to pieces, Aristo was there to witness it. Not one, but three of his uncles were executed in public. "I saw them hang," he told a reporter for the *New York Herald Tribune* in 1954 (although the hangings happened forty miles outside Smyrna). He also told that reporter and others that his aunt Maria, Socrates' only sister, who was married to Chrysostomos Konialidis, was burned to death by the Turks together with their infant daughter in a church in Thyatira. It's true that Chrysostomos Konialidis was seized by the Turks and later killed, and it's also true that five hundred Greeks died when the Turks barred the exits of the burning church in Thyatira, but Onassis' aunt Maria was not among them, for, according to Merope, "Maria died giving birth to her fifth child before the Anatolian catastrophe." But Maria's six-year-old daughter, Antiopi, was lost during the days of the atrocities, and when she was located many years later by her brother, Nikos Konialidis, she was married to a Turk and did not want to rejoin her Greek relatives.

Smyrna was where Onassis had lived the happiest as well as the most traumatic years of his life, and as the *Christina* approached the dirty, crowded, noisy harbor, he entered his own past: the donkey carts and camels and screaming *hamals* unloading cargoes on the waterfront, his old neighborhood rising up the hillside, the narrow, terraced streets of Karatas, some of them no more than stone staircases, still filled with peddlers pulling wheeled carts beneath the ornate, overhanging closed balconies where the veiled women of the Muslim households could watch the activity below hidden from the gaze of passersby. "Whenever he returned to Smyrna, he was profoundly affected by the visit," the captain of the *Christina* told me.

Onassis insisted on taking everyone ashore for the sentimental journey. His high school still looked in 1959 (and does today) much the same as it did when he was its most rebellious student: its large cream-colored neo-classical buildings with Ionian columns stand in an enclosed campus shaded by ancient palms and fir trees that are draped with brilliant swaths of bougainvillea. The young students still wear the navy blue uniform and white blouse Aristo wore at Evangheliki Scholi, but now classes are taught in Turkish rather than in English and Greek. Today the main entrance is dominated by a giant, glowering bust of Kemal Ataturk, the man who launched the sack of Smyrna in 1922, on a gray granite pedestal. Behind it, carved into the gray marble wall in foot-high letters, is the inscription: WHAT AN HONOR IT IS TO SAY, "I AM A TURK."

As he led his guests through the shady campus, Aristotle bragged of his success there. He told how he had nearly won a place on the Olympic water polo team and how he had graduated near the top of his class. "I was supposed to go to Oxford next, to study architecture," he said. "I already had bought my wardrobe for England before the massacre began." Onassis did excel at water sports, but as for his claims of academic honors, his classmates remember quite the opposite.

After causing major mischief in every school he attended, he was granted entry to Evangheliki because his father, Socrates, pleaded with his friend Michael Avramides, a teacher at the school, which had been founded in 1733 under British auspices. Avramides would regret persuading the school to accept the boy, writing years later: "The son was as terrible as the father was kind. . . . Even when he was young, you could see that he was one of those people who would either destroy themselves or succeed brilliantly." The young Aristo quickly earned distinctions chiefly for pranks and truancy. One day he and a friend wired all the electric bells to go off every time he tugged on a wire. Money his father gave him to tip the staff at the school was used to buy his friends cigarettes and drinks. He favored brawling and swimming in the harbor to sitting in class, and hitched rides on the ferryboats that plied the waters. He liked to grab on to the stern and pull himself aboard, causing consternation among the veiled Turkish ladies who were seated in the back section to avoid being seen by men. "In the fifth term at Evangheliki he pinched the young woman who taught us English and got paddled for it, but it didn't bother him," recalled his classmate George Katramopoulos.

Onassis' school in Smyrna (Izmir) as it appears today

The only area in which Aristotle applied himself with any determination was water sports: sailing, rowing, water polo, and swimming. The greatest disappointment of his youth, two months before the catastrophe of September 1922, was failing to win the title of "Victor Ludorum," or champion of games, for which he had been training all year, rowing for hours every morning to improve his endurance. His uncle Omeros, one of the four judges, had coached the boy in sports, just as his other favorite uncle, Alexander, had guided him through adolescence and acquainted him with the company of women. (His father was rather aloof and completely absorbed in his business; Aristotle turned to these two uncles as father substitutes and would mourn their early deaths all his life.)

The young Onassis never graduated from Evangheliki, despite his claims to the contrary. After their records were destroyed in the Anatolian disaster, a group of his classmates were reunited in Athens and compiled a registry of the school's graduates to present to the university entrance boards. His friends hopefully included the name "Aristotle Onassis" near the bottom of the list, but their elderly headmaster vehemently crossed it out.

Onassis drove his guests to the foot of the stone staircase leading to his old neighborhood of Karatas, and they climbed up to the corner building where he had lived until the Turks usurped the villa. The wrought-iron grille over the front door, the front stoop with its pebble mosaic, the barred windows that look down on the waterfront below—all these were still there, although somewhat dilapidated. The sight of these familiar stones and steps, trees and vines filled Onassis with such emotion that his string of recollections trailed to a halt, Maria recalled.

Aristo may have been remembering the first time he and his sister Artemis came back to this place, in 1955. In the summer of 1998 Merope described that visit to me just as Artemis had recounted it to her: "They knocked on the door and a woman opened it and invited them in. When Artemis walked into the living room she saw a piano in the middle of the room, walked over, touched it affectionately and started to cry. 'This is the piano I practiced on,' she told Aristo in Greek. The woman who lived in the house looked at them in surprise and said—also speaking in perfect Greek—'Are you Greek? I'm a Muslim Greek from Crete. We came over here in the exchange of populations and they put us in this house.' "

As he stood now before the door whose grille still bore his father's initials, gazing down at the familiar view of the waterfront, Onassis told his sister he felt as if he was once again ten years old, playing on the steps that led down to the harbor as the sun slowly set and the adults of the family looked on from the shade of the grape arbor.

Socrates and his cronies would be smoking their Turkish hookah waterpipes, as the women, padding in their soft slippers, brought them silver trays bearing small cups of Turkish coffee, glasses of water, candied fruits in syrup, and cloudy glasses of ouzo. The gramophone would send the wailing, keening melody of a Turkish *halk* song out into the evening air, and if the *kefi* of the moment or the high-proof anise liqueur inspired them, the men might stand and dance a few steps of the slow and hypnotic *zembebkiko*—the eagle's dance—demonstrating their skill and strength. Such images as well as the scents of saffron and honey, wood smoke and goat cheese, lemon blossoms and jasmine, the aromatic meatballs in tomato sauce that Hadji-néné would make especially for her grandson—these were the madeleines that transported Onassis as he stood on the cobblestoned road outside his now empty childhood home. It was futile to try to describe his teeming memories to his guests, because neither the Britons nor his own wife, reared in England and America, had experienced the food, music, and tumultuous family celebrations that molded his youth. Only Maria, who had lived in prewar Athens surrounded by neighborhoods of tenements overflowing with refugees from Anatolia, could understand the sadness evoked by the plaintive wailing *rebetika* songs and the joy conjured up in

Onassis beneath a portrait of his lost mother, Penelope

Aristo's breast by a recitation of elaborately spiced dishes rich with currants and pine nuts.

The group's final stop was the Archangel Michael Greek Orthodox Cemetery, where Onassis' mother, Penelope, was buried in a grove of cypresses, usually planted in cemeteries as a symbol of the resurrection. (The Greek cemetery in Smyrna was later plowed over and a stadium was built on the grounds.) Penelope had died slowly of an infection after a botched kidney operation when her son was only eight years old. Now, as he stood at her simple gravestone, Onassis spoke of how beautiful she had been, with her huge dark eyes and chestnut hair, how gentle and quiet in her manner. The sad fact was that Aristotle could scarcely remember his mother's face. He had only one old sepia-colored photograph of her as a young woman gazing petulantly at the camera, with a high-necked lace yoke over her dress and her hair piled on her head in the manner of a Gibson girl. Her son had commissioned an oil portrait based on that photo and had it hung over his desk on the *Christina,* but he was later to learn from older relations that it wasn't a good likeness. Onassis once remarked to Churchill, "You told me, Sir Winston, your father died very young. If he had lived to your age you might not have had to struggle so hard. Your life would have been easier, and you might not have done what you did. . . . My mother died when I was six. If she had lived, I might not have worked as hard as I have done."

At the harborside, en route back to the *Christina,* Onassis pointed out to the Montague Brownes the exact spot where he plunged into the water on the darkest night of the catastrophe and swam, dodging bullets and dead bodies, to the American ship that would take him to safety. He did not mention that he had been ferried to the battleship in the motorboat of the American vice consul while dressed in the uniform of a U.S. sailor.

The *Christina* sailed out of Smyrna at 12:55 p.m. after a visit that had lasted only four hours but encompassed more than fifty years of memories. As the guests gathered on the rear deck for lunch, Onassis' stories of his youth continued, the tide of his memory turning now toward his adolescence. After lunch, out of earshot of the children, Onassis regaled Callas and the others with tales of his early erotic adventures. He was only twelve, he told Maria, the first time he tried to lose his virginity to a pretty young laundress who worked in the house, but his stepmother came home, interrupting the experiment under way atop a pile of soiled linens in the basement. She suspended the proceedings before they could reach their intended conclusion, and fired the laundress. Aristo had better luck with a comely French tutor whom his father had engaged for his summer vacation. The young woman received him in her home on a sweltering summer day, clad in a light dressing gown that was nearly transparent, "exposing her ample bosom," as Onassis recalled.

All French irregular verbs immediately vanished from his memory and he spoke to her in stammering Greek, saying, " 'Mademoiselle, you are indecently dressed. You are arousing me against my will. If you continue to dress in such fashion nothing can stop me from violating you!' Not at all taken aback at my frankness," Aristo recalled later, "she burst out laughing. I urged her on to the sofa and without hesitation showed her my admiration. She was my first mistress."

Girls of good family, on the other hand, could not be approached with such impertinence. Aristo had developed feelings of a higher order for a Jewish Spanish girl who lived in his neighborhood of Karatas. He called the dark-eyed beauty Luna-e-Kinze, he explained to Maria, because she was only fifteen. Aristo pursued Luna in courtly style, gathering his friends under her window to serenade her with Italian *cantadas.* He even challenged a rival suitor, a wealthy Armenian boy named Spartalis, to a fight for the girl's affections. But Luna-e-Kinze proved unyielding, and in any case her parents eventually whisked her off to South America.

Aristo did not suffer long, and sought consolation in Demir Yolu, the red-light district of Smyrna. In 1921 he even led a dozen of his awed classmates on a tour of the quarter after dutifully securing his professors' permission to skip morning classes and attend services for St. Barbara's day. His boyish charm, his bronzed, muscular (if somewhat small) physique, and most of all, his father's wealth and the resulting access to the best in tobacco and liquor, all made him a great favorite of the professional ladies.

Aristo's favorite brothel in Smyrna, he confided to Maria (in Greek, of course, lest his British guests understand him), was Fahrie's. The alluring odor of the ladies' body powder and musk perfume and the smoothness of their silk-stockinged legs inspired recollections that would arouse romantic longings for the rest of his life. Here he collected the wisdom and experience of the prostitutes of Smyrna. "One way or another, sweets, all ladies do it for the money," an old Turkish whore had advised him. He mused that in every society, money and sex are inexorably intertwined.

The long nights of conversation on board the *Christina* had been filled with confessions and reminiscences, shared secrets and charged glances, yet aside from a bit of furtive hand-holding when no one was looking, Onassis and Maria had carefully refrained from physical contact. On board the yacht there was simply nowhere they could enjoy secure privacy, and in any event Onassis would not relax the chaperone rule whereby the hapless Montague Brownes were typically the guardians of propriety. All these scruples only exacerbated the building sexual tension. Very likely, for Onassis, recounting his youthful sexual adventures to Maria was as much a displacement of frustrated longings as a crude though effective means of seduction.

Maria listened to these tales of conquest with her eyes glistening. She had never heard a man speak of such things so frankly, and she was fascinated with Aristo's attitude toward sex. All her experiences with sex until now had been negative. Her mother had resented and despised her father and had become hysterical, even suicidal, when he directed his sexual energy into extramarital liaisons. In Athens, Litsa used sex as a means of acquiring food, money, and attention from enemy officers and perhaps encouraged her daughters to do the same. In wedlock, Maria told her friends, she learned that "sometimes a wife has to fulfill her marital duties" in order to ensure a husband's protection and happiness. No one, until Onassis, had suggested to her that sex could be joyful, natural, even invigorating for a woman as well as a man. It was a startling and liberating concept to a woman who had been brought up to think of sex as an unpleasant duty, and Onassis' crude tales of his youthful adventures were profoundly exciting to her.

Meneghini, of course, couldn't understand precisely what Onassis was saying but evidently he somehow got the drift, for when he wrote about the visit to Smyrna many years later, he described Onassis leading him and Maria personally, like Dante's Virgil, through the infernal red-light district.

"Near the port we went to various local dives, which Onassis knew intimately," he wrote in *My Wife Maria Callas.* "At five in the morning I managed to persuade him to return to the yacht. He was so drunk he couldn't stand up." The ship's log, however, makes it clear that the *Christina* was in Smyrna for only four hours, from 9:02 a.m. on August 4 to 12:55 p.m., when it sailed north toward Istanbul. Battista's fervid memories of a visit to the brothels of Smyrna, repeated by several other biographers, were complete fiction.

That afternoon, during the siesta hour, the schism between Maria and her husband deepened with another battle about her career. Callas later described the episode to friends, including Mary Carter, her Paris friend Vasso Devetzi, and Stelios Galatopoulos.

Perhaps responding to the increasing influence he sensed Onassis had over Maria, Meneghini sought to regain control, announcing several new engagements he had set up for the rest of the year. As he boasted to her about the record fees he was going to demand, Callas in effect fired him as her business manager, citing his clumsy combativeness with the leading opera houses, his lack of languages, his generally offensive manners and outrageous demands. She told him that from now on she would manage her own career.

Their argument exploded into shouting, and Maria, disgusted and worried they would be overheard, stormed out of their stateroom. On the deck at the stern of the ship, near the swimming pool, she discovered Onassis leaning on the railing, staring into the gathering dusk at the silhouette of a large land mass. It was a typical sight, according to Captain Kostas. "He rarely came to the bridge but liked to go to the stern and watch whatever port we had just left disappear on the horizon."

Maria walked to his side, and after some moments of silence, Onassis told her that the land in the distance was the island of Mytilene, where he had been taken when he left the burning city of Smyrna in 1922. Here the young Onassis had searched one refugee camp after another for his lost family.

As they talked, Maria realized yet another essential thing they had in common: "Although he was getting out of life all that he thought he wanted—he was a very hard-working man with amazing drive—he felt that something vital was eluding him," Galatopoulos remembers her saying. "I listened, and to a great deal that he said I could find a parallel in my own life. It was daybreak when I returned to my cabin."

On the way to Istanbul, the *Christina* had to pass through the Dardanelles. It was in these straits that Sir Winston, during World War I, suffered one of the most painful moments of his career. As the first lord of the British Admiralty, Churchill had proposed to force open the Dardanelles and then capture the Gallipoli Peninsula and Constantinople (now Istanbul). An Allied fleet destroyed the forts at the entrance to the straits and advanced part way up, but on March 18, 1915, they were forced to turn back after several ships struck mines. The engagement ended disastrously: the Allies withdrew, and 43,000 British troops were killed, taken prisoner, or missing in action.

According to the Onassis biographer Willi Frischauer, Sir Winston had expressed a wish at the beginning of the 1959 cruise to visit the graves of those who had fallen at Gallipoli and the Turkish government replied with a warm welcome. Everyone on the boat, however, especially Onassis, Lady Clementine, and Anthony Montague Browne, felt that the emotional upheaval would be too much for the old man. They talked him out of his plan and Onassis instructed the captain to pass through the Dardanelles in the early-morning hours of August 5, when Churchill would be sound asleep. This did not prevent the former Old Naval Party from musing mournfully on the tragedy at dinner that night, "in a meditative historian's mood," according to Montague Browne.

During the next day, cruising the Turkish coast past sleek wooden *gulets* and huge freighters and tankers moving between the Aegean and the Black Sea, the passengers on the *Christina* had ample time to gossip about what had happened so far during the cruise and what might lie ahead. Meneghini later wrote that he had no clue to the relationship developing between his wife and Onassis until the day they arrived in Istanbul, but this seems highly unlikely. Everyone else on the yacht (with the continuing exception of Sir Winston, perhaps) was aware of the growing intimacy between the diva and their host.

Still lacking sea legs and increasingly ignored by his wife, Meneghini blundered on with his attempt to "improve his acquaintance" with certain of the other ladies on board, his unwanted attentions soiling more than one dress as he played footsie under the dinner table. His most frequent victim was Nonie Montague Browne. "Poor Meneghini didn't know what to do. His Maria, whom he adored, was slipping out of his reach and he was unable to stop it," she told me in early 1999. "He became a disillusioned, unable to stop it," she told me in early 1999. "He became a disillusioned, sad chap and I paid the price because he was always seated next to me and he kept ruining my shoes in a pathetic effort to prove that he could still attract a woman."

On that night of the fourth, as the *Christina* passed quietly through the ill-starred Dardanelles and into the Sea of Marmara, everyone had retired in anticipation of the day they would spend in the fabled city of Istanbul. Maria and Aristo sat up on deck late. Most of the time they were silent, watching the occasional spotlights from the land, while Meneghini sulked in his stateroom below, perhaps vainly hoping that Istanbul would prove a less disagreeable stop than Smyrna. In fact, the former capital of the Byzantine empire was the place where Maria and Onassis would consummate their affair, and Meneghini would later record the arrival there as the day "destiny changed my life."

10

AT THE CROSSROADS

An aged man is but a paltry thing,
A tattered coat upon a stick, unless
Soul clap its hands and sing, and louder sing
For every tatter in its mortal dress,
Nor is there singing school but studying
Monuments of its own magnificence;
And therefore I have sailed the seas and come
To the holy city of Byzantium.

William Butler Yeats, "Sailing to Byzantium"

Approaching Istanbul, the passengers on the *Christina* glimpsed a fairy-tale vision worthy of the *Rubáiyát* of Omar Khayyám. Minarets rise like forests of cypress trees over the city's five hundred mosques and surround immense domes like those of Aghia Sofia, the Blue Mosque, and Suley-maniye Mosque, which are set ablaze by the rising and setting sun, glowing as bright as the fabled jewels of Topkapi Palace.

The only major city in the world located at the crossroads of two continents, Constantinople was for centuries the capital of the Eastern Roman Empire, keeping alive all the art and wisdom of Greek and Roman civilization through the Dark Ages, until it fell to the Ottoman Turks in 1453. In 1923 the name was officially changed to Istanbul, a corruption of the Greek words *eis tin poli*, meaning "to the city."

The *Christina* entered the Sea of Marmara on Wednesday, August 5, and anchored at noon at Buyukada, the largest of the Princes Islands, twelve miles southeast of Istanbul. On these islands Byzantine princes lived out their exiles, and in the nineteenth century wealthy Turks built elegant summer homes there. They are cool havens of parks and gardens, horse-drawn carriages and quaint buildings, including the traditional wooden *yakli*, whose balconies, curtained by wooden fretwork, overhang the water.

"As soon as the luxurious yacht was anchored in front of Buyukada," the Turkish newspaper *Hurriyet* reported, "boats and motorboats full of natives of the island as well as journalists came near to the *Christina* just to see the famous people and the famous yacht. . . . Meanwhile, the son of the billionaire businessman Onassis made some speed shows around the island with his speedboat."

While Alexander was amusing the journalists with his daredevil stunts, a launch arrived at the *Christina* bringing aboard the dignitaries Onassis had invited for lunch: the Turkish prime minister, Adnan Menderes, his foreign minister, Fatin Rustu Zorlu, both their wives, and the British ambassador, Sir Bernard Burrows, with Lady Burrows.

Onassis had intended this luncheon as an attempt at a diplomatic rapprochement in the wake of the growing Cyprus crisis, but the enormous bitterness toward Menderes among the Greeks already on board threatened to sabotage the plan.

Ever since the outbreak of violence between Turks and Greeks in Cyprus—the powder-keg issue Onassis had dared to raise with Sir Winston on their first meeting in 1957—relations among England, Turkey, and Greece had been extremely volatile. On the night of September 6, 1955, a pogrom was launched in Istanbul against the large Greek population whose roots there went back 104 generations. (The city was founded in 660 B.C. by Greek colonists, who called it Byzantium.) In one night, more than four thousand Greek shops were plundered, more than two thousand Greek homes were vandalized and robbed, and twenty-eight Greek civilians were killed, including a monk. Forty-one churches (including two Roman Catholic) were torched. Fifty-two Greek schools were stripped of their furniture, books, and equipment. The total damage to Greek homes, churches, schools, and businesses was estimated at between $150 million and $300 million ($2 billion to $4 billion today).

The main target of the attack was the Ecumenical Patriarchate, the seat of the Eastern Orthodox church, which is situated in a neighborhood of Istanbul called the Phanar ("lighthouse"). The rioters desecrated two Greek cemeteries, opening the tombs of past patriarchs and scattering their bones. According to a British journalist, the next day the Greek quarter looked "like the bombed parts of London during the Second World War." More than 30,000 ethnic Greeks fled what has been called the most destructive pogrom executed in Europe since the infamous Kristallnacht, when Nazis attacked Jews and their communities in November 1938, on the eve of World War II. (Continued persecution eventually reduced the original community of more than 100,000 Greeks to fewer than 3,000.)

These atrocities, which had taken place only four years earlier, were still fresh in the minds of the Greeks aboard the *Christina* when Onassis announced that Prime Minister Adnan Menderes, the man considered responsible for planning them, was coming for lunch with Sir Winston. "How could you invite this man on board when his hands are still wet with Greek blood?" Maria demanded in outrage. Onassis explained that he was doing it for the benefit of his good friend, Patriarch Athenagoras, whom they would meet the following day. According to Captain Kostas Anastasiades, Onassis felt it would help the besieged patriarch if the prime minister were to see that powerful individuals, including Winston Churchill, cared about Athenagoras' welfare and the future of the Patriarchate.

This explanation quieted Maria, Artemis, and others who would have preferred to throw Menderes overboard. They were polite to the Turkish politicians and their wives throughout the luncheon, and afterward all gathered on the deck near the swimming pool for photographs. According to *Hurriyet,* "While posing, the Turkish Prime Minister gave some information about Istanbul to the famous soprano Maria Callas."

After cordial farewells all around, Menderes went ashore beaming. He saluted Sir Winston and Onassis and left, accompanied by the British ambassador. He had no foreboding that his moment of glory—in fact, his life—was nearly over. Within eight months, the Turkish army would seize the government in a coup, try him for abuse of power, and hang him.

The *Christina* next sailed into the straits of the Bosphorus for a dramatic passage through the heart of Istanbul. As the ship passed the Golden Horn, a narrow inlet where pleasure craft anchor, views of the city that spreads over seven hills unfolded. As they proceed north up the Bosphorus, ships pass ornate white marble palaces and pavilions on the European side, where the sultans took their pleasure amid the beauties of their harems and their exotic aviaries and zoos. The white facade of Dolmabahce Palace stretches for six hundred yards along the shore, with a vast reception salon boasting fifty-six columns and a crystal chandelier that weighs four and a half tons. It was near this palace, at the Dolmabahce Marina, that the *Christina* docked at 5 p.m. that afternoon so Sir Winston and the other guests could go ashore for a tour of the ancient city, including a visit to the famous Hagia Sophia church built by Justinian I, now a museum.

The Turkish papers photographed the special Fiat jeep being carried ashore on a small boat while Sir Winston descended from the gangplank in his navy commander's cap, still delighting the crowd with his victory salute. With Onassis at the wheel of the jeep, he was driven on a tour of Istanbul

Inside the Hagia Sophia, Istanbul. From left: a Greek consular official, Theodore Garofalidis,
Tina, Meneghini, Artemis, Nonie, a Turkish official, Maria, Lady Churchill, Celia Sandys,
Diana Sandys, Anthony Montague Brown, and the British ambassador's wife

that included stops at Dolmabahce, Topkapi Palace, and Sultanahmet Mosque. Finally Churchill and the Fiat were ceremoniously returned to the yacht.

The next morning the passengers hurried to dress. The Greeks were to go ashore to meet and receive the blessing of Patriarch Athenagoras, the spiritual leader of the Eastern Orthodox church and its 150 million members. For them, this was the equivalent of entering the Vatican for an audience with the pope, although the Turks had seized so many of the Patriarchate's extensive holdings that it now occupied only a small corner of its formerly grand domain. After the visit, the patriarch was expected to come on board the *Christina* for a luncheon in his honor.

Onassis had arranged for all the non-Greeks to be taken in the meantime on a tour of the city's famous sights, including the Blue Mosque and Topkapi Palace. Then they would be conveyed by boat up the Bosphorus for their own lunch, hosted by the British consul, after which they were scheduled to return to the ship just in time to meet the patriarch before his departure.

"At 10 a.m. the first Chris-Craft brought Mrs. Churchill, Lady Sandys and her daughter to the Marina from the yacht," *Hurriyet* reported. "While Mrs. Churchill went to see Topkapi Palace and other historic sightseeing places, Lady Sandys and her daughter went to the British consulate." An hour later, according to the press, another Chris-Craft left the yacht, this one carrying only Onassis and Callas. They attempted to go to Dolmabahce Marina, but when they saw the crowd waiting for them on shore, they decided not to land and changed direction, heading toward Leander's Tower (called Kiz Kulesi by the Turks), which stands on a small island about two hundred yards off shore at the entrance to the Bosphorus. European writers have celebrated this as the spot where Leander drowned trying to join his beloved Hero, although it was probably the Hellespont, to the south, that he tried to cross.

Onassis showed Callas the romantic sight from the privacy of the small boat he was piloting. The pair, no doubt frustrated by their desire for each other and eager to be away from the accusing eyes of Meneghini, managed to steal a few moments alone, but they returned to the boat after a brief interlude. According to the Turkish press, several Chris-Crafts soon carried ashore the entire party who were to visit the Patriarchate, including Callas, Meneghini, Tina, and Ari.

Onassis had spent a great deal of time and effort organizing and choreographing this day. He wanted to make sure that the Greek Orthodox Christians like Callas would have an unforgettable experience visiting the Patriarchate and that the non-Greeks would also enjoy themselves without being forced to endure conversations and rites which, he felt, they would find tedious and alien to their own religious traditions.

While the English passengers set out for their day of sightseeing (with the exception of Sir Winston, who remained on board), Maria donned her most modest dress and covered her hair with a scarf to visit the holiest place and the holiest man in the Eastern Orthodox world. Meneghini, who had evidently decided not to let her out of his sight, insisted on accompanying the group to the Patriarchate, even though he would not understand a word that was said there.

Eleven years after the Roman emperor Constantine was converted to Christianity in A.D. 313 by the vision of a cross in the sky, he decided to move the capital of the Roman Empire to the site of a Greek city on the Bosphorus called Byzantium. There, at the gateway between Europe and Asia, he built the "New Rome," which he named Constantinople. The entire Christian world was then divided into five sees, each headed by a patriarch, among whom the pope in Rome was considered to have the primacy of honor.

After 787, however, a schism between Rome and the patriarchates of the East slowly began to develop. The split of the church into two branches—represented by the two heads of the Byzantine eagle, seen in most Orthodox churches—is usually dated to 1054, the year the pope excommunicated the patriarch of Constantinople and the patriarch in turn excommunicated the pope. Today the patriarch of Constantinople is considered by Orthodox Christians to be the "first among equals," but he is not seen to be endowed with moral infallibility, as Roman Catholics believe the pope is, and he is not the administrative leader of Orthodox churches in countries like Russia and Greece, which are autocephalous, or self-ruling.

Religion is by custom and culture central to the life of every Greek, even if he or she rarely attends church. Greeks celebrate their saint's day rather than their birthday. They light candles and hang votive figures on household icons to ask for a saint's intercession in any of life's problems, from an ailing child to a misplaced object. Whenever a business or household is established, it must be blessed and evil spirits exorcised with holy water, ideally administered by a priest. Both Onassis and Maria Callas were steeped in Orthodox tradition and honored it throughout their lives. Maria prayed and crossed herself—in the Orthodox way, from right to left—before every performance she gave, and when Onassis inaugurated the offices of Olympic Airways in New York in 1966, Archbishop Iakovos, the leader of the Greek Orthodox church in the United States, was there to bless the building on Fifth Avenue. (It is now the New York showroom of Versace.)

When Battista Meneghini and Maria Callas wanted to marry, in Italy in 1949, they had great difficulty obtaining permission from the church because Maria was not a Catholic and Meneghini's family objected to the union. On April 21, 1949, just before Maria was to leave for a long singing engagement in South America, Meneghini managed to find a vicar in his hometown of Verona who would facilitate the papers and a priest willing to marry them—not at the church altar but in the sacristy, which was used for storage. They rushed through the ceremony before two witnesses. "There among broken chairs, headless statues, funeral palls covered with dust, and century-old canopies and banners, we became husband and wife," Battista wrote in his memoirs.

Although Maria prayed regularly with her husband in Catholic churches in Italy, she never lost her primal emotional connection to the Greek Orthodox church in which she had been raised. Just after her marriage, she wrote to her new husband from Argentina, "The other evening I went with a Greek journalist and a lady to the Greek Orthodox church to light a candle for us and my *Norma*. You see, I feel our Church more than yours. It's strange, but it's so. Perhaps because I'm more accustomed to it, or perhaps because the Orthodox Church is warmer and more festive." Meneghini confirms this: "Despite having married a Catholic, she remained Greek Orthodox and was closely bound to her Church. . . .

Faithful to her beliefs, Maria wasn't very sympathetic toward Rome's Pope."

Her patron saint was of course the Virgin Mary. According to Meneghini, she carried everywhere with her a small Cignaroli triptych of the Holy Family painted on wood, which he had given her in 1947. Before one performance in Vienna she became hysterical when she realized she had left the painting behind, insisting she could not go on without it. According to Meneghini, "It was necessary to telephone a friend in Milan and importune her to go to our home and then fly to Vienna with Maria's talisman."

Callas had an extremely personal and rather self-centered idea of her relationship with God, as several friends have pointed out. Nadia Stancioff wrote: "She once said to me, 'God was good to me, Nadia. I'm not saying all the credit is his. No, I earned my place at the top the hard way, but he did give me success beyond my expectations.' " John Ardoin, in whom Maria frequently confided, said something similar to me: "She saw everything in terms of herself. I mean, if it was raining, she would say, 'Why is it raining? I wanted to go shopping. Why is God doing this to me?' "

Like many Greeks Maria would cross herself whenever she passed a church or when she felt she needed a little divine help. On every August 15, the feast day of the Virgin, Maria celebrated her name day and her friends would remember her with phone calls and gifts. Prayer was a daily part of her life, according to Meneghini, even on the early days of the cruise: "In the evening we knelt together in our cabin and prayed before the little painting of the Madonna from which Maria was never separated. This was our relationship until August 7."

To visit the venerable Patriarch Athenagoras in Orthodox Christendom's holy see would be for Maria one of the most solemn and moving moments of her life. It would probably not even have occurred to her to compare this experience to the earlier occasion when she and Meneghini had been received by the pope in Rome (and she had rebuffed the pontiff's entreaties rather flippantly). Onassis was by now well aware of Maria's strong religious feelings and knew how much it meant to her to visit Patriarch Athenagoras.

Over six feet tall, with a long white beard that extended to his waist, Athenagoras had personally officiated at Aristotle and Tina's wedding in 1946. Born in 1886 in the Epiros region of northwestern Greece in a village called Vasilikon, he had swiftly climbed the hierarchy of the church, becoming bishop of Corfu before being enthroned as archbishop of North and

South America in 1932. In this post he managed to end the long political feud between republicans and royalists that had rent the Greek church in the United States and polarized most Greek-American communities. So successful was Athenagoras as a peacemaker that President Truman personally intervened with the Turks on his behalf and convinced them to waive for him their restriction that the ecumenical patriarch be a Turkish citizen. With the suspension of this qualification, Athenagoras was allowed to become the patriarch in Istanbul in 1949, a position he held until his death in 1972.

The pilgrims from the *Christina*—the group included Aristotle and Tina Onassis, Artemis and Theodore Garofalidis, Maria Callas and Battista Meneghini, and the ship's captain, Kostas Anastasiades—entered the walled environs of the Patriarchate at noon. After stopping at the church of St. George to light the customary candles (Onassis made an offering of a $100 bill for his), they were escorted into the patriarch's wood-paneled reception room lined with dazzling icons and redolent of incense. Within, the imposing figure of the seventy-three-year-old Athenagoras in his black robes and black stove-pipe headdress (called a *kalimmafki*) and draped in a black train that framed his long white beard and hair, looked very like yet another icon, a Byzantine rendering of St. Nicholas.

The patriarch called Onassis and Callas to the front of the group. As they stood together before him, he blessed them, placing a hand on each head. In sonorous Greek he lauded them as "the world's finest singer and the most famous mariner of the modern world, a modern Odysseus." He thanked them for the honors they had brought to Greece and then he said prayers on their behalf.

Although he didn't understand Greek, Meneghini, in the back of the group, saw the effect the prelate's words had on Maria and became so agitated that he protested out loud: "But she's already married!" Someone in the group managed to hush him, whispering the vain assurance that this was, after all, only a blessing.

Meneghini's apprehension of the patriarch's benediction as some sort of bizarre marriage ceremony may have amused the others, but the blessing's significance could not have been more profound. From the moment Athenagoras blessed Onassis and Maria together as a couple, Callas felt free to follow her heart. Her religious and moral scruples had been torturing her, but now her mind was suddenly made up. And Meneghini, who for eleven years had devoted every day to observing her, realized this. "Maria remained profoundly troubled afterward. I could see it in her eyes, which were luminous and wild," he wrote.

Maria later told several friends, including Vasso Devetzi, that the visit to the Patriarchate was the catalyst for her decision to leave her husband for Onassis. Instantly it seemed clear to her that her destiny lay with her fellow Greek, who, as she imagined, had just been joined with her with the patriarch's blessing. The realization transformed her, and she longed to tell Aristo, but he was too preoccupied to listen to or notice the change in her. He was bidding farewell to the patriarch, declaring that the entire staff of the *Christina* was eagerly awaiting His All-Holiness's arrival on board.

Athenagoras was due to board the *Christina* at 1 p.m. For this visit Onassis had insisted on the best Greek cuisine, the best service, the cleanest ship—everything had to be perfect for the spiritual head of the church. The plan for the patriarch's visit was to cruise slowly down the Bosphorus and back. Before the patriarch's arrival, Anthony Montague Browne noticed his host huddled in earnest conversation with Captain Kostas and asked him what was wrong. "All sailors believe a priest on board brings bad luck," Onassis explained. "I was saying to him: 'This guy is one hundred priests' value. And there is an eight-knot current running. So be very, very careful.' "

The Montague Brownes and all the non-Greeks besides Sir Winston had vanished by the time the patriarch came aboard in his long black robes and wearing a large jeweled pectoral cross on a heavy gold chain that nestled against his flowing white beard. Sir Winston, seated in his chair on deck, was somewhat taken aback at the sight of this Eastern apparition, trailed by a parade of lesser prelates in elaborate robes and jewelry. Athenagoras came over to Churchill, placed a hand on each of his shoulders, then leaned over and began to chant in Greek, invoking God's blessings on the famous statesman.

According to Onassis' biographer Willi Frischauer, Churchill became increasingly agitated as he felt himself smothered in the robes and hair. "The heavy cross and chain dangling from his neck was banging against Churchill's face, his beard was tickling the bald dome. It was a most uncomfortable situation and Onassis . . . had to act quickly," Frischauer writes. "The last thing he wanted was a fracas between his distinguished friend and the highest cleric of the Greek Orthodox Church. Sidling up to Churchill, he whispered in his ear: 'It's quite all right, Sir Winston. The Patriarch is praying for you!' Winston's anger dissolved into a broad smile. The lunch that followed was an animated affair."

In fact, the conversation got a little too animated for Onassis' taste; he was terrified of offending either Sir Winston or Athenagoras. Sometime during the lunch, Artemis, who'd had a bit too much to drink, said something that caused both Onassis and her husband, Theodore, to wince and then pray silently that she'd shut up before she created a scandal. Signals, meaningful glances, and whispers were exchanged, and suddenly a member of the crew appeared. He murmured into Artemis' ear that an urgent telephone call was awaiting her if she would kindly go to her stateroom to receive it.

Later Theodore Garofalidis, Aristo's co-conspirator, recounted the incident to Nonie Montague Browne, but he didn't specify what exactly Artemis had said when she spoke out of turn. Onassis' older sister was an extremely religious person. She may have made some potentially inflammatory remarks about the recent persecution of the Greeks by the Turks in Istanbul, which reminded her of the atrocities in Smyrna suffered by her family. Or she may have made an indiscreet remark in the presence of the prelate about romantic activities and undercurrents on board the *Christina* which she felt worthy of censure by his high moral authority. Whatever Artemis said, it was disturbing enough to her brother for him to order the crewman who brought word of the spurious phone call to lock her up in her room for the remainder of the visit.

Apparently oblivious to—or perhaps grateful for—Artemis' sudden disappearance, Patriarch Athenagoras enjoyed himself immensely during the lunch on the *Christina* and Nonie recalled that the British contingent returned just in time to be introduced to the patriarch and kiss his ring, after which he "left smartly." Onassis escorted Athenagoras ashore, to the Dolmabahce Marina, and, in a final diplomatic gesture, told the crowd of reporters that he would offer "his yacht to the Turkish and Greek leaders for one cruise, if they would establish democracy on Cyprus."

Onassis no doubt heaved a sigh of relief as he ordered Artemis released from her temporary prison. It had been a day of delicate logistical problems and he had managed to stave off disaster so far. But the day wasn't over. Maria, who had been flushed with emotion and nearly speechless throughout the lunch, told Aristo that she wanted to speak to him in private.

That night there was exuberant feasting, drinking, and dancing. Meneghini sulked below, while Maria danced nearly every dance with their host. According to what Meneghini told Italian reporters a month later (when he was giving press conferences nearly every day about his wife's and Onassis' treachery), that was the night Maria and Onassis consummated their love and his wife told him their marriage was over. "The evening of August 6, Maria told me that she wanted to leave me" (*Gente,* September 25, 1959). Meneghini's statements varied from one day to the next, however: "It was in fact on the eighth of August that Maria Callas told her husband frankly that their life together was over forever and that her destiny was tied to a new love, to Aristotle Onassis" (*Oggi,* September 24; the story cited Meneghini and the notations he had shown the reporter from his diary of the cruise). Later, in his memoir, he named August 7 as the day everything changed. "Before that date I noticed absolutely nothing that could have foreshadowed the tragedy."

Maria herself confided later to several of her closest friends that it was after their last night in Istanbul that she and Onassis first made love. Among those was Mary Carter, to whom she gushed like a smitten adolescent when she visited her in Dallas only two months after the cruise. "She had this girlish quality about her and she was clearly madly in love," Mrs. Carter told me when I interviewed her in her home in Cuernavaca, Mexico, in early 1999. "Maria said that all she wanted was 'to be his woman.' She wanted to quit singing and spend the rest of her life with Onassis and didn't care about anything else. She said he was a great lover, well endowed, and very imaginative. She experienced her first orgasm that first time they made love."

The first time would never have happened, however, if Maria hadn't managed to justify it to herself. "At the beginning of the cruise, Onassis started flirting with her and then told her he wanted her," Mrs. Carter said. "But she told him she couldn't start anything unless she decided to end everything with Battista, and he had to be sure he was prepared to leave Tina and be with her. He insisted that he was ready and that Tina would welcome the end of their marriage because she wanted to be with someone else too. Maria thought about it and then finally made her decision."

Until the day Maria managed to convince herself that God condoned her union with Onassis, she had expressed a hidebound traditionalism respecting marital fidelity and was in fact caustically judgmental toward anyone who took his or her marriage vows lightly. When Mary Carter first met Maria in 1957, Carter was having a flirtation with the actor Laurence Harvey. One night in New York she arrived for dinner with Maria at the Forum of the Twelve Caesars with Harvey on her arm. "She turned on him and said, 'What are you doing here?' " Mary Carter recalled. "He became so upset he got up and left. Later I asked Maria to have him invited to Onassis' party for her at the Dorchester in London and she refused. 'You have no business seeing that man,' she told me. 'He has a wife and you have a husband and you'd both better remember that.' "

Meneghini, too, writes that, because Maria's own parents had had an unhappy marriage and had separated, "she had a rigid, puritanical concept of matrimony. She could not accept, for any reason, that two married people could be unfaithful. . . . Ingrid Bergman and my wife were good friends. One day we ran into Ingrid, who had just been separated from Roberto Rossellini. . . . My wife reproached Bergman and said that from that moment they could no longer be friends in the way they once were."

Despite these views, on August 6, 1959, after receiving the blessing of the patriarch, Maria went to Onassis and told him she was finally ready to leave her husband for him. "Maria made the decision, not Onassis," Mary Carter said. "She told me, 'I went to him.' " Nadia Stancioff also reported the connection between the visit to the Patriarchate and Maria's initiating the affair. "She confided to a friend that it was on the evening following the blessing that their union was consummated."

The Montague Brownes and Captain Kostas all believe that it would have been impossible for Maria and Onassis to stage their first sexual encounter on board the *Christina*. But according to the couple's own confessions to friends, it did indeed take place on that August night. And since the *Christina* left Istanbul at 6:20 p.m. on Thursday, August 6—a fact confirmed not only by the *Christina*'s log but also by the Turkish newspapers—there is little doubt that somehow, on that night or in the early-morning hours of August 7, Onassis and Callas, on board the *Christina*, found the opportunity to capitulate to the passion that had been building in them throughout the cruise. Maria herself never explicitly disclosed where the act took place, but Onassis, typically, was not so reticent. He would reveal both the affair and the site of their first tryst to close friends when the *Christina* reached Athens three days later and his sister gave a dinner for all the passengers at her house in the seaside suburb of Glyfada.

The night they left Istanbul, Meneghini, still disturbed by the events of the day, left the others on deck to go below early—or perhaps Maria told him to retire. He noted in his diary, according to his friend and collaborator Renzo Allegri: "Maria always dances with Onassis. She has let herself go like I've never seen before. I am almost happy about this. Maria is still a young woman, and if she enjoys herself it will do her good."

At six-thirty on the morning of August 7, Maria, flushed and nervous, returned to her stateroom and confronted a frantic Meneghini. By his own account, although everything had changed that night, he didn't know it until "a few days later." Other reports say that Maria replied to his accusing questions by declaring flatly, "It's over. I'm in love with Ari."

None of the surviving passengers on the *Christina* heard any altercations from the Meneghini stateroom and there are no witnesses to the scene between Maria and her husband as dawn broke over the Aegean Sea, but considering her penchant for brutal honesty and her determination for complete resolution before taking up with Onassis, it's likely that she spoke frankly to the man who had shared her life and career for the past eleven years. Soon the guilt, recriminations, and doubt would set in. But in her exultation over her first real sexual fulfillment, things seemed simple, clear, and right to Maria on that morning. Later Meneghini would say, "It was as if a fire was devouring them both."

Those who best knew Maria agree that she met and fell in love with Onassis at a moment in her life when the burdens of her career and her faltering voice had begun to tell on her, and her disenchantment with her husband—and his managerial incompetence—had reached a critical point. Until now, Maria had poured all her energy and passion into her art. Suddenly this seemed too hard and thankless a life. She was ready to direct her energy and passion into physical love and to get her satisfaction from the attentions of a devoted lover rather than the applause of a faceless audience.

Maria had truly loved Meneghini for the eleven years of their marriage, that was clear to everyone, but she had loved him as a mentor and older father figure and had never experienced the kind of headlong, irrational sexual pleasure that she found with Onassis. "Psychologically, I think she had lost the need for a parent figure and was now craving a sexually fulfilling husband-lover, a role Titta [Maria's nickname for Battista] could no longer fill," wrote Nadia Stancioff. "Her devotion was slow to fade, but she was increasingly irritated by Titta's professional possessiveness and by his obsession with the Callas career as a money machine. . . . When she finally understood [that he had squandered her money unwisely], she burst open like a steam valve. . . . What she now saw was her 'Santo Benedetto' without the halo she had created for him: a potbellied, unsophisticated little gargoyle."

Even after Maria was faced with the censure of a scandalized world and her own inner qualms about what she had done, she would still defend her love for Onassis to friends as being above reproach because it was fated. "I was not a home breaker, nor was he," she insisted. "Tina was going to leave anyway. It was something that had to happen. I had to follow my destiny."

Another friend, Prince Michael of Greece, who came to know Maria well when she lived in Paris, said later, "It was that sense of destiny, that Greekness that she and Onassis had in common. She was profoundly Greek."

When Maria and Prince Michael spoke of destiny, they were alluding to a deeply held belief among Greeks that dates back to ancient times and was best expressed in Plato's famous *Symposium:* the idea that each person is half of what was once a whole and spends his or her whole life searching for the other individual who will make him complete.

In the *Symposium,* as the greatest minds of ancient Athens debate the nature of love at a banquet in 416 B.C., the playwright Aristophanes speaks up and explains the atavistic origin of our need to search unceasingly for our missing part: "And when one of them meets with his other half, the actual half of himself . . . the pair are lost in an amazement of love and friendship and intimacy, and one will not be out of the other's sight, even for a moment: these are the people who pass their whole lives together; yet they could not explain what they desire of one another."

This idea—that for each of us there is only one individual who will complete and fulfill us—was often cited by those who saw Aristotle Onassis and Maria Callas together, for they seemed so much alike that it made sense, especially to fellow Greeks, that they were the two complementary halves of the same person. "Maria and Aristo were like twins who could never be separated," said Korinna Spanidou, a physical therapist who later came to know both of them well. "They were both Greeks, of course, but more than that, they almost seemed to be halves of the same person." (Korinna, who was encouraged by Onassis to read the books in the *Christina*'s library and then discuss them, remembers a long conversation with him about the *Symposium* and Plato's concept of the two souls.)

Aristo's sister Artemis, who watched the affair develop from the very beginning, saw the striking similarities between the two as a danger, not a blessing. She later told Kiki Feroudi Moutsatsos, an Onassis secretary, that she believed Maria was a perfectionist who, when she couldn't be sure of meeting the highest standards of her art, didn't want to sing anymore. Artemis believed that Aristo "took all the passion that she poured into her voice and provided another outlet for such energy and ardor: him. He redirected the sensuality she had previously poured into her music." But, Artemis added, "she will never make him happy. They are too much alike. They are both big bosses. How can they ever live together without killing each other?"

On the night of August 7, the ship sailed past the Northern Sporades Islands, a landscape of unsurpassed beauty and dangerous hidden shoals. Nonie's diary entry: "We dined and star-gazed to 2:30!" That exclamation point meant that she was once again pressed into service as chaperone, and suggests what a euphemism "star-gazing" had become for the nocturnal conversations of Aristotle and Maria. By this time everyone on board, even the cuckolded husband, was aware of their feelings for each other. Now that they were lovers in fact, their pantomime of discretion and propriety was becoming an increasingly threadbare disguise.

11

THE JOURNEY BACK

The beginnings and endings of all human undertakings are
untidy, the building of a house, the writing of a novel, the demolition
of a bridge, and eminently, the finish of a voyage.

John Galsworthy, *Over the River*

From the Patriarchate—the holiest spot in Turkey for Orthodox Christians—the *Christina* sailed west through the Northern Aegean until it came within sight of Mount Athos, the most sacred site on the Greek mainland.

The Holy Mountain of Greece is a wild, roadless outgrowth of rock—the easternmost section of the three prongs of the Chalkidhiki Peninsula—extending into the Aegean and connected to the mainland by a narrow ribbon of land just over a mile wide. Officially Mount Athos is not a part of the Greek nation, but is an independent monastic republic of Greek, Russian, Bulgarian, Serb, and Romanian religious communities. For more than a thousand years the peninsula has been occupied by men only, monks and hermits who retreated from civilization to spend their lives here in meditation and prayer. They once numbered more than 20,000, but today only about 1,500 remain in the twenty monasteries and hermit caves. The monks never eat meat, and spend a minimum of eight hours a day at prayer. They follow the Julian Calendar, which is thirteen days behind the Gregorian calendar used by the rest of the Western world, and a bizarre Byzantine clock with hours of variable length to ensure that sunset is always at twelve o'clock. The famous injunction against entry to "every woman, every female animal, every child, eunuch and smooth-faced person" is still officially in force, except that beards are no longer required.

On the seventh of August, as the *Christina* sailed around the Holy Mountain, the passengers used binoculars to peer inside the community and were amused to observe that the monks were looking back at them through equally high-powered lenses.

After it had traced the perimeter of the mountain, the *Christina* spent another night at sea, moving south toward the Cycladic island of Mykonos and its satellite, Delos. The yacht arrived at Delos at 9:55 a.m. on Saturday, August 8, according to the captain's log. Mount Athos is a bastion of Christian self-denial and the life of prayer, but Delos, the legendary birthplace of Apollo and Artemis, was in ancient times the center of a more hedonistic religion. Now uninhabited except by guards, the island was once sacred to the Ionian Greeks, and its oracle rivaled that of Delphi in importance. During Hellenistic times, Delos was covered with magnificent temples and villas of a wealthy regional merchant community. Pilgrims came to worship Apollo and Artemis, leaving sacrifices, treasures, and statues behind, including a row of archaic stone lions, five of which still stood guard over the shrine when the *Christina*'s guests visited it.

Among the more peculiar statues surviving to honor the gods is a phallus erected in 300 B.C. outside the Sanctuary of Dionysos. This might have proved awkward to explain to the Churchills, but the day was sweltering, the visitors huddled in the scant shade of the tourist pavilion, and only Anthony Montague Browne elected to walk through the sacred precincts under the relentless sun and gaze thoughtfully up at the immense penis pointing toward the sky.

After spending three hours at Delos, the *Christina* sailed to the nearby island of Mykonos, the playground of international visitors to Greece. Famous then as now for its nude beaches and raucous nightlife, Mykonos' main town is composed of whitewashed houses that look like melting sugar cubes, and winding streets barely wide enough for a donkey to pass, created as a maze to confound invading pirates. After lunch, the passengers walked along the picturesque harborside, where art students sketch the outdoor tavernas and the row of windmills that stand like sentinels on the hills above. They admired the self-important pelicans, the mascots of the island, cadging for fish and leftovers in the harbor. In August, when the rich and spoiled youth of Greece, France, and other European countries flock to Mykonos, even the birds fear for their lives amidst the ceaseless revels.

Nearly four hours after arriving at Mykonos, at 5:45 p.m., the *Christina* sailed to the island of Tinos, a place of pilgrimage for all Greeks. They come to venerate the famed icon of the Virgin Mary, which is believed to have the power to heal the ill and infirm. Pilgrims flock to Panayia Evanghelistria (Our Lady of Good Tidings), offering the gold and silver votive figures that fill the huge church to beseech the Virgin to intercede for them. Many crawl on their knees from the port to the church to show their devotion. Twice a year, on the feasts of the Annunciation (March 25) and the Assumption (August 15), the famous icon is paraded outside the church as thousands prostrate themselves in its path praying for a cure.

According to Captain Kostas, it was Maria who persuaded Onassis to take the *Christina* to Tinos so they could make a brief visit to the church to pray before the icon of her patron saint, the Virgin Mary. They stayed on the island for only an hour and fifteen minutes, enough time to light a candle and ask the Virgin's intercession. The island was already preparing for the feast of the Assumption a week later, when the gathering multitudes would scarcely leave room to set foot in the harbor.

The *Christina* left Tinos at 8:10 p.m., and now Onassis focused all his attention on Churchill, perhaps afraid he had been neglecting him while spending so much time with Callas. He was even seen sitting next to the old man during the cocktail hour and feeding him caviar with a spoon.

Now that tensions were becoming heightened among Tina, Maria, Meneghini, and Artemis, Onassis was at pains to keep the hostilities from impinging on the comfort of the Churchills. "He was trying very hard," Celia Sandys remembers. "All he really wanted was for my grandfather to enjoy himself and for Maria to be happy and for Tina not to make a drama. My grandparents couldn't know what was going on."

Onassis was always known for his impeccable solicitude toward his guests. "Ari was basically a very sensitive, warm, kind man," Nonie recalls. "I don't mean in business, I mean as a man to travel with. I've been on eight cruises with Onassis and I got to like him more and more as a friend. He was a very charming, philosophical person to talk to. Never rude to his staff. At least never in front of anybody. Which is totally different from Niarchos. He did a lot of little things. He understood we weren't all wildly rich."

During an earlier cruise to Morocco, in 1958, a dealer in antique caftans came on board and managed to sell the expensive garments to most of the guests, except for the Montague Brownes, who blanched at the prices. That night at dinner, when most of the women appeared in their new finery, Onassis said, "Oh dear, we've got one too many of these dresses. Nonie, do you think you could possibly wear it?"

"Like the gesture of breaking his own wine glass to ease Diana Sandys's embarrassment, it was an example of how Ari always tried to make everyone feel comfortable," Nonie concluded. "He was tactful and kind that way."

This time, however, it would take every ounce of Onassis' extraordinary tact and diplomatic skills to get the *Christina* party back to Monte Carlo without any outbursts of marital discord being noted by the crew or the reporters who awaited their arrival in every port.

As the *Christina* headed toward Piraeus, the port city that serves Athens, Aristo attempted to distract his volatile company with reminiscences of his first arrival there in 1922 as a young refugee from the Smyrna atrocities. Like Maria, he had painful memories of Athens and its environs, and as they sailed closer to the busy harbor, choked with oil tankers and cruise ships, Onassis told his guests the rest of the story that he had begun in Smyrna.

As soon as the U.S. tanker *Edsall* deposited young Aristotle—dressed in an American sailor's uniform with the remainder of the family's fortune taped to his body—on the island Mytilene, he was surrounded by fellow Anatolians pleading for news of loved ones back in Smyrna. The island was overflowing with refugees, many of whom were dying of typhoid and dysentery. Some of the exiles, finding very little food but plenty of wine here, preyed on their fellows, stealing anything of value they could forage from the rags and baskets and bundles their victims had carried out of the cataclysm.

Aristotle went from one refugee camp to another seeking his sisters and stepmother. He questioned everyone he met and studied messages left pinned to trees and names scrawled on walls and doors. Finally, at a camp near the foot of the Hill of Olympus, he found his family—a total of seventeen women and children, including his sisters, aunts, and cousins. As the only man in the group, the eighteen-year-old put himself in charge of the family's welfare. They still had some money, and he told them he would buy their passage to Athens as soon as possible. In the meantime, Aristotle and Artemis enquired everywhere on the island for news of their grandmother, Gethsemane. The old woman had sailed from Smyrna later than Aristotle's sisters; she had refused to go until her son Socrates forced her to leave the house in the company of a neighbor, who promised to get her on a boat to Greece. At that point, her trail was lost. Despite the reward Aristotle offered for news of her, none of the countless people he asked could help him.

After a month of living in the squalor of the camp, Aristotle and his clan of seventeen women and children escaped to the port of Piraeus on a Libyan freighter. They were part of the flood of 1,500,000 Anatolians streaming into the country whose five million mainland Greeks were scornful and even hostile to the new arrivals.

When Aristotle located his uncle Omeros, who'd left for Athens months before the disaster, he learned the fate of his grandmother. As Merope later told it to me, their Hadji-néné and the neighbors from Smyrna had found themselves crowded onto a boat allegedly bound for Greek soil, but they soon realized that the Turkish captain had no intention of taking them there. The passengers mutinied and forced him at gunpoint to leave them on the island of Samos. Eventually, Gethsemane managed to find passage on a ship headed for Athens, but onlookers reported that when she reached into her apron to pay for her ticket, two Greek men sitting nearby spied her cache of gold coins tied there. They started shoving the old woman and finally knocked her down. Feisty to the last, Gethsemane fought back, but she suffered a heart attack and died on the deck of the ship. She was seventy-five years old.

When Gethsemane reached the Greek mainland for the first time, she was carried off the ferry as a corpse. Her descendents buried her in the Anastasios cemetery in Piraeus. Aristotle would often visit her grave there and spoke in Turkish to the old woman, who had never learned Greek. She had reared him after his mother died and he now felt the same sense of loss and loneliness he had felt from the earlier death. (The old woman left her mark on him. "Very often," he told his guests on the *Christina,* "my sister Artemis complains that we didn't have the opportunity to study during our youth. So I tell her, 'Why are you complaining? We graduated from the University of Grandma Gethsemane, which is worth ten universities.' ")

Once in Athens, the extended family were settled in rooming houses near the harbor; eventually they moved to a large house in the prosperous Castella district on the heights overlooking the port. But when they were joined by Omeros, a power struggle developed between the young man and his uncle over who was in charge of the family while Socrates was imprisoned in Smyrna. Aristo had the advantage of possessing the mother lode of family money he had carried from Turkey. He decided that he should go to Constantinople, where his father had many influential acquaintances, and try to win Socrates' freedom with a liberal dose of bribes and networking. The uncle disagreed, arguing that Socrates was a resourceful man and with his many Turkish friends he would find a way out of prison on his own. Against Omeros' protests, Aristotle booked passage to Istanbul on an Egyptian passenger ship, the *Abbazia,* of the Khedivia Line, which sailed under the British flag.

On board the *Abbazia,* Aristo was struck with wonder as he strolled through the first-class dining room and saw beautiful women in evening gowns and jewels and men in dinner jackets dancing to an orchestra that played Broadway show tunes. This vision of luxury and elegance made an impression on the young refugee that he never forgot. Although he was shooed back to his own quarters by a steward, Onassis later told friends he had seen enough to vow that this was the way he wanted to spend his life.

Onassis considered it a strategic necessity on this trip that he be dressed expensively, book a room in the best section of Istanbul, and generally play the high-roller while he conducted his negotiations there. During his three weeks of wheeling and dealing, he handed out approximately $20,000 in bribes, a small fortune in 1922. He also made an impression on the young women who worked as paid dancing partners in the bars and cafés around Cumhuriyet Caddessi.

By the time he returned to Athens, Aristo had spent most of the Turkish lire he had spirited out of Smyrna. Socrates was soon released, and he arrived in Athens not long after his son. Aristo was convinced that he had obtained his father's freedom, but both Omeros and Socrates himself complained that the boy had squandered the family's cash needlessly. According to Merope, the actual reason for Socrates' release had nothing to do with the Turkish lire the youth had spread around Istanbul. Instead, she said, "A Jewish merchant who was [Socrates'] friend had been beaten by the Turks to make him tell them which Greeks in Smyrna were active in Greek patriotic organizations and he gave the name of Socrates and two of his brothers. But when Socrates was put on trial, the man defended [him and his brothers] and said he had been forced to speak against them."

This Jewish merchant was Bohor Behadava, the very man who had employed Socrates as a clerk for two years when he first arrived in Smyrna. That merchant's recantation, not his son's negotiations, won Socrates' release, according to Merope. In any case, Aristo was upset that his father didn't appreciate his efforts, and hard feelings festered between them. "The tension mounted when our father told Aristo that he wanted him to go to Oxford and become an architect. My brother was never big on school and he fled to Argentina, where he was joined by our cousin Nikos Konialidis, whom I later married."

Onassis recounted to his guests the story of the falling out with his father, still evidently heartbroken by Socrates' callous ingratitude. "You know how it is, people forget quickly," he said. "They may have been on the verge of death, but the moment they're safe, all the recriminations and curses come pouring out. I saved his life and he behaved like an accountant!"

These wounds of estrangement would fester in Onassis for the rest of his life, even after Socrates eventually relented in his reproach and became a partner in his son's fledgling business efforts. (Socrates suffered from angina and never quite recovered from the stress of his imprisonment. He died of a heart attack in 1932, at the age of fifty-eight, and was buried in the family vault at Anastasios cemetery, next to his mother.)

The economic situation in Greece was difficult, and was exacerbated by the constant influx of desperate refugees. According to his former classmates from Smyrna, Aristotle spent the first months of exile in Athens trying to find a way out of the country. He considered going to the United States, but soon learned that immigration quotas there were prohibitively restrictive. Then he thought of Buenos Aires, where the family had some distant relatives. Although his father strongly opposed the boy's leaving Greece following the recent family trauma, Aristo managed to obtain a Nansen permit—a special visa that was valid for a one-way trip for refugees going to a country of resettlement—to Argentina. With $250 in his pocket, he boarded a ferry in Piraeus for passage to Brindisi, Italy, the first leg of his journey. There, on August 27, 1923, he boarded the immigrant ship *Tomaso di Savoya,* along with a thousand other steerage-class passengers jammed into holds, to travel to the New World. Typically, Onassis soon bribed a deckhand to let him sleep on deck in a round cage designed to enclose the ship's stern lines, a much more comfortable berth than the ones below.

As Maria listened to this tale and the *Christina* pushed on toward Piraeus, she could almost imagine she was hearing her own story. Like Onassis, she had sailed out of that harbor for the New World, bitter, estranged from her parent, and determined to make a success on her own, with help from no one. The ship she had boarded departed twenty-two years later than Aristotle's, but they were fired with the same anger and ambition, and by 1959, both of them had succeeded far beyond their youthful dreams. "We both started from zero and reached the top only thanks to our own will and our own abilities," she would later tell friends.

The passengers on the *Christina* were eager to make landfall because on that night, Theodore and Artemis Garofalidis would be hosting a dinner dance at their seaside villa in the Athens suburb of Glyfada. It promised to be the festive climax of the trip. The yacht pulled in as close as possible to shore and anchored at 10:17 a.m. on Sunday, August 9.

Two cornerstones of the Greek character are expressed by the words *philoxenia* and *philotimo. Philoxenia* means "hospitality," but the literal translation is "love of strangers." A Greek, whether rich or poor, will vie with his neighbors to extend the hospitality of his house to anyone who happens along, even if it means killing and cooking the family's only lamb.

Philotimo denotes pride, sense of honor, or self-esteem, and it is closely tied to the responsibilities of hospitality. On board the ship, while Onassis was the host, his self-esteem was dependent on making his guests happy, but when the *Christina* docked outside Athens near the Garofalidises' villa, he enjoyed a respite as Theodore's *philotimo* and *philoxenia* came into play.

Theodore Garofalidis was universally adored by the other passengers. "He was a sweet old dear," Nonie recalls. "He and I used to gossip together. He was the one person I could talk to best. Ari said, 'I don't know what's with Theodore and Nonie but they totally understand each other.' We sort of had a nice little *tendresse* between us." Montague Browne recalls that hunting was Theodore's passion—he went on long hunting trips in the north of Greece several times a year—and on board the *Christina* they passed pleasant hours together shooting clay pigeons. "Ari once said to him—he spoke in French because Theodore didn't understand English— '*Voyez Théodore. A part de la médecine et la chasse, c'est un enfant.*' Apart from medicine and hunting, he's a child."

When the travelers came ashore in the launch, Theodore personally drove them through Athens in an air-conditioned car and escorted those who wished to see the Acropolis up the famous hill at the heart of the city to view the sacred stones and columns of the Parthenon. Then he drove them back to his home, which adjoined Onassis' in Glyfada, where they could spend the afternoon swimming in the turquoise bay, basking in the sun on its white sand beach, or waterskiing with Kostas Koutsouvelis, Alexander's tutor. That night Theodore made sure that the dinner dance in the garden of his villa, under trees strung with lighted Japanese lanterns, was the most pleasant and most festive of the many parties they had enjoyed on their cruise.

Among the guests (later invited to lunch on board the yacht) was the movie tycoon Spyros Skouras, a Greek-American who was the son of a shepherd from Corfu. Skouras, the chairman of 20th Century-Fox, could speak no language fluently and often admitted that no Greek could understand his Greek and no Englishman his English. He was also famous for his malapropisms. In *Long Sunset*, Anthony Montague Browne recalls:

> *As we leant on the ship's rail looking at dolphins, Skouras said: "I've a great idea for a movie. It will be about the Benzedrines." I pondered. "You mean about the drug-taking generation?" I hazarded.*
>
> *"I don't know if they took drugs or not. I mean the Benzedrines' Empire in Constantinople."*
>
> *Enlightenment dawned. "Oh, you mean Byzantines?"*
>
> *"Benzedrine, Byzantines, it would make a great movie."*

Skouras suggested to Maria Callas in the garden at Glyfada that she consider undertaking a movie role in some film. At least that's what she told her husband she wanted to discuss with Onassis when she and Ari stayed up late that night on the *Christina*. According to Meneghini's memoirs, he gave up on the party and returned to the yacht at 4 a.m. but Maria was too excited to consider going to sleep.

Another guest at the party in Glyfada was Ettalia Maria Papanikolaou, whose late husband was financial adviser to the former Greek king. Lilika, as she is called, spoke to me at her home in Politea, a suburb of Athens, in 1999. She had known Onassis ever since he was the Greek consul in Buenos Aires and she was a girl of thirteen who sailed into the city's harbor on her father's ship in 1936. She remembers how impressed she was when the youthful consul bought her "biscuits, chocolates and a bottle of eau de cologne with mirrors on the bottle." Her father was a friend of Stavros Livanos', and Lilika became a good friend of Tina Onassis' after her marriage to Aristotle. At the party in the Garofalidises' garden, Lilika recalls, Tina came in first and confided to her that Ari and Callas were having an affair; then the new lovers arrived together.

"I will tell you about that terrible night. My God, that night!" Lilika told me as she asked her daughter to pour her a glass of champagne. "There was Maria Callas. And that poor Meneghini, the poor ill-fated thing [*kakomiris*]!

"First Tina says to me: 'You know what's been going on? That whore has thrown herself at him and Aristo has been taken in. You will see.' Then Aristo comes into the garden. And he says to me, 'Come and sit next to me, Lilika.' And there was Maria Callas, and *po! po! po!* what they were saying! I'm ashamed to repeat it in front of you. He was saying, 'Tell her, Maria, tell her what I did to you in the *varka* [small boat]. Tell her how I did it to you.'

"I got up," Mrs. Papanikolaou continued. "I said, 'Don't talk in front of me like that!' He takes my hand and says, 'Sit down, Lilika.' He was talking in Greek, of course, so the others couldn't understand.

"What had happened to him was a craziness," Lilika continued. "You know what they call that illness, that happens to men: *andropsoenia*— poverty of virility. When a man starts to feel that he's losing his virility, he tries to show off. A man, a real man who wants to fool around, he goes and gets a mistress and does it *quietly*, but a man who's showing off in front of his wife, his sisters, his friends, he's not a real man."

Onassis' unmannerly behavior at the party seems incompatible with the painstaking decorum and propriety that the Montague Brownes and Captain Kostas report he maintained during the cruise. He had been drinking, and being among his more earthy Greek friends, relieved of his sacred

Lilika Papanikolaou admonishing Onassis

obligations as host, he may have been anxious to show his wife, whose own lover was less than half his age, that any sexual dysfunction he had experienced with her (and which she had not failed to describe to Reinaldo Herrera) was no impediment to his new love. If that was his intention, Onassis was hardly above a coarse frankness, even bragging, about his tryst in the launch with Maria—especially when speaking to a woman who he knew was close to his wife.

Onassis' boast, as reported by Lilika Papanikolaou, suggests that he and Callas had found their long-elusive privacy on board the yacht in one of the launches that were stored on the upper decks of the *Christina,* near the Piaggio airplane. An examination of the plans of the *Christina,* which show where the small lifeboats, sailboats, etc., were stowed, suggests that they would probably have chosen the largest launch, on the port side of the boat deck, just forward of the plane. About twenty-six feet long, with an enclosed cabin, it would have served nicely to protect them from the eyes of anyone happening by. That launch was situated toward the stern on the same deck as the dining room and lounge and the kitchens, one deck below the Onassis suite and one above the guests' staterooms.

Following the dinner party, Lilika says, she had a heart-to-heart conversation with Tina Onassis. "She asked me, 'What shall I do?' and I said, 'You go to your bedroom and sleep in your bed.' " All the passengers of the

Christina went back to the yacht, which was to leave Glyfada at 5:40 a.m. the next morning. According to Meneghini's memoirs,

> *Onassis and Maria wanted to continue the festivities on the yacht. "I'm going to bed," I said. I was more dead than alive, and I fell asleep immediately. I awoke at 9:30 the next morning and realized that Maria was not there. I was worried and I went around the yacht looking for her. I ran into Onassis, who was smiling and ebullient. He said that he had been to sleep and had already shaved. A horrible suspicion passed through my mind. If Onassis had been asleep, then where had Maria been? I felt faint. I went to my cabin and she was there, having just returned. "You gave me a big fright," I said. It seemed as if she didn't hear me. She was vague and preoccupied. She began to rhapsodize about the beauty of the night, and the magic of the dawn over the sea. Then, suddenly changing her tone and assuming a derisive, offensive attitude, she launched into an acrimonious tirade, telling me that I should stop being her shadow. "You act like my jailer," she said. "You never leave me alone. You control me in everything. You're like some hateful guardian and you've kept me hemmed in all these years. I'm suffocating!" Then she began to criticize my shape, my way of doing things. "You're not adventuresome, you don't know languages, your hair is always uncombed, you can't manage to dress smartly."*

Meneghini's dogged shadowing of Maria was fraying her nerves. According to Mary Carter, Maria told her shortly after the cruise that "when she and Onassis clicked, they naturally wanted to be alone together whenever possible, but everywhere they went, there was Meneghini. They would go to see some sight and Meneghini would insist on going along. They'd jump off the yacht for a swim and he would get in the dinghy and follow Maria along. She was furious with him. 'He wouldn't leave me alone,' she complained to me [in Dallas]. 'Well, Maria,' I told her. 'He *is* your husband and you *are* the only one he can talk to.' But she thought it was very inconsiderate of him not to leave her alone with Onassis. She said Tina was not intrusive. She kind of liked Tina—thought she was very sweet, very friendly, not very smart, but very sweet."

Following this early-morning confrontation with her husband in their stateroom and a final uncorking of all the resentment she had bottled up, Maria made no further effort to be civil to Battista. According to his account, she no longer even came back to the stateroom to sleep, only to change her clothes and bathe in the morning.

.   .   .

On Monday, August 10, the morning of Maria's confrontation with her husband, the *Christina* sailed through the Corinth Canal, then anchored in the Bay of Corinth, thus retracing its path from the first days of the cruise. In the calm, protected bay, many of the passengers went overboard for swimming or waterskiing before lunch was served on the top deck.

Meanwhile, Anthony Montague Browne, who had business in Athens, took the Piaggio to fly into the city and back. A licensed pilot, he had been a Royal Air Force fighter in Burma during World War II. As Anthony prepared for takeoff, eleven-year-old Alexander Onassis pestered him with questions about his flying exploits. The boy had always been fascinated with planes, motorboats, racing cars—anything with an engine—and he longed for the day when he would earn his own pilot's license.

The Montague Brownes and many other Onassis friends have fond memories of Alexander, who grew up into a sensitive, considerate, and self-sacrificing young man. But as a child he was spoiled, rambunctious, and overindulged. He managed to annoy and alienate most of the guests who sailed on the *Christina,* including Maria Callas, and she soon became the main target of his animosity. Montague Browne recalls that during this cruise "Alexander was rather tiresome. One day I put him in the pool and took away the ladder so he couldn't get out. It wasn't very deep, and he never told his father because he knew he'd get in trouble. He was fascinated by airplanes and he wanted to know what military aircraft were like and what you did before a mission and did you have bad nerves and all that. He was fascinated by flying, but he had bad eyesight like his father."

In contrast, Christina, then eight, was a sensitive, shy child who was somewhat dominated by her formidable English nanny, Miss Lehane. "She was a sweet little girl and very good," Nonie recalls. " 'Oh Miss Lehane, can't I do this or that?' she was always saying to her governess—a tow-headed, beaky sort of woman who looked a little bit like a hen. She certainly didn't mean to be unkind or nasty, but she made Christina turn on one side in the bed so she could have the light on to read: 'Christina, you're not to turn until later,' that sort of thing. But Christina used to get her own back. Particularly when we went to Mykonos. It was rather rough. It got very choppy in the little speedboat, and she said, 'Oh, Miss Lehane, I've never seen it like this! I think we're not going to make it!' Miss Lehane was clutching her and trying not to be sick."

Anthony, too, remembers Christina fondly. "When we got to places, she used to say, 'Daddy'—she spoke to him in English—'Daddy, may I have twenty dollars?' He'd say, 'What for?' 'I want to buy something.' So he'd give her twenty dollars and she'd go and buy him and Tina little presents. So sad. A very engaging child."

Both the Montague Brownes remember Ari teasing and playing with his children constantly, letting them push him into the swimming pool, complimenting them on their clothes, kissing them all over with the demonstrative paternal affection that is typically Greek. "He was absolutely sweet with his children," Nonie said emphatically. "Make no mistake, he was a very loving father to them both. They were often with us on board."

Genevieve Roy, a Frenchwoman who was a tutor to Alexander and Christina until she married the *Christina*'s captain, Kostas Anastasiades, in November of 1958 and settled in Athens to raise their children, recalls that Onassis, and especially Tina, outrageously favored Alexander over Christina. "Tina adored Alexander but was not very nice to Christina," she told me. "She called him 'my angel' and 'angel face' and always criticized Christina's looks. Alexander picked up on that and would lock his sister in her room when people came around and tell her she was too ugly for people to see. Tina would buy presents for Alexander but nothing for Christina. I would buy something for the child out of my own pocket and Tina would say, 'You mustn't do that. Christina must get used to it. Alexander's going to get eighty percent of everything in the end.' She really neglected the girl. I remember when Christina would come home from school with a medal or award, she'd go to show Tina and her mother would be asleep and not want to be disturbed."

As the yacht sailed out of the Bay of Corinth on August 10 to begin the three-day passage across the Ionian Sea and up the western coast of Italy to Monte Carlo, the atmosphere on board the *Christina* was far less festive than at the beginning of the cruise. There were no more glamorous parties or historic sights on shore to anticipate. The sea became rough once they left the protected waters of the bay, and Meneghini sulked in his stateroom, as miserably seasick as ever and now with an added bitterness over Maria's blatantly scornful treatment.

The Churchills, too, spent much of their time below as the heavy seas caused the ship to roll perilously. The only passengers who seemed oblivious to the lurching of the ship were Maria and Aristo, who spent most of each night on deck or, in bad weather, in the wood-paneled library called the game room, where, seated before the sapphire-blue fireplace faced with lapis lazuli, they talked quietly through the night. Often, according to Anthony Montague Browne, who was usually nearby, they would invade the ship's galley for a snack in the wee hours of the morning.

After midnight on the second night at sea as the *Christina* steamed toward Monte Carlo, Tina Onassis got up and, finding herself alone, took a walk around the ship. According to Meneghini's memoirs, she wound up in his stateroom. "We are both miserable," he says she told him. "Your Maria is downstairs in the lounge in my husband's arms. Now there is nothing more that can be done. He has taken her away from you. I'm especially sorry for you. I had already decided to leave him, and this will be my opportunity to initiate divorce proceedings. . . . Poor Battista, but also poor Maria. She'll learn soon enough what kind of man he is."

Meneghini relates that after Tina left him he was "in a piteous state" until Maria returned to the room at 6:10 in the morning; she refused to answer his questions. His wife didn't speak to him the entire next day and did not reenter their room until five the next morning. "She told me the sea was splendid, even though it was squally. Nothing else," he wrote. "I prayed to God that the accursed cruise would end soon. I was certain in my heart that, once we arrived back at our home, everything would return to normal."

As always, Meneghini's account has to be viewed with considerable skepticism, with an eye toward his self-serving, self-pitying alterations of fact. Nevertheless, there are revealing details in his story, such as Tina's confession that she was already looking for an opportunity to leave Onassis. Another is the telling statement that, despite the bad weather, Maria came in at five on the last morning of the cruise rhapsodizing that the "sea was splendid." And there are some corroborating third-party reports that, late on the second-to-last night of the cruise, Tina did get up and discover Maria and Aristotle together in the lounge and then told Meneghini about it. According to Peter Evans she later repeated the story to a lover, saying of Meneghini: "I could see by his face that he was beyond doing a thing about it."

It seems likely that Tina discovered Onassis and Callas in each other's arms—kissing at most—on a night when the ocean was so rough that they believed everyone would be confined to their rooms and asleep. Rather than confront them, she went to speak to Meneghini, hoping to ignite a scandal as she had with the episode of the Greek meal they ate alone together. Her plans were foiled by Meneghini's reluctance to take on his host. If Ari and Maria had wanted to make love, they could have returned to the launch, but it's unlikely that they took such a risk again during the last days of the cruise.

On Thursday, August 13, the *Christina* churned through a rough sea before entering the harbor of Monte Carlo and docking at 11:10 a.m. As usual, a crowd of photographers in hired boats snapped away feverishly at the passengers waiting on deck to disembark. The photographic record of this moment is intriguing. One shot reveals the obliviousness of the very young and very old to the foregoing intrigues: Sir Winston, in a huge wide-

Maria gazing at Ari at the end of the cruise

brimmed white hat and three-piece suit, and young Alexander, in only a bathing suit, are both slumped in the wicker chairs, as if half asleep. In another photo, the principals seem not much changed either: Meneghini, in a suit and tie, glowers as usual; Maria is cool and calm in a short-sleeved white-on-white cotton shirtdress with a wide leather cinch belt; Tina is jauntily clad in a halter blouse and shorts; and Onassis, in shirtsleeves, distractedly mans the phone. All are chatting civilly but look a bit bored and not very congenial, not so unusual perhaps for two couples of recent acquaintance who had just spent three weeks together at sea. The only plainly happy faces to be found are in a photo that shows Maria and Onassis standing close together, nearly touching: as Onassis speaks into the phone, Maria smiles at what he's saying (both are wearing dark glasses). In another, she walks down the gangplank with Onassis one step behind; Meneghini is not in the picture. In his memoirs Battista wrote: "On August 13 . . . we arrived at Monte Carlo. Two hours later we were in Nice's airport. By five in the evening, we were back in Milan. Between us, for the entire trip, there was a glacial silence."

Most of the guests, including the Churchills, left the *Christina* with no evident awareness that anything momentous had happened. "I left very promptly at the end of the cruise," Montague Browne told me. "I had dreadful hay fever and I was going to a place in Switzerland, up in the mountains, for a fortnight to get over it. Nonie flew straight on to London." Sir Winston drove to nearby Cap d'Ail, where he was to be the guest of Lord Beaverbrook at his Villa Caponcia. The sixteen-year-old Celia Sandys didn't even see the Meneghinis go, though they were the first to depart. She was with Kostas Koutsouvelis just beyond the entrance to Monte Carlo's harbor. "By that time I had got up the nerve to talk to him and he was coaching me in waterskiing," she said. "He might have taught me a lot more, but I was so backward in that area, I'm sure I discouraged him."

Aristotle and Tina Onassis maintained their cordial demeanor as the last guest disembarked. The facade of their marriage was intact to all observers, though the Meneghinis' union, troubled from the outset of the voyage, seemed more openly in tatters at the conclusion: "I was absolutely certain that Maria had totally dropped her husband. Absolutely, totally," Nonie told me.

Still, none of the minor players in this drama suspected that within days, the romance between Maria Callas and Aristotle Onassis would become the focus of relentless international scrutiny, their every word, every movement, every meal reported hourly, as the world watched, riveted by the spectacle of two fabled marriages unraveling in public.

12

PAS DE QUATRE

The greatest griefs are those we cause ourselves.

Sophocles, *Oedipus Rex*

Some of the most respected biographers of Onassis and Callas have written that the fateful 1959 cruise of the *Christina* ended in Venice. A few accounts accurately describe it as ending on August 13 in Monte Carlo, where the guests disembarked, but then make the error of saying that the *Christina* sailed from Monte Carlo to Venice for the annual film festival carrying no one but a forlorn Tina and her two children, who expected at every stop that Onassis would join them, only to be disappointed.

That is not what happened during those tumultuous weeks in late August and early September when the world press first got wind of the Callas-Onassis affair. The truth was told to me by two witnesses who sailed with Tina on the *Christina* from Monte Carlo to Venice. One of them was her twenty-five-year-old lover, Reinaldo Herrera.

During the twenty-five days before Tuesday, September 8, when Maria made the public announcement that her marriage to Meneghini was over, the four protagonists—Ari and Maria, Tina and Meneghini—engaged in a complicated *pas de quatre.* Onassis ricocheted between Monte Carlo, Milan, and Venice in his amphibious Piaggio plane, Maria was either secluded in Milan or traveling with Aristo, while Meneghini was driving daily between his country house in Sirmione on Lake Garda, his mother's home in nearby Zevio, his lawyer's office in Turin, and the villa he and Maria owned in Milan.

Onassis had begun the affair with Callas convinced that he could be with his new mistress and keep the rest of his life—his wife and children—as well. Maria, on the other hand, once she committed herself to Onassis, wanted to eliminate both Meneghini and her singing career from her life and spend all her time with Aristo.

Tina had been persuaded by her parents to persist in the charade of a marriage she was tired of for the sake of appearances, but eventually she realized that the scandal of the Onassis-Callas affair was so overwhelming, even her father couldn't ask her to stay with Ari. As for the loquacious cuckold, Meneghini, he acted like a bellows to accelerate the entire debacle, fanning the flames of publicity whenever they threatened to die down.

Interested observers would need an atlas and a timetable to keep track of the confrontations, cover-ups, ruses, press conferences, attorneys' meetings, heated battles, and recriminations that kept Ari, Maria, and Meneghini scurrying about like rats in a maze. A primary source for these day-to-day developments until the press picked up the scent is Meneghini's diary, which relates what happened after they returned to their villa on Via Buonarotti in Milan on August 13. Maria told Battista that she wanted to stay on in Milan but that he was to go to Sirmione, their country home. Meneghini prepared to leave for Sirmione by 9 a.m. the next day and when he went to say good morning to Maria she asked "without preamble: 'What would you do if I no longer wanted to stay with you?' I felt the blood rush to my head. Everything around me started spinning. I managed a little laugh and said, 'Oh, I'd retire to one of those rocky gorges where the monks live on Mount Athos.' . . . I've begun to realize the enormity of the tragedy engulfing me."

Meneghini departed, stopping in Zevio to visit his ailing mother, then went on to Sirmione and wrote that he was surprised and disappointed that Maria did not call him that night.

Meanwhile, Onassis was winging from Monte Carlo to Milan in the Piaggio, flown by his pilot, Angelo Pirotti. He had left Tina and the children behind on the yacht in Monte Carlo, pleading pressing business matters. That night he managed to dine with Maria in Milan without being noticed by the paparazzi.

The following day was August 15, the feast of the Assumption (one of the most important holidays in Italy and Greece, where it is celebrated as the Dormition of the Virgin Mary)—marking the beginning of Ferragosto, when nearly everyone takes to the road for a two-week holiday. August 15 was also Maria's name day, and at 8 a.m. on that Saturday, Meneghini telephoned her from Sirmione. "She returned to the subject of wishing to be alone in Milan," he writes. " 'I rest better,' she explained. 'If there's news, we can keep in touch by phone.' "

Within the next four hours, however, Callas abruptly reversed herself.

Evidently she and Onassis had been having serious conversations about their relationship, and as usual she could not defer speaking her mind once she had made it up. "Maria telephoned at 12:15 and asked me to come to see her immediately in Milan," Meneghini writes. " 'Right away, without losing a minute,' she emphasized. 'I have decided to discuss things with you and inform you of everything. I cannot put it off any longer. Come, your Maria is waiting for you.' "

Perplexed by the phrase "your Maria," Meneghini drove to Milan, and when he arrived, he found that his wife had prepared a meal for him. When he ate it, "to placate her," she commented disagreeably, "You never change: you never lose either your sleep or your appetite." Then Maria closed the door so the servants couldn't hear and "came right to the point. With an icy voice, she said: 'It's all over between us. I have decided to stay with Onassis.' "

Meneghini reports he was too dumbfounded to reply, but Maria "continued, and her voice was almost sweet: 'Ari and I have been caught up in this twist of fate and we are unable to combat it. We have done nothing wrong. We have behaved according to the rules and we have not crossed the bounds of honesty, but he can no longer be apart from me, and I cannot be away from him. He is here in Milan.' "

The first confrontation between the two rivals took place in the Milan villa at ten that night, and it's clear, even from Meneghini's self-serving account, that Onassis was in control of the negotiations. He tried to be friendly while stealing Meneghini's wife as tactfully as possible. Onassis arrived "dressed in a strange outfit so that he would not be recognized." Meneghini says he began the conversation, admonishing the adulterers to be aware of the "sin you are committing, the lives you are ruining." "It seemed as if I were speaking to two twenty-year-olds in love," he writes. "Onassis tried to comfort me by saying that he himself had gone through a similar experience" (a reference, perhaps, to his own confrontations with Tina's lovers). " 'These are things that happen in life,' he told me. I wanted to kill him."

Evidently, though, Meneghini offered only passive resistance. At 3 a.m. he retired, and Maria remained downstairs with Onassis for another hour. "When she came to bed I pretended to be asleep. She slid into bed slowly, into her usual place, and then dozed off. I was trembling like a leaf. Perhaps I was feverish. At six I got out of bed and without disturbing anyone, I left my home. As I closed the door behind me, I was weeping." When the sixty-four-year-old Meneghini stopped to see his mother, who was still unwell, he evaded her questions as to why Maria wasn't with him. He then continued on to Sirmione.

The next day, Monday, August 17, Maria called Meneghini to say that she would be coming to see him. He told her, apparently regretting his earlier meekness before Onassis, that he wanted to meet with him again. Maria called back in the afternoon to say that she and Onassis would come together to Sirmione at once; Aristo had to leave immediately afterward "on business."

"At eight an enormous car passed through the gates of my villa," Meneghini writes. "Maria got out, followed by Onassis, Bruna (our maid in Milan) and the two poodles, Toy and Tea. The chauffeur remained at attention. Onassis was euphoric. He greeted everyone warmly, loudly. His breath smelled of alcohol.

"Maria must also have been drinking," Meneghini continues. "She was acting peculiarly. I had never seen her this way. We ate at nine. Maria behaved like a silly, stupid child." Perhaps Maria was giddily proud to be showing off to her lover the beauties of her home, but according to Meneghini, "Onassis was not enthusiastic. He told me, 'You have a nerve confining a woman like Maria to the edge of a puddle like this lake.' "

Around eleven, the battle began in earnest. "I was no longer passive and subdued, the way I was two days earlier," Meneghini reports. "I taunted Onassis and fought him every inch of the way. . . . He accused me of being cruel and of hoping for their unhappiness. Then I really lost my patience and lit into him. I insulted him and called him the epithets he deserved."

The outburst, however, seemed only to strengthen Onassis' resolve. "I will never give up Maria," Meneghini quotes him as saying, "and I will take her away from whomever it's necessary, using whatever means, sending people, things, contracts and conventions to hell." At this point they were shouting back and forth, Meneghini writes, and he reports that Onassis said, "How many millions do you want for Maria? Five? Ten?"

Meneghini implies that Onassis was rudely offering to pay him to give up his wife, but it is more likely he was telling him he knew that Maria's value for her husband was primarily financial, and he was prepared to compensate him for the loss.

Meneghini continues: "It was now three in the morning. . . . I said that I was going to bed. 'Then let's shake hands,' Onassis said. 'I don't shake hands with refuse like you,' I replied. 'You invited me on your damned yacht and then you stabbed me in the back. I am placing a curse on you that you may never have peace for the rest of your days.' "

Meneghini's malediction, if he did utter it, would surely have unsettled Onassis and also—especially—Maria, for they were both deeply superstitious. Having delivered himself of it, he went up to bed, leaving Maria downstairs with Onassis. "I rested on the bed, fully dressed," Meneghini reports. "At four, Maria tiptoed into the room. She took some piece of clothing. I assumed she would return shortly, but by five I hadn't seen her. I got up and went downstairs. There was no one there. There was only the poodle Tea, sleeping in her usual spot. Onassis' limousine was no longer in the driveway. I looked into Bruna's room, but her bed was unmussed."

Only two hours later, at seven o'clock on the morning of Tuesday, August 18, Maria telephoned Meneghini from Milan asking him to "send Ferruccio, our butler, with her passport and the Madonnina, the little painting I had given her the day we met, and which had been our companion for twelve years of struggles, disappointments, tears and also happiness." It may have been her passport that Maria was looking for when she came into the bedroom earlier that morning, if she was planning to fly off with Onassis. In any case, she accompanied him back to Milan and Onassis departed from the airport near Verona, back to the Riviera and the *Christina*, anchored in Monte Carlo's harbor.

Maria took only one poodle, Toy, with her, leaving Battista custody of Tea and separating the two dogs that had been like the children they never had. In addition to Toy, she took her maid, Bruna Lupoli. It appears that there may have been a struggle initially for the loyalties of this close retainer. That morning, when Meneghini sent Maria her belongings with Ferruccio, he also sent a handwritten letter addressed to Bruna, which I have uncovered.

My Dear Bruna,

You know, you know everything! Incredible, this tremendous reality! And you, who, alone, can reach into the soul of the signora, of my and your signora, get close to her with your heart and tell her a word, one only!

I beseech you with my hands together and pray that God bless you and that you stay.

Good bye Bruna, I confide in you.

Your S. Battista Meneghini

Sirmione, Tuesday, 18, Aug. 1959

It would be but one of his many unanswered prayers, for Bruna would remain with Maria from that day on.

The next day, Thursday, August 20, Meneghini wrote in his diary that Maria had "telephoned at two in the morning to inquire how I was. She called again at ten in the morning. She was almost sweet with me." It seems an odd reversal, but if Onassis told Maria that he had to go back to the *Christina* with Tina and her friends and wouldn't be able to see her for a while, it is not inconceivable that Maria, suddenly alone in Milan, would become solicitous about how her husband was getting on without her. The feeling was in any event short-lived. Onassis unexpectedly appeared back in Milan, and when Meneghini tried to contact his wife that Friday, she was nowhere to be found. Ferruccio informed him that Maria was "out with friends."

In fact, Maria had left town that evening. On Saturday, August 22, Meneghini drove to Turin to work with his lawyer. "On the return trip I had trouble with my Mercedes and had to stop in Milan," he notes disingenuously. "I arrived at Via Buonarroti at seven. Maria wasn't home. She had left with friends the night before. She had written down her address: Hotel Hermitage, Monte Carlo. . . . *Stampe Sera* mentioned that Maria Callas had been seen driving through Cuneo [in northwestern Italy] on the way to Monaco some 250 miles from Milan with Aristotle Onassis."

Meneghini spent the weekend in the Milan villa, from which he evidently barraged Maria with phone calls. When the phone went dead on Sunday, he made numerous complaints to the phone company before learning that the service "had been cut off following 'a request for termination of the contract.' " He took the train to Sirmione at eight. There, in his study, he wrote: "I feel so frighteningly sad without Maria."

By Monday Maria was back in Milan, and on Tuesday she informed Meneghini by phone that she wanted possession of the house in town as well as her jewels. He replied uncertainly, "These are matters to be discussed." She also told him to stay in Sirmione and, evidently following the advice of Onassis, who had spent the weekend worrying that the affair might be leaked to the press and cause problems with Tina, she urged Meneghini "not to speak of the dissolution of our marriage with anyone. 'The name of the other person absolutely must not be mentioned,' she said. 'Ari and I are the ones who are disgraced, the unfortunate parties. Everyone will blame us for this.' "

The next day, still clearly under the guidance of Onassis, Maria phoned Meneghini again and asked that his housekeeper, Emma, "bring her clothes, lingerie and evening dresses. She was most insistent that I send all of Elsa Maxwell's letters to her. . . . She invoked all her patron saints to come to her aid, 'because [her words] I need to have peace.' "

Meneghini proceeded to lecture Maria about the sanctity of the matrimonial bond and the dim view that the church took of such behavior as hers. "You have committed an unspeakable sin," he told her. "You have ruined my life." She replied, "You have had a full life. You must be prepared to step aside. I, on the other hand, have my entire life before me and I want to enjoy it. I was with you for twelve years. That is enough now."

Meneghini reports, "There were no telephone calls" on the following day, Thursday the twenty-seventh. He did not know that Maria and Ari had left Milan for another long weekend on the French Riviera. On Friday he went to Turin to visit his lawyer and fumed to him that Maria was treating him this way and getting away with it. "I suggested denouncing my wife and Onassis. He pointed out that Maria is an American citizen and therefore could not be incriminated." (In Italy at that time adultery was a crime that could bring imprisonment.)

The pressing business that required Onassis' presence back in Monte Carlo was a dinner party to be held on board the *Christina* for Prince Rainier and Princess Grace of Monaco on Friday, August 28. The other guests, according to the newspapers, were the friends that Tina had invited aboard to sail with her to Venice, plus Greta Garbo, who wore "a simple print afternoon dress and her habitual dark glasses . . . the Maharani of Baroda adorned with precious jewels, Prince Aldobrandini and the Count and Countess Bernadotte." The reporters crowded on the dock were surprised to see Princess Grace arrive looking pale and in pain, with her arm in a sling made of a silk scarf imprinted with the royal coat of arms; she had suffered an allergic reaction to a wasp sting earlier in the day.

The dinner was to be the kickoff for the cruise to Venice. As soon as the royal couple returned ashore, Captain Kostas was to set sail for a four-day trip to Venice, with a stop at Capri on the way. Ari was to be the host and Tina the hostess.

The group Tina had invited was quite a far cry from Ari's mismatched guests of the previous voyage. All were rich, sophisticated, glamorous aristocrats, and all were one to three decades younger than Ari. (Tina was now thirty; her lover, Reinaldo Herrera, only twenty-five, was less than half Onassis' age.) Also on board: the Italian prince Francesco Aldobrandini and his wife, Anne-Marie; the Spaniard Jaime Campo Florida (who later became Count Casa Lombillo); the British socialite Peggy Scott Duff; and Lady Stella Ednam, called Baby, recently divorced from the English duke who later became Viscount Ednam.

This cruise was an elaborate charade. Each of the guests was pretending to be with one person while actually involved with another, or, as Reinaldo put it, "We all had double connections. I was supposed to be with Peggy, but was really with Tina. Peggy was supposed to be with me, but was being pursued by Francesco. Jaime was with Lady Ednam."

Onassis was perfectly aware of the romantic entanglements aboard the *Christina*, including his wife's liaison with young Reinaldo. "Ari was never angry with me," Herrera told me. "He just didn't want to lose possession of Tina." (Ari's sister Artemis was also on board, and he could count on her to keep him informed about what was going on.)

When I interviewed her in her Manhattan apartment in 1999, Peggy Scott Duff (now Mrs. Hans Kertess) showed me an album with photos taken on board the *Christina* forty years earlier. Like Tina, all the guests were svelte, stylish, and attractive enough to be posing for a *Vogue* fashion spread as they lounged around the swimming pool. Peggy herself had long blond hair and a sultry pout. Reinaldo tended to leave his shirt open or go shirtless to show off his muscular chest, and he wore a gold chain and religious medals around his neck. (Herrera, who is now married to the fashion designer Carolina Herrera, still wears those charms, including one that was a gift from Tina which portrays the infant Jesus with a lamb.)

These socialites plus Greta Garbo, Garbo's lover, George Schlee, and the Maharani of Baroda were among the twenty assembled on the night of Friday, August 28, to dine on the afterdeck with Prince Rainier and Princess Grace as the *Christina*, festooned with strings of lights, rocked gently in the harbor of Monte Carlo.

Ari had ensconced Maria in a suite at the Hermitage Hotel with a dramatic view of the *Christina* and the harbor far below; now, on board, he held forth at the head of the table in his white dinner jacket. The Dom Perignon flowed freely, as did the cosmopolitan conversation, flowing from French to English to Italian without pause. Princess Grace, however, was not enjoying herself. Her arm was now painfully swollen, and her mood was not improved when Peggy Scott Duff greeted her with the question "Did you forget to feed your dog?" "[Grace] left the Christina at midnight accompanied by Rainier and Onassis as far as the boarding wharf," noted the *Corriere della Sera*'s reporter. "Their early departure was surprising because usually parties on board the luxurious yacht go on until three or four o'clock in the morning." Ari led his guests of honor to their chauffeured limousine, decked with Monegasque flags, which was waiting to carry them up the winding road to their hilltop palace.

The reporter further noted that Onassis had taken great "precautions to conceal the names of his guests on board. . . . After Grace and Rainier left, Onassis' guests danced until the early morning hours and afterward only a few of them disembarked. Onassis was apparently so irritated by the publicity given to this party that he had his guests who were not staying on board the *Christina* for the cruise taken ashore in small boats so that the curiosity seekers could not put together the complete guest list."

No doubt Onassis was trying to hide the fact that he and Tina were being accompanied on their cruise to Venice by the young man whom the Italian papers already referred to as Tina's "flame." When I spoke to Herrera in 1999, he described the unexpected conclusion to the dinner party for the prince and princess. It was after 2 a.m. by the time Ari escorted the

Jaime Castelbarco, Tina Onassis, and her young flame Reinaldo Herrera.
Behind them is young Alexander Onassis, playing with a toy boat.

last guest ashore. As Herrera and Tina watched from the yacht's rail, Ari started to reboard the yacht, but suddenly, with one foot on the dock and one on the gangplank, he paused and looked up. As it started to rise in preparation for departure, Onassis jumped back to the dock and waved the *Christina* away, shouting that he'd join them later, maybe in Capri—he had some unfinished business on land. Tina, standing next to Reinaldo, was astonished by his sudden departure.

It's not hard to imagine what Onassis might have been thinking as he prepared to sail off to Venice and looked up at the guests awaiting him. There was his wife with her twenty-five-year-old lover. There were several other young, spoiled, aristocratic couples who would spend the cruise cavorting with each other. These people of inherited ease were accustomed to following the seasons from one playground to another. They were not his kind of people.

To Maria, Aristo was a young, vital, sexually exciting man (especially compared to Meneghini). Tina, on the other hand, viewed her husband as someone from another generation. "You must realize, he was older than her mother, and she wanted to have—not just fun, she wanted to have youth, which she never had," Herrera told me. "She was a virgin when she got married. Of course Ari tried to make love to her [before the wedding], but she said at first she felt very funny about it, like an old uncle was trying to seduce her. But then she was very flattered, when she got to love and admire him a great deal."

Herrera emphasized to me that Tina always was very fond of Ari and admired him until the end of her life, but he also suggested that by the time of his own affair with Tina, Ari's age had become an impediment to intimacy with his wife: "Tina told me that he was having sexual problems and had difficulty performing," Herrera said. "I don't know if that was only with her or with women in general, but he was definitely having problems."

Onassis' sexual dysfunction was also described by Lilika Papanikolaou, the long-time Onassis family friend to whom he first revealed his affair with Maria. "I'll tell you something that was told to me by members of his family," she confided to me. "The father of Onassis started to suffer from impotence at the age of fifty, and Onassis experienced the same thing at the age of fifty, like his father."

But if Onassis indeed suffered from some organic condition, it clearly did not affect his physical relations with Maria, who told friends that he was a skilled, patient, and energetic lover. Once their affair began, Callas, one of the most famous women and most admired artists in the world, wanted nothing more than to devote herself completely to him, something that had long ago ceased to interest his wife Tina.

As Onassis stood with one foot on the gangplank and one on the ground, he reached a characteristically hair-trigger decision to jump back onto the harborside and abandon the *Christina* to Tina and her guests, choosing to play the ardent lover on land rather than the cuckold at sea. The ship sailed at 2:25 a.m. on Saturday, August 29, headed for Capri and then Venice.

While Onassis was with Callas in the Hermitage Hotel in Monte Carlo, Maria's husband was meeting with his lawyer in Turin. From there, Meneghini drove to the house in Milan, where Bruna told him that Madame was in Nice. "I noticed that Maria had left without taking her little painting of the Madonnina from which she had never been separated. I asked Bruna how this could have happened, and she replied, 'That painting no longer matters to Maria.' "

That weekend Meneghini's fury grew to the bursting point. At a dinner in Sirmione, he heard one of the guests repeat a rumor she'd heard at Consuelo Crespi's party in Milan that Callas and Meneghini were separated. Seething, he drove to Milan that Sunday night and discovered that Maria was still not there. A frustrated and bitter Meneghini confided to his diary: "When Maria had some little temperamental flare-up in the theater, the press jumped on her back. Now that she has been running around with Onassis for almost a month after having left her husband, not one reporter is on top of the situation." He knew that Callas, and especially Onassis, were terrified of a scandal in the papers. It now occurred to him how to get his revenge.

On Monday, August 31, Meneghini lingered in Milan all day and even called Maria's cardiologist. "He informed me that on her last visit, only four days before, her heart was fine. 'It has returned to normal,' he said. 'Her blood pressure, which has always been dangerously low, has climbed to 110. We should thank the Lord for the benefits your wife has received from that cruise.' " Meneghini was not thankful, and as he drove back to Sirmione, he decided he would not suffer in silence much longer.

The next day, Tuesday, Meneghini heard a rumor that Maria would be lunching in Milan with the impresario Sander Gorlinsky, and he scooted back to the city to inject himself into the meeting, only to learn Maria was still in Nice. Bruna told him that Callas was expected around noon the next day, and he stayed all night in the Milan house, although the maid strongly suggested that he leave early, before Maria arrived.

Desperate to see his wife, Meneghini headed for Malpensa Airport, determined to ambush her there. "I assumed that she would be arriving in Onassis' little two-engine plane." He parked the Mercedes near the exit ramp in the sweltering sun. "I never took my eyes off the runway. Each time I spotted a tiny aircraft, my heart started pounding." When he left the car to get some air, Meneghini ran into a friend who asked what he was doing there and he replied, "I'm here to pick up Maria." The bewildered friend told him that he had just seen Maria leave by another exit. Defeated, Meneghini limped off to Sirmione. He had told Bruna that he would be back in Milan the next day. Meanwhile, Ari had flown in with Maria, kissed her good-bye, and taken off again for Venice, where the *Christina* had dropped anchor in the harbor at 10:40 a.m. It was Wednesday, September 2.

Peggy Kertess recalled a mortifying misadventure that occurred the day the yacht anchored in the Grand Canal: "When we got to Venice I remember Peggy Bancroft came aboard with about twenty of her friends to show them the *Christina*. (Mrs. Thomas Bancroft was a Manhattan socialite described in 1958 as "the queen of New York.")

"They were walking in and out of all the staterooms and I needed to go to the loo, so I went upstairs to the Onassis suite and used their bathroom," Peggy continued. "I sat down on the toilet and looked to the side and there was a glass partition and in the adjoining bathroom were all of Peggy Bancroft's twenty guests, looking towards me! I was so mortified, my water-works shut down for a year, I think. Later I found that while I could see into the room where they were, all they could see of the alcove I was in was a one-way mirror." (Herrera thereafter referred to it as the "see-through loo.")

Tina's guests on the *Christina* had first read news reports of the Onassis-Callas sightings during their stop in Capri, but Tina wasn't overly concerned, according to Herrera. "The pressure started coming two days before we landed in Venice. There were cables and phone calls. Tina was annoyed, not with jealousy, but she felt the scandal was not good for the children and for her family. She was on the telephone with her father all the time. But once we got to Venice we went to all the parties and the balls."

Reporters covering the film festival recorded that on the day the *Christina* docked, "Tina joined society friends for a coffee chat at the fashionable Lido beach with Elsa Maxwell." What the reporters (and probably Maxwell) didn't realize was that the society friends basking in the sun, including Reinaldo in an open-necked white shirt and beige slacks, smiling beside Tina, had sailed into Venice with Tina. Because Onassis was expected at any moment—in fact, he'd been expected at every stop along the way—Herrera was aware that he had to appear to the press to be a casual friend who'd just run into Tina. It would be hard to explain to a gossip columnist and meddler like Elsa Maxwell—especially in the conservative moral climate of the 1950s—that Tina's plan was to sail on the *Christina* with both her husband and her young Latin swain. As the papers picked up the scent of the Ari-Maria romance, it became even more important for Herrera to stay out of the scandal. But any evasions would prove pointless. "In Venice," according to Reinaldo, "Elsa told Tina, 'Ari's in love with Maria and Maria's crazy about him.' That's when Tina learned that word was getting around about them.' "

Onassis' Piaggio landed at Lido Airport at 4:26 that afternoon. Four days later, London's *Sunday Pictorial* published a breathless report that summarized the events of the week hour by hour. It stated: "Although he had parted from Mme. Callas only 90 minutes earlier, he demanded an urgent telephone call to be put through to her in Milan. He returned to his yacht but at 10:15 the next morning he phoned Mme. Callas again. Then 35 minutes later [on Thursday, September 3] he was winging his way back to Milan. After landing at Milan he took a taxi to Mme. Callas' villa."

After promising Tina that he would catch up with the cruise along the way, Ari had finally reached the *Christina* only after its arrival in Venice, and then he departed abruptly the next morning, leaving his wife without an escort to the festival's kickoff party, a reception given by Countess Volpi di Misurata at her palace on the Grand Canal. Tina was described as attending

Tina and Herrera in Venice

the party alone but looking "serene and lovely." The same article mentioned that her supposed "flame," Reynaldo Herrera [*sic*], was seen in her company in Venice.

It is interesting to speculate about Tina and Ari's exchange during their brief encounter on Wednesday night. One conversation aboard the *Christina* was reported to me by Herrera. It concerned Ari's desire to retain Tina as his nominal wife while in effect sponsoring her happiness with her lover. According to Herrera, "He said, 'Reinaldo, don't marry Tina. I'll get a property in France and you and Tina can spend as much time as you want there, and we'll spend summers together.' " There is no record of Tina's response to this extraordinarily civilized proposal whereby everyone could have his or her cake and eat it too, but Ari's abrupt return to Milan the next morning clearly was not on Tina's social calendar.

Meanwhile, back in Milan, the paparazzi were waking up to the scandal unfolding before their eyes. Shortly after Onassis called Maria on Thursday morning to tell her he was coming back, Bruna called Meneghini in Sirmione to say that Maria was not feeling well, and, Meneghini writes, "Maria had Bruna ask me to postpone the trip [to Milan] for a few days so she could rest quietly at home." On that Thursday, September 3, Ari and Maria were seen dining at the Rendez-vous restaurant in Milan's Porta Venezia Gardens, serenaded by violins. Later they were photographed dancing at Montemerlo, a popular night spot, where they lingered until 3:10 a.m. The proprietor told reporters, "Mr. Onassis particularly asked for a dimly lit corner. He left a £30 tip." After they left the nightclub, they were photographed arm in arm going into the Hotel Principe e Savoia, where Onassis had booked a suite. Maria was carrying a bouquet of red roses.

Thursday was also the day, according to the *Sunday Pictorial,* that eleven-year-old Alexander Onassis spent two hours waiting at the airport in Venice for his father to come back, but his wait was in vain.

On Friday, nearly every literate person in Italy knew how Ari and Maria had spent the previous night. Among the last to find out was Meneghini, who left at 5 a.m. to visit his attorney in Turin and called as he passed through Milan to ask about his wife's health. "She's better," Bruna told him. Meneghini quarreled with and fired his attorney, perhaps because the counselor refused to let the irate husband denounce his wife in public. As he drove back to Sirmione in the early evening, Battista had an unpleasant surprise: "At the toll booth on the highway I saw on the front page of one of the afternoon papers an article describing a rendezvous between Callas and Onassis. . . . Unwell my foot!" Furious, he telephoned Bruna and exploded: "My room and office," I told her, "must always be ready and in order, because I intend to come to my own house whenever I please."

That afternoon, according to the newspapers, Ari and Maria lunched together in Milan, then retreated to Maria's villa, where they were joined by a lawyer. Later, according to the *Sunday Pictorial,* "Mme. Callas saw Aristotle off at the airport. There were tears in her eyes."

By this time, both the *Christina* in Venice and Maria's villa in Milan were under siege by the press, and Tina warned her guests to get off the yacht before they were dragged into the whirlpool of gossip. "Peggy and I left because somebody leaked that Tina and I were having a flirt and that I was on board," Herrera told me. They retrieved their passports from Madame Rocaserra, the yacht's *gouvernante* (housekeeper), and left the next morning by launch for the Bauer Grünwald Hotel, where they "sat in the lobby with newspapers in front of our faces so no one would recognize us. The press were looking for anyone connected with Onassis. We were literally hiding behind pillars."

The next day they arranged for a car and chauffeur. After a stop in Florence they headed for the Grand Hotel in Rome. They had almost no money between them. "When we got to the Grand," Herrera recalled, "Lorenzo, the concierge, who was the best who ever lived, said, 'No problem whatsoever, your excellency.' And he paid for everything—food, clothes—until money was wired to me from Venezuela. I even gave a party and he paid for it!"

Reinaldo recalled his escape from the scandal as a farce worthy of a silent film. "The papers were full of headlines like 'Where is Young Herrera Hiding?' " he told me. "The press were looking for me everywhere." He called the British publisher Lord Beaverbrook, who counseled him to give an interview, " 'but make sure you are very dull and boring.' So I gave a press conference in the Royal Suite and said I was on a brief holiday and would soon leave on business. I made sure Peggy was visible, and when they asked me about Tina, I said, 'We're friends, but any suggestion of romance is ridiculous. I know Mr. Onassis as well as Mrs. Onassis.'

"We stayed in Rome for ten days, and by this time my father was beside himself. He called me and said, 'Get out of there. Come to Paris and then go home to Caracas.' So we flew to Paris after paying the driver. By now I had money, which had been sent to me by my father." Peggy Kertess confirmed his account.

Maria Callas couldn't so nimbly flee the press hounding her in Milan, because she was scheduled from September 2 to 10 to rehearse and then record *La Gioconda* at La Scala for EMI. On the first day of rehearsals she was escorted by Peter Diamand, the director of the Holland Festival and later the Edinburgh Festival. "One really had to protect her physically from the press and the photographers," he said later. "Anyone who was with her was interrogated: 'How do you know Madame Callas?' . . . 'I am her Egyptian hairdresser,' I said to one Italian reporter who proceeded to print it in his newspaper, together with all the details I gave him about how her hair goes all soft and smooth when she's singing Violetta and all crisp and wild when she's Medea."

Despite conscientiously fulfilling the commitment Meneghini had made for her, Maria enjoyed a brief respite from the tumult. Aristo flew the Piaggio to Turin's airport to avoid the army of reporters waiting at the Milan airport. After hiding out at "a beauty spot in Piedmont," the lovers returned to Turin's airport on Monday so that Maria could resume recording at La Scala.

Monday, September 7, marked the high point of the Venice Film Festival: Elsa Maxwell's annual masked ball at the Hotel Danieli. Two years earlier Maxwell had introduced Onassis to Maria at this annual celebration and had then written, "I have never given a better dinner and ball in my life.

It had a flare of such joy and happiness." She would not feel the same way about the one she gave in 1959. This time her friend Tina's mood was notably less festive as, having promised everyone her husband would be there, she turned up without him by her side. Nevertheless, she posed with a brave smile, resplendent in a white pleated gown with a diamond brooch at the point of the deep décolleté. Its artfully draped folds clung to her slender body, suggesting a Greek goddess. Her blond hair was piled high on her head, and in a string bag she carried what seemed to be a large and evil-looking eel. (Elsa Maxwell had decreed that this year everyone was to wear or carry something "very ugly." Many of the guests wore grotesque masks and Elsa herself sported a huge false nose.)

The most observed and sought-after guest, Tina was photographed dancing in the arms of Count Brando Brandolini. The press reported that she maintained a dignified silence against their harangue. Finally, though, Tina could no longer bear their hounding questions about the whereabouts of her husband; she left the party early and fled alone for the sanctuary of the yacht. The next morning aboard the *Christina,* Tina received a social visit from Elsa Maxwell, who had some advice for her friend in this difficult situation.

With every other party to the scandal eluding them, the members of the press concentrated their attentions on Meneghini at Sirmione, and he did not disappoint them. He issued daily statements of operatic hyperbole: "Maria is Medea. . . . Onassis has his billions and he wants to have his tankers shine with the name of a great actress," he told one Italian reporter; to another he said, "This Onassis is a madman. He's a madman like Hitler. . . . He thinks he can buy anything and everything with money." He also said that Onassis admitted to him that he wanted to marry Callas. This verbosity was a far cry from the offerings of the other jilted spouse; in Venice, Tina could only mutter through clenched teeth, "You must realize all this is something I would rather not talk about."

Onassis was still in Milan with Callas, trying to stem the flood of accusations coming from Meneghini and to salvage his marriage. On Tuesday, September 8, Maria made a public statement in a bar near La Scala, declaring that it was true that her marriage was over, but not because of a romance with Onassis. "I confirm that the break between my husband and myself is complete and final. It has been in the air for quite some time, and the cruise on the *Christina* was only coincidental. . . . I am now my own manager. I ask for understanding in this painful personal situation. . . . Between Signor Onassis and myself there exists a profound friendship that dates back some time. I am also in a business connection with him. I have received offers from the Monte Carlo Opera and there is also a prospect for a film." She told reporters there was "no sentimental link" between her and Onassis, adding, "He is only a good friend of mine assisting me in a difficult moment."

The papers reported that Meneghini came from Verona to Milan on September 8 but that he and Maria did not meet. "She is here to complete a recording," reported the Associated Press. "He came from their summer home near Verona for a meeting of his attorneys with his wife's lawyer. Reporters said they heard loud agitated voices coming from the locked room in a fashionable hotel where the four-hour conference was held."

On the same day, Onassis made two statements that would be quoted around the world, the first one in Milan, where he was cornered in the "gilded lounge of the Hotel Principe e Savoia." According to newspaper reports, he "adjusted his smoked glasses, smiled sweetly at the reporters, and said inscrutably, 'I am a sailor and these things may happen to a sailor.' " Later in the day he flew to Venice, but not before discounting the rumors as "fairy tales . . . silly inventions."

When Onassis arrived on board the *Christina* in Venice, however, he was enraged to discover Tina gone. Her patience exhausted at last, she had grabbed the two children and fled as soon as she heard the sound of his Piaggio approaching. Captain Kostas Anastasiades remembers this event vividly because he became the target of his employer's anger. He told me, "The two children had been taken to the Lido to swim. Christina and Alexander had gone in separate Chris-Crafts. When she saw the Piaggio approaching, Tina came to me and asked me for her passport, which I gave her. What could I do? She told me to call the Chris-Craft and have the children brought to the train station. Then she took another Chris-Craft and went on shore to the station. When Onassis' plane arrived, we had no fast Chris-Crafts left and we sent him in a slow one. He was furious because he felt that if he had a fast one he could have caught up with Tina and the children. He got angry at me and accused me of setting things up deliberately, so that he couldn't catch up with them."

According to Reinaldo Herrera, Tina went to the home of Brando Brandolini in Venice before going to the train station. (Her brother, George Livanos, told me, however, that Tina flew from Venice to Paris in a private plane furnished by Gianni Agnelli, the brother of Brandolini's wife, Christina.) As soon as Onassis realized that Tina had eluded him, he stormed up to the *Christina*'s bridge and began making phone calls to his father-in-law, Stavros Livanos, in Paris, where he guessed Tina was headed with the children.

Much later on the same day, reporters discovered Onassis at Harry's Bar in Venice. It was hardly a place to evade them and, feeling expansive after a few drinks, he offered up what would become the most oft-repeated comment to come out of the scandal: "Friends have described me as a sailor. Sailors do not usually go for sopranos. But I would indeed be flattered to have a woman of her class fall for me."

The remark triggered an avalanche of further speculation, including Elsa Maxwell's. In her column of September 11, she wrote that she had spoken to Onassis "last night" about the rumors. She claimed she hadn't discussed the crisis with his wife (which was untrue) and added, "I hope the whole affair ends well for all concerned. It is an unpleasant story." Posing the question of whether Callas and Onassis would marry, she answered herself: "I guess not."

The whole imbroglio was now reaching operatic proportions, and it was inevitable that someone would cast the roles. Taking a cue from Meneghini's description of Maria as Medea, *Time* magazine's September 21 issue naturally selected Maria as Soprano, Meneghini as Bass, Elsa Maxwell as Baritone, Maria's mother as Contralto, Onassis as Tenor, and Tina as the Mezzo-soprano. Pointing out that Meneghini, "after years of silence now kept delivering some of the best lines," *Time* quoted one of his outbursts: "I was building a little masterpiece. Then I fell in love with my masterpiece and I married her. I created Callas and she repaid me with a stab in the back."

Onassis, having drowned his sorrows and loosened his lips in Harry's Bar, ordered his exhausted pilot to fly the Piaggio back to Milan the next day, September 9, for a quick meeting with Maria, no doubt to work out plans in light of Tina's hasty departure. Then he continued on to Paris. ("Never has the Piaggio flown so much since he bought it," the pilot, Pirotti, was heard to groan.) Describing his relationship with Miss Callas, Ari told the swarming French reporters: "Friendship—it is too simple," and "No one wants to believe me. I have only affection for Maria. She is a childhood friend of my sister's. I have known her for twenty years. And I have never heard her sing." (That last was patently untrue, for he sat through her performance of *Medea* in London on the evening of the party he gave for her at the Dorchester Hotel.) He then rushed to his father-in-law's home on Avenue Foch to confer with Stavros Livanos and plead with Tina for a reconciliation.

But Tina now wanted only one thing—her freedom—and at last her father was ready to see things her way. The staid and old-fashioned Greek patriarch had heretofore counseled forbearance even as his daughter's marriage degenerated into a sham—after all, there were children involved, as well as the union of two huge Greek fortunes. But now he had to agree with Tina. With Onassis and Callas on the front page of every newspaper in the

Flying high to lie low, Ari picks up Maria at the Brescia airport.

world, he could hardly ask his daughter to endure any more public humiliation. He realized, too, that this scandal offered the best opportunity to end a
long-troubled marriage without any blame on his daughter or dishonor to
his family.

It was a naive hope, even for a man of Onassis' formidable powers of
persuasion, to think he could hold on to his wife while indulging his new
passion. All the same he was crestfallen, even despondent, at his failure
when he flew back to the *Christina* on September 10. But as he mulled
things over and repeatedly phoned Maria, he began to rally, to recharge his
native optimism. If Tina was going to walk out of the marriage and reject his
offer of a polite charade of togetherness, then he was ready to show her he
didn't care.

On the morning of Friday, September 11, the long-suffering Pirotti flew
Onassis to the Brescia airport, near Milan, to collect Maria, who had completed her recordings for EMI the day before. She was wearing dark glasses
and a full-skirted dark shirtwaist dress with a nautically knotted sash at the

collar. Onassis, in shirtsleeves, helped her aboard the plane. Traveling with her, as ever, were Bruna and Toy. (Meneghini, still delivering the best lines, told the press: "You'll see, if everything is split and we have to divide our poodle, Maria will get the front and I will end up with the tail.") The lovers returned to the *Christina* in Venice, to the shock and consternation of the crew, who had expected their boss to come back with his wife and children. Tina was popular with all hands because she always took an interest in their families and personal welfare. "When Maria came on board, we were surprised," Captain Kostas told me. "It was not a happy time. Callas was put in her usual cabin, the Ithaki. She seemed very happy."

Onassis' sister Artemis was the only other passenger on board, according to the captain. As the sun sank lower, the yacht prepared to depart for Greece. Onassis went up to the bridge and, in a flamboyant gesture of farewell and defiance, personally sounded the ship's siren: several loud triumphant blasts. It was his way of broadcasting that he and his lover, Maria Callas, were sailing off together toward their own country and they wanted the entire world to know it—there would be no more hiding for the sake of propriety.

An engineer on the *Christina,* Demetrios Demetriades, later interpreted the significance of those blasts of the siren in Venice a bit differently to a reporter: "I don't know if you can imagine what it is like to be Greek, but for us, the heroes of the old legends are sometimes very real. And we knew what those blasts on the yacht's siren meant. They were telling Italy that Maria Callas, the Greek woman who had become one of them by her marriage to Meneghini, was with her own people again. The spotlight of the world was now on the *Christina.*"

13

GOING PUBLIC

Gossip is mischievous, light and easy to raise,
but grievous to bear and difficult to shake.

Hesiod, *Works and Days*

As the modern-day Odysseus and Medea sailed off toward Greece with a triumphant flourish of bells and sirens, the world's fascination with their romance continued to grow. Onassis made no secret of his bond with Maria—at least at the beginning of this cruise. According to Captain Kostas, "When we were sailing through the Straits of Messina, we passed some ferryboats loaded with people. Onassis and Callas went up on the top deck and the people all waved at them and shouted, 'Good luck!' "

While Onassis and Maria were flaunting their togetherness, the other actors in the opera buffa did not neglect their roles. The day after the *Christina* left Venice, Meneghini, from Sirmione, belittled the Onassis-Callas affair in one of his most long-winded press conferences. Speaking to United Press International by telephone, he said that Onassis and Maria "are in love like children," and noted that whereas he had "devoted my entire life to her . . . Onassis has no interest in Maria's artistic life." Three days later he added, "I still love her" and told reporters that he "would wage an all-out court battle in any divorce action his wife Maria Callas or the money of Onassis begins anywhere in the world."

Tina, in Paris, refused to talk to the press, but at one point she made a statement about the cruise through her secretary: "I am not at all worried about my husband and Maria being thrown together. They are old friends. I would like to accompany them but I have to get the children back to school."

After long consultations with her parents, her sister, Eugenia, and brother-in-law, Stravros Niarchos, Tina enlisted the services of one of America's most famous divorce lawyers, Sol Rosenblatt, and began floating trial balloons about her reaction to the scandal through the gossip columnist Cholly Knickerbocker (the pseudonym of Igor Cassini), who kept providing updates on the battle in his column for the *New York Journal American*.

In his September 15 column, a day after the *Christina* had docked in Glyfada with the lovers aboard, for example, "Knickerbocker" hardly sounded like an objective reporter. He wrote:

> *The biggest gossip of Europe continues to be the Callas-Onassis "romance."*
> *. . . When asked if he would marry Callas or whether he was in love with her, [Onassis] said, "This would be news—but only the day I choose to give it." "And your wife, do you love her?" a reporter asked him. "She's my wife," came the abrupt and cryptic answer.*
>
> *As to the wife—lovely petite Christina Livanos Onassis [the columnist consistently got Athina's first name wrong]—I spoke to her in Paris after she had escaped from Venice unnoticed by the hordes of clamoring reporters. . . . Tina has kept a dignified silence during the entire affair, which must have indeed been unpleasant for her.*
>
> *Callas is a very ambitious woman. Meneghini was the first step to success. Now Onassis would crown her career, so Meneghini had to go. But . . . Onassis is no easy fish to catch. . . . I don't believe for one moment that he intends to marry her. . . . He couldn't care less what people say or think of him. That's why he took off with Callas on a cruise to Greece despite the scandal in the press. He told his wife he was going off with Callas—and that's life, he explained. He told her that he hadn't minded last Summer when everyone was talking about her "romance" with a handsome young Venezuelan.*
>
> *But Ari never said that he wanted a divorce. And for that matter, neither does Tina. . . . Callas, of course is trying hard. It was she who kept the publicity going and Onassis won't have an easy time losing her. But I will make a bet, and so will all their friends, that the future will still find Ari and Tina Onassis together—with Maria Callas singing a loud solo.*

This column contains some astute observations about the marriage but many misrepresentations as well—including the claims that it was Maria who was courting publicity and that Tina didn't want a divorce. It's clearly informed by Tina's efforts to get her case before the public eye and provoke her husband's next move. At about the time Onassis and Maria were arriving in Greece, Sol Rosenblatt flew to Paris to consult with his client and her parents before returning with Tina to New York City via London. The children joined her a few days later.

The *Christina*'s trip to Athens was not just a honeymoon cruise for Maria and Ari. Onassis needed to attend a business meeting with the directors of Olympic Airways, his favorite among his "hobby enterprises." (He had taken over a small, unprofitable Greek airline, TAE, for a mere two million dollars in 1956—making himself the only private citizen in the world who owned a national airline—and promptly renamed it.) In an effort to keep the clamoring reporters at bay as they docked in Glyfada, Onassis invoked the aid of the Greek navy, which sent sailors to clear the jetty of gawkers a half hour before the *Christina* arrived. When the yacht's launches came ashore, Theodore Garofalidis announced loudly to a navy officer, "Madame Callas left the *Christina* at Brindisi." This did not discourage the members of the fourth estate, who could see that she was on the top deck. Launches brought the Olympic Airways executives onto the ship for their meeting with the chairman of the board.

Soon after the *Christina* anchored in Glyfada near the two neighboring villas owned by Onassis and his sister Artemis, a crew member was dispatched to buy all the foreign newspapers so that the lovers could catch up on their reviews. Finally, after some days of suspense, Onassis and Maria came ashore to go nightclubbing outside Athens.

On September 17, Onassis hired a plane to fly Maria (and Bruna Lupoli) to a concert she was to give in Bilbao, Spain, which Meneghini had long ago scheduled for her. Captain Kostas told me: "He gave her a special plane from Olympic Airways, which was fitted with a bed in it so she would be fresh for the performance." But by now Maria was so deeply in love and so distracted by her adventures that her singing career seemed no more than a nuisance. She longed to give up performing altogether. She walked through the concert in Bilbao like a robot, and received a chilly reception. Then in the Athens airport on the way back, she foolishly told reporters that Bilbao was a "silly little engagement." Needless to say, her disdain did not go over well in Spain.

Time magazine reported: "To the disappointment of her Spanish audience, she barely managed to rise above middle C, moving one critic to write: 'The Bilbao public demonstrated perfect manners in not showing greater disgust.' Then it was back to her sailor man, who was having something of a crisis himself."

Maria's mother, hunted down by reporters in New York, was happy to join the chorus. Like Meneghini, she loved talking to the press any time she could publicize her relationship with Callas and shoot a poisoned arrow at her daughter via the media. Evangelia Callas was easy to find in New York, where she was selling jewelry at the Manhattan shop of Madame Joli Gabor, the mother of Zsa Zsa. (The two had met during a television program featuring women with famous daughters, and Madame Gabor, moved by Evangelia's complaints of penury, hired her at once.) Asked about the scandal, Litsa spoke with a previously undemonstrated affection for her hapless son-in-law: "Meneghini was a father and a mother to Maria. Now she no longer needs him. But Maria will never be happy: my soul says it. Women like Maria can never know real love." To another reporter she carped: "I was Maria's first victim. Now it's Meneghini. Onassis will be the third. Maria would marry Onassis to further her limitless ambition."

Vengeance was perhaps cold comfort to Evangelia, who had long tried to get her daughter's attention by complaining to the press, writing letters begging for money, asking relatives to arrange meetings, even selling dolls that she dressed to represent Maria in her various opera roles. But despite Evangelia's efforts and all the family's attempts to effect a reconciliation, Maria grimly refused ever to speak to her mother again.

The rift first opened in 1950, when Maria flew from Italy for a triumphal series of concerts in Mexico City. On her way she stopped in New York to see her parents and found her mother in the hospital with an eye infection. She impulsively invited Evangelia to join her as soon as she was well enough to travel, whereupon the woman made a miraculous recovery. By displaying her new wealth and fame and the adoration of her fans, Maria undoubtedly hoped to impress her mother. Evangelia had dreamed of such a moment all her life, and when she arrived in Mexico, she found herself celebrated as the mother of the diva. Her hotel room was filled with flowers every day, and she was showered with invitations to embassy events, diplomatic receptions, premieres.

There were lavish gifts from Maria, too, and she gave her mother almost every dollar of the fees she made from the tour. In the end Evangelia was so reluctant to return to New York and her failing marriage that she stayed on after her daughter had left. But during the last days of the visit, Maria and her mother had a fight that would divide them forever.

Dozens of reasons have been postulated for the estrangement of mother and daughter, but after speaking to various Callas friends and relatives, I have concluded that the terrible sin for which Maria could not forgive her mother was quite simple, and as old as the story of Cain and Abel.

The first clue was given to me by Callas' friend Giulietta Simionato, the mezzo-soprano, who traveled with Maria during their Mexican tour.

She told me that Callas was wearing two diamond rings, and during her visit, Evangelia asked, "Why don't you give me one of your rings to give to Jackie?"

"The rings were the first two diamonds Battista had given to Maria," Madame Simionato told me when I interviewed her in Milan. "I remember, they were like two stars when she did *I Puritani* in Catania. We had gone together to get them at Farone, the jewelry store in Milan. I could even tell you the prices," she added. When Evangelia suggested Maria give one of the gems to her sister, the diva tartly replied, "No. When my sister works like me and meets a man like Battista, so too will she be fortunate and have jewelry. But Battista gave me this and I'm keeping it!" Mme. Simionata was shocked. "They argued, and almost punched each other. I said, 'Excuse me, but I have to go rest.'"

Jackie Callas confirmed this story in 1999 and also told me of another incident that, for Maria, was the last straw. Still courting her mother's love and approval, Callas took time out between performances in Mexico to shop with Evangelia, buying her a mink coat to wear at her social engagements in Mexico and in New York during the winter. Evangelia, however, had not yet learned her lesson. "They had a second fight when Mother saw a nice mink cape in the store and asked Maria to buy it for me. Maria hit the ceiling," said Jackie.

The episodes of the diamond rings and the mink stole, however dramatic, were by no means the only flash points of this acrimonious trip to Mexico in 1950. Evangelia was talking about divorcing her husband and Maria was desperately trying to dissuade her. She was still angry at her mother for taking her away from her father and moving to Greece in 1937. Evangelia herself complained that during her stay in Mexico, Maria used her as a laundress to wash her underwear (which was black from the makeup Maria had to wear for *Aida*). Years later, Evangelia would continue to wonder why Maria refused ever to see her or speak to her again, but clearly, having failed in this final effort to capture the primary spot in her mother's heart, Maria resolutely shut the door.

After the Mexico trip, the relationship disintegrated in an angry exchange of letters. When Evangelia wrote asking for more money, Maria advised her to get a job and, failing that, to "go and drown yourself"—a barb that was prominently featured in a *Time* cover story on the diva. Evangelia cursed her daughter in kind. "I have embraced you, my child, many times," she wrote (in Greek) in a letter to Maria that I have obtained. "But if I embrace you just once more, my embrace will become a heavy chain around your neck forever. Then you will see how you sing and what happiness you can expect."

For the next twenty-five years, Evangelia continued to publicize and exploit her relationship to her daughter in every way she could, and Maria's godfather and sister tried repeatedly to persuade the singer to reconcile, or at least communicate, with her mother. Maria may well have had frequent occasion to ponder the traditional Greek belief which holds that no other oath is as potent as a mother's curse, but she would remain characteristically unyielding to the day she died.

While the press were hounding Maria's mother and her husband for juicy quotes about the scandal, Tina Onassis was guarding her silence but making plans. She had arrived in New York saying she was going to enter her children in school there. (In fact, she eventually enrolled them in a Paris lycée.) She was seen dining with her lawyer, her brother, George Livanos, and "some friends from Brazil" at Henri Soulé's Pavillon restaurant. Reinaldo Herrera provided her with moral support during these stressful days, but he had to be extremely discreet so as not to undermine Tina's position as the injured party in the divorce dispute. "The lawyers told us we couldn't see each other in New York," he recalled. But the couple did arrange to meet in Puerto Rico during this time, she coming from New York on a private plane and he flying from Caracas, he said.

As soon as Aristo's business in Greece was finished, he and Maria sailed back to Monte Carlo, where she disembarked. She then flew straight to London for a scheduled concert at the Royal Festival Hall on September 23. Her performance received much better reviews than her engagement in Spain—"One of the most dramatic and memorable nights in London's music," gushed one critic. Nevertheless, Maria knew her voice was beginning to fail her, and the tensions and distractions of "la scandale" did not help her concentration.

Furious at her husband's melodramatic statements to the press after she sailed away with Onassis, Maria warned Meneghini from London, according to his memoir, "Be careful, Battista: one day or another I'm going to arrive at Sirmione with a revolver and I'm going to kill you." His response was no less heated: " 'Fine,' I shouted at her, 'and I'll be waiting to machine-gun you down.' " He concluded sadly, "That was the final break: violent and irreparable. It seemed impossible to believe that we were so in love only a few weeks before." It would be the last time in their lives they spoke to each other.

On September 28, Meneghini filed for a legal separation in Brescia, Italy, despite having loudly vowed two weeks earlier to fight Onassis and his millions to the end and win Maria back. ("Italian law does not permit divorce and if a legal separation is granted, neither party would be free to remarry in Italy," the *New York Times* pointed out.) The suit did not mention Onassis by name but charged that Maria's behavior was "incompatible with elementary decency." Meneghini claimed, "After a cruise in which we both took part alongside of persons who are reckoned the most powerful of our time, the attitude of Signora Callas changed abruptly in an altogether unexpected and unforeseen manner." It was then that his formerly "loyal and grateful wife," he said, began going to nightclubs and keeping company with a man "whom she described as her lover." The settlement hearing was eventually scheduled for November 14.

A small news article, dated October 11, states: "Operatic star Maria Callas was reported today to be back in the villa which her husband occupied last Monday. Madame Callas had been living in the villa since their marriage broke down last month. When her husband, Signor Meneghini, moved in while she was shopping, she said she would not return till he left. He moved out last night." Sometime in October, Meneghini had evidently made an effort to take over the Milan villa by right of possession, but by month's end Maria was securely entrenched.

Hunkered down in her Milan bunker, Maria seemed to be avoiding many of her acquaintances. Her friend Helen Rochas later said, "She suffered from a 'back-street complex'—of being the mistress. She needed the conventional status symbol of being a wife." It seems likely that shame was at the root of her new reticence. Nicola Rescigno, one of the diva's favorite conductors, whom I interviewed at his home in Rignona, outside Rome, observed that "as a person Maria was rather simple and quite conventional." When she informed him of her decision to leave her husband, her greatest concern was the reaction of Rescigno's mother, who lived in Queens and took a maternal interest in Maria. " 'Please tell her not to think too badly of me,' Maria pleaded," said Rescigno.

But not all the reproach Maria suffered was self-inflicted. Giulietta Simionato, her lifelong friend and colleague, told me she herself was among the many in Milan who berated Maria for cuckolding Meneghini: " 'You have behaved badly with Battista,' I told her, because I could scold her. She accepted everything from me. I said, 'The way you were in love with Battista, how could you fall in love with Onassis also?' " And, typically, the direct assault galvanized the guilty Callas, who shot back, "I believed that I was in love, but now I understand that what it was with Battista wasn't love. It was gratitude! Because I hadn't known love until I met Onassis!"

Elsa Maxwell, once first among Callas' defenders, aligned herself with Tina and against Maria whenever she spoke of the scandal. A few years later, in 1963, Maxwell would publish *The Celebrity Circus,* a frothy collection of anecdotes about her famous pals. In it she writes at length about Maria, "my musician of musicians, my diva of divas, a woman who has had a profound influence on the last few years of my life, an artist who has given me great joy, and great disappointment." But her admiration gives way to a sense of bereavement and elegy: "She has the mien of a goddess, yet she can rage like a spoiled, stupid child. She is a genius, and a witch. . . . Our friendship . . . blew cold when I discovered her incapacity for lasting friendship, for loyalty, trust, truth or honesty." Maxwell's coup de grace is fortified with the starchy moralism of the 1950s: "I have not been able to defend her or explain her as a person since August of 1959, when Tina Onassis invited her and Meneghini aboard the Christina for that fateful cruise."

Even in this withering indictment, however, Maxwell cannot repress her profound ambivalence and does rise to the formerly beloved's defense: "When she and Meneghini separated, she learned that he had not even paid for the jewels he had given her. She realized further that during her marriage she had not learned to write a check, nor had she, at any time, more than a few francs in her purse. She had met no one socially, gone nowhere. She had been kept a child. . . . What is ahead for this extraordinary woman, I cannot say. But I know one thing: when I once wrote that she had forever removed opera from the dustbin, I said a mouthful!" Perhaps the most telling gesture in the schizophrenic Celebrity Circus is the dedication: "To M.C. With great admiration and affection and love."

Under the weight of public criticism, Maria couldn't bear to face her Italian friends in Milan. She took refuge on the Christina with Onassis, spending most of her time there between performances. But she found she could speak more frankly about her love affair with her American friends like Mary Carter, whom she saw while in the States for scheduled appearances in Kansas City on October 28 and in Dallas, where she did two performances of Lucia di Lammermoor, on November 6 and 8, followed by two performances of Medea, on November 19 and 21.

Maria landed at New York's Idlewild Airport on the morning of October 27. She was being guided toward a limousine waiting to take her to La Guardia Airport and the plane for Kansas City when she was ambushed by reporters and a hailstorm of questions about her affair with Onassis. As the flashbulbs popped in her face, Maria abruptly lost her cool, slipping from the role of dignified diva known for enunciating a Garboesque "I want to be left alone" into that of a frightened and furious New York native who howled in less than melodious tones: "Get those wires out from under my feet. Lay off, will you?!" By the time she got to the theater, Maria was tense and unprepared to go on; she told her friend Larry Kelly of the Dallas Civic

Opera Company, who had come to Kansas City, "I've only come because of you." There was a bomb scare at the Midland Theater, and the audience, which included the former president Harry Truman, had to be evacuated for a time, but in the end Maria sang to boisterous applause. Then she headed to Dallas, accompanied by Mary Carter, who had flown up from Texas.

It was during this reunion with her old friend in Dallas that Maria gushed about Onassis and his lovemaking skills. Given her own complicated love life, "Maria Seconda" was much less judgmental than Maria's circle in Italy. "She was ecstatic," Mary Carter told me. "She wanted to give up her career, give up everything and be with him." Maria described every detail of Onassis' attentions: "She said he always took time to satisfy her. That had never happened to her before. She was in heaven! She said that she was madly in love with Onassis, that performing was a chore for her now and all she wanted was 'to be his woman.' She had this girlish quality about her."

The trip to Dallas was plagued by mishaps that strained Maria's already taut nerves to the breaking point. The company's shortage of funds was mainly to blame, Mary Carter told me. "For the *Lucia,* the company hadn't paid the costumer in Italy and he hadn't sent Maria's costumes. I called Stanley Marcus, and Neiman's outfitted her for the role. She was so upset, she missed the E-flat in the mad scene. After the performance she went back to the dressing room, muttering to herself, 'I had the note. What happened?' When she got back to the dressing room she hit the note solidly half a dozen times to prove to everyone and herself that it was a fluke." (In the second performance of *Lucia* she eliminated the E-flats altogether.)

Maria told her friend Giovanna Lomazzi, "I gambled my career tonight, my career ends here." Lomazzi, who together with Bruna had accompanied Maria to the United States, shared a hotel suite with her during the trip to Dallas. She told me when I interviewed her in Rome in 1999, "After that performance, about three a.m. I heard her sobbing. I tried to comfort her, to reassure her, but she couldn't stop. It was so difficult to handle the situation. She continued to cry until the morning. For her, singing was a great struggle and she realized she no longer had the strength to fight on her own terms."

Maria had to cancel her scheduled Dallas appearance in *The Barber of Seville* and fly to Italy to attend the settlement hearing with Battista on November 14. Callas' and Meneghini's appearance in Brescia drew crowds to the door of the courthouse, eager to witness the latest act in the drama. She was accompanied by another Italian friend, Carla Nani Mocenigo, who later described Maria's mounting terror as they arrived in the town to face the assembled crowd, who had cheered Meneghini when he entered the courthouse earlier.

Desperate to postpone the ordeal, Maria insisted they stop at a pharmacy on a secluded side street to buy a nail file. The salesgirl, overwhelmed by Callas' presence, made the diva take some perfume samples as a gift. Characteristically, Maria was so pleased and distracted by the offering of the tiny bottles that she was still examining them as she walked through the crowd of reporters and gawkers on the courthouse steps, who stared at her in silence. Carla ordered that she stop playing with the perfumes "on such a serious occasion." Maria put the samples in her purse and took off her glasses. "Now I'm fine," she told her friend. (Maria was extremely nearsighted, and often used this technique to ease the paralysis of stage fright; without her glasses, she could see neither the audience nor the conductor.) "Meneghini will be nothing but a blur."

The hearing lasted six hours. When it was over, the separation was legal and Maria had been awarded the Milan townhouse, most of her jewelry, and the income from her recording royalties, while Meneghini got Sirmione and all the jointly held real estate. The paintings and all other valuables were to be divided equally.

When Maria flew back to Dallas to complete her engagement there (she was scheduled to sing Medea on November 19), she discovered that the airplane seat next to hers had been reserved for a giant arrangement of red roses from Onassis; it was the kind of extravagant, romantic gesture that was typical of him and never ceased to enchant her.

Only eleven days later, on November 25, Tina Onassis finally made her move. She filed for divorce in the New York State Supreme Court on the grounds of adultery (the only grounds then admissible in New York). She asked for custody of Alexander, eleven, and Christina, nine. That evening she called a press conference at her Sutton Square home, and as she listened tearfully, her attorney, Sol Rosenblatt, read her statement to the reporters:

> *It is almost thirteen years since Mr. Onassis and I were married in New York City. Since then he has become one of the world's richest men, but his great wealth has not brought me happiness with him nor, as the world knows, has it brought him happiness with me. After we parted this summer in Venice, I had hoped that Mr. Onassis loved our children enough and respected our privacy sufficiently to meet with me—or, through lawyers, with my lawyers—to straighten out our problems. But that was not to be.*
>
> *Mr. Onassis knows positively that I want none of his wealth and that I am solely concerned with the welfare of our children.*

I deeply regret that Mr. Onassis leaves me no alternative other than a New York suit for divorce.

For my part I will always wish Mr. Onassis well, and I expect that after this action is concluded he will continue to enjoy the kind of life which he apparently desires to live, but in which I have played no real part. I shall have nothing more to say and I hope I shall be left with my children in peace.

Ari and Maria were aboard the *Christina*, which was anchored in Monte Carlo, when Tina's statement—a self-portrait as a martyred wife and saintly mother—came out in the New York papers. Costa Gratsos, Ari's head of operations in the United States, who read it to him over the telephone, quipped, "This stuff's been written by lawyers and scored for Jascha Heifetz."

Despite Tina's claims that she wanted none of her husband's wealth, Onassis later told the journalist Willi Frischauer that Sol Rosenblatt was putting forward massive claims on behalf of his client. Frischauer reports that in the end, Tina kept her jewelry, worth an estimated four million dollars, as well as the Sutton Square home and its contents.

The bombshell in Tina's divorce suit was the name of the "other woman." She charged that her husband had engaged in adulterous conduct "by land and sea in the United States, France, Monte Carlo, Greece and Turkey from 1957 up to the present time" with a certain "Mrs. J.R." This was soon revealed to be Tina's old school friend Jeanne-Marie Rhinelander, whom she had introduced to Ari back in the days when they were living at the Château de la Croë on the Riviera, and whom she later discovered in bed with her husband when she paid an unannounced visit to La Bastide, Rhinelander's house near Grasse. There was a strategic reason behind Tina's decision to name her friend. If she had named Maria, Ari could quickly countersue, citing Tina's long affair with Herrera. She had to name a corespondent whom Ari had slept with *before* Tina's own adulterous affairs began.

"Onassis still didn't want to agree to a divorce, until Tina told him she had a key to the safe deposit box in Panama that had all the bearer shares of his corporation in it and if he wanted the key back he had to cooperate," Reinaldo Herrera told me. "Finally, he did. All this, of course, was suggested by Sol Rosenblatt, who was a brilliant divorce lawyer. And I know what she paid him. One million dollars, which was a lot of money in 1959."

After Tina's statement, Ari quickly went into action. He moved Maria from his yacht into a suite at the Hermitage Hotel, and issued a comment of his own: "I have just heard that my wife has begun divorce proceedings. I am not surprised, the situation has been moving rapidly. But I was not warned. Obviously I shall have to do what she wants and make suitable arrangements." Then he drove to Grasse to talk to Jeanne-Marie Rhinelander, a woman with a history of emotional problems. He was worried that she might panic or lose her temper at being dragged into the fray and say something that would only make the situation worse. Ari's diplomatic skill and charm seem to have prevailed. The tall divorcée eventually gave up an earlier threat to sue for slander and issued a statement showing remarkable composure: "I am an old friend of Mr. and Mrs. Onassis. I am astonished that after so many years of friendship of which everybody knew, here and in the United States, Mrs. Onassis should try to use it as an excuse to obtain her freedom. . . . I repeat that I know Mr. Onassis and that I remain a devoted friend."

On the night that Tina's statement appeared in the press, Onassis dined in Monte Carlo with Prince Rainier and Princess Grace. Callas was not there. Soon thereafter, as Ari ranted and complained to friends and barraged Tina with calls pleading for a reconciliation, Maria tactfully retreated to Milan, to her home on Via Buonarotti.

Friends of Onassis' reported him moping around Monte Carlo day and night. Spyros Skouras said that Ari "sobbed like a child" in his suite at Claridge's after pleading for an hour on the phone with Tina to change her mind about the divorce. Ari himself later told Stelios Papadimitriou that he would go to the farthest edge of Monte Carlo's harbor, where the waves pound the rocks, and howl with grief and frustration over the loss of his wife.

It is remarkable how long he continued to imagine and wish he could retain both wife and mistress. Ari and Tina were hardly happy together and hadn't even shared their lives and interests in the last years of their marriage, but Tina was Onassis' possession, his "third child," as he often remarked to friends, and she was the mother of Christina and Alexander. Earlier, when quizzed by reporters in Venice as to whether his private cruise with Maria meant a separation between himself and his wife, Onassis replied nervously, "I don't like to think about it. We've been married for thirteen years. A father would be crazy if he wanted to separate his children from their mother." It was a fight—this time for a reconciliation—into which Ari drew an impressive troop of conscripts. Everyone intervened in the fray, from Princess Grace and Elsa Maxwell to Lady Churchill, all trying to convince Tina to reconcile. But having seen the light of freedom at the end of the tunnel, she remained unmoved by the sentimental appeals of her well-intentioned friends.

Ironically, many months later, when Tina finally got the divorce she had wanted for so long, she and Reinaldo Herrera did not seize the opportunity to marry. In fact, Tina's freedom eventually led to a bittersweet parting between the young lovers.

Herrera told me his father had warned him, out of a strong sense of propriety, to stay away from Tina and remain at home in Caracas during the divorce proceeding. "In those days, one paid attention to his parents. So I promised I would. Tina was very annoyed: 'Why have you abandoned me? Why aren't you here?' But I had promised my father. So I stayed in Caracas for almost six months."

When the divorce was final, Herrera immediately went to New York and began seeing Tina again. "But we had a big problem with Alexander. Ari kept calling the boy and talking to him for hours and he became uncontrollable. One day we came home and all the windows in the Sutton Square house were broken. Alexander had gone around breaking them because she was seeing me.

"My father was in a state about the whole thing too, and we decided not to see each other for a few weeks. I went to Venezuela and my father later told me Tina was seeing someone else. I finally came up to New York and we met at the Carlton House Restaurant on Madison, which was, and is, a very sedate place where we were not likely to run into any people we knew.

"We decided we should break off for a while. We agreed we wouldn't see each other for three years. We both cried."

It was a sad Christmas season for all the players in this game of marital musical chairs. Onassis in Monte Carlo continued to sulk, rant, and plead for a reconciliation. Meneghini in Sirmione kept all Maria's things just as she'd left them, even her cosmetics and perfumes on a shelf in their bedroom and the green jacket she'd left behind, hanging on a door. To the end of his life, everything would remain in pathetic readiness for Maria's return.

Meanwhile Maria celebrated her thirty-sixth birthday quietly in Milan. Only a few days later her archrival, the soprano Renata Tebaldi, opened at La Scala in *Tosca* after an absence of five years, and received triumphant applause and an onslaught of flowers. Milan's opera lovers, to whom Callas had so long been the reigning deity, now were enthralled by Tebaldi. When asked whether she would attend the opening, Maria declined without a trace of envy or regret: "Now that Renata Tebaldi returns to La Scala, public attention should be focused on this important event without direct or indirect interference of any kind. I have closed many chapters this year; it is my sincere wish that this chapter too be closed."

Singing at La Scala or anywhere else was far from Maria's mind, and she stayed quietly ensconced in her villa on Via Buonarotti with only Bruna and her poodle Toy for company. Just as she never for a moment looked back longingly on her marriage once she made the decision to leave

Meneghini for the man she considered to be her destiny, she now resolved unflinchingly to forget about her once all-consuming art.

Even Onassis' insistence that she keep singing to remain in the public eye could not persuade her. After her last performance of *Medea* in Dallas, Maria had no more engagements scheduled. She would not sing in public again until August of 1960—a silence of nine months. Maria had more important things on her mind. As she celebrated the end of the most tumultuous year in her stormy life, she was indeed planning to close one chapter and open another. She was already almost five months pregnant with Aristotle Onassis' child.

14

THE SECRET SON

If we cease to grieve,
We may cease to remember.

Plutarch, *Letter of Consolation to His Wife*

In all the books, articles, and dramatizations of the love affair between Maria Callas and Aristotle Onassis, the defining moment is seen to be the abortion that the tycoon reportedly forced Maria to have in 1966, despite her lifelong desire for a child.

It makes a good fulcrum for the drama of their relationship and fits the popular conception of Onassis as a selfish brute, indifferent to both Maria's art and her feelings, and of Callas as a woman who sacrificed everything for the love of a man who discarded her when she was no longer useful to him. There is only one problem with this story—it isn't true.

The tale of the abortion was first reported in Arianna Stassinopoulos' biography *Maria: Beyond the Callas Legend,* published in England in 1980, three years after the diva's death. (It appeared in 1981 in the United States as *Maria Callas: The Woman Behind the Legend.*) "Now, at the age of forty-three, she found herself pregnant," writes Stassinopoulos, placing the event in 1966–67.

All her instincts, everything in her that longed for life, wanted a child. Onassis did not. It was painful enough to have the man she adored reject instead of celebrate the child of their love, but he went further: he warned her that if she went ahead and kept the child it would be the end of their relationship. She was pitched into a torrent of doubt, fear, confusion. Her decision betrayed everything real and life-giving in her for the sake of a relationship that was increasingly tenuous and unreal. The aborted baby, at the moment when she longed for a new source of energy and meaning, was her life's greatest might-have-been. . . . Her choosing to give in to Onassis' will was the turning point. Her second great dream was slowly souring into nightmare. From then on their quarrels were only temporarily mended: they never really ceased.

Most subsequent books about Callas have followed a similar line, some of them specifying that the procedure was performed aboard the *Christina* in the summer of 1966. The abortion is also the harrowing climax of the play *Master Class,* by Terrence McNally, which has been performed in most major cities around the world. In an agonized speech in the second act, McNally has Maria movingly recount the pain it caused her to obey Ari's command:

> *I have news, Ari, such great and wonderful news. I'm going to have your child. No, our child, our son. I would not insult you by giving you a daughter. And we will name him Odysseus for the greatest Greek hero of them all, like you, and because he wandered the world the longest, like me, until he came home to love.*
>
> *No, I don't need your child to feel like a woman. I am a woman. I don't need anything. Some people would say I don't need you. I want a child. Your child. I love you. There, I've said it.*
>
> *Don't ask me to do that. Why would you ask me to do that? What do you mean, you've changed your mind? I'm not a young woman. This may be my only chance. I'll give up anything, my career even, everything I've worked for, but not this.*
>
> *Then don't marry me. I won't do it. You can't make me. I won't let you make me!*
>
> *Don't leave me! I've been alone all my life until now!*
>
> *O child I will never see or know or nurse or say how much I love you, forgive me.*
>
> *It's done, Ari.*

In fairness to Stassinopoulos, McNally, et al., it must be acknowledged that this Sturm und Drang was not made up out of whole cloth. After Onassis married Jacqueline Kennedy, Maria did tell a number of close friends that he had forced her to have an abortion two years earlier. Arianna Stassinopoulos cites three of Maria's friends—Edith Gorlinsky, Anastasia Gratsos, and Nadia Stancioff—as sources. Nadia recounted Maria's words in *Maria Callas Remembered,* published in 1987: " 'At first I couldn't believe he was serious,' she said on our way from Athens to Tragonissi in the summer of 1970. 'He said, "I don't want a baby by you! What would I do with another child? I already have two." The decision was torture. As you know, Nadia, I don't believe in abortion. It took me four months to make up my mind. Think how fulfilled my life would be if I'd stood up to him and kept the baby.' " Even Mary Carter, one of the most reliable observers of Callas' life, who spoke to me extensively about her twenty years as the diva's close friend, repeated the details Maria told her of an abortion that happened aboard the *Christina* in 1966, when Captain Kostas Anastasiades brought a doctor aboard.

Maria may well have had her reasons for telling her friends this wrenching tale of Onassis' cruelty after he left her for Jacqueline Kennedy, but three years of investigation, research, and interviews throughout the world have turned up no evidence that the abortion ever happened. However, I have found strong proof, including documents that Maria left behind in her private papers, that she did become pregnant by Onassis, not in 1966 but at the very start of their relationship, in 1959, and that she gave birth on March 30, 1960, in Milan to a baby boy, who died of natural causes later that day.

The published allegations that Maria became pregnant and that Onassis forced her to abort the child so incensed Meneghini that he sent a telegram about Stassinopoulos' book to the *London Times* in 1980 protesting the charge and insisting that his wife was unable to conceive a child. "But my telegram was published most inconspicuously," he complained to Stelios Galatopoulos, an opera critic who had befriended Maria. In his biography *Maria Callas: Sacred Monster* (published in Great Britain in 1998 and in the United States in 1999), Galatopoulos writes: "In one of my meetings with Callas as late as the spring of 1977, she specifically spoke about children: 'I would have been the happiest of women, if I had children and a happy family of course—surely the greatest ideal in life.' "

Galatopoulos adds that, after Maria's death and before Stassinopoulos' book was published, he asked Meneghini why they never had children.

Unable to conceal his tears, Meneghini said, "From the very beginning of our marriage we both dreamed of having a child. Any man would have been happy and indeed proud to have had children with this wonderful woman!" He then produced the medical report of 1957 [by consultant gynaecologist Carlo Palmieri], which diagnosed malformation of the womb. There was no remedy other than through a dangerous and highly experimental operation which might offer some faint hope but with severely damaging effects on her health and voice. Maria decided against it. The gynaecologist also diagnosed symptoms of early menopause and prescribed a series of injections which delayed it for about a year."

When Meneghini read of the alleged abortion he was overwhelmed with disbelief that Maria, who had the menopause before the age of thirty-five (a year before her separation from her husband) had become pregnant at forty-three and subsequently got rid of the child. He also felt that even Onassis (who was not Meneghini's favourite person) would not have acted in this way—no man would in the event of such a miracle—and that such information was false and published solely as lucrative sensationalism.

Galatopoulos is one of the few Callas biographers to conclude that the reports of the abortion are fiction. "In reality the child would have been her greatest weapon in keeping Onassis," he persuasively argues. "Even so, he married another, but Maria and Onassis maintained and deepened their friendship to his death. We are speaking here of a strong-minded woman with deeply rooted moral and religious values."

Many of Maria's published letters confirm her longing to have a child from the time she married Meneghini in 1949 and her bitter disappointment that the wish hadn't been fulfilled. On December 20, 1949: "I have to report again—still no baby! I had my period the eighteenth, right on schedule, along with a headache fit for our worst enemies. We must be patient. . . ." On June, 6, 1950: "Dear Battista, I have to make a confession. I want so much for us to have a baby. I also believe a baby would be good for my voice and my bad skin. What are your thoughts?"

The ostensible reason she could not fulfill her hopes of conceiving—what Meneghini called "malformation of the womb"—was, as Maria told several friends, a tipped uterus, a fairly common condition that makes it difficult, but not impossible, to conceive. A more likely reason for her problems in conceiving was Meneghini. He never did father a child by any woman, and Maria told her good friend Giovanna Lomazzi in Milan, while she was still married to him, that "she would like to have a child but Battista was too old and it was not possible to have a child with him."

Whoever was to blame, it is important to note Meneghini's reference to the fact that Maria's gynecologist, Carlo Palmieri, was giving her "a series of injections which [lasted] about a year" and that these injections, intended to stave off menopause, began in 1957.

Almost certainly the injections were estrogen hormones—the same therapy prescribed for women with infertility problems. A leading Milan gynecologist who was practicing at the time, Professor Gianbattista Candiani, recalled that in the late 1950s, if a woman was suffering from symptoms of premature menopause, she would be treated with Premarin, an estrogen hormone that would promote the continuation of a regular menstrual cycle. This would also be used, followed by another hormone, if she wanted to get pregnant. He said that if infertility arose from the inability of the uterus to hold the egg, then the Premarin alone might be enough to promote pregnancy.

If Maria had been receiving these injections regularly for at least a year (and perhaps two) beginning in May of 1957, then by the time she slept with Onassis in August of 1959, she might have been superfertile. She could well have conceived on her first sexual encounter with a man who, unlike her husband, was certainly capable of siring a child.

Maria did indeed conceive a child in early August of 1959 when she began having sex with Onassis. Upon learning that she was pregnant, she was overjoyed—but doubtless the news would not have made Aristo very happy. Callas and Onassis were both still married to others at the time.

Judging from Onassis' reaction to Tina's second pregnancy and his declared intention to have only one heir, it is likely that when he learned the news, Aristo would have asked Maria to have an abortion. Whatever he said to her, Maria firmly rejected the idea. As Galatopoulos points out, she had always wanted a baby, she had strong moral and religious objections to an abortion, and a child would have been her greatest weapon in keeping Onassis. Maria's ex-husband, many close friends, and her sister, Jackie, all insist that if she ever managed to conceive, no one and nothing—not even the fury of her lover Onassis—could make her destroy it. "Maria always wanted a baby so badly that there is no way that anyone, including Onassis, could have made her consider an abortion," Jackie Callas Stathopoulos told me.

Whatever arguments were raised by the unexpected conception, there is evidence from those closest to Maria that the couple made plans for the child's arrival. They began looking for a house in Switzerland where Maria would live and raise it. Between themselves they referred to this as "the Swiss project."

When Maria declined the invitation to attend Renata Tebaldi's triumphant return to La Scala in Milan just before Christmas of 1959, declaring "I have closed many chapters this year," she was nearly five months pregnant. She would not appear in public for the next several months, but did grant one notable exception: an interview that appeared in *France-Soir* on February 13, 1960, under the headline: LA CALLAS TOLD ME: "I NO LONGER FEEL LIKE SINGING . . . I WOULD LIKE TO HAVE A CHILD."

The interview, by Marlyse Schaeffer, is fascinating when one considers that Maria was nearly seven months pregnant at the time. The reporter describes how she encountered Maria at the Paris Opéra, evidently trying to avoid being seen, "so pale in her little black, slightly out-of-date ensemble, with her modest makeup, her new short hair." Ms. Schaeffer was surprised that Maria looked so commonplace, like an American tourist. "The proof, nobody recognised her." But when the reporter asked the *diva incognita* for an interview, she agreed to a meeting the next day in her apartment at the Ritz Hotel.

Maria received Schaeffer punctually, to the reporter's further astonishment, but declared immediately: "I have a horror of journalists, I give you fifteen minutes." Before long Schaeffer observed "a sudden need to confide (in the end she spoke for an hour and forty minutes . . .)."

As Maria poured forth her confessions—"Yes, Onassis and I have been very close. But it's not because of that, that Tina Onassis asked for a divorce. She's been thinking about it for two years"—Schaeffer noticed that the soprano's famously beautiful and slender hands had developed "thickened joints." These swollen extremities and the voluminous dress of "stiff faille" that Maria wore might have suggested she had something to hide, but Schaeffer indicates no suspicions to that effect.

Maria continues: "They have named me the Tigress. Of course I laugh, I hold my head high. . . . I am very proud. . . ." Then, "on the verge of tears," she speaks of turning down singing engagements and of being alone:

"I didn't say yes to L'Opéra for Medea, didn't say yes to La Scala, to Covent Garden. I no longer have a desire to sing. I wish to live, to live like any other woman. . . ." Her eye was becoming again black, terrible. . . . She added: "Perhaps it amuses you to think that I also had the desire to have a baby one day, that I wished for it, asked my husband. . . . Meneghini (she put all the scorn of the world in these syllables) answered me: 'That would make you lose a year of your career.' For he, he thought about my career. Much more than me. . . . But now, I refuse to sing. I can last for some time longer with the sale of my records. Then, we shall see. . . ."

Her voice low, whispering: "I want to live . . . to have a baby; I'm thirty-six years old, with no one in my life, and I do not even know if I am capable of giving the day to a being [i.e., giving birth]. . . . Do you understand? Do you understand this? What a lovely story to write: La Callas would like a baby. . . ."

She looks at me, as if to assure herself that I could understand, oblivious to the time passing, the maid, Bruna, who tidied the jumble of minks, the "Ritz" which stirred around us. . . . I had just had one hour and 40 minutes of an extraordinary spectacle.

Maria, secretly pregnant, is cornered by a photographer in Paris.

It seems plain, in retrospect, that this interview, granted impulsively, was Maria's way of telegraphing her case to the public: she was explaining her decision to give up her singing, everything, in order to have a child. At the same time, she was undeniably anguished and was worrying that she was going to lose Onassis because of his unhappiness about the breakup of his marriage, just when she needed him most.

There is also a photograph of Maria from this time in Paris—one of the most poignant ever taken. She sits huddled in the back of a chauffeured car, swathed in a fur coat, her hair now in an above-the-shoulder bob as Onassis had told her to cut it. She is pale, mournful, downcast, and very much alone in the back of the large limousine.

Shortly after the interview, Maria returned with Bruna and Toy to her villa in Milan. The time of her confinement was approaching and she would be getting little moral support from Onassis. He was scheduled to leave on March 8 for another long cruise with Sir Winston and Lady Churchill. This time they would be sailing from Gibraltar to Tangier to Las Palmas and then across the Atlantic Ocean to Barbados and the Virgin Islands.

To make matters worse, her mother, living in a seedy hotel room in a decaying section of New York, had just published *My Daughter Maria Callas,* in which she rehashed at book length her stories of Maria's ingratitude and cruelty. In interviews Evangelia gave from her rundown abode, she attributed Maria's tantrums and character pathologies to a head injury she suffered in a car accident at the age of five. She also took the opportunity to advertise her interest in finding herself a rich husband, now that she was separated from Callas' father.

The vindictive book cut Maria deeply at a moment when she was most vulnerable, as Vicky Anthopoulou, the niece of her close friend the Greek pianist Vasso Devetzi, explained to me. As a student in Paris from 1980 to 1987, Vicky lived with Vasso and heard her aunt's daily stories about Callas. "Often Maria would say that she had never read her mother's book, in order to avoid discussing it," Ms. Anthopoulou said. "In truth, however, for days after she received it and read it, she closed herself in her room and did not speak to anyone. . . . At the critical moment when her hopes were about to be fulfilled, the man she loved and the father of her child had abandoned her for another cruise with his friends, and her own mother was not by her side to help her but on the contrary was stabbing her in a vicious way."

As Maria usually did when her mother burst into print with criticisms of her, she wrote to her godfather, Dr. Leonidas Lantzounis, who lived in New York and acted on her behalf in dealing with her mother's outrageous behavior. She asked him to handle the problem, and she wrote lines that carried more significance than he could guess: "I don't want to sing anymore. I want to live, just like a normal woman, with children, a home, a dog." This was Maria's goal as she entered the eighth month of her pregnancy.

While her mother was attacking her in print, Onassis was sailing farther and farther away on the *Christina*. His guests were the Churchills, the Montague Brownes, Churchill's elderly doctor, Lord Moran, and his wife, and Theodore and Artemis Garofalidis. Though a hemisphere away, he called Maria daily from the yacht. The cruise was due to end April 3. But Maria's loneliness at his absence slowly gave way to dread at the prospect of his return.

She feared having him see her swollen and nine months pregnant. She felt ugly and awkward and wished he could find her slim again, and holding their baby in her arms. Although well aware of Aristo's insistence that no child would ever challenge the primacy of Alexander—the alpha and omega of his father's affections—she longed for the baby to be a boy. She was sure that, once Onassis saw the son they had made together, he would love it as much as she did. In the hope of presenting her returning lover with a fait accompli, Maria spoke to Dr. Palmieri (who died in 1992 at the age of ninety) and pressured him to deliver the child early—by cesarean section—as soon as it was safe to do so. Dr. Palmieri apparently agreed to do as she wished.

Early on the morning of Wednesday, March 30, Callas arrived at Clinica Dezza on Via Dezza 48 accompanied by Bruna. She was anesthetized and Palmieri made a horizontal incision below her navel. He delivered a baby boy. Soon, however, the tiny infant began to have difficulty breathing. The clinic was not equipped to deal with the crisis and an ambulance was called to rush the baby to a better-equipped facility. On the way, seeing that the baby was about to die, a nurse baptized him "in the air." She gave him the name Maria had told her she had chosen if it was a boy: Omero Lengrini.

The surname is a mystery—it may have been the pseudonym under which Maria had registered at the clinic—but Omero, not a common first name in Italy, has an unmistakable significance. Omeros in Greek—Homer in English—was the name of Onassis' uncle, the one who had trained him to become a champion swimmer in Smyrna, had given him his love of the sea, and had died of a heart attack in Athens in 1944. It seems an inescapable conclusion that Maria and Onassis together had chosen this name for their son. Aristotle had given the name of his other favorite uncle, Alexander, to his son by Tina.

When Maria awoke from the anesthesia, Dr. Palmieri told her that her son had died. His lungs, the doctor said, had not been strong enough. Bruna sat beside her mistress and wiped away her tears. What would prove to be Maria's only chance for the child she had always longed for was now dead and cold and she hadn't even seen him.

While Maria lay in the clinic, there was a call from Onassis on board the *Christina*. He had called the house on Via Buonarroti and learned where she was. He asked Bruna, his voice tense with concern, what was going on. Had Maria become ill? Were there problems with the pregnancy?

Without answering him, Bruna handed the telephone to her mistress, then sat there and listened as Maria told her lover that their son, Omeros, had been born and had died; had lived his entire life in the space of two hours. Alexander Onassis was still the first and the last.

Municipality of Milan
Civil Service Branch
Bureau of Vital Statistics
"Extract from a Resume of the Birth Certificate"

Year 1960 Number 0615 Register 08 Part 1 Series A

The 30th day of the month of March
of the year one thousand nine hundred sixty
at the hour of eight and zero minutes
at the house listed as Via Dezza number 48

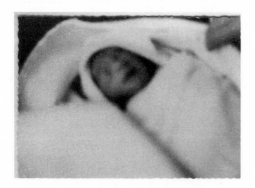

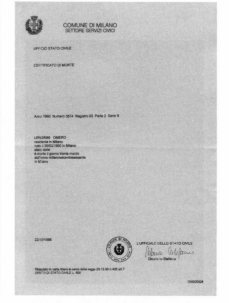

The secret love child was born and died on the same day, March 30, 1960, in Milan.
Here, a picture of the dead infant, and Milanese documents attesting to his short life

in the municipality of Milan
was born LENGRINI, OMERO

Marginal notation: *Died in Milan 30/3/1960.*

A rubber stamp on the "reminder of the birth certificate," which refers to this document, reads:

Born alive and died before the announcement of the birth.

The tiny body of Omero was buried in a cemetery in Milan beneath a small stone. But before the burial, a photograph was taken of the baby. It's an odd photograph, matte black-and-white, only three inches by four inches, with scalloped edges—odd because it's out of focus, although it bears a photographer's stamp on the back. Despite the poor quality, the image is unmistakably that of a dead baby—mouth open, eyes closed, cheeks sunken—wrapped in a white blanket with fabric draped around his head like a hood. The body is in some sort of white-lined container. The stamp on the back reads "Ottica Zeta, Buonarroti 5, 481-846 Milano." It is the mark of Zeta Optics, a shop only a few doors down the street from Maria's villa at Buonarroti 40.

The story of this baby's birth and death has never been told. Maria spoke of it to only three people: her lifelong and obsessively loyal servants, Bruna Lupoli and Ferruccio Mezzadri, and the Greek pianist Vasso Devetzi, who became Maria's closest Paris friend at the end of her life.

After Maria's death in September 1977, Vasso Devetzi made herself the keeper of many of Callas' private papers. In 1986, as the tenth anniversary of the death approached, Vasso felt a responsibility to put down her memories of Maria in a book, which she told a writer friend would be "the only authentic testimony." It would be "the book of remembrances," he recalls her saying—that "she wanted to write about her Great Friend, the Great Diva, the Divina, as she called her . . . so that at last a dam might be erected against the endless lies and myths that had collected, greatly enlarged, of course, around the legend of her friend. . . . She wanted to rescue, to tell the few details she knew about her, so that she herself could at some point depart from this life unburdened."

Needing help with the book, Vasso asked her friend Vasilis Vasilikos, a Greek journalist and the author of the political thriller *Z*, to come to her apartment in Passy to hear the true story of Maria's life. (His recollection of Vasso's statement is quoted in the previous paragraph, translated from his original Greek.) Vasilikos did agree to come, and brought with him his companion, a woman who aspired to be an opera singer. Vasso offered to help the woman in her career if Vasilikos would listen to her memories and then write the book about Maria.

Every morning for about three weeks, according to Vasilikos, Vasso Devetzi brought from "the Great Diva's archives" piles of letters, contracts, interviews, photographs, even tape recordings of her telephone conversations, but she would never allow him to take notes, use a tape recorder, or even hold and read the documents himself. Finally succumbing to frustration—and an "emotional crisis" with his love—Vasilikos returned to Greece, but not before Devetzi had extracted from him a promise "that you will not speak about this story, you will not write anything. . . ."

A year later, after Vasso Devetzi died, Vasilikos broke his promise. He wrote a novella in Greek based on his experiences in Paris, using fictitious names for all the characters (he called Vasso "Zoe" and referred to Maria only as "the Diva"). It was published in a book of stories and essays called *The Eviction* (*To Sfrato*). The section about Maria was entitled "Chronicle of a Testament That Was Not Written" and subtitled "About the Diva." Only two lines are devoted to the birth of the child of the diva and the tycoon, mentioning that it happened during an attempted delivery the same year they met, and that the child died two hours later, after being baptized "in the air" with the name Angelo.

Vasso Devetzi died in September of 1987 with the burden of Maria's unwritten testament still weighing on her soul. At that point, her archive of Callas documents disappeared.

Eventually, however, certain papers relating to the life and death of the infant Omero came into my hands, including the blurry photograph of the small corpse and copies of other official documents relating to the boy's birth and death. The events to which these documents testify are known firsthand by two people alive today—Bruna and Ferruccio, Maria's servants, who cared for her every day until her death.

Bruna Lupoli lives in a small villa in Travagola Pedavena, the provincial Italian village where she was born in 1921. Her loyalty to her mistress is unwavering and she has steadfastly refused to speak to reporters, scholars, friends, fans, or anyone else who asked about Maria. But in 1999 she agreed for the first time to answer some key questions. I was able to put these to her only through an intermediary, a person who had been close to Vasso Devetzi in the years after Maria's death, when Bruna and Ferruccio would often gather at Vasso's home in Passy to reminisce about their beloved mistress. (Every year, on the anniversary of Maria's death, September 16, Vasso held a memorial service and Bruna would always come to Paris from Italy to attend it. After church they would pay a visit to Père Lachaise cemetery, where Maria had been cremated, then go back to Vasso's apartment to sit and talk of their departed friend.) My written inquiries were posed to Bruna over the course of many telephone conversations. Because the subject was so painful, she could endure only a few questions each time. The description of the birth and death of Omero given above is based on her recollections, and is supported by the picture and documents left behind by Maria in her private papers.

Bruna was the one person who shared every secret of Maria's life from the day she entered the Meneghinis' service in 1954 to the day Callas died in her arms in the Paris apartment at 36 Avenue Georges Mandel. Maria herself once spoke about Bruna's importance to her in an emotional outburst that was taped by John Ardoin:

> *If you can't trust your husband or your mother, to whom do you turn? When I go back to Paris, you know who takes care of me and who I know will always be there? My maid Bruna, who adores me and who has been a nurse, sister and mother to me. She is only two years older. When I was in the hospital she didn't want the nurse to touch me, for she was ashamed to humiliate me, to have a nurse clean me. Imagine that such a person should exist today. . . . They are very rare. But she shouldn't have been there. It should have been my mother and my sister. . . . The people who have been the closest to me have hurt me the most. . . .*
>
> *After nine years, not a child, not a family, not a friend! That's very little, you know. And you say, God, why? Why should these things happen?*

Bruna was categorical concerning Maria's reproductive history: "Madame never had an abortion in 1966, 1967, or any other time. She never got pregnant except that one time when the baby was delivered in the eighth month and lived for one day. She had a scar in the lower section of the middle of her stomach because the baby was delivered by cesarean." (The existence of this scar was also confirmed to me in 1998 by Korinna Spanidou, the physical therapist who worked for Onassis and Maria on the *Christina* in the summer of 1964. "I didn't ask her what it was from, because I didn't want to be intrusive in case it was for some gynecological procedure," Mrs. Spanidou told me.)

"Mr. Onassis was very upset when he called her at the clinic and learned the boy had died," Bruna continued. "They were going to buy a house in Switzerland and raise the boy there. I never heard either of them talk about not having it. She was never pregnant before or after that time. I am certain of that."

*Ferruccio Mezzadri (right), Maria's former butler, sits with the author
in his home, a shrine to his former employer.*

Maria evidently also spoke of her 1960 pregnancy to Giuseppe di Stefano, the noted tenor who was her lover near the end of her life. When I
interviewed him in May of 1998 at his home near Lake Como, however, he
said, "I never believed her story." He was familiar with Maria's habit of casting herself as a victim and he mockingly imitated the sound of her voice
uttering her complaint: "Nobody noticed that I was pregnant!" With a
laugh he added, "How could I believe her, that she was pregnant all that
time and nobody noticed?"

Not so dismissive of the pregnancy was Ferruccio Mezzadri, Maria's
butler from October of 1957, when he was twenty-two years old, until she
died twenty years later. Like Bruna, he left Meneghini's employ and followed Maria to Paris after she split with her husband. Like Bruna, Ferruccio
has rejected every request to speak about his dead mistress, but he did agree
to meet me and answer questions at his home, Villa Nova, near Bussetto in
northern Italy, on March 10, 1999. A cherub-faced man of sixty-three when
I interviewed him, Ferruccio is fifteen years younger than Bruna; like her, he
never married, but devoted his life to Maria until the end.

Receiving me hospitably in his two-storey house, which he built on the
plot of land where he was born, Ferruccio brought me coffee prepared
Greek style, just as Maria had taught him. His walls are completely covered
with paintings and photographs of Callas, and the material remains of her

life, such as her eyeglasses, pens, and combs, are preserved in glass cases like the relics of a saint.

Ferruccio indignantly rejected the idea that Maria had ever had an abortion, as dramatized in the play *Master Class:* "This never happened. Madame would not have done such a thing, no matter who asked her," he insisted. "I've heard about the play. It was performed here, but it is all wrong."

But when I asked him about a baby, born on March 30, 1960, who died the same day, and when I showed him the birth and death certificates, Ferruccio's faced turned pale and he swallowed hard before asking me, "Who told you about this?"

When I then showed him a copy of the photo of the dead baby and told him it had been named Omero, for Onassis' uncle, Ferruccio did not deny the authenticity of the documents but said only, "I'm sorry, but this is not something I will discuss."

While Maria was recuperating from the operation at the Clinica Dezza, Onassis was ending his cruise in Puerto Rico. Shortly after he had flown the Churchills back to London (on an Olympic Airways jet specially equipped with actual beds) he was seen dining with Tina in Paris. Some viewed this meeting as another effort at reconciliation—Lady Churchill, in particular, had expressed her hope that Tina and Ari would get back together—but it was more likely an attempt by Ari to convince Tina to soften the terms of the divorce suit and not sue on the basis of adultery with Jeanne-Marie Rhinelander. His maneuver may have worked: soon thereafter, in June, Tina slipped into Alabama to obtain a "quickie" divorce on the basis of mental cruelty. At approximately the same time, Ari and Maria traveled together to see the Château du Jonchet in Eure-et-Loir, with the intention of buying it.

If he was secretly relieved that the infant son had died at birth, Onassis never admitted it to Maria. In fact, on his return from the cruise he was more affectionate and more attentive to her than he had ever been. That spring of 1960 marked the beginning of what she would later describe as the happiest period of their relationship.

Nevertheless, with the death of the boy, Maria had lost the most important potential weapon in her battle to keep Aristo always by her side, and she knew it. Much later, after he had waffled for nine years about marrying her and then suddenly married Jacqueline Kennedy, Maria was quoted as saying bitterly: "I should have insisted that he marry me in 1960. Then he would have done it."

The death of her son would haunt Maria until the end of her life. "Madame went to visit her son's grave whenever she was in Milan and sometimes made special trips from Paris just to go there," Bruna told my intermediary: "I would go with her. Many times at night when she would get drowsy and start to fall asleep she would start talking about the boy: 'If only I had my son. If only my son was with me.' " (Bruna refused to reveal what cemetery the baby was buried in and added, "Anyhow, the grave isn't still there after all these years.")

The socialite and Onassis crony Vivi Crespi described to me a telling incident that occurred on board the *Christina* in the early 1960s. "I remember once, Onassis was giving a dinner for Sukarno [the president of Indonesia] on the yacht," she said, "and Sukarno said to Maria, 'Madame Callas, you are so beautiful, so charming, so talented, you are truly among God's most favored creatures.' And she turned and looked at Onassis and said loudly so he could hear, 'Yes, but I want a baby with the man I love.' "

In the summer of 1960, Maria and Onassis lived together on the *Christina* in the harbor of Monte Carlo, coming ashore nearly every night to dine and dance in the Maona nightclub. As they visited France to shop for a château, she was sure that they would soon be wed. Maria was very much in love and she still believed that God was looking after her welfare. She was only thirty-six years old and it seemed that her dream of a home, a child, and a dog could be fulfilled.

Nicola Rescigno, one of Maria's favorite conductors and a close friend, recalls her joy and tremulous hope at that time: "She loved to dance," he told me when I interviewed him at his home in Rignona, Italy. "I once asked her to dance with me, and she said, 'No, Nicola, you're too short. Neither of us will look good.' Then when she was dancing with Onassis, I said, 'Maria, he's shorter than I am.' 'But I'm in love with him!' she said. She really loved him. She wasn't interested in his money. She wanted a son by him. She told me she wanted that more than anything else in the world. She told me that right at the beginning, after she left her husband for him. I'm sorry she never got her wish."

The story of the birth and death of Omero raises a perplexing question: If Maria did give birth to a much-wanted son in 1960, then why did she never mention it to anyone except her servants and Vasso Devetzi (and later her lover, di Stefano)? And why would she later create a tale of an abortion forced on her by Onassis in 1966 or 1967—an abortion that evidently never happened?

The answer probably lies in Maria's own feelings at the time she began to circulate the story. Here is how Vicky Anthopoulou interprets Callas' actions, on the basis of her aunt's recollections: "The dramatic event that occurred and cost her so much was for Maria very painful and very personal, too much to have it passed on to others. She wanted to keep it a deep secret inside her, to have it fade from her mind if that was possible, to save it from becoming the subject of careless discussion. Her resort to a story about abortion was more suited to her and more acceptable to anyone who would hear it. It fulfills a part of the truth, telling about her pain at not having a child, and it satisfied her need to discuss the subject. In addition, it gave her the opportunity to establish that she was capable of having a child, in contrast to everything Meneghini was saying—that she was sterile or was the victim of gynecological problems. Finally, with this story she found a way to attack Onassis at a time in her life that she felt wounded by him—this was also something she needed."

Throughout her life, Maria demonstrated a habit of portraying herself as the victim. Her mother's abuse, her husband's greed and self-interest, her colleagues' treachery—she exaggerated every wrong done to her, every sign of betrayal from those around her.

After Onassis left her for Jacqueline Kennedy in 1968, Maria, filled with rage, found it more comfortable to tell friends the story of an abortion that he demanded she have on board the Christina in 1966 or '67. (Captain Kostas told me, "It never could have happened on the *Christina*. I was in charge of the keys to the ship's hospital, which was always locked, and no one could open it without getting them from me. I would know if an abortion—or any other medical procedure—took place on board.")

It is significant that Callas never mentioned an abortion, or even being pregnant, to any of her friends such as Mary Carter, Anastasia Gratsos, and others until after 1968, when she was furious at Onassis for marrying Jacqueline Kennedy. It seems apparent from the fact that no information was found about the alleged 1966 abortion in her private papers and that she did not tell anyone about it until after her break with Onassis two years later, that the tale of the abortion grew out of Maria's anger over Aristo's betrayal and her own conflict over contributing to the accidental death of their premature son in 1960.

"In the critical hours when Maria was waiting for her pregnancy to end," Vicky Anthopoulou added, "the absence of Onassis (perceived by Maria as indifference and abandonment), the publication of her mother's book (which revived in her the trauma and the problems involving her relationship with her mother)—these made Maria very conflicted. On the one hand, everything in her craves that child. On the other, however, deep inside her is an inexplicable fear. As the time draws near, her agony rises.

She doesn't understand why she's so nervous, so anxious. She can't wait any longer. She wants to have, right away, that which she always feared she would never have. . . . Of course, no one will know what she felt in those secret moments. What is certain is that once again, at a critical point in her life, Maria was left to face her fears and anxieties all alone."

As for the abortion described by Maria to friends and reported by Stassi-nopoulos, it was obviously easier for Callas to create a scenario in which Onassis was to blame for the baby's death than to admit to herself any responsibility for the infant son who had been born and died and buried in a Milan cemetery with only four people—herself, Bruna, Ferruccio, and Onassis—to mourn him or even to know his name.

15

THE GOOD YEARS

On this dark earth, some say
the thing most lovely
Is a host of horsemen, some,
lines of foot soldiers
Others a fleet of ships, but I say
it is the sight
Of the one you love.

Sappho, *Fragments*

The birth and death of their son seemed to bring Onassis and Maria closer together. After Tina's Alabama divorce made her split from Onassis official on June 25, 1960, Maria was convinced that Aristo would marry her once she had solved the problem of getting her own freedom from Meneghini. She had wed him in Italy, and under Italian law at that time there was no recognition of divorce. Later Battista would write: "Using an acquaintance as an intermediary, Maria tried everything to persuade me to sign [a divorce agreement], but I refused . . . and she despised me even more." Nevertheless, on August 10, when reporters questioned Onassis and Callas—already disporting themselves like newlyweds in their favorite Monte Carlo hangout, the Maona nightclub—Maria did indicate that they planned to marry. The next day Onassis said she was only joking.

Maria now lavished all her energy and affection on Onassis, the way his mother had when he was a small child. An engineer on the *Christina* wrote that, shortly after returning to Monte Carlo, Onassis came down with a fever and stayed ashore in his apartments above his office at the Sporting Club on the harbor, while Maria remained on the yacht. "During the ten days Onassis was ill," the engineer said, "she visited him daily, taking specially cooked food from the galley to him in the chauffeur-driven car that called for her at the ship."

Panayiotis Zigomalas, who served as the captain of the *Christina* for eight months in 1964–65 while Captain Kostas was on another assignment, also remarked on her doting care of Onassis, "like a protective mother," he told me. "Onassis always walked around in shorts, bare-chested, and whenever a bit of wind kicked up, [Callas] ran to get him a shirt and sweater. She watched carefully to see that he didn't drink too much."

Maria, who liked to call Ari "my pasha," was the only woman, except for his mother and his sister Artemis, to spoil him and wait on him the way a traditional Greek wife is expected to do. Captain Kostas remembers that when Onassis was negotiating Olympic Airways agreements with the Greek government and the discussions dragged on into the night, Callas would pace nervously, asking, " 'Have you heard anything? When is he coming? What are you preparing for him?' She would often send the cook to bed and prepare pasta meals for him by herself."

Maria's devotions must have seemed a homecoming to Onassis after all the years he felt ignored by his Americanized wife, who had excluded him from her life and interests. Here was the adoring care he had felt since his youth to be his unalienable right, and it seems to have inspired a reciprocal tenderness. Stelios Papadimitriou, Onassis' lawyer, told me that Ari was extremely solicitous of Maria; he would, for example, order all his employees to remove their shoes and not use the elevator when she was asleep in the living quarters above the offices in Monte Carlo.

Onassis had once explained to a friend his decidedly Anatolian attitude toward women: "I find that a woman loses long-standing privileges in important spheres, where she has always been considered as queen of the hearth and family, in trying to claim territories which, since the creation of the world, have belonged to male domination." For him, tending the hearth was not only a woman's sacred obligation—it was the source of her glory. But when it came to Callas' career, his traditional attitudes ran up against his competitive instincts. Mary Carter told me that, contrary to what many have suggested, Onassis had no desire for Maria to give up singing: "She did and he didn't. He told me, 'Mary, you talk to her. Everyone will forget her if she stops singing. But Dallas, Chicago, that's all too far. She should stay in Europe—Milan, Paris, Monaco, London, and once in a while, New York." He knew that if she did not appear in public, her devoted fans would soon find someone else to replace her as the *diva assoluta*.

Aristo's prodding Maria to sing was not enlightened benevolence toward her but a function of his egotism: he valued her fame, and he felt responsible for ensuring her continued success after supplanting Mene-ghini in her life. Whatever his beliefs about the proper place of woman, Onassis was no ordinary man and he felt it necessary to his reputation to have a consort whose status enhanced his own. As he explained to Anthony Montague Browne, who always considered the affair with Maria to be a disastrous mistake, "I, for good or ill, am a person who's well known. I had to go with a personality—somebody who's someone in her own right—and Maria was that."

Whether it was on account of Aristo's insistence or an encroaching guilt at having been silent so long, in July of 1960 Maria attempted to make a recording of Verdi and Rossini arias for EMI and traveled to London for the studio sessions, conducted by Antonio Tonini. But the months of neglect-ing her daily regime of vocal practice had taken their toll, and Maria, ever the perfectionist, was horrified when she listened to the recordings. She refused to give permission for their release. She had scheduled a concert in Ostend, but her confidence was now shaken. Callas traveled to Belgium, but on the morning of the concert she awoke to find her voice completely gone, and the engagement was canceled. She retreated to the *Christina* in despair, terrified at the prospect of two performances of *Norma* she had already agreed to do in Greece in August at Aristo's urging. She now felt incapable of singing anything in public.

That same summer, Onassis arranged another cruise with the Churchills, the Montague Brownes, and Artemis and Theodore; the *Christina* would sail from Venice to the Dalmatian coast (where tea would be taken with Marshall Tito) before heading to Greece. This time, however, Onassis told Maria she could not be included. In the years ahead, there would be three more cruises with the Churchills, but after the first, infa-mous one that began the affair, Maria would never again be invited to sail with the elder statesman. Onassis knew that having the notorious "other woman" along would raise eyebrows, particularly those of Lady Churchill (who was devoted to Tina), and he set retaining the Churchills' good opin-ion of him above all else.

To Maria, Onassis blamed the decision not to include her on Montague Browne. In his memoirs, Montague Browne describes how, dining one time in Monte Carlo with Onassis and Maria, he was surprised to find Maria treating him with a "maximum freeze." When he asked what he'd done, she replied, "You know what you've done. Be careful. Not for nothing am I called the Tigress!" He later queried Ari, who sheepishly confessed his ploy.

. . .

Maria had not sung in public since the *Medea* in Dallas in November of 1959, nine months earlier. On her first trip back to Greece in 1957, when her cancellation of the opening concert at Herodes Atticus Theater had been answered with cruel attacks, she had lamented to a Greek reporter, "Seven years of my career were spent in Greece. The blood in my veins, my character, my thoughts all are Greek." Now, at Onassis' insistence, she would return to appear at the ancient theater of Epidaurus, eighty miles from Athens, in August of 1960. His aim was not only for Callas to reclaim the world spotlight but also for him to be seen triumphantly bringing his new consort back to the land they both considered their spiritual home.

Like Callas, Onassis the Anatolian professed a deeply felt essential Greekness. In fact, he considered Hellenes of the diaspora, like him, to be more Greek than those born and raised within the country. "We are like orphans who were deprived of their real mother and long for her embrace," he once said. As a sailor, a wanderer, and a former refugee, he consciously identified with Homer's Odysseus, and much of Onassis' lifelong striving, like his hero's, can be understood as an effort to get back home. To become the preeminent tycoon in Greece (and trump his rival, Niarchos), he had bought the national airline, proudly renaming it Olympic Airlines. This he envisioned as the first step in an ultimate plan to move the headquarters of all his enterprises to Greece. Now he was arriving on his private yacht with the world's most famous diva as his consort for a historic performance at the ancient theater where the masterpieces of Aeschylus, Sophocles, and Euripides had been staged.

This would be the first opera ever performed at the theater of Epidaurus, built in the fourth century B.C., which is considered to have perhaps the best acoustics in the world. For her appearance there, Maria chose her signature role, her favorite—Norma. She had long felt that Bellini's opera, whose central character is a Druid priestess, was the most ideally suited to her talents, and she knew the stakes were high: if she couldn't achieve a triumph in *Norma* in her homeland, it would be a humiliation not only for her but also for Onassis. Maria arrived in Epidaurus to begin rehearsals toward the end of July. At that time there was no hotel nearby, and so quarters were prepared for her at the museum at the ancient site so she could avoid the long journey by road every day.

By the scheduled opening night, August 22, the *Christina* was anchored in the bay of Old Epidaurus, announcing the triumphal homecoming of the two most celebrated living Greeks. But a torrential rain poured down on the open theater as if by some whim of angry gods, forcing a cancellation. The twenty thousand waiting in and around the stadium had to slog home through the mud, and traffic clogged the highways back to

Athens. Some muttered that it never rained like this in Greece, especially not in August. Maria naturally perceived a bad omen, and her anxiety reached new heights.

On the rescheduled opening night, August 24, the theater was again packed and the surrounding hills were carpeted with Greeks. Many in the audience had never attended an opera. Maria appeared on the ancient proscenium dressed in a long, dark draped gown with a flowing train. The audience gasped. Someone near the front released two white doves, and the twenty thousand onlookers rose to their feet, roaring their welcome. The ovation was one of the greatest of her career and she had not yet sung a note.

As Callas began to sing the recitatives, she was terrified that her voice would fail her once again. Since her last performance, in Dallas, she had suffered the birth and death of her son and the realization that her instrument was no longer fully under her control. On this night she was so overcome with emotion that the notes began to wobble as soon as the first ones left her throat. Yet she continued. As she raised her face to the moon—a priestess invoking the gods during a rite in the sacred forest of pre-Christian Gaul—she seemed to absorb the magical powers of this ancient site under the Greek sky.

Whatever may have been lacking in the voice, she more than made up for with the magic of her acting. Callas gave a heartbreaking performance as the tragic druid priestess who has secretly borne two children to the Roman proconsul Pollione, only to learn he has betrayed her by falling in love with the vestal virgin Adalgisa. To take revenge, Norma decides to murder her two children as they sleep, but is so moved by the sight of them that she changes her mind and offers up her own life in a fiery ritual of atonement.

The Norma that Callas sang on August 24, 1960, in the theater of Epidaurus became one of the legends of her career. The critics called it a "miracle" and many detected a new tenderness, "a real mother's feeling," in the way she interacted with the children on stage. Franco Zeffirelli was not the only one to note Callas' identification with her heroine: "In a way it was her own story. Maria, after all, is a high priestess—the high priestess of her art. Yet, at the same time, she is the most fallible of women." Nor was he alone in proclaiming the transcendence of her performance, in which, he said, "Maria created the maximum of what opera can be. In a lifetime, one can see many great things in the theater, but to see Maria Callas in *Norma,* what is there to compare to it?"

One of the many transfixed Greeks watching Callas that night was Amalia Karamanlis, the wife of the Greek prime minister, who had also been among those who observed the imbroglio when Churchill's daughter spilled wine on the British ambassador aboard the *Christina* a year before.

Nearly forty years later, the former Mrs. Karamanlis still vividly remembers the magic of Maria's performance at Epidaurus: "She held her arms closed, crossing her arms over her chest, with a palm on each shoulder. She started singing and her voice was rough, not prepared. At a certain moment, she opened up her hands and one arm shot up toward the sky. Seeing that, I made my cross. You'd swear she was going to pull down a star from the heavens at that moment."

As the former first lady of Greece recalled the effect Callas' performance had on her, she succinctly described the catharsis that results from all great art: "People need love stories. Life is ugly and you need something to identify with which makes you feel beautiful. Maria took me out of my self that day in Epidaurus. We were reaching for the stars together. While she was weeping for Norma's lost love, I was weeping for my own lost loves."

At the end of the evening, under the same stars that had illuminated the performances of the ancient tragedies, the ecstatic crowd crowned Maria with a wreath of laurel leaves. It was a triumph she would never surpass. Her father, George Callas, was sitting in the front row. He had met her lover, Onassis, for the first time at Epidaurus and had watched the dress rehearsal with him. Onassis found the former pharmacist to be a kindred soul—a true Greek who, like him, enjoyed the elemental pleasures of life, including food, wine, and women.

Unfortunately, Onassis' appreciation of opera was not as highly evolved as his other passions. Maria's friend Giovanna Lomazzi, who like others pointed out that "he knew nothing of opera and singing," sat next to Onassis at the dress rehearsal. She later recalled: "At the beginning, Norma comes out, sings, and leaves, and then the mezzo-soprano comes out. Onassis turned to me and asked, 'Is this Maria again?' " Onassis himself once mocked his own ignorance of opera, saying, "To me it sounds like a lot of Italian chefs shouting risotto recipes at each other." At Epidaurus, he decided to skip the opening night performance and proceed directly to the celebration on the *Christina*.

Among those who had been invited back to the yacht for the party after the performance was seventeen-year-old Marina Karella, an artist and the assistant to *Norma*'s stage designer, Yiannis Tsarouchis. Today she is married to Prince Michael of Greece. When I interviewed the couple in Paris in 1999, she recalled having lost both her shoes as she navigated the delirious crowd on her way to the *Christina*. "When I finally made it on board I was surprised to see that Onassis greeted Callas as if she were just an ordinary guest. He never mentioned the great triumph she'd just created. Onassis seemed primarily concerned that his important guests were looked after.

He'd say to Maria, 'Make sure that so and so gets more champagne.' The strangest thing of all to me was that she didn't seem to mind a bit. She was perfectly happy just being his hostess, scurrying around carrying out the duties of a good Greek wife."

Four days later, Maria again sang Norma in the theater of Epidaurus, despite having developed a fever for which the doctors advised her to stay in bed. The performance was another triumph and, at Onassis' suggestion, she donated her ten-thousand-dollar fee to establish the Maria Callas Scholarships for young singers in Greece.

Filled with new confidence, Maria recovered her health on the *Christina* and then flew to Milan to record *Norma* for EMI. Comparing the recording to one of her earlier ones, John Ardoin wrote, "This *Norma* is more giving, more many-sided, more complex and drawn in finer lines. . . . There are certainly signs of fatigue, but a depth of emotion and a dense, rich vocal colour too which makes her druidess a pitiable as well as a noble figure." It seems likely that the experiences of the past year—her love for Onassis and the tragedy of the lost son—had added depths and shadings to her portrayal, even though the voice was now weaker.

Celebrated by the Greek people as their greatest living artist, Maria was lifted to a level of happiness that she had never known. Shortly after her triumphant opening night she asked Onassis to take her to Tinos to visit the miraculous icon of the Virgin Mary as they had done a year earlier, after they first consummated their love. Maria wanted to go to the church of her patron saint, the Madonna, to light candles and give thanks. Coming out of the shrine, somberly dressed in black from head to toe but looking "exuberant and smiling," Maria encountered Stelios Galatopoulos. She confessed to him what she had discovered: "It is wonderful to be happy and to know it right at the time you are."

Things were going well for her on all fronts. Her father arranged a meeting with her older sister, Jackie, whom Maria had not spoken to for a decade. After the trip to Mexico in 1950, when Callas and her mother had their final altercation, Jackie incurred Maria's wrath by taking their mother's side. Now George Callas was determined to bring his daughters together, and Maria agreed to meet Jackie and her father for lunch in Glyfada, where the *Christina* was moored. (Her mother was still living in New York, still trying to extort money from Maria with complaints to the press and the welfare authorities.)

Jackie Callas was born in 1917, six years before Maria. When I met her on several occasions in her home in Athens, I found the eighty-one-year-old woman implausibly fresh, slender, and beautiful. (She attributes her uncanny youthfulness to the regimen of stretching exercises she has done

*The author with Jackie Callas, Maria's older sister, and her husband,
Dr. Andreas Stathopoulos, at their home in Athens*

every day since adolescence and to her happy marriage to Dr. Andreas
Stathopoulos, twenty-four years her junior, whom she married in 1983,
when she was sixty-six.)

While Maria had recently fallen for a shipowner who would never
marry her, Jackie was nearing the end of her own decades-long "engagement" to another shipowner, Miltos Embiricos, whose family did not
approve of the union. He was slowly dying of cancer at the time of the sisters' reconciliation, and Jackie was nursing him through his last illness.
(Embiricos would finally die in 1963 after his brothers halted an attempt at a
deathbed wedding, leaving Jackie to lament, "I was forty-six years old. I
had given him twenty-eight years of my life.")

According to Jackie, on Thursday, September 29, she and her father
took a bus from Athens to Glyfada, where they met up with some friends
from Jackie and Maria's youth in Athens, including the physician Ilias
Papatestas, who had been Maria's first love. They all gathered outside
an expensive seaside restaurant, Psaropoulos, waiting for the diva to come
ashore. When Callas finally appeared, Jackie felt she was meeting a total
stranger. "The Maria I had last seen, the Maria I knew, was fat and awkward,
ill tempered and greedy; here was this vision of refined elegance."

The Greek newspaper *Ethnos* reported that after the meal, "Father Callas was heard to say, 'May God grant that we are always as happy as we are now' and then someone else, whose voice was not Maria's said, 'The nightingales have reunited.' "

Maria then took her father, sister, and friends aboard the *Christina* for an hour to have tea, but also, of course, to show off the famous tycoon and the luxurious quarters. After returning to shore, George Callas told the assembled reporters: "As you can see, I am the father of two beloved daughters, one of whom from now on will live with me here and the other far away, for she does not belong to me but to all the world, which so loves my child."

Maria would see Jackie again, especially on her return to Epidaurus the following year, but their meetings would always be tense with the leftover rivalries of childhood and the diva's efforts to impress her older sister with her new glory and status.

Callas now felt emboldened to return to La Scala despite the controversies that had alienated her from her Milanese fans and from the theater that she considered her musical home. On December 7, 1960, five days after her thirty-seventh birthday, she appeared as Paolina in Donizetti's *Poliuto* before an audience so illustrious that Onassis must have preened at the power of his mistress's name. On hand were Prince Rainier and Princess Grace, the Begum Aga Khan, Gina Lollobrigida, Elisabeth Schwarzkopf, and Elsa Maxwell, who had flown over specially from the United States. The prince and princess were hosting a supper party for Maria after the performance. The couturier Balmain had donated sixteen thousand carnations, which were woven into garlands and draped over the six tiers of the gilded theater. They inspired Elsa Maxwell to describe the scene in her gossip column as a vision from the Arabian Nights.

The production was fraught with problems. The director, Luchino Visconti, had walked out during rehearsals in protest against the Italian government for trying to censor his film *Rocco and His Brothers*. He was replaced as Callas was preparing her role. She had chosen *Poliuto* partly because the music did not demand the vocal gymnastics that she could no longer summon at will. Still, the memory of her last appearance in Milan and the fickleness of her voice overcame her, and Maria was paralyzed with stage fright. Giulietta Simionato remembers that a nurse was called to give her a "vitamin shot" so that she'd have the strength to go on. She heard Maria muttering to herself backstage, "If I don't do a good job tonight, I'll kill myself."

The performance was not a disaster, although the reviews were mixed and Maria's anxiety mounted over each of the five nights. As the holidays approached, Callas' fans realized that for the first time since 1947 she'd

Callas at La Scala, applauded by Prince Rainier and Onassis

notched only two public performances during the year—at Epidaurus in *Norma* and at La Scala in *Poliuto*. The frequency barely increased in 1961, and Maria did not sing in public again until May. After each of her increasingly rare appearances, she would rush back to the sanctuary of the *Christina* and her pasha. Like Onassis, she felt more at home on the ship than anywhere else on earth. She didn't practice on board; she didn't even think about singing, and of course the neglect of her voice would only hasten the decline of her failing powers.

Once, after a three-week cruise on the *Christina*, Princess Grace scolded Maria for not having practiced once. Franco Zeffirelli, visiting her in the Paris apartment that Onassis had rented for her on 44 Avenue Foch, down the street from his own apartment, later recalled that he also accused Maria of not practicing. It was clear she hadn't touched a piano keyboard for months, he told her. " 'How do you know?' Maria asked. I said 'Look at your fingernails,' and she . . . made a beautiful gesture with her hands, like a little girl, and said, 'Yes, all right, but I've been distracted. . . . I am trying to fulfill my life as a woman.' "

Maria had never before enjoyed such freedom from the rigors of her work. She was thrilled to give up the grueling rehearsals, the nights of studying librettos, the strenuous daily vocal exercises, the terrible stage fright before every performance, and the merciless criticisms whenever she missed a single note. The lazy routine on the *Christina* now suited her perfectly. She and Ari both loved swimming, staying up late into the night talking, dancing and drinking. Whether aboard ship or at the Maona nightclub, which had been built in Monte Carlo's harbor in the hull of an overturned barge, they were typically toasted by friends, including the Rainiers, Bette Davis, Greta Garbo, Margot Fonteyn, Elizabeth Taylor and Richard Burton, and a hodgepodge of titles.

For the first time in her life Maria felt loved for herself and not for her ability to sing for her supper. She told Artemis, Aristo's older sister, "Everyone in my life has used me. Aristo is the only person I have ever met who does not take something from me. Instead, he offers me everything. Everything I could ever want." Despite these loving words about her brother, Artemis would never accept Maria or learn to like her. She remained loyal to Tina and she felt that Maria was not of a sufficiently high-born family for her adored brother.

Artemis' rejection was also fueled by Alexander's furious resentment of the singer. Those who knew the couple regard this familial resistance as the primary reason why Onassis did not marry Maria. Miltos Yiannakopoulos, Aristo's intelligence gatherer, told me when I interviewed him in Athens in 1998 that "Onassis tried everything to get the boy to come around. He even sent me to talk to Alexander about a year before he married Jackie and the boy wouldn't budge. 'If he marries that whore, I'll never speak to him,' he told me, and he meant it. Maria was nothing of the kind, of course. I don't think she ever looked at another man while she was with Onassis. But the boy despised her, and his hostility was the reason Artemis was so much against her."

Onassis' younger sisters, Merope and Kalliroe, were more sympathetic toward the diva, as were their husbands, both of whom were great opera lovers and had been fans of Callas' since the beginning of her career. Nikos Konialidis, the husband of Merope, once leaped to the singer's defense in a conversation on board the *Christina* when a woman remarked, "How lucky you are, Maria! Such an important man fell in love with you! We must all envy you!"

Maria only listened thoughtfully, but Konialidis interjected, "In this case Aristo is the lucky one. Fifty years from now, nobody will remember Onassis, while Maria's name will never be forgotten. Perhaps then he will borrow some of her immortality, thanks to this love affair."

Maria also managed to find an ally in the family in Onassis' niece Marilena Patronikola, the daughter of Kalliroe and Gerasimos Patronikolas, who was only a year older than Alexander. She spoke to me several times in Athens. Marilena told me that Maria welcomed her as "the only one in the family who liked her" and often invited her to come aboard the *Christina*.

Callas was especially understanding of her teenaged missteps: "Once I caused a big *fasaria* [upset] in the family," Marilena recalls. "My father was always a womanizer, and I was with him at dinner at one of his hotels, the Miramar, on Rhodes, when he said he had to dance with this young blonde because she was a tour director and brought lots of business to the hotel. Then they both disappeared.

"I knew at what cabana she was staying," Marilena continued, "and I went there and heard them inside. I told my mother and all hell broke loose. My aunt Artemis called me and started screaming: 'Do you want to destroy your mother?' Then Uncle Aristo started chewing me out for telling tales. But Maria took me aside. She talked to me quietly and told me not to blame myself; sometimes marriages don't work out and perhaps it's better for people to separate than to stay together, being miserable and fighting all the time. She made me feel much better."

Having spent a lot of time on board the *Christina* playing with the Onassis children, Marilena disputes the oft-repeated story that her uncle Aristo didn't like music and never listened to Maria sing. "He was proud of her talent," she told me. One night during dinner, Marilena's uncle invited Maria to come to the piano and favor the guests with a song. "As she played, she sang 'Casta Diva' from *Norma* and then the Ave Maria," Marilena recalls. "I looked over at Uncle Aristo and he was crying. We were all crying, because she sang so beautifully."

According to Marilena, her aunt Artemis always blamed Maria for breaking up the marriage to Tina and it was she who kept the children's hostility against the singer inflamed. "Uncle Aristo fought with Artemis a lot, but he was very vulnerable to her because they had become so close after their mother died." Indeed, the only flaw in Maria's happiness during those first years on the *Christina* was her treatment at the hands of the children, especially Alexander, who never missed an opportunity to make her life miserable while they were aboard during summers and school vacations.

Once the divorce became final and Tina received custody of Alexander, twelve, and Christina, nine, she enrolled them in schools in Paris and left them supervised by servants and their Onassis aunts while she celebrated her freedom. Following a party in Monte Carlo, she headed off to ski in St. Moritz, where, speeding down the run named for Niarchos, she fell thirty feet and shattered her right leg. Niarchos dispatched his private plane to bring a leading bone specialist from England to Switzerland to examine his sister-in-law. The doctor advised that Tina be moved to Oxford, where he could supervise her treatment, but warned that it might be a year before she could walk without a cane.

Onassis hurried to England to his former wife's bedside—a trip that little comforted his present mistress—but the rumors of a reconciliation were groundless. While convalescing—and bored to death in bucolic Oxford—Tina was introduced (by Lady Clementine Churchill, some say) to Sonny Blandford, the son of the tenth duke of Marlborough. By the time her cast was removed, she had agreed to marry the thirty-five-year-old aristocrat. The wedding took place on October 23, 1961, in Paris. Ten-year-old Christina wore a fur hat her father had brought her from Moscow. Later she said she wore it "as a secret sign of allegiance to Daddy."

Despite the wedding, the Onassis children refused to give up their hope that their parents would one day get back together. On the *Christina* that summer and every summer thereafter, they continued to treat Maria with complete scorn. Korinna Spanidou, the masseuse, recalls, "Alexander would never eat at the dinner table with us when Maria was on board, not once. He always went to eat with the crew." When she tried to take an afternoon nap he would launch into a noisy barrage of waterskiing and speedboating. When she bought them carefully chosen gifts from Harrods, the children would leave them conspicuously on deck, not even bothering to open them.

One of Alexander's best friends, the son of another Greek shipowner, told me that despite Callas' efforts to win them over, "Alexander and Christina called her 'the Ugly One' (*e aschimi*) and 'the Singer' and twisted the name Callas into '*Kolou,*' which means 'big ass.' "

Onassis was so happy with the reception in Greece of Maria's *Norma* that he persuaded her to agree to return to Epidaurus in August of 1961. Both were especially pleased that this would be a completely Greek production. The opera to be performed was *Medea,* which takes place in Corinth, not far from Epidaurus. The director was Alexis Minotis, who had mounted *Medea* with Maria in Dallas and London in the 1950s to great acclaim, and he had been a close friend of Onassis' since 1922; they met when both were new arrivals to Athens. The costume designer was the renowned Greek painter Yiannis Tsarouchis. The only non-Greek in the team was the conductor, Nicola Rescigno, but he had conducted previous productions of *Medea* with Maria and Minotis and was almost part of the family.

The opening night was scheduled for August 6. Maria rehearsed doggedly around the clock for four days, even insisting on sleeping in the drafty museum so as to be as close to the stage as possible.

All of Greece wanted to be in the theater that night to hear Callas sing Medea, and her friends came from all over the world. One of them was Mary

Carter, whose arrival from Dallas was characteristically filled with misadventures. The Grande Bretagne Hotel had lost her reservation and so she called Maria at Epidaurus. Mary insisted it was an emergency and Maria was called out of rehearsal. " 'What am I going to do?' I asked her. 'Buy cigarettes, buy a bottle of vodka, get a car and come down,' she said. . . . Then just as I was putting everything in the taxi, the police arrived and arrested the driver for murder. But they were very nice when I mentioned that I was going to see Maria. They put me in another taxi and took me to Epidaurus."

She arrived at the Xenia Hotel to find Maria having dinner with a group that included Larry Kelly, EMI executive Walter Legge, the conductor Thomas Schippers, Elsa Maxwell, Alexis Minotis, and Baroness Maggie van Zuylen, a Paris friend of Maria's. Space was at such a premium at the Xenia, Mary Carter recalls, that "Larry slept on the roof and I slept in the hallway next to the WC. Maria was staying in a room above the museum with no hot water, but she didn't complain. She was so happy then, nothing could upset her."

The dress rehearsal of *Medea* was performed free of charge for a full house of Greek peasants from the neighboring countryside. On the day of the opening, eastbound traffic on the main road between Athens and Epidaurus was closed to accommodate all the vehicles streaming toward the ancient theater.

Maria did not disappoint them. Nicola Rescigno told me her phenomenal energy was so intense that night that when "she had to walk up this ramp . . . she did it with such fury it took five strong stage hands to hold the wall supporting it to keep the whole set from collapsing."

The Greek prime minister, Karamanlis, was there along with most of his cabinet. So were Elsa Maxwell, La Scala's general manager, Antonio Ghiringhelli, and Wally Toscanini, who had come even though she was then not on speaking terms with Callas. After watching Maria as the sorceress who murders her own children, Wally said to Gian Carlo Menotti, "I began to cry. I had to forgive her because I knew what she was going through. She was losing her voice . . . and . . . *he* was there, in the audience. You could almost see the blood coming out of her vocal cords. She gave an incandescent performance, out of despair. All she wanted was to be loved."

(In fact, Onassis was one famous face not present in the audience that night. Sailing on the *Christina* toward Egypt on pressing business, he missed Maria's greatest triumph in Greece, which brought her seventeen curtain calls. But he would be there for the second performance, a week later, on August 13.)

In the front row, beside Maria's father, was her older sister, Jackie. This was the first time she had seen and heard her younger sister perform since Mary Kalogeropoulos became Maria Callas. In *Sisters,* Jackie would recall an awkward tenderness following the performance: "My fumbling praise must have seemed genuine enough. 'I didn't realize,' I said, and then let it trail away. . . . We embraced. We understood each other. . . . I left her to be devoured by her admirers." What Jackie could not at that moment comprehend was that the celebrated sister, with whom she had only recently been reconciled, had changed. "She had grown tired of the struggle; the nerve-racking effort wearied her, she dreamed no longer of curtain calls and applause; she had had them in abundance. What she wanted now was a child, and that I too had been denied."

Not everything had changed, though. Their next meeting was at a luncheon at the Glyfada home of Artemis and Theodore Garofalidis. Maria, in a foul temper, overheard their host tell Jackie that he'd heard she had a lovely voice. According to Jackie, Maria turned into the Tigress, snarling, "Who has a voice? I have a voice!" Garofalidis said, "Yes, Maria, we all know that you're a great artist, but now we're talking about your sister." (Jackie had in fact once given a concert in Greece in a brief attempt at a singing career.) As Jackie recounted the rest of the story to me: "Maria said, 'I'm a singer, but you're a *gria* [old lady]. You started singing too late.' This was in 1961. If I was a *gria* then, what am I now?" Jackie concluded, smiling. "I think Maria could have said it more tactfully."

Before the *Christina* sailed away from Glyfada, Maria issued one more invitation to her sister to come aboard for tea. The diva sat in her luxurious stateroom fondling her jewelry and couture clothes and asked Jackie what she should wear. According to Jackie, Maria said finally, "I hear you're jealous of me," to which Jackie replied, "I'm lucky. I'm not a jealous person. I'm sorry for anyone who is, it must be a terrible feeling." Callas was never to forget entirely the years she had spent as a fat, pimply, myopic younger sister to the lissome blonde. She dropped the subject of jealousy and seemed to warm to her again as she led her off the yacht to the harbor. But even though Onassis' car and chauffeur stood waiting nearby, she directed her sister, "You should be able to get a bus over there."

Despite the lingering tension between them, Maria seemed happy that she had reconciled with her older sister, for she continued to stay in touch with her, if only sporadically. Until the end of her life, Callas would telephone Jackie in Athens unexpectedly, usually late at night, sometimes for a brief chat or to ask her to obtain and send to her medications that she couldn't get in Paris. Sometimes, according to Jackie, Maria would launch into long rambling monologues about her life, in which she poured out her frustrations, longings, and fears.

Aristo and Maria sailed away from Epidaurus on the *Christina* trailing clouds of glory, but two months later, when Maria sang Medea at La Scala, which she had considered "her" opera house, her voice was so wobbly that the entire audience began to hiss her. She silenced them by turning Medea's fury toward Jason into Callas' rage at the audience, shaking her fist at the gallery and shouting the libretto's words "cruel man" and "I have given everything to you" directly at her attackers.

Onassis realized the terrible burden Maria bore trying to continue her career despite her voice's inconsistency, and he considered other ways to perpetuate her celebrity. He encouraged her to consider a career in films. Onassis was intrigued when the producer Carl Foreman, a guest on the *Christina,* offered Callas a part in the 1961 film *The Guns of Navarone,* opposite Anthony Quinn. Maria was unsure, but Onassis reportedly volunteered, "Give her ten days and if she's no good, okay, dump her, get somebody else—and I'll foot the bill." But when Foreman pressed the offer, Maria's courage failed and she turn down the part (which was eventually taken by the Greek actress Irene Papas). Aristo was furious: "I get up every day of my life to win!" he shouted. "I don't know why you bother to get up at all."

To Maria the answer was clear. Onassis was the reason she got up every morning. He suggested she cut her hair short and she did it. He told her not to wear glasses and she learned to wear contact lenses. If, when she sat down at the table to dinner, he indicated that he didn't like what she was wearing, she would get up and change. All she wanted was to please him, and usually she succeeded.

Both Maria and Aristo increasingly felt more at home in Greece than in Monte Carlo or Paris, and they preferred drinking ouzo with fishermen at a seaside taverna to sipping martinis with the gilded crowd of film stars, maharanis, and titled layabouts who were their usual companions. At the same time that Prince Rainier was planning a financial coup that would ultimately eliminate Onassis' favored tax status in Monte Carlo and force him to sell his controlling interest in the Société des Bains de Mer—the group that virtually ran the tiny country—Onassis himself was trying to expand his presence in Greece. As the new owner of the national airline, he had already proved a formidable entrepreneur. Now he was bent on establishing himself as a landholder. Not the least of his motivations was the fact that his rival Niarchos had just acquired the five-thousand-acre island of Spetsopoula near the bustling tourist island of Spetses. He was creating an aristocratic pleasure park and had stocked the island with game to turn it into a paradise for hunting—his passion.

Onassis was delighted to learn, in the summer of 1963, that the deserted Ionian island of Skorpios was for sale by its owners. Originally he had yearned to buy Ithaca, the legendary home of his idol, Odysseus, but he finally had to admit that the notion was impractical: the island's 58,000 inhabitants would be reluctant to move. At least Skorpios was close enough— only ten miles to the north—that Onassis could see Ithaca from the highest point. In addition to Skorpios he purchased Sparte, another deserted island nearby, in order to ensure perfect privacy, and began sketching plans to turn his new acquisition into the kind of domain he had always dreamed of—one worthy not merely of a tycoon, but of a Greek hero or even a king. (At first he even talked about re-creating the ancient Cretan palace of Minos, one of the wonders of the ancient world, on the summit of Skorpios.)

Skorpios, shaped like its namesake the scorpion, was an ample four hundred acres, and the price was right—only $110,000. It had a few problems—no source of fresh water, for one. It was rocky and barren except for a pink stucco neoclassical house, called the Pink House, and a tiny stone chapel, built by the earliest known owners of the island, the Mavridi brothers, in 1894. There was also an unsettling rumor that a previous owner— perhaps one of the Mavridis themselves—had been mysteriously killed there in a hunting accident. But Onassis knew that by pouring enough money into the island he could achieve the private paradise he had always wanted. Besides the main house and guest cottages, he would have orchards, exotic vegetation, bougainvillea, jasmine, groves of oleander. There would be roads and a harbor big enough to accommodate the *Christina* and private coves in which one could swim far from prying eyes. (He had to import tons of white sand for the beaches.)

There would be a farm with all sorts of domesticated animals and a farmer to look after it. (When the farm was all finished, it was reported that, at the suggestion of Swiss agriculturalists, Onassis had the livestock serenaded with classical music to keep them tranquil and productive.) Water would be brought over from the nearby town of Nidri on the island of Lefkada every day until desalinization plants could be set up. He would import and plant all the biblical trees and plants that his grandmother Gethsemane had told him grew in the Holy Land: the almond, olive, and fig trees, the cypress and pine trees, palms and oranges and lemons. It would be Onassis' own Garden of Eden.

. . .

For Maria, despite the bliss of being with Aristo, the early sixties were not without trials. In Milan, Meneghini asked the civic tribunal to annul their separation by mutual consent and in its place to install a separation order that blamed Maria for the breakup of their marriage. In the end his effort failed.

In February of 1962, when Maria sang a concert at the Royal Festival Hall in London, she suffered her first blows from the English press. "It has been clear for some time that her voice has been sinking in pitch," said one critic. "Her voice is now quite ugly and even out of tune," wrote another. Though Maria and Ari's friend the shipowner Panaghis Vergottis gave her a lavish supper party after the concert, Onassis, in the throes of some transactions of his own, was not there to offer his much-needed moral support.

Callas was more successful when she sang selections from *Carmen* at Madison Square Garden in New York on May 19, 1962, to mark President John F. Kennedy's forty-fifth birthday. (The role of the sultry gypsy, meant for a mezzo-soprano, was now more suitable for her vocal range.) But the lore of that evening would forever belong to Marilyn Monroe, who sang her breathless "Happy Birthday, Mr. President" clad in a skin-tight sparkling dress. Jacqueline Kennedy was not present.

Two weeks before the Kennedy birthday performance, Maria's mother tried to kill herself with an overdose of medicine (just as she had done thirty years earlier when her husband was forced to sell his pharmacy). Evangelia left notes to Maria and to the public next to her bed before taking the pills. She was rushed to Roosevelt Hospital, where doctors pumped her stomach. One of the doctors informed Callas that a psychiatrist who had examined her mother "felt that while she is an unstable personality, it is reasonably safe to return her to her present environment." But Maria appealed to her godfather, Dr. Leonidas Lantzounis, for help in placing her in an institution, "maybe in Europe where things are cheaper." When Callas arrived in New York for the concert, she refused Lantzounis' suggestions that she meet with her mother.

Following the Kennedy gala, Maria went immediately back to Milan to sing Medea at La Scala, but she was in agony from a severe case of sinusitis, which made high and long notes excruciatingly painful. Those "dreadful performances," as the critic Pierre-Jean Rémy calls them, seemed to signal the end of her career as an opera singer. On June 3 Maria made her dramatic entrance on the stage at La Scala, cloaked in black, her face hidden, and as she sang the first words, "I am Medea!" her voice cracked. It was "unbearably sad to watch, her voice on the point of giving out, she somehow struggled through the part," Rémy wrote. "After 3 June 1962, a date to be remembered, Callas never again appeared on stage at La Scala, nor, her voice and strength failing, did she return to Epidaurus that year. . . . She was undergoing the second of her great vocal crises."

At the end of 1962 a letter came from the New York City welfare department saying that her mother had applied for public assistance and that Maria was "responsible for her support to the extent of her ability to contribute." Again she put the problem in the hands of Lantzounis, who worked out a settlement stipulating that Maria would pay two hundred dollars a month if Evangelia would promise not to do anything to draw publicity to herself or her daughter.

By the beginning of 1963 there was nothing left in Maria's life but her relationship with Aristo. They sailed together and dined nightly in Monte Carlo with those who by this time were known as the jet set. This dazzling group now included Prince and Princess Radziwill—Stas and Lee. Lee, of course, was the former Lee Bouvier, the sister of the first lady of the United States, Jacqueline Kennedy.

In 1963 Lee Radziwill was a very beautiful woman only twenty-nine years old, but it was perhaps her connection to the American president that Onassis found most intriguing. While Maria was scheduling a concert tour of Europe for late May and early June of 1963, Onassis was planning another cruise for the Churchills, and he invited the Radziwills to come along. Other guests included Sir Winston's son, Randolph Churchill, and his grandson Winston Jr.; Vivi Crespi; Jock and Meg Colville; and the Anthony Montague Brownes.

Anthony Montague Browne later recalled that voyage, which began on June 8 and passed through the Greek isles, including Skorpios, as the "last and least fortunate" cruise. During the course of it, Randolph Churchill drank too much at dinner and began to rage against his father, creating such a scene that Onassis had to find a ruse to lure him off the boat the next day. (Randolph was a journalist, and Onassis secured him a rare interview with the Greek royal family to force his departure.)

With Maria absent for the sake of the Churchills, Onassis took the opportunity to improve his friendship with Lee Radziwill, who, according to Anthony Montague Browne, "had a striking, high-cheekboned, almost Red Indian face, but didn't have much to say." Stas (or Stash, as some called him) did not seem to be the jealous sort. He "later did some rather successful property deals, with Ari's support," recalls Anthony.

Shortly after this cruise, rumors of an affair between Lee Radziwill and Onassis began to circulate. The columnist Drew Pearson asked in the *Washington Post*, "Does the ambitious Greek tycoon hope to become the brother-in-law of the American President?" Meneghini, eager as ever to hold a press conference, announced in Milan that Onassis had left Callas for Princess Radziwill, adding, "I always knew their friendship would have a sad ending for Maria."

Maria herself was not blind to what was going on. She was all too familiar with Aristo's reputation for seducing high-profile women, and he had no doubt bragged to her about his affairs with the likes of Eva Perón, Veronica Lake, Gloria Swanson, Greta Garbo, and even Jeanne-Marie Rhinelander. But those involvements seemed like ancient history. Lee Radziwill was perceived by Callas as a clear and present danger to her relationship with Aristo, which was all she had left by now. Still, when Maria came back aboard the *Christina* as soon as it returned from the Churchill cruise (Lee and Stas Radziwill had left early, in Italy) she did her best to keep quiet and distract her pasha from any temptations that he might have found on the holiday.

Ed Klein, in his book *Just Jackie,* cites a conversation that occurred on the terrace of Bunny Mellon's estate on Half Moon Bay, Antigua, in which Lee Radziwill announced to a group of friends that she was going to marry Onassis. Her husband, Stas, needled her in front of the others: "But my dear, what makes you so certain that Ari wants to marry you?"

Whether or not Lee had such plans, it's unlikely that Onassis' interest in her was serious. He viewed her primarily as a conduit to the president and first lady of the United States. When tragedy struck the Kennedys, Onassis jumped at the chance to offer a cruise on his yacht to help Mrs. Kennedy recover.

On August 7, 1963, Jacqueline Kennedy collapsed in pain and was rushed to a hospital, where a four-pound son was born six weeks early and was immediately baptized Patrick Bouvier Kennedy. Like Maria's son, he had severe difficulty breathing, and on August 9, after forty hours of struggling to live, he lost the battle.

Lee Radziwill, who was in Athens at the time, flew to Washington and then flew straight back to Ari, confiding to him her sister's deep depression. Maria, evidently present during the conversation, later told Nadia Stancioff: "I was astonished she hadn't stayed with her sister. She repeatedly told us how undone Jackie was by the death of her baby. Both Aristo and I felt badly about it, so he extended an open invitation to the president and Mrs. Kennedy to join us on a cruise."

But when Jacqueline Kennedy eventually flew to Athens to board the *Christina* on October 4, 1963, two important guests were missing: the president of the United States and Maria Callas. According to Nadia, Maria later told her: "I was in Paris. Aristo had kicked me out! He told me he couldn't have his 'concubine' on board with the president and first lady of the

United States. That was just an added insult to the fight we'd had a month before when I discovered an empty Cartier box with a love note from Aristo to Lee. A couple of nights later, I saw the bracelet it had contained, on her wrist! How could they! How did they dare have an affair right under my nose? I still can't get over their nerve. I have the proof. I've hidden the note and box. But tell me, how could she accept those dirty diamonds?"

Mary Carter, to whom Maria made her feelings clear, recalls Maria's desperate jealousy of Lee Radziwill: "When she found out in 1963 that he was having an affair with Lee Radziwill," Mary Carter said, "she was so upset she overdosed, and he found her on the floor in Paris. He walked her around, fed coffee into her, and called a doctor. Now, I'm not so sure she didn't have some kind of backup arrangement so that if Onassis didn't find her, Bruna or Ferruccio would. But he did."

John F. Kennedy was worrying about the 1964 election campaign when his wife told him excitedly that she was going on a Greek cruise on the *Christina*. Like everyone else who read the newspapers, Kennedy knew the stories, largely exaggerated, of the Dionysian revels aboard Onassis' yacht. It was bad enough that his sister-in-law was linked to such a controversial figure. "For Christ's sake, Jackie!" he exclaimed, "Onassis is an international pirate!"

Lee and Stas promised to chaperone Jackie, but the president ordered his undersecretary of commerce, Franklin D. Roosevelt, Jr., and his wife, Susan, to go along as well, saying, "Your presence will add a little respectability to the whole thing." JFK also sent a memo to his press office suggesting that, in order to disassociate the trip from Onassis himself, it should be reported that the *Christina* had been "secured" by Prince Stanislas Radziwill from Onassis. "If asked, we should state that Onassis is not expected on the trip, at least not in the beginning," Kennedy wrote.

Onassis gamely volunteered to stay away from the cruise altogether to calm the president's fears, but Jackie said that was out of the question. She asked her sister to tell Ari she "could not accept his generous hospitality and then not let him come along."

Mrs. Kennedy flew into Athens on Wednesday, October 2. The eleven-hour flight stopped in Rome, where she asked for oxygen while reclining in first class. "She had not been ill," according to the *New York Times*, "just very tired, and the altitude had affected her." Two days later, on Friday, October 4, after "a gay shipboard dinner party," the *Christina* set sail from the port of Piraeus, headed for Istanbul, and then the island of Mytilene. Onassis was nowhere to be seen. He didn't show his face on deck until the third stop, when the ship was approaching his native Smyrna. The first lady

Jackie Kennedy's controversial 1963 cruise on the Christina, *shortly after she lost her baby. Onassis stands between her and Franklin D. Roosevelt, Jr., sent on the cruise as chaperone by JFK.*

sent Franklin Roosevelt, Jr., to Ari's stateroom to insist that he give them a personal tour of the town. Onassis was, of course, more than happy to show them his old neighborhood and all his childhood haunts.

Photographs appeared in newspapers around the world of Onassis leading Jacqueline Kennedy by the hand through the Turkish city. Maria, reading the papers in Paris, told Panaghis Vergottis: "Four years ago, that was me by his side, being beguiled by the story of his life . . . although I'm sure he makes most of it up. Memories demand too much effort."

The president saw the same photos and called his wife on the *Christina* to suggest that she cut the cruise short, but she refused. Jackie had always been fascinated with Greek literature and history and it had been her dream to visit these places with a guide who could make the gods and myths come alive for her. Onassis was just such a guide.

At the end of the cruise, Onassis bestowed on his guest of honor a farewell gift: a stunning diamond and ruby necklace reportedly worth fifty thousand dollars. Lee was crestfallen to see what her reward was for bringing her sister aboard the *Christina*. She wrote to John Kennedy, making an effort to joke about it, that Ari had showered Jackie with so many presents she couldn't stand it—because all she'd gotten from the tycoon were three little bracelets that Caroline wouldn't even wear.

When Jackie Kennedy got back to Washington, still raving about her trip, she was faced with all the negative publicity it had engendered. Feeling guilty, she agreed to her husband's demand that she accompany him to Texas the following month, to help garner votes for the reelection campaign.

On November 22, 1963, when an assassin's bullet cut Jack Kennedy's life short in Dallas, many around the world found their lives profoundly affected. But Maria Callas, reading in the French newspapers about Kennedy's murder, could not have suspected that the assassination was the beginning of a series of events that would forever alter her future and the relationship that had become the center of her existence.

16

COLD WIND IN EDEN

An object in possession seldom retains
the same charm it had in pursuit.

Pliny the Younger, *Letters*

Onassis was in Hamburg, Germany, checking on the construction of his
newest tanker, the *Olympic Chivalry,* when he heard the news of John
Kennedy's assassination. He called Lee Radziwill in London and she asked
him to accompany her and Stas to Washington for the funeral. The next day
Onassis received an official invitation to attend the funeral and to stay at the
White House—one of only half a dozen extended to people outside the
immediate family. Some of Princess Radziwill's friends insist that she had
Onassis invited because he had helped console her sister after Jackie's baby
died. Others believe Lee hoped that giving him entrée to the Kennedy inner
circle might revive Ari's interest in her.

Inside the White House on Sunday, November 24, 1963, Onassis discovered the raucous atmosphere of an Irish wake. He found himself joking
and clowning with Bobby Kennedy, Ted Kennedy, Robert McNamara, Ken
O'Donnell, and Dave Powers, as well as other family members and close
friends. After teasing Onassis about his fortune, Bobby Kennedy produced
a bogus contract pledging half of it to the poor of Latin America. Keeping a
straight face, Onassis signed it in Greek. He also found time during the
weekend to spend a few minutes with Jackie Kennedy in the family quarters
and to offer her some words of consolation.

Just over a week later, Onassis was back in Paris with Maria, celebrating
her fortieth birthday at Maxim's. They seemed as close as ever, although he
couldn't hide his elation at having been admitted to the inner circle at the

White House. If Callas was holding a grudge about being excluded from the Jackie Kennedy cruise on the *Christina,* she hid it well. She still considered Lee Radziwill to be her primary competitor for Aristo's attention. As though to remind her lover of why he had first admired her, Maria threw herself impetuously and obsessively into preparing for a lavish production of *Tosca* for the Royal Opera House at Covent Garden in London, scheduled for January of 1964.

Maria had contacted Franco Zeffirelli and told him she would perform only if he agreed to direct. In just six weeks, they put together a production of *Tosca* that many critics say has never been surpassed. So completely did Maria immerse herself in the work during rehearsals that she didn't notice when a candle set her wig on fire: she kept on singing as smoke billowed from her head. In another rehearsal the trick knife that she used to stab the villain, Scarpia, failed to retract and she nearly killed Tito Gobbi, her beloved colleague, who had the role of the wicked chief of police.

On opening night, Maria had bronchitis and a temperature of over one hundred degrees, but she refused to let her condition be announced to the audience. She was, in Zeffirelli's words, "a walking disaster area." Standing in the wings, the panic-stricken diva was fiercely gripping the director's hand and "crossing herself over and over in the Orthodox manner." When the first chord sounded, he pushed her out. "I looked down at my hand, which was bleeding from where her nails had cut into my palm. It was like stigmata and I cherished the wounds for weeks."

The production and the costumes, including Maria's long, gold-embroidered stole, became famous. Zeffirelli said that when he brought the stole to Maria during rehearsals, she took it, "starting to practise those gestures—twitching the edge, letting it slide down her arms—that brought such drama to her movements." Of the pair of long gloves that Callas slowly unbuttoned and peeled off in one scene, Zeffirelli recalled, "It was almost as if she were stripping, exposing herself, tantalizing Scarpia. This was Maria the actress at her best." It was also during this production that they created the celebrated rape scene in which Gobbi grasped Maria's hands as she beat on his chest and spread them into the image of a crucifixion. With the aria "Vissi d'arte," the showpiece of the opera, Maria offered an impassioned summation of her life: "I lived for art, I lived for love."

Callas' instinctive dramatic talent set her apart from every opera star before or after. As the *New York Times* music critic Harold Schonberg wrote following her death: "Callas triumphed because of brains and temperament rather than intrinsic beauty of voice. . . . Everything she did was musically and dramatically interesting. . . . Others merely sang. Callas lived her roles."

Alexis Minotis, who directed Maria in *Traviata* and *Medea* and was himself a renowned interpreter of ancient Greek tragic heroes, considered her one of the greatest actors he'd ever seen in any field. He often described how, as the dying Violetta in *Traviata,* she achieved an effect he had witnessed only once before in his life, at a performance by a legendary Japanese actor who was revered in his own country. John Ardoin related to me what Minotis had told him: "Callas did it in the last act of *Traviata*. Like the Japanese actor, she died with her eyes open and you could see the light go out of her eyes. . . . Minotis said it was the most incredible moment of dramatic truth he had ever seen."

The London critics wore out their superlatives describing Maria's comeback in *Tosca*. Convinced that she had conquered her problems with The Voice, she agreed to do a series of recordings in the spring in Paris. Most, however, would never be released, owing in part to an unsettling surprise in the middle of the sessions: she received a telegram saying that her father was critically ill in New York and had remarried. His new wife, Alexandra Papajohn, a family friend since Maria's childhood, had been living with George Callas for many years.

Maria was outraged by her father's unexpected nuptials, for which she would never really forgive him. She wrote to her godfather: "I want nothing to do with the doctors or his newly acquired family. . . . I authorize you to take over, on my behalf, this situation as if I was there. . . . He has his wife to take care of him—he chose her (at such an age!). . . . All he has to do is keep on that way and not bother me any more. . . . I hope the newspapers don't catch on. . . . Then I'll really curse the moment I had any parents at all."

In a subsequent letter she wrote: "If he is very bad off let me know by cable or telephone—and if he is at the end one day—take care that he dies well taken care of because of course if he dies in bad hands or things like that I alone will be blamed. I'm sending you from now on $200 also for him. But remember I'm not maintaining any wife." Despite her anger, Maria paid all the bills for her father's hospitalization, which amounted to more than four thousand dollars.

In early spring of 1964, she began rehearsing with Zeffirelli for a production of her signature opera, *Norma,* to open in Paris on May 22. The director suggested that she avoid the risk of the high notes. Most of the audience would never know the difference, he told her, "and those that do won't care." But Maria refused to compromise the music in any way. " 'You might be right, but *I'll* know,' she said fiercely, 'and *I'll* care.' "

Zeffirelli spared no effort or expense to make the Paris *Norma* a showcase for Maria's mature sensuality. "The original Callas Norma had been a virginal creature, almost the Casta Diva [Stainless Goddess] she invokes,"

"What a pity this woman never had a child": Callas with child actors in Norma

he wrote. "Now she was an altogether more romantic creature, someone who has loved and who is now a passionate woman, not an untouched priestess." He created on the stage an enchanted forest whose colors changed with the seasons, which Zeffirelli described: "beginning in spring with everything green, then hot summer when she has arranged a tent for shade, then a third act of red and yellow autumn as the tragedy begins, and finally a burned-out, blackened winter. It was the right setting for her. Here Maria, denied children of her own, could sing her heart out for Norma and the children they were trying to tear from her. It was the other half of the passionate Maria in *Tosca* and could never have been done before the episode with Onassis."

Describing how well Callas worked with the child actors in *Norma,* Zeffirelli said, "When the premiere came, Maria was so tender with them. Immensely tender. Like a real mother. My God, what a pity this woman never had a child."

The quality of her Norma and the resulting reviews varied with hair-raising unpredictability from day to day. Zeffirelli would never forget the nerve-wracking anticipation as she began the first act. "Would she make it or not, would her voice hold out?" But it was Maria's fourth performance of *Norma,* when Onassis was in the audience, that started a riot. Together with Onassis in the royal box sat Princess Grace and the Begum Aga Khan. Those scattered elsewhere included Rudolf Bing, Charlie Chaplin, Yves St. Laurent, and many members of the French government.

From the first notes it was clear that Maria was in trouble. Many, including the French critic Claude Samuel, would recall wincing again and again with every missed note. Particularly with Aristo in the audience, she was determined to wrestle The Voice into submission, but in the final scene it broke on a critical high C.

The audience exploded in whistles, boos, and catcalls. Drawing herself up to her full height, Maria raised her hand and stopped the orchestra; she signaled them to start over again. This time she hit the note perfectly, and the crowd turned on itself, erupting into two warring factions, for and against Callas. When the curtain came down, the fighting didn't abate. Hand-to-hand battles broke out in the elegant corridors of the Paris opera house. Finally the French authorities had to be called to quell the disturbance.

A shaken Maria left the opera house in Aristo's Rolls-Royce, desperately in need of consolation, exhausted by the weakness of her voice and the volatile reactions of her fans. (She later asked Zeffirelli, "Oh, why can't I sing Norma in a forest all alone, me and the moon, instead of having to go through this?") Onassis was there to supply the sanctuary she needed. The couple returned to the *Christina* and sailed to Skorpios for the summer.

Onassis was completely obsessed with the creation of his own paradise that year, and there was no limit to what he would spend to realize his vision of Xanadu. A British writer, Charles Graves, whom he impulsively invited to fly with him to Skorpios to see the work in progress, reported the staggering scale of the undertaking: "Alongside a jetty an enormous tank-landing craft was disgorging road-mending materials to dozens of workmen stripped to the waist. . . . Nine kilometres of roads are planned and six are already completed. . . . Bulldozers are clearing seven acres of pasturage. . . . Each morning, except Sunday, Onassis went ashore, long before I had breakfast in bed, discussing points with the architect or the foreman, returning [to the *Christina*] for lunch at two o'clock and then going back to Skorpios."

Onassis wanted to plant the island with every flower and tree he remembered from his childhood in Smyrna, including fields of fragrant tobacco. Entertaining a very few visitors (among them his sister Artemis) he was totally content living with Maria on the *Christina* anchored in the small harbor as he labored with his own hands, day by day, often bare-chested and wearing only shorts to show off his impressive physique. His children, however, still resented Maria's presence and would not deign to come to see their father's proud creation.

Panayiotis Zigomalas, who was temporarily the captain of the *Christina* for eight months during late 1964 and 1965, told me that Onassis invited him to bring his wife and spend Christmas on Skorpios, since Aristotle and Maria would be alone. When Zigomalas asked why his children weren't coming, Onassis replied that Christina was in the States and Alexander in Athens. "You know, they want to be with their friends." But the captain tracked down Alexander and convinced him to surprise his father, saying how much he regretted that he hadn't spent more time with his own father, who had just died. Alexander agreed to fly back from Athens with him on the company plane, "but we dropped him off in Lefkada so he would come on his own and it wouldn't look like a setup. Onassis was on deck when he saw this dinghy coming toward us, and when he saw that Alexander was on it, his eyes filled with tears. He embraced the boy as if he hadn't seen him in twenty years."

Earlier that year, in June, Korinna Spanidou, then twenty-five, a physical therapist who worked in the orthopedic clinic of Dr. Theodore Garofalidis in Athens, had been brought aboard the *Christina* to treat Onassis for a neck problem. Soon she was hired as a permanent member of the staff to administer daily exercise and massage to him and Maria.

An able conversationalist and curious reader who was encouraged to browse in the ship's library, Korinna was regularly welcomed at the master's dinner table when no important visitors were aboard. "I believe that I owe a great deal to Callas' reluctance to invite people on the *Christina,* as Onassis used to do," Korinna wrote in her Greek-language reminiscences of these years, *Onassis As I Knew Him.* A close observer of their long private periods aboard ship, she got to know the couple as few others would.

Except for weekends when he stayed on the island, Onassis usually left early in the morning, taking his Piaggio to Athens. He usually returned at lunchtime. "Around two we ate, then he had a siesta and, around five o'clock, he would say cheerfully: 'Where would you like me to take you, girls?' "

A rare photograph of Callas and Korinna Spanidou
aboard the Christina, *showing off their toned bodies*

The evening would then continue with some sailing or even a rowboat ride with Onassis rowing, a picnic on a beach or a visit to a nightclub or taverna on one of the nearby islands. There were always baskets packed with delicacies, including the dark homemade bread that Artemis sent to the ship daily and Aristo's favorite appetizer, brick-colored sea urchin eggs, which the sailors would gather for him by diving into the ocean when there was a full moon. Other favorite foods which he had flown in from around the world included caviar from Iran, oysters from the Pacific, salmon and trout from Norway and Sweden, even marinated camel meat from Cappadocia. "Besides these, the chef prepared his own specialties, which were also superb, since he had been the head cook of Iran's shah," Korinna recalls. "The serving of appetizers and drinks was a ritual which frequently lasted two or three hours. . . . Then Onassis would wink and say, 'We are going to eat a simple steak and salad!' But this was a lie: the most delicious foods in the world were waiting for us at the table."

In her reminiscences, Korinna evocatively describes a typical night on the *Christina:*

The breeze carries the sounds of the crickets and the powerful scent of jasmine from Skorpios, mixed with the saltiness of the sea. In the darkness, three people, Callas, Onassis and myself, under the light of the stars, are listening to the music of the waves. It is late . . . everyone on the boat is asleep. The spark from the cigar in Onassis' hand flickers. . . . I am certain that the silence will soon turn into a slow chat, almost a monologue. . . . I have never seen him so relaxed, in such good mood and so carefree as that summer. Abandoned to the memories of a life full of extraordinary adventures, he wanted to confess them and to place them as an open book at the feet of his beloved Maria. During those evenings, he bared his soul to us. Callas was listening to him intently and bombarded him with many questions. . . . She would turn to me and say, full of enthusiasm, "Did you hear, Korinna? But what you are telling us, Aristo, is fascinating!" She was an indefatigable listener and he an unsurpassable narrator.

Korinna administered exercise and massage to Maria and Ari every day on board the ship, though "between the two, Callas was more systematic." Despite the flabbiness of certain parts of her body, owing to her considerable weight loss, two areas, Korinna noticed, showed astonishing muscular development: "the muscles of the neck and those of her stomach and abdomen were like iron. The first time she started exercising she told me proudly: 'Give a punch to my stomach with all your strength!' I had the impression that my hand hit iron armor. Through her diaphragm and breathing exercises, she had succeeded in having tremendously strong abdominal muscles." The extraordinary diaphragm and abdominal muscles of an opera singer who had practiced every day since childhood had doubtless helped Maria hide her pregnancy four years earlier.

When I spoke to Korinna Spanidou in July of 1998 at the Grande Bretagne Hotel in Athens, she told me that Maria was proud of the slender body she had achieved and worked hard to maintain it. "I remember once I went to Onassis' apartment in Monte Carlo to give her a massage. She was lying in bed completely nude but with all kinds of jewelry on her as if she was going to Maxim's. 'Aristo likes me this way,' she said. And she was very beautiful with her hair down and her lovely neck and ears all bejeweled. She gave herself totally to him without any condition. 'Nothing comes before what I feel for this man,' she once told me."

Korinna recalls that when Maria put on even a pound, she would take diuretics, although "she did not dare to take them in [Onassis'] presence, because he yelled that they would affect her heart." Nor did Onassis have any patience for dieting. Whenever Maria dared to try to refuse the offerings of the maitre d', Aristo would reproach her heatedly, says Spanidou: " 'The chef is killing himself all day in the kitchen to please us,' he would say. 'You can't ignore these people.' "

With covert dieting and self-medicating, Maria maintained her hard-won figure, but she was not so assiduous about keeping her most precious physical asset in shape. According to Spanidou, "On the *Christina* Maria rarely, if ever, exercised her voice. The fact is that she had abandoned it." She would tell Korinna, "This is the first time in my life I feel fulfilled. Until now, I lived for my career. I worked without stop, not knowing anything else of life."

But it was obvious to those who visited Maria and Onassis on Skorpios that fissures were starting to develop in their private paradise. The creation of Skorpios was Onassis' particular pride and he would take no suggestions from his lover. Spanidou recalls that when Maria innocently commented on the enormous expense of shipping and transplanting fully grown cypress trees onto the island, Onassis shot back a cutting reply: "Keep in mind that anything that has to do with my pleasure and entertainment, I like to buy it ready. I do the same with my mistresses. I make sure they are broken in before I acquire them."

It was an outburst without any reason, Korinna observed.

"I don't understand. What do you mean?" Callas asked him, upset.

"Exactly what I said," he repeated.

When Onassis exploded at Maria, according to their friends, she would either return fire in Greek, or dissolve into tears and run out of the room, but she would quickly get over her anger. Korinna describes one morning when she came to Maria's cabin for their regular session and found "an unrecognizable Callas. She was pale, with black circles under her eyes; she was a mess." Maria told the masseuse, "I'm leaving for Paris. I'm going to Bruna. . . . Would you like to come with me, Korinna?" Before Spanidou could respond, the telephone rang. "Onassis' voice was heard. 'Maryo, take Korinna and let's go on a ride with the speedboat. The weather is good.'

"She jumped up like a little girl, very excited, and she started getting dressed. She had forgotten everything! Onassis was like that. His anger would disappear as fast as it would rise."

Often friction broke out when Maria's profound native shyness—the true self that lurked behind the imperious diva—clashed with Onassis' self-promoting plans, as happened during the summer of 1964, when he attempted to trade on Maria's fame to wangle a deal to get fresh water for Skorpios delivered from the nearby island of Lefkada. Onassis promised the people of Lefkada that if they would agree to provide him with the water, Callas would sing in their public square. When he told Maria, according to Korinna, she exclaimed, "You must be crazy, Aristo! It's out of the question! First, I have abandoned the exercises, and my voice is not obeying me any longer, and then, how is it possible to sing in an open space without acoustics and without a microphone? . . . I absolutely refuse to make a fool of myself."

According to Korinna, when the appointed hour arrived, he advised everyone to prepare for the visit to Lefkada, but an outraged Callas declared that she would not come. Then Onassis became furious. " 'You'll come whether you want to or not.' . . . In a short while, we saw Onassis bringing Maria. Forced into the boat, she was silent and had a long face. He sat beside her, nudging her with his leg, telling her in a manner that did not accept any objections: 'You hear what I'm saying? You'll sing, no matter what!' "

After the mayor of Lefkada introduced her in the village square, Callas did get up to sing, "as if she was an automaton." But soon her voice flooded the square, at the beginning in low, velvet tones, "then it mounted in all its intensity and passion as she sang arias from *Cavalleria Rusticana* and I do not recall what else." The islanders burst into a delirium of cheers, according to Korinna, and the local barber offered the most moving tribute. He ran to his shop and returned with the cage holding his favorite canary and presented it to her. Callas came to adore her canary. Not long after, with increasingly typical intolerance, Onassis released the bird while they were having coffee on deck. "He claimed that he did not like to see birds imprisoned in cages," Korinna recalls.

Few celebrities enjoyed the pleasure of the *Christina* that summer, Korinna remembers. The most frequent guests were Artemis, her husband, and Ari's closest friend in the fraternity of shipowners, Panaghis Vergottis. Maria had first met the seventy-year-old Vergottis at the lavish dinner Onassis gave for her at the Dorchester Hotel in London after her performance of *Medea* in 1959. She came to consider the old man a father and mentor as she became alienated from George Callas. Vergottis cared deeply for Maria—some even say he fell in love with her. Of all Onassis' friends, he knew the most about opera, and his Old World elegance and genteel appreciation of Maria's talents ensured him a special place in her heart. Although Vergottis, who lived in a suite at the Ritz in London, had the air of an English gentleman, his heart was entirely Greek, and he took a nationalistic pride in Maria's success.

When Aristo and Maria had a falling out, Vergottis was always the diplomat between the warring lovers. He was more understanding than Onassis of Callas' fears that her earning power was fading. "I am always careful," she often said, "always afraid that I will die, or live the end of my life in poverty." In the aftermath of the Paris *Norma,* Maria had to face the fact that she could not count on her voice to bring in enough to maintain her lavish lifestyle forever. Aristo advised her once again to consider starring in a film. But the more pragmatic Vergottis suggested investing in a ship as the most reliable path to financial security.

In September of 1964, Vergottis heard of a ship for sale in a Spanish shipyard. The asking price was a bargain because the company that had ordered it had backed out of the contract. Vergottis offered $3.6 million, 25 percent cash with the balance on mortgage over eight years. Then he flew to Greece and told Aristo and Maria his plan: Callas would buy a 25 percent holding in the company, Vergottis would buy a 25 percent interest, and Ari would buy the remaining 50 percent. Then Onassis would transfer 26 percent of his share to Maria as a gift, giving her a 51 percent controlling interest in the ship, which would be managed by Vergottis.

Eventually Vergottis acquired the ship, called the *Artemision II,* for only $3.4 million, even less than his first offer because prices had declined in the meantime. In late October the three new partners met in Paris for a dinner at Maxim's to celebrate the deal they dubbed Operation Prima Donna. Maria was delighted to have joined the ranks of shipowners.

In the winter of 1964 the two lovers went for a visit to the United States. While there, Onassis had a meeting with Jacqueline Kennedy that would shake his relationship with Callas to its foundations, according to Maria's friend Mary Carter. "Maria came to New York with Ari and he called Jackie Kennedy to see how she was doing," Mary Carter told me. "You know, after she moved to New York, Jackie used to have these Sunday brunches at her apartment. She immediately invited him. He said to Maria: 'Hey, Jackie invited us to brunch on Sunday at her place.' Maria said, 'Are you sure she invited both of us?' He had someone call to ask, and was told, 'Regrettably, there is only one place still available and the invitation must be limited to Mr. Onassis.' " When Onassis arrived at Mrs. Kennedy's new fifteen-room apartment at 1040 Fifth Avenue, overlooking the Metropolitan Museum of Art, he immediately divined the reason for the exclusive invitation. "All the guests were men. The only woman present was Jackie."

Jacqueline Kennedy's refusal to entertain Maria made it unmistakably clear to Onassis that the president's widow considered him a possible swain. Until then he had been linked with her sister, Lee, but now he suspected that he might have a chance at a bigger conquest—in terms of prestige, the biggest in the entire world. The one thing Ari, a competitor to his core, could not resist was a contest. As always, he would play to win.

"The way Jackie snared him was classic," Mary Carter told me. "She set a trap for Onassis and caught him. She had very little money after JFK died and debts piled to the ceiling. When she was invited on the cruise by Ari, she saw how he lived and spent money and how he treated her sister Lee. A smart woman can get any man if she makes it her life's goal."

Shortly after Ari's first brunch at Mrs. Kennedy's, huge bunches of red roses began arriving at the apartment regularly, with Onassis' card attached.

All Maria's friends agree that she did not immediately notice her lover's romantic interest in the most famous woman in the world because the new year that began shortly after their New York visit proved to be especially stressful for the singer. The trouble began early in 1965, when her fledgling career as a shipowner ran aground.

The ship she had bought into, the *Artemision II*, developed engine problems on her maiden voyage, and Vergottis, who was as superstitious as his fellow Greek partners, declared it "an unlucky ship." He took Maria out for another dinner at Maxim's in January of 1965 (Aristo was in Athens) and persuaded her to change the terms of the partnership by converting her $168,000 investment into a straight loan that would pay her 6.5 percent interest. She liked the idea of steady interest and he assured her that she could at any time exercise the option on her twenty-five shares in the company. She later said that Vergottis told her, "As I love you very much, I think this is a better way. . . . If, which I doubt, the ship does not do well, you can always pull out, and you have had the interest on your money."

The next day, when Maria called Athens to tell Aristo, who had already given her his twenty-six shares, what Vergottis had convinced her to do, Onassis said he did not see any sound financial reason for the change. Maria replied, "Never mind, let us not hurt Mr. Vergottis' feelings. He is doing his best for me."

Onassis was preoccupied with business problems of his own. Prince Rainier was preparing to strip him of his controlling interest in Société des Bains de Mer (SBM), the company that owned Monte Carlo's major assets, a move that would eventually force Onassis to sell his shares for ten million dollars, less than a third of what he felt they were worth.

Maria was also distracted, worrying about her voice as she prepared for the commitments she had made for 1965: eight performances of *Tosca* at the Paris Opéra in February, followed by two in New York at the Met in March, then back to the Paris Opéra in May for five performances of *Norma*, before concluding with *Tosca* at Covent Garden on July 5.

The performances of *Tosca* in Paris that began on February 19, 1965, were so well received by the French, who were thrilled with the lavish production, that Maria was even persuaded to sing for an extra, ninth, night on March 13. The next day she flew to New York, to prepare for a very different *Tosca*. Maria had always resented the Met's notoriously ugly scenery, its shoddy old costumes, and, worst of all, the woefully inadequate rehearsal time allotted. She had not sung there for seven years and so her performances were sold out far in advance. Some fans, hoping only for standing-room tickets, camped out for days before her arrival, sleeping on the pavement under a huge banner that read WELCOME HOME CALLAS.

When the curtain was raised for the opening performance, Maria's first word, "Mario," uttered off stage, before her entrance, provoked four minutes of applause that forced the orchestra to stop and wait. The ovation was even greater than the one that had greeted the arrival of Jacqueline Kennedy minutes before. It was the only time the widowed first lady would be outshone by Callas.

Maria's performance was interrupted by applause so often that the opera ended an hour later than scheduled. All the critics exulted over the homecoming of the legend. They feverishly celebrated her acting, her singing, her hands. But Harold Schonberg, writing in the *New York Times,* was notably clearer-eyed: "This was supreme acting, unforgettable acting. But now we come to matters vocal, and the story is less pleasant. Miss Callas is operating these days with only the remnants of a voice."

Maria was staying at Onassis' apartment at the Pierre, but Aristo was not with her in New York during this appearance. Mary Carter, however, flew that morning to see her. After lunch with Maggie van Zuylen and Vergottis, Maria, Larry Kelly, and Mary Carter went shopping to buy Onassis bathing trunks. When they couldn't find any in his waist size (42) Maria asked Mary to buy some for him at Neiman Marcus in Dallas. (At the doting lover's request, Mary Carter would get a dozen of the bathing trunks in different colors.) Callas did manage to find a yellow rain hat. "It rains so much on Skorpios and we walk a lot." And having found a bathing suit with a mesh center, she insisted Mary buy one too. " 'My waist is much narrower than yours, but I think it will fit,' she told me in her brutally honest way. In 1965 she still had hopes that she and Onassis would get married. 'I think we will be spending a lot more time on Skorpios,' she told me, smiling happily."

After Maria's triumphant return to the Met, when she was cheered by her American fans, including Jacqueline Kennedy, expectations were high that she would also conquer Paris with the *Norma* that was based on Zeffirelli's London production of the previous year. Norma, Maria's signature role, was also one of her most difficult roles, and she was terrified of reliving the fiasco that had started a riot at L'Opéra in 1964. Her fears were exacerbated by an abrupt fall in her blood pressure, a dry throat due in part to an unseasonable heat wave, and the news that Meneghini was trying to get the courts to blame Maria officially for their separation, which if he succeeded would entitle him to a larger share of their property.

On opening night, May 14, 1965, Maria had to be pumped full of tranquilizers and vitamins. Before the curtain went up, the house manager announced that the diva was not in good health and declared, "Nevertheless, Callas will sing, but she begs for your indulgence." Her singing proved adequate, but her nervousness was compounded by feuding among the cast members, and the tensions took their toll on the ensuing nights.

In the third performance, Maria's close friend, Giulietta Simionato, was replaced in the role of Adalgisa by Fiorenza Cossotto, who decided to make the opera a personal duel. The two sopranos are supposed to sing in close harmony while holding hands, but whenever Maria would signal the end of a note, Cossotto would hang on for a few extra seconds, driving her own claque of fans wild with excitement. Inevitably, Cossotto would reach and hold the high notes that Callas couldn't get.

Maria's nerves grew worse with each performance, and by the last night, May 29, she was desperate. Her doctor advised her to cancel the performance, but she wouldn't. During their important duet Cossotto nearly drove her off the stage, and it was clear by the end of the third act that Maria could not continue. When the curtain came down, she collapsed on the stage and was carried to her dressing room. There would be no fourth act. In fact, Maria would never sing at L'Opéra again. A friend who went backstage said: "She seemed almost dead. That night she understood that she could not sing Norma again. When Callas understood that, she ceased being Callas."

There were still four performances of *Tosca* in London at the end of June hanging over Maria, and though she knew she couldn't do them, she also refused to cancel. She was well enough to attend the Rothschild ball in Paris on the Friday before her London rehearsals were scheduled to start, but then she disappeared for several days, leaving the British papers to wonder what had happened to her. Covent Garden's general administrator, David Webster, flew to Paris to plead with Maria, but ultimately he replaced her in the first three performances. He did persuade her, however, to appear for the last night of *Tosca*, which was a royal gala to be attended by the Queen. But by then the British fans who had eagerly bought the tickets for the first three performances were furious. When she did finally appear, on July 5, she gave merely a serviceable performance to a less-than-enthusiastic audience.

After she left the stage that night, Maria must have suspected the truth—that she would never again be able to sing an entire opera. In fact, she wouldn't even try to sing in public at all until eight years later.

Maria returned to Skorpios to lick her wounds, but the idyllic life she had enjoyed the year before was now marred by outbursts from her lover that cut her more deeply than the catcalls and boos of Paris or Milan. Many visitors to the *Christina* in the summer of 1965 described how Ari would often taunt and belittle her in public about her fading voice when he wanted to be cruel: "What are you? Nothing! You just have a whistle in your throat that no longer works," he would rail.

And he became even more controlling and proprietary about his private kingdom of the *Christina* and Skorpios, constantly reminding Maria, when she tried to make even minor changes to her stateroom: "Never forget, my darling, you are not the housewife here. You are only a guest."

Onassis knew that the best way to hurt Maria, especially in public, was to criticize her appearance. Like any woman who began life as an unattractive, unloved child, she never felt secure in her beauty. "Her nose was too big, her eyes too big, yet in a theater from a distance, she was stunning," John Ardoin told me. "She was a beautiful woman in a kind of strange way, but I don't think she ever believed it. Although Callas the great diva basked in the adoration of her fans, Maria the woman always felt fat, unattractive, and unloved. But she wanted Maria to be as important as Callas, and Onassis provided that opportunity. She had never liked being Maria before."

Maria was always fishing for compliments. Zeffirelli recalls her constant refrain: "Franco, don't you think I look pretty in this dress, and what about my suntan? You know, darling, for years they wanted me as white as the camellias in *Traviata,* but can you play Violetta all your life?"

It was when she would try this ploy on Onassis that his cruel wit was most inspired. John Ardoin recounted for me a well-known story that was told to him by Larry Kelly, who had gone to pick Maria up one night in Paris. "She was dressed and all ready, but she kept changing her dress, asking 'How do I look?' It soon became apparent that they were going to be joined by Mr. Onassis. They went to dinner and during the course of the meal she had on this little hat—a round thing with veils—and she kept posing, trying to draw Onassis' attention to the hat. Finally she said, 'Ari, you didn't say anything yet about my hat.' He looked her up and down and said, 'Harmony, my love, harmony.' She said, 'What do you mean?' and he replied, 'Either get a bigger hat or cut down your nose.' "

At the same dinner, Callas propped her legs up on a nearby chair, as she was wont to do on account of her bad circulation. Larry Kelly, who was balding, had just undergone a painful series of hair transplants. According to Ardoin, "Onassis asked Larry all about it, and meanwhile Maria's leg was up on the chair and Onassis was fondling her. He said, 'Poor Larry, he spends so much money to put hair on his head and Maria spends so much money to take hair off her legs!' That's how he was, as far as an eloquent lover!"

The fights between Maria and Onassis escalated, sometimes becoming physical. Marilena Patronikola remembers how, as a sixteen-year-old, she tried to protect Christina, then thirteen, from witnessing a row aboard the yacht. "We were in the main salon," she told me, "and Maria said she was leaving the next day to go to Milan or Rome. My uncle said, 'You can't go. I've invited important people on the boat.' . . . But she said she was going anyway. He told her, 'No, I won't allow it.' She said she wasn't asking for permission, she was going. Whack! He hit her. She exploded and flew at him, hitting him hard. She was bigger than he was, and she gave as good as she got." Panaghis Vergottis, who was there, tried without success to separate the combatants, and when Marilena heard Christina coming down the hallway, she "rushed out to keep her from coming to the salon while they were still at it. I remembered a friend of mine who lost her voice after seeing her father beating up her mother and I didn't want Christina to be traumatized."

During the tumultuous summer of 1965, Onassis put himself in charge of negotiating a project that was proposed to Maria: a film version of Puccini's *Tosca* directed by Zeffirelli, who was convinced that Callas would be "the new Greta Garbo."

Panaghis Vergottis, too, was wildly enthusiastic about the project, as he told her when she flew to London to console him on the death of his brother. Even though Maria had made outrageous demands (according to Zeffirelli) for percentages of the gross as well as a huge salary, a compromise was struck and all parties seemed ready to sign the contract in Monte Carlo. But first Maria would take the contract back to the *Christina* to show Aristo. After two weeks her agent, Sander Gorlinsky, got a call to come at once to the *Christina* from London.

As soon as Gorlinsky got there, Onassis began to carp about the agreement, raising one objection after another. At one point, when Maria asked a question, Onassis shouted, "Shut up! Don't interfere, you know nothing about these things. You are nothing but a nightclub singer." Onassis finally offered to buy the rights and produce the film himself, but Gorlinsky believed he was being disingenuous and wanted only to defeat the project and thereby reinforce Maria's fears and self-doubts.

Zeffirelli, who believed that "to capture her *Tosca* would surely be one of the artistic monuments of our time," has a slightly different take on the fiasco. He found Onassis "eager to help" and to accept the support of Lord Brabourne and Tony Havelock-Allan of British Home Entertainment, the government-backed film company.

Onassis invited Zeffirelli and the two Britons aboard the *Christina.* When the director arrived, Onassis was all smiles and insisted on personally piloting the Chris-Craft on a tour of the island, "just the two of us alone." During the excursion Onassis stunned Zeffirelli when, to celebrate the sunset, he suddenly quoted lines from Dante in Italian. In his autobiography Zeffirelli puzzled, "Had he learned it parrot-fashion to impress? Was he a genuine lover of poetry? I was never able to fathom the man. . . . He was a mass of contradictions—hence his peculiar fascination for Maria." (Onassis' now deceased adviser Professor Yiannis Giorgakis once told me that often when Ari was anticipating an important meeting, he would call Giorgakis ahead of time and ask him to research some bons mots or literary allusions appropriate to the occasion.)

Zeffirelli describes a rather uneasy dinner aboard the *Christina* that followed the tour. Maria kept saying, "I'm only doing this because Ari insists I should go into movies. You know, Franco, I've been through hell all my life, worked like a slave, and look what happened—Meneghini stole everything. . . . But if Ari insists I do it, I'll do it, though I'd rather stay here and relax."

According to Zeffirelli, "The main difficulty for us was that Herbert von Karajan [a renowned conductor and the artistic director of the Vienna State Opera] had acquired the film rights to the opera and was insisting on producing it with his company. This would never tie in with the Covent Garden production, which we wished to use as the basis for the film. Nor was it likely that he and Maria would work together." Maria agreed: "Two prima donnas in a show are too many," she said of the volatile conductor. "If Karajan is involved, then I'm not interested."

Onassis then proposed to buy out von Karajan himself, and as the director and the British film executives were debating this tactic, "there was a quite unexpected outburst," according to Zeffirelli. "Maria and Onassis had been talking together in Greek, as they now did constantly, when suddenly he yelled something at her with almost a snarl of rage. While the three of us watched in blank amazement, a full-scale Greek row took place—shouting, arm-waving—until Maria burst into tears and ran from the deck."

Zeffirelli reports that he later left Onassis drinking brandy and went down to Maria's suite. "She fell into my arms and sobbed her heart out. When the first spasm ended she started to talk through the racking sobs, telling me about Ari, how he was the first to make her feel like a woman, the first really to make love to her, and how afraid she was of losing him."

(Stelios Galatopoulos, however, writes that Callas told him the fight was staged to furnish her an excuse to walk out, leaving the negotiations in the hands of Onassis.)

The next morning, according to Zeffirelli, Onassis announced that he would give him ten thousand dollars in development money; later an Onassis aide delivered to the director in Rome a paper bag full of cash. The plan collapsed, however, when von Karajan flatly refused to part with the rights to *Tosca*.

Many have suggested that Zeffirelli's film faltered on Onassis' sadistic penchant for humiliating Maria, but the director himself has conceded that Callas' lover cannot be blamed. In fact, Onassis offered to provide the money to buy the rights from von Karajan, but when the conductor refused to sell them, the project could not proceed, as Zeffirelli acknowledges. Soon after things fell apart, Maria called Zeffirelli and demanded the return of the ten thousand dollars. She was shocked to hear him tell her it was gone and he wasn't paying it back, it was spent on "development" of the projected film, and besides, Onassis wouldn't miss it. According to Zeffirelli, Maria replied: " 'It was my money. He made me pay it out of the little I have left.' . . . Then she was screaming, 'Give me my money back, give it to me, you understand?' It was the other Maria, the woman who hoarded cash with Meneghini, the Maria who resented paying her father's hospital bills and who loved shopping in Woolworth's."

But Maria's anger had less to do with her native frugality than with her avowed commitment to avoid even the appearance that she was exploiting Onassis' fortune. In fact, Callas was so insistent about paying her own way that some, like Amalia Karamanlis Megapanou, the former first lady of Greece, found it embarrassing. "Once when she was with Onassis, we were dining together and she wore an elegant diamond brooch—not heavy," Mrs. Megapanou recalled. "She insisted on saying that she bought it from the last royalties. 'A present to myself,' she said. We didn't doubt it. She felt the need to add, in front of him, that when she traveled alone on Olympic she always paid."

The failure of the *Tosca* film precipitated a fatal crisis in Maria's friendship with Panaghis Vergottis. When he heard that she had backed out of the project, the elderly shipowner called to upbraid her for ignoring his advice; it was essential, he believed, for her to film *Tosca*. Maria lost her temper and said something—it has never been established what exactly—that offended

Vergottis so deeply, he would never forgive her. A letter of abject apology she wrote him the very next day was of no avail.

When she saw that a reconciliation was not possible, Maria sent Vergottis a telegram asking that her loan be converted back to shares in the ship they jointly owned, so that control of the vessel would not remain in his hands now that he was angry with her. He replied curtly that, contrary to his earlier assurances, she had no right to such an option. Onassis entered the fray, battling with his old friend on Maria's behalf. The rift became permanent when the two accidentally ran into each other in Claridge's in London and Vergottis picked up a bottle of whiskey and threatened to throw it at Onassis' head. Later, Ari threatened to sue for Maria's shares of the ship; Vergottis warned that if the couple dragged him into court, their names would be soiled with scandal in the press.

Maria and Onassis did sue, and the case began to make its way through the British courts. Meanwhile, Maria turned her attention to a maneuver to try to settle the most important issue in her personal life. In the spring of 1966 she discovered that, according to a Greek law passed three years before her 1949 wedding to Meneghini, the marriage of a Greek citizen was recognized as valid only if it had taken place in a Greek church. She and Meneghini had been married in a Catholic church in Verona, and in the dusty sacristy at that.

If Italian law would never allow Callas a divorce, she reasoned that she could nullify her marriage by becoming a Greek national. Then, she was sure, Onassis would make their relationship official. To do this she would have to renounce her American citizenship. State Department documents I have obtained show that she applied in person on March 18, 1966, to the American embassy in Paris under the name on her birth certificate: Sophie C. Kalos. One of the documents states: "Mme. Kalos gave as her reason for renouncing her American citizenship her relationship with her estranged husband from whom she cannot obtain a divorce in Italy. . . . Mme. Kalos says that, if she has only Greek nationality, she is legally free from her husband, and that he can no longer make demands on her income and otherwise harass her." Other documents I uncovered in Greece show that "Maria Kalogeropoulos" had requested registration on the rolls of the municipality of Athens even earlier, on March 7.

At the beginning of April 1966 Maria announced that she was renouncing her American citizenship. Meneghini told the press, "As far as I am concerned, Maria will always be my wife." Onassis, when queried by reporters, was as usual carefully noncommittal: "All along, we have explained that we are very close, good friends," he announced. "This new event changes nothing. Of course, I'm very happy that her seven years of struggle have ended so well. It is wonderful for her to be a Signorina again."

These breezy words must have felt to Maria like so much salt rubbed in her wounds, for despite her insistence that she wanted only to free herself of Meneghini's "demands on her income" and harassment, her most profound ambition was for her love for Onassis to be sanctified by marriage. "Maria had a deep, religious, peasant's morality and she desperately needed a marriage certificate to make her feel all right about her behavior," said her friend from Milan, Giovanna Lomazzi. She would have to settle for other gestures and commitment while the elusive Onassis kept his options open.

Aristo did at least buy her the home he had promised—if not quite the house and garden she had been hoping for. "What do you want with a house? You know what a house costs to keep up? Besides, you wouldn't know how to decorate it," Mary Carter says he told Maria over lunch at the Ritz early in 1966. "So eventually he bought her the apartment on Georges Mandel, but she really wanted a house."

The apartment was on the third floor of a six-storey mansard-roofed building at 36 Avenue Georges Mandel in the toney 16th arrondissement, not far from the Arc de Triomphe, and was within walking distance of Onassis' home on Avenue Foch. Looking out of the towering French windows behind the wrought-iron balustrade on her balcony, Maria could see the leafy green park where well-heeled Parisians walked their dogs. And she could watch the leaves of "her" chestnut tree change with the seasons. As the years passed, Callas would become reluctant to leave the confines of her home, apparently satisfied to view the world from behind her curtains.

In her villa in Milan, Maria had indulged a taste she shared with Meneghini for a grotesquely ornate haut-bourgeois style. Now, though by no means embracing simplicity, she at least avoided the same mistakes by hiring Georges Grandpierre, a devoted fan of hers, to decorate the rooms. He filled the apartment's high-ceilinged public salons with lavish antiques and Renaissance paintings, gilded chandeliers and light fixtures that would have looked at home in Versailles. The curved marble fireplace, topped by a huge Empire mirror with gilded vines, supported two golden candelabra and a clock "au chinois" in bronze and gold carried by two figures of kneeling Chinese men, with a young Indian prince perched on top. The *salon rouge* was filled with the kind of chinoiserie that Onassis loved: enameled pagodas, a pair of bronze and cloisonné temple dogs with movable tongues—almost the twins of the ones on the *Christina*—a pair of bronze elephants carrying perfume burners on their backs. One might well have

Maria on stage, Maria off stage: in her Paris apartment

expected Tosca or Aida to walk in at any moment and launch into song. As the biographer Arianna Stassinopoulos wrote, "It was less a home than a tomb for a legend."

Everything in the apartment was in rigid order and there were no personal mementos in the public rooms. Callas indulged her former taste a bit more in the bedroom by salvaging some of the furniture she had owned with Meneghini: a rococo set consisting of carved and painted bed, bureau, and side tables, all in a bombé shape, lavishly lacquered in jonquil yellow, then heavily painted with flowers. Over the carved and upholstered bed and slightly to one side was an oil painting of the Virgin and Child. There was a touchingly childish note on an ornate armchair near the bed, where a plush toy, a large koala bear, sat. But even here an odd regimentation prevailed: Maria had Bruna bag and label every article of clothing, including every glove, handbag, and shoe, and catalogued each object according to where the diva had bought it and where she had worn it.

In contrast to the grand and impersonal public rooms, Maria created little sanctuaries for herself in her small study and the opulent bathroom, which was pink and white marble with mirrored walls. Its furnishings included a settee and large armchair, a telephone and record player, hanging plants and golden fixtures (like those in her stateroom on the *Christina*).

A candid photo taken by a friend in the 1970s shows her seated in her small study, which she had filled with the awards, photographs, caricatures, and stacks of books and librettos that had been banished from the more formal rooms. The snapshot shows a bespectacled Maria sitting in a chair in her study wearing white slippers and a blue robe, with no makeup and no jewelry except a large cross on a chain around her neck. She looks relaxed and at home, as she never was in the more glamorous public rooms that she had created as a stage setting for La Callas.

Though Maria implied to friends that she had bought the Georges Mandel apartment herself, it was in fact purchased by Onassis. Documents I have uncovered show that it was bought by two Panamanian companies: Westchester Corporation Ltd. and Trenton Inversion Company Inc. The companies, both owned by Onassis, bought the apartment for Maria and continued to pay the monthly common charges after she and Aristo parted and even after he died. Maria held the bearer shares, which gave her ownership of the apartment.

With her singing career at a standstill and Onassis taking more and more frequent trips to the United States, Maria spent her days decorating the apartment before moving in. She wrote to her former teacher and friend Elvira de Hidalgo in April of 1966, "I found an apartment and am dedicating myself to it for the moment. That way, I won't get too tired trying to work on both my voice and the house. . . . I need to talk to you, but have so much to do for this little apartment. . . . I'm much calmer now, but tranquillity is certainly not synonymous with happiness."

Maria had a painful hernia operation shortly after moving to Avenue Georges Mandel. As she explained to John Ardoin years later, Bruna attended her in the hospital and refused to let the nurses touch her.

The following spring, in April of 1967, Maria and Onassis had to appear in court in London for the suit against Vergottis. During the proceedings, their former friend tried his best to fulfill his threat to besmirch their names and re-ignite the scandal of their affair in the newspapers. At one point, after repeated personal questions posed by Vergottis' lawyers, Maria said, "We are here because of twenty-five shares for which I have paid, and not because of my relations with another man." When Callas was asked, "Do you regard yourself now as a single woman?" she paused, then answered, "In Italy no, elsewhere, yes." Onassis maintained his usual sangfroid about their relationship. When asked, "Did you regard her as being in a position equivalent to being your wife if she was free?" he answered, "No. If that was the case I have no problem of marrying her; neither has she any problem of marrying me." Then the counsel asked him, "Do you feel obligations toward her other than those of mere friendship?" Onassis replied, "None whatsoever"—a strategically considered reply that surely stung his fellow plaintiff.

After ten days of wrangling, the court found against Vergottis and ordered him to transfer twenty-five shares in the company to Maria and pay all her and Ari's legal costs. The judge said the case had "many of the elements of Sophoclean tragedy." Vergottis appealed.

That summer of 1967 was filled with battles and tensions between Aristo and Maria. The writer Willi Frischauer had been invited to join the couple on Skorpios to write Onassis' authorized biography, and every day the tycoon poured himself more enthusiastically into creating a heroic version of his life story for posterity. Frischauer recalled that Maria was annoyed when he and Onassis showed up late for meals; she fussed and worried, "like an irritated suburban housewife."

Maria knew that Onassis pursued other women, and she probably learned the identity of her primary rival in the fall of 1967, when Onassis hosted a mysterious dinner party for a special guest at Avenue Foch. He told his servants, Eleni and George Siros, to stay in their quarters all evening; he would serve the dinner himself. The guest, of course, was Jacqueline Kennedy, and if Eleni Siros ferreted out this information, she probably whispered it to Bruna, who was her close friend in Paris.

Maria continued to feel confident of Aristo's love for her, perhaps willfully deluding herself as his formerly earnest devotions gave way to sportive cruelties. He played out a sadistic little joke in November of 1967 when a reporter waylaid the couple coming out of Régine's in Paris at two in the morning. Asked whether rumors of an impending marriage were true, Onassis grinned and said, "You are late. We are already married. We married fifteen days ago. It was a wonderful thing." The reporter, taking him at his word, wrote up an exclusive for the next day's papers, noting that the couple appeared "particularly gay and lighthearted."

A week or so later, Maria was at the Hotel Pierre in New York. She wrote the following letter to Elvira de Hidalgo, revealing that her armor of denial was still intact: "Dearest Elvira, I drove you crazy, didn't I? You see what being in love does! . . . Aristo treats me so lovingly. He sends you his love and thanks you for being so understanding and such a dear friend to me. Please forgive my follies, we all have them, haven't we? Don't you find Aristo has changed for the better?"

Gossip columnists in the United States began noting the frequency with which Onassis was seen dining with Jacqueline Kennedy in Manhattan, at El Morocco, "21," and Greek restaurants like Dionysos and Mykonos. They inferred surprisingly little from such sightings. The pair were almost always with others, and anyway, the press were sure that the main contender for the Widow Kennedy's hand was the handsome, elegant, and eminently presentable former British ambassador to the United States, David, Lord Harlech. Few even considered the possibility that the successful suitor might be the short, swarthy Greek tycoon who had long been under J. Edgar Hoover's paranoid scrutiny.

On January 20, 1968, at the beginning of the most turbulent year of her life, Maria wrote to Elvira de Hidalgo again. Her letter spoke mostly of her efforts to retrain her voice. She had worked out a "new system," she said, tape-recording her voice at home to study its problems. "It's a long process, but I have a great deal of patience," she wrote. "I'll manage, just as I have in the past. If it's meant to be, okay. If not, I'll forget it. Basically, I have Aristo. What more could I want?"

Presumably Maria had read the newspapers and heard the gossip about all the time Aristo was spending in New York. But whether the possibility had not occurred to her or she simply could not bear to acknowledge it, the truth was increasingly plain: Onassis was rapidly slipping out of her grasp.

17

ON THE ROAD

Stay away from places that once bore
Silent witness to your love
For they hold the seeds of sorrow.

Ovid, *Remedia Amoris*

Nineteen sixty-eight was a watershed year in which the universal status quo was wracked by unexpected upheavals—student revolutions, political riots, and horrifying assassinations. It seemed as if the world was having a collective breakdown.

The mellow Age of Aquarius karma of the early sixties turned sour as students rioted in the United States and Paris, police clubbed demonstrators at the Democratic National Convention in Chicago, and the Tet Offensive battered Vietnam. President Lyndon Johnson announced that he would not run for reelection, then four days later Martin Luther King, Jr., was assassinated on a motel balcony in Memphis, bringing violence and rioting to cities throughout the United States. The next day, four thousand troops had to be sent to restore calm in Washington, D.C., after angry rioters looted and set fires in response to King's murder. In New York, students at Columbia seized and occupied the university's buildings for a week, until they were removed and arrested during a predawn raid by a force of more than a thousand policemen. A more violent student revolution erupted in Paris and paralyzed the whole country.

The social and political earthquakes would continue throughout the year, ending with a holiday season marked by three U.S. astronauts quoting from the Book of Genesis as they orbited the moon on Christmas Day. It was a year of fundamental and permanent changes.

Nineteen sixty-eight was also a critical year for the love affair of Maria Callas and Aristotle Onassis. Although at first they seemed untouched by the tumult, insulated by their wealth and fame, the events outside their doors would impinge on their personal life and change their relationship forever. They caused Maria to suffer her own breakdown as she made a bizarre, directionless journey through the western United States looking for help and the strength to go on.

In March and April, Callas was sailing with Onassis on their annual winter cruise in the Caribbean. Although most biographers say that they were estranged by this time, I have obtained two letters that Maria sent from the *Christina* to Bruna at 36 Avenue Georges Mandel, which make it clear that at the time she still believed all was well in her life with Aristo.

On March 19, Maria wrote from Nassau: "Just now we are going to Trinidad, then returning to Guadalupe, next maybe the Bahamas (Jamaica). Many wonderful things!" On April 3, from Jamaica: "We have made a marvelous voyage. . . . I'm already tan without being in the sun—imagine! I'm trying to diet. . . . I was inflating, we'll see if I can stick to it. I sing every once in a while. But there are a lot of people around and I don't feel like doing it. . . . The Signore wants us to go to New York toward the end of the month. I think maybe I'll go so I could study with the fine pianists of the Metropolitan and Dallas. I haven't decided yet. I will write you what clothes to send." In a postscript she added: "The 2 dogs are having a marvelous time. They adore the boat. It's incredible!"

The next day, April 4, Martin Luther King, Jr., was shot to death in Memphis. The ensuing civil unrest in the United States would little disturb Maria and Aristo in the calm seas around Jamaica. But after Callas left the ship in mid-May, a number of events that month and in the first two weeks of June would herald a cataclysm much closer to home, one that would drive her to the edge of a breakdown. By June Maria's tone and outlook were completely transformed. On June 16 she wrote from Paris to Elvira de Hidalgo:

I'm pretty well, considering the circumstances, but I feel as if I'd received a tremendous blow and haven't recovered from it yet. I received three telephone calls: one I didn't answer, but the other two I answered and they were disastrous for me.

As I told you, he's irresponsible and disgusts me. I'm in Paris and will try to reorder my thoughts in the midst of so much pain. I'm trying just to survive during these months. I'm not forcing myself much because I'm not very strong mentally or psychologically. I can't even think where to go to get some rest. I feel so lost after so many years of work and sacrifice for him, that I don't even know where to go. Isn't that incredible? If you want,

Maria and Ari in Nassau, shortly before Jackie Kennedy came between them

write me here. At least I feel all right for the moment here in my own home. An affectionate hug. I hope you won't worry too much about me, my dear lifelong friend.

In a brief interval, things with Aristo had changed and would never be the same. The undoing of Maria's happiness, like the making of it, began with a carefully calculated cruise aboard the *Christina*.

Easter fell on April 14 that year, and, unbeknownst to Maria, when Ari left her to fly to New York, supposedly on business, he instead collected Jackie Kennedy in his private plane and shuttled her to Palm Beach to spend the holiday with her children. He refused to exit the plane with her in Florida, with photographers lurking. After Jackie disembarked, Ari flew on to Nassau to be with his daughter before reboarding the *Christina* on April 21 to spend Greek Orthodox Easter with Maria.

Onassis somehow managed to convince Maria to disembark from the

Christina on May 18 and fly to Paris via New York on the pretext that the yacht would soon be starting back for Skorpios and there was no point in her making the tedious seventeen-day return voyage. Then he set about preparing the ship with great secrecy for an important guest. He told his sister Artemis to fly in from Greece because he wanted her along on the cruise, but he didn't tell her why.

On May 25, 1968, while the *Christina* was anchored in St. Thomas, Captain Kostas Anastasiades, Chief Engineer Stefanos Darousos, and Artemis Garofalidis were sent to the airport to pick up an anonymous but very important guest. Nervously, Ari waited behind on the yacht. He ordered the oil painting of Tina to be removed from its place over the fireplace (something he would never do to placate Maria). In its place he hung the portrait of his mother that he had commissioned.

According to Captain Kostas, Onassis had Jacqueline Kennedy fly into St. Thomas, a U.S. possession, to avoid a check through customs that would call attention to her presence. Accompanied by a single Secret Service agent, she appeared in the airport's V.I.P. lounge wearing a brown Valentino suit and was embraced and kissed by a surprised and delighted Artemis.

As soon as Mrs. Kennedy came aboard the *Christina*, speculation began among the crew, who only seven days before had seen Maria disembark to fly to New York and eventually to Paris. "Telis," as Jackie called him, was awaiting her in a fit of nervous anticipation, but once he had greeted the former first lady, they both began to relax. She and Onassis spent a peaceful, romantic four days sailing around the Virgin Islands. The engineer, Stefanos Darousos, told me that, although his boss carefully avoided any public display of affection, the consensus of the crew was that he and Mrs. Kennedy had become intimate by this time. "They touched often, you could sense the electricity between them," he recalled, contrasting it with their behavior on the first cruise, after Jackie had lost her baby. "We had seen many times how the Boss behaved with women he was pursuing, and there was clearly something going on between them."

The only other guest, besides Jackie and Artemis, was Joan Thring, the personal assistant to Rudolf Nureyev. At Ari's request, she alone had stayed on board when the guests on the previous cruise were asked to disembark at St. John the day before Jackie's arrival. Ari conscripted Joan to stay close to Jackie when photographers were around so that no one could snap a picture of him and Mrs. Kennedy alone together.

According to Joan Thring, Onassis and Jackie were alone during their afternoon teas, when they talked intently. Several biographers of both have speculated that it was in the course of these tête-à-têtes that the tycoon first suggested marriage. But it's just as likely that Jackie may have been the one to raise the subject. Dorothy Schiff, the former publisher of the *New York Post,* who was close to Mrs. Kennedy at the time, later wrote in her book, *Men, Money and Magic,* "Jackie wanted to marry Onassis more than Onassis wanted to marry Jackie."

Jackie and Ari had a lot to discuss on that Caribbean cruise. But by the time Mrs. Kennedy disembarked in St. Thomas on Wednesday, May 29, nothing had been decided. Many problems had to be solved before the pair could seriously consider marriage. There was the question of their conflicting religions and Onassis' divorce. There were Jackie's young children, Caroline, eleven, and John Jr., eight, who might be reluctant to accept the sixty-four-year-old Onassis as a stepfather. There was the all-important question of money. And there was also the question of Maria Callas.

Though the world press as yet had no inkling that Mrs. Kennedy and Mr. Onassis were romantically involved, some of their intimates were finding out. Jackie went to her brother-in-law, former attorney general Robert Kennedy, who had become her adviser and mentor since her husband's death, and told him of the marriage discussions, it was later reported. Bobby Kennedy was horrified when he heard Jackie's news. He had called Onassis a "complete rogue on a grand scale," but he couldn't tell her what to do with her life. He asked only that she postpone any announcement until after Election Day. Bobby was running for president and Jackie had promised to help him campaign, but he could easily imagine what her romance with the shipowner could do to his standing in the polls. She agreed to everything he asked.

(On May 17, a week before the widowed first lady boarded the *Christina,* President Lyndon Johnson received from J. Edgar Hoover a reply to a White House name-check request concerning Aristotle Socrates Onassis, according to the Onassis biographer Peter Evans. LBJ's interest in the shipowner may not have been inspired solely by Jackie's romance with him. According to Evans, a friend had told the president on April 3 that Onassis was negotiating a massive secret deal with the colonels who had seized control of the Greek government in a coup a year earlier. The agreement, code-named Project Omega, provided for the construction of a refinery near Athens, through which Ari planned to process crude oil bought from the Soviets. Project Omega would be the biggest business deal of Ari's career. His growing involvement with the former American first lady could be invaluable in facilitating it.)

On June 5, 1968, in the kitchen of the Ambassador Hotel in Los Angeles, minutes after his speech declaring victory in the California primary,

Robert Kennedy was shot by Sirhan Sirhan, a young, mentally unstable Palestinian Arab. He died twenty hours later.

His assassination would not only void Jackie's promise to wait until after the election to make her interest in Onassis known, it would also drive her to Aristotle Onassis for consolation and protection. At Robert Kennedy's funeral in St. Patrick's Cathedral in New York, those who approached her were alarmed to see she no longer could muster the stoic strength that had inspired the world during her husband's funeral five years earlier. Lady Bird Johnson later said that after the Mass, "I called out her name and put out my hand. She looked at me as if from a great distance, as though I were an apparition."

A funeral train took Bobby's casket and eleven hundred invited guests from New York to Washington in a sort of traveling Irish wake that was well lubricated with alcohol, but Jackie sat very still in a private car. Those who spoke with her remarked that she seemed almost incoherent, confusing Jack's and Bobby's assassinations, thinking she was still the first lady, apparently unaware where she was and who was dead.

If Jackie herself had any residual doubts about the wisdom of a union with Onassis, her grief over this second Kennedy murder and her fear for herself and her children may very well have convinced her that she could not afford to live outside the protective cocoon that such a man could furnish. "If they're killing Kennedys, then my children are targets," she said at the time. "I want to get out of this country." After Bobby's death, she was certain that she wanted to turn her back on the nation that worshiped her yet killed those she loved.

On the day that Robert Kennedy was assassinated, Onassis, aboard the *Christina,* was almost at the midpoint of the journey from Puerto Rico to Greece. He did not disembark until he reached Skorpios on June 16. But where was Maria Callas while Jackie was cruising on the *Christina* with Aristo, then grieving at the funeral of Robert Kennedy? The diva later told a reporter that she spent May and June in Milan to avoid the student uprising in Paris, *"les événements de mai,"* which turned the streets of the French capital into a war zone between roving bands of riot police and youths. Yet according to her agonized letter of June 16 to Elvira de Hidalgo, Maria was "in Paris and . . . just trying to survive during these months. . . . I'm not very strong mentally or psychologically."

Callas had apparently learned of Jackie's Caribbean cruise and Aristo's serious intentions toward the widow, although, judging from his previous behavior, he was probably quite adept at keeping his mistress in the dark about his other amatory activities for as long as possible. Callas certainly had sounded completely happy in the letter she wrote Bruna only weeks before Jackie boarded the *Christina*. Back in 1959, when he began his affair with Maria, Ari believed for longer than anyone else that he could keep his wife and have his mistress too. In the spring of 1968, he probably also imagined that he could continue his relationship with Maria—of whose devotion he was certain—while negotiating for the hand of the illustrious widow. In any case, several of his friends say that Onassis never expected the marriage to Jackie to happen, and some doubt he really wished it. "He wanted the world to know that the most famous woman in the world had chosen him, but he thought he would find a way out of it until the very end," Alexis Minotis, one of his closest friends, told me shortly after Onassis' death.

Diplomatic maneuvers took up a lot of Onassis' time that summer—and the prime mover in the negotiations may have been Jacqueline Kennedy. She launched a campaign to convince her family and friends that Onassis was a worthy suitor and to entreat the Catholic Church not to denounce her for such a marriage.

During one June weekend she brought "Telis" to see her mother and stepfather at the Auchincloss estate in Newport. Jackie perhaps did not realize that Janet Auchincloss, who inevitably considered Onassis their social inferior, had formed a strong dislike of him ever since a previous encounter with him in London: she had stormed his suite in Claridge's a few years earlier looking for her other daughter, Lee. Onassis, in a dressing gown, coolly informed her that Princess Radziwill had just left.

Jackie had better luck when she introduced Onassis to her former mother-in-law, Rose Kennedy, at Hyannis Port. Rose described the visit in her memoir, *Times to Remember*: "I have a memory of him one summer day on our front porch sitting rather scrunched up in one of our tall, fanback white wicker chairs. . . . The white paint on the wicker was beginning to flake, as it always does. . . . And knowing of Onassis' fabulous wealth and style of life—islands, yachts, and villas with retinues of servants—I wondered if he might find it a bit strange to be in such an informal environment as ours. If so, he showed no sign of it. He was quietly companionable, easy to talk with, intelligent, with a sense of humor and a fund of good anecdotes to tell. I liked him. He was pleasant, interesting, and, to use a word of Greek origin, charismatic."

At that point, however, the woman whom Jackie affectionately called *belle-mère* did not yet realize that Onassis was being proposed as a successor to her son in the widow's life. As for Jackie's father-in-law, Joseph Kennedy, the patriarch of the Kennedy clan, he had suffered a major stroke in 1961 and so was unable to speak intelligibly. It is unclear whether the old man realized that both he and Onassis had once enjoyed the favors of the same woman: Gloria Swanson, who was Joe Kennedy's longtime mistress and had been a brief fling for Ari.

Between long weekends during which he charmed Jackie's family and friends, arriving each time with armfuls of gifts for Caroline and John, Onassis was busily jetting back to Maria. After the brief cruise with Mrs. Kennedy, the *Christina* had left St. Thomas at 12:10 a.m. on May 30, stopped briefly for supplies in San Juan, Puerto Rico, and then crossed the Atlantic with its owner aboard, to arrive in Skorpios at 7:50 a.m. on June 16, 1968—the same day that Maria, in Paris, wrote her brokenhearted letter to Elvira de Hidalgo.

With his expectation—and gift—for having it both ways, Onassis managed not only to win over Jackie's intimates but also somehow to sweet-talk Maria into joining him back on the *Christina* in Greece for their annual summer stay on Skorpios. She flew there to be with him, despite having written only a week earlier that he was "irresponsible and disgusts me." She may well have been deluding herself, but whatever Aristo said, it was enough to convince her that they still had a future together. She arrived on June 23 and awaited her old friend Lawrence Kelly, whom she had invited to join them on the yacht.

Larry Kelly, the cofounder of the Lyric Theater of Chicago and the Dallas Civic Opera, had been among the first in the United States to recognize her unique talent, and he remained one of her most loyal friends. After a performance of *Madame Butterfly* in Chicago in 1955, a sheriff entered her dressing room to deliver a summons from a former agent who was trying to sue her. The cameras caught Maria, still in her makeup and kimono, her face twisting in anger as she shrieked at the process servers. Kelly snuck her out of the theater and hid her at his brother's house, and then patiently listened all night as the diva raged against her enemies. He was a small, dapper, handsome man with great charisma. His hairline was receding at the temples and he tended to wear three-piece suits in light colors. He was bisexual, and everyone who knew him, men and women alike, seemed to fall in love with him. To Maria, he was frequently a lifesaver.

Maria desperately needed such a friend in the summer of 1968 because, without her realizing it, the negotiations in the Onassis-Kennedy alliance were rushing irreversibly ahead. On Jackie's thirty-ninth birthday, July 28, Rose Kennedy organized a family dinner party at Hyannis Port. By then Jackie had told Teddy Kennedy, now the de facto head of the clan, that she intended to marry Onassis. Sometime in late July, Teddy called Onassis to say they needed to talk. Ari invited him to come to Skorpios along with Jackie.

Larry Kelly coaxed Maria back to music.

Maria and Larry Kelly were sitting on the deck of the *Christina,* watching the sun sink behind the island's verdant hills punctuated by the needle-like cypresses, when Onassis appeared on deck, poured himself a scotch, and told Maria that she would have to return to Paris at the beginning of August and wait for him there. Guests were expected on the *Christina* and she couldn't be aboard.

She looked at him in shock. No one was in Paris in August, especially the Parisians—especially in this worst of all summers.

"Go back to Paris and wait for me," Onassis repeated. "I'll join you in September."

Maria knew, without his saying the name, who was coming aboard, and she couldn't bear to be evicted on Jackie's account. She realized that she had made a mistake in allowing Aristo to win her back after the revelations of May, but she couldn't control herself. When it came to her love for Onassis, Maria had no pride, no *philotimo.* She was simply his woman, and no matter how much he humiliated her, she would endure it.

Larry Kelly observed how Onassis was treating her. He grieved that Maria had abandoned the opera stage and her daily vocal practice. But he was also sure that her singing career and her voice could be coaxed back to the heights they had once achieved. He would not let her suffer any more of Onassis' abuse, he told her.

John Ardoin, a close friend of Kelly's before becoming one to Maria as well, told me that Kelly made her get off the boat in 1968 and took her to

Paris. "He said, 'Now pack your bags, you're going to America—you need your buddies. I'm going to Rome to see Nicola Rescigno and I'll be back very soon.' When he got back to Paris a week later, he found Maria at the American Hospital. She had overdosed with sleeping pills. She claimed it was an accident, that she just took too many pills inadvertently. That may be true, but how do you draw the line between not caring how many pills you take and trying to commit suicide? He got her out of the hospital and brought her to America."

Mary Carter told me the same story, adding a further detail: "Maria got off the yacht in such a hurry that she left most of the jewels Onassis had given her in the safe on the ship. Naturally, he later gave some of them to Jackie."

Many of Callas' friends and acquaintances believe that leaving the *Christina* in anger rather than yielding quietly in August of 1968 was a fatal tactical error. Miltos Yiannakopoulos, Ari's friend and adviser, told me, "All of it wouldn't have happened, the marriage to Jackie wouldn't have happened, if Maria hadn't rushed off the *Christina* in a huff in the summer of 1968. It was a catastrophic mistake because it angered Onassis and left the field completely to Jackie. Ari was bound to Maria, and while he liked to have an occasional affair on the side, he wouldn't have been able to leave her and hook up with Jackie if Callas hadn't left him. She made the same mistake Tina made in 1959. It was the biggest mistake Maria ever made in her life."

This opinion was echoed by Panayiotis Zigomalas, the captain of the *Christina* from late 1964 to 1965. He told me, "Onassis knew no one loved him like Maria did, and if she had been patient and hadn't taken off in 1968, he wouldn't have let Jackie move in and take him from her. It was a big mistake to leave."

After Maria's overdose, Larry Kelly felt a trip would help raise her spirits, and he turned to another Callas friend, Mary Carter, for support. "He said 'I'm coming to New York with Maria. Can you please meet us there?' recalls Mrs. Carter, but she had to stay in Dallas to get her children ready for school. With considerable apprehension, Kelly escorted the heartbroken Maria to New York City at the beginning of a peripatetic journey intended to distract her from her despair.

When they got to Manhattan, Maria stayed for a few days with Costa Gratsos, who was Ari's close friend and the head of his American operations, and Gratsos' wife, Anastasia. She poured out her grief to her friends: "I have lived the most beautiful years of my life next to Aristo, and I have lived the worst." Gratsos had always been very fond of Maria and he felt that she was the one woman Onassis should have married. At this point, Callas still believed that Aristo would repent of his behavior, would telephone her and beg her to come back. She told Gratsos that, as she traveled with Larry Kelly, she would call him from every place she went to give him her telephone number in case Aristo wanted to reach her.

From New York, Maria and Larry called Mary Carter and said they wanted to visit her in Dallas. "I said to them: 'You can't come to Dallas in August. Birds don't fly, the weather is so ghastly.' " she recalls. "Maria was in a desperate state. She wanted to go somewhere, anywhere."

Larry Kelly next contacted the wealthy industrialist David Stickelbar, a good friend who lived in Kansas City, Larry's hometown. Stickelbar was an executive in his father's firm, Stickelbar and Sons, which made machinery for the baking industry. He offered to put up the wanderers in his spacious home and he enlisted a friend, Sue Blair, to join them and to travel with Maria until Mary Carter could take over. Kelly must have felt that propriety demanded a female traveling companion for Callas and that it would take more than one person to keep up the diva's spirits and prevent further acts of self-destruction.

Mrs. Blair, a former model then married to the *New York Times* correspondent William G. Blair, had never met Maria when she got Stickelbar's call. "Maria arrived sometime in late summer," Mrs. Blair told me. "Then she, David, Larry Kelly, and I all flew in David's company plane to Colorado Springs. I think she stayed in Kansas City only about three days." (Mr. Stickelbar recalled, "I suggested going to Colorado Springs to get Maria out of the house because she was a bit of a handful.") Mrs. Blair said that Maria had so much luggage with her, it overflowed the luggage bin of the small plane and had to be stowed in the bathroom as well. When they got to Colorado Springs, they stayed at the Garden of the Gods Hotel.

According to John Ardoin, Larry Kelly had pledged not only to see Maria through the shock of Onassis' treachery but also to help her line up American engagements and jump-start her career. As they began what turned into a six-week odyssey around the United States and Mexico, he spoke optimistically of Callas' career. She politely agreed, but without conviction. Wherever they went, she spoke vaguely of making commitments but kept changing her mind. The truth was, she didn't really want to go back to singing; the only thing she wanted was for Onassis to come back, and every day she waited for his call.

After three days at the Garden of the Gods, the four pilgrims—Maria, Kelly, Stickelbar, and Blair—drove over the mountains to Santa Fe, where they stopped at the Rancho Encantado, which had just completed extensive renovations.

Mrs. Blair was struck by the difference between the volcanic persona she had expected and this woman who was "very gracious to everyone she met." She also noted that "her speaking voice was very flat, not melodious at all, and she loved to do very simple things like going to dime stores and buying makeup, eating corn on the cob. She didn't talk about Onassis. My impression is that she thought she was going to get him back. What she talked about was her jewelry, how Meneghini had kept the best of it and it had all been bought with her own money. She talked about how much she regretted not having children. I said to her, 'How can you be bothered about that when you have what you have?' She replied, 'What could be more wonderful than having a child?' "

The kindness Mrs. Blair remarked on was evident in Maria's agreeing to help a Santa Fe artist named Ford Ruthling who was involved in a folk art museum outside the city. Callas visited the museum to bring it publicity, spending several hours there posing for photographs. Coincidentally, while Maria was at the museum, Mrs. Blair ran into a friend, John Ardoin, who was then starting his career as a music critic in Dallas and was in Santa Fe to review a performance of the Dallas Civic Opera. She invited him to lunch with Maria and the others. Although Callas was initially upset at seeing a stranger and a journalist at the table, according to Mrs. Blair she was very gracious.

Ardoin told me that this was not actually the first time he had met Maria, but it was the beginning of their close friendship. Before the summer was over, the diva would pour out her bitterness and anger to Ardoin on tape, opening up her heart in a way she never had done before.

Mary Carter (then Mrs. Robert Mead) joined the group in Santa Fe, permitting Sue Blair's return to Kansas City. An intimate friend, "Maria Seconda" became a sounding board to whom Maria confided her agony and grief about Onassis.

Callas had always been an insomniac (as was Onassis); now, according to Mary Carter, she became dependent on prescription drugs to get her through the night. Almost certainly her overdose in Paris was not a suicide attempt, but the result of self-medicating to the point where she could no longer remember how many pills she'd taken. For the rest of her life, especially in times of stress, she would be caught in, or on the verge of, this spiral of dependency. Still hoping that Onassis would call her, says Mary Carter, Callas insisted that they move out of the newly renovated Rancho Encantado, whose luxurious appointments did not yet include telephones in the rooms.

"That drove Maria crazy," Mrs. Carter recalled. "How could he call her if she didn't have a phone?" The group decamped to the La Fonda in town, but there were no available rooms. "So we are in the lobby, trying to figure out what we're going to do, and Maria said to me, 'I've never been to Las Vegas. Let's go to Las Vegas.' So I called Moe Dalitz right from the lobby of the La Fonda, and he got Maria and Larry suites at the Desert Inn." (Moe Dalitz was the organized-crime figure who oversaw gambling interests in Las Vegas for Jewish gangs and Mafia families back East. Construction of the Desert Inn was started in 1947 by the gambler Wilbur Clark, but he ran out of money to finish it, so he sold a 74 percent share to Dalitz and his friends.)

Wilbur Clark, who managed the hotel, treated the group royally, according to Mrs. Carter. He collected them at the airport in a big white limousine and personally escorted Maria to some of the stage shows. "She told me later he kept saying to her how thrilled he was to have someone 'with real class' at his hotel." Maria enjoyed herself in Las Vegas, but after three days with no call from Onassis, she told the others that she wanted to leave. Mrs. Carter arranged reservations for them in Los Angeles with Joe Drown, who owned the Bel Air Hotel. Kelly left to return to Dallas "for a breather," while the two women faced California alone until he returned and they resumed their journey.

Like Ken Kesey and his Merry Pranksters and thousands of other Americans in the summer of 1968, Maria Callas, Mary Carter, and Larry Kelly found themselves on the road, wandering the western parts of the country, choosing destinations on a whim. They weren't quite sure where they were headed, but for Maria, it would have been enough to arrive at a sense of peace—any relief from the anger and anxiety of her frantic wakeful nights that continued until she took enough pills to quiet the roaring in her head. Everywhere they went, she waited for the phone to ring, expecting to hear Aristo's voice begging her to come back. But as the days passed, she began to realize it wasn't going to happen.

Los Angeles represented the nadir of Maria's misadventures. As more and more things went wrong, she felt her self-esteem and courage melting away, until soon she would be afraid to leave the side of Larry Kelly, who seemed to be her only anchor.

One day while Kelly was away, according to Mrs. Carter, the two women were invited to dinner by Joe Drown. "We sat at a glass-topped table and Maria noticed that Joe was looking at her legs through the glass and she became very self-conscious and tried to bury her legs under the chair." (Maria's legs were always her worst feature—swollen and thick at the ankles—and when she was under stress, they became even more swollen until they appeared grotesque.) After this uncomfortable meal, Callas went

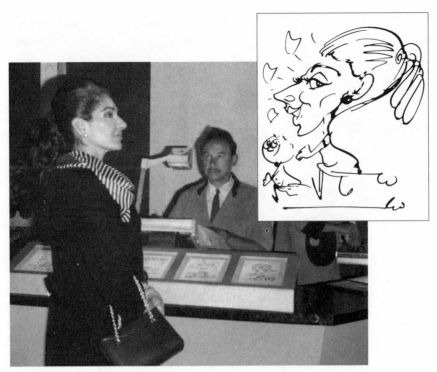

Maria posing for a caricaturist at Disneyland

back to her room to discover that she had been robbed. "The jewelry that she was not wearing was taken and she found a belt on the bed," Mary Carter said. "The security people told her that the thief had brought the belt to strangle anyone he might have found there." Maria was so nervous at hearing this that she took two Nembutal (the barbiturate she took every night of her life).

It was strange to be rootlessly wandering in her own country; her English sounded odd because of all the years Callas had been speaking Italian, and she felt particularly alien in the drawling, rowdy West, a region and a part of American culture she had never known. Still, her friends tried to distract her, and there were pleasant moments amid the agonizing ones. Mary Carter gave me a snapshot of Maria posing with great seriousness for a bemused caricaturist at Disneyland. "Maria absolutely loved it," Mrs. Carter told me. "She went on all the rides and exhibitions. She was like a child."

Later Mary Carter's then husband, Bob Mead, came to L.A. and they all went to dinners with the likes of Baron and Marilyn Hilton, the director Mervyn LeRoy, and Meredith Wilson, who wrote *The Music Man.* The fuss everyone made over Callas took her mind off the silence from Onassis, but

Waiting for the call: Meredith Wilson at Callas' left, film director Mervyn LeRoy in foreground, and Mary Carter, obscured at right, among others, at a dinner in Hollywood

her thoughts would always return to him. Throughout the ten days in Los Angeles she continued to leave her number with Costa Gratsos for Ari.

The next stop was San Francisco, where they went out nightly to the city's famous restaurants, "but she didn't want to be with strangers," Mrs. Carter recalled. "Still no word, still more anxiety." Leaving Maria with Kelly, Mary Carter went back to Dallas to check on her children. From there she called a friend who might put them up for a while in Pebble Beach, and the woman asked if she could arrange a Callas interview with a mutual friend who worked on a San Francisco newspaper. "I called Maria, and she agreed with one proviso—that the article not mention Onassis. The reporter got the interview, wrote the article, and the first words read: " 'JUST DON'T MENTION THAT RAT.' "

The *San Francisco Chronicle* article is benign and does not mention the offending subject again except to state, "Obviously . . . her romance with Aristotle Onassis is over." It quotes Maria as saying she intends to return to the opera stage and notes the presence in her entourage of Lawrence Kelly. The reporter, Frances Moffat, also observed:

The past several years as the companion of Onassis and being part of the international social set gave her the first opportunity to relax from the highly disciplined regime that goes with opera success. Mr. Kelly remarked on this score: "These have been the first years she's been with people her own age. I remember her as a very old 29-year old."

"Don't Mention That Rat" appeared on Wednesday, August 21, 1968. On the same day, the *New York Times* featured a banner headline reading: CZECHOSLOVAKIA INVADED BY RUSSIANS AND FOUR OTHER WARSAW PACT FORCES; THEY OPEN FIRE ON CROWDS IN PRAGUE. The *Times* also noted that the former president Dwight Eisenhower was on his deathbed, and that Mayor Richard Daley had ordered 5,649 Illinois National Guardsmen for round-the-clock duty in Chicago beginning on Friday to head off threats of "tumult, riot or mob disorder" during the Democratic National Convention. (Earlier in the month, on August 2, at the Republican National Convention in Miami Beach, Richard Milhous Nixon had been nominated for president on the first ballot, an event the *Times* called "a remarkable comeback.")

In the wake of Moffat's article, Maria was eager to get out of town. Mary Carter suggested that they travel to the historic and fashionable resort town of Cuernavaca, Mexico, where she owned a house. It sounded like a wonderful idea to Callas, but she soon discovered a problem that threatened to stop her odyssey cold.

Olympic Airways was holding her Greek passport; now they said they couldn't get a her visa for Mexico. Finally, Costa Gratsos, who knew that negotiations between the Kennedys and Ari were becoming very serious and felt increasingly sorry for Maria, called Luis Echeverria, Mexico's secretary of the interior (later he was elected president of Mexico) for assistance. The visa was granted and the group stayed in Cuernavaca two weeks. Gratsos made sure that huge bouquets of flowers greeted Maria when she arrived in Cuernavaca and later in Dallas, but Maria liked to pretend, at least for John Ardoin's benefit, that the flowers were from Onassis. By now, Callas was so depressed, she didn't want to leave the house. "She had lost all her self-respect and she was truly amazed to discover that people still loved her, still cared for her and admired her," Mary Carter told me.

Still, her friends did all they could to keep her entertained in Cuernavaca. Mary Carter called Canfield Hines, a wealthy socialite based in South Carolina, and asked him to invite the group to a party at his estate nearby, but when the invitation came, Maria refused to go. When they threatened to leave without her, Mary Carter told me, "Of course she imme-

At a Cuernavaca nightclub: Larry Kelly, Mary Carter, Mrs. Roscoe Holder,
Callas, Robert Brady, Roscoe Holder, and David Stickelbar

diately agreed to come. She was afraid to stay home alone. She had a marvelous time."

Bob Brady, who owned a trucking company in the Midwest, asked
them to his house (which is now a museum). On September 2, Maria signed
the guest book there and met Roscoe Holder, the brother of the entertainer
Geoffrey Holder. Afterward the group went to a nightclub in the red-light
district. "Maria was fascinated and kept looking at the little cubicles, with
the prostitutes standing in front of them trying to entice customers inside,"
Mrs. Carter recalls. "Before going to that club, we both decided to put on
dresses that wouldn't draw any attention to us, and both of us picked out
simple Pucci dresses, but when we walked into the club it had these hot
lights that picked up all the colors. We lit up like Christmas trees." A photograph I found in Cuernavaca shows Maria in the tawdry interior of the El
Bohemio nightclub, apparently enjoying herself among a group that
includes Roscoe Holder, his wife, Bob Brady, Mary Mead, Larry Kelly, and
David Stickelbar.

By this time, Maria was in a state of complete denial, trying to pretend
that there was nothing wrong in her life while she was coming apart emotionally. "She walked around with a radio, almost like a boombox, playing
jazz all the time," Mary Carter told me. "When they would occasionally play
opera she'd say, 'Change the station. Let's hear some *good* music.'"

To make matters worse, while at Mary Carter's estate, Maria slipped
and fell on the marble floor, tearing the cartilage of her ribs so that when she
talked or laughed one could hear a little clicking sound. After that, her

friends started calling her "Maria Click," but she was in such severe pain that Larry Kelly decided they would have to take her to Dallas for medical treatment.

Mary Carter's doctor in Dallas, Buck Shaw, said the cartilage would repair itself and gave Maria some codeine for the pain, but it made her violently ill. When John Ardoin came to visit her, he found the room full of flowers, which she pretended were from Onassis but were really from the sympathetic Gratsos, who, according to Carter, had told everyone who would listen that Onassis was crazy to give up a woman like Maria for Jackie, and had probably told the Boss himself as well. "But Ari never called Maria during the entire trip," Mrs. Carter said, "and while her anxiety lessened as time passed, it still wasn't easy to be with her during this period."

While Maria was blindly following Larry Kelly from Kansas City to Santa Fe to Las Vegas to Hollywood to San Francisco to Mexico, Onassis was busy on a more directed course and he shuttled back and forth between Skorpios and New York as the negotiations with the Kennedy family reached a fever pitch.

In early August, Jackie and Ted Kennedy came aboard the *Christina* at Skorpios, for the cruise that Maria had been told would not include her. To welcome the late president's younger brother on board, Onassis threw a raucous Greek bouzouki party complete with the smashing of plates and glasses, and he made sure that some attractive blond women were brought from Athens to please Teddy, who he knew to have much the same interests as his older brother Jack.

One of the members of the bouzouki band brought aboard was Nicos Mastorakis, an undercover reporter for a Greek tabloid. Mastorakis carried a concealed camera, and when a rather inebriated Teddy became increasingly friendly with one of the blond women, he began snapping pictures. A bystander noticed what he was doing—some say it was Jackie's sharp eye—and the reporter was relieved of his camera and film. According to *Time* magazine, "Later, police detained the intruder overnight until he agreed not to publish any photographs he might have smuggled off the ship."

Mastorakis' report of the party includes the following lines:

The musical evening begins with pepper tips, red ripe tomatoes, spinach puree, black caviar and liquor. Teddy drinks ouzo, permanently. Jackie prefers vodka at first. . . . A crooner sings and Jackie is rapt with fascination. From time to time Onassis . . . translates with whispers in her ear the words of the song and she stares with those big eyes. The bouzouki music

reaches its peak and Teddy gets up and tries to dance. . . . Teddy returns to
his ouzo. Onassis loves one particular song:

> *These are bitter summers*
> *And you have taught me to spend them with you*
> *And the sky was filled at dawn with dead doves.*

The laughing face of the Greek Croesus framed by his ashen-gray hair
darkens as he hears these words. His eyes cannot betray him easily behind
those thick glasses. But the drooping corners of his mouth show that the 'bit-
ter summers' remind him of too much.

After the infamous party, Teddy stayed on Skorpios for two days of
hard bargaining with Onassis while Jackie decorously absented herself
from such mercenary discussions by going back to Glyfada with Artemis to
investigate the shops of Athens. Teddy began by pointing out the world's
and the Kennedy family's possible objections to the match. When it finally
got down to dollars and cents, Onassis later told friends, the senator mentioned that in marrying Ari, Jackie would forfeit the $175,000 a year she got
from the Kennedy trust, as well as her widow's pension of $10,000 a year
from the government. Ari for his part insisted that he would be generous,
but would not endanger or diminish the inheritance of his own children.

Once Teddy and Onassis had reached an agreement of sorts, the details
were sent to André Meyer, the chairman of the Lazard Frères investment
banking firm in New York. Meyer, who had long advised Jackie on financial
matters, was completely opposed to the marriage and he rejected the terms,
offering a counterproposal that included a twenty-million-dollar cash settlement up front. Nearly apoplectic, an enraged Onassis flew to New York
City to confront Meyer face-to-face.

While Onassis was tussling with the Kennedys and their counselors, Callas
was convalescing at Mary Carter's home in Dallas. It was during this ten-
day visit that Maria announced to the press her plans for a comeback. "Next
season, I shall sing again at the Dallas Opera. Lawrence Kelly and Nicola
Rescigno have been my friends for a very long time. It was with them that I
made my debut in America. And it is with them that I would like to return to
the stage." Unfortunately, the announcement was vague about dates, and the
comeback in Dallas would never happen.

While in Dallas Maria agreed to give a taped radio interview to her new
friend John Ardoin, the music critic for the *Dallas Morning News* since
1966, who also had a local radio show on musical matters.

After they had taped the interview at his house, Ardoin told me, Maria suddenly seemed overwhelmed and began to cry. He tried to comfort her, but she was inconsolable. "I felt very awkward and didn't know quite what to do about it, so she excused herself, went to the bathroom, pulled herself together, and came back out," he said. "She looked me straight in the eye and said, 'Have you got another tape?' and I said, 'Sure,' and she said, 'Put it on.' I didn't know what was coming."

Maria began an hour-long confessional, a rambling lament about the injustice of her fate. "Her parents had no use for her, her sister . . . then she went into a big thing about Onassis—a kind of bloodletting," Ardoin told me. "I said to Larry Kelly the next day, 'What in the world do I do with this?' He said, 'She knows what's coming. She wants to have someone hear her story.' So I called her and I said, 'What do I do with this? Do you want me to publish it?' She said, 'No, just sit on it. Keep it for your notes.' "

John Ardoin gave me a complete transcript of the interview, which he kept to himself until after Maria's death, quoting only the less intimate sections in his books about her music. The rambling monologue is a unique document because Maria had never spoken so intimately and frankly about her feelings before, nor did she again. In every other press conference and interview she gave during her lifetime it seemed to be Callas speaking, playing a role. This, however, was Maria pouring out her bitterness. At no point does she refer to Onassis by name, only as "they" or "he." But her heartbreak at his betrayal and abandonment, which by now she realized to be permanent, seeps into every line. Here are some extracts from the tape in Maria's peculiarly idiosyncratic English:

> All honest, or dishonest people must know that whatever you do you're going to pay a price for it. . . . I am a woman and . . . I'm undefended. I've been undefended all my life. . . . The world is full of unjustness. . . . You have to keep your dignity. Now dignity can be misunderstood for high-hattedness, or superiorness. . . . Nobody thought when they tear me down, "How is this woman feeling, how is she taking it, is there anybody to hold her hand, it must be hell." Well of course it's hell, and then you have to go sing. . . .
>
> Glory terrifies me because you're quite uncomfortable up there. But other people around you, . . . they get drunk. It's a wine that goes to their head. . . . It's been a lonely life. Lonely. It would be so nice to come home, John, and have a nice honest shoulder to lean on. . . . If you don't even trust your husband or your mother, who do you trust? . . . The world has gone a bit haywire. . . . There's one standard for music and that is perfect musicianship. . . . Same thing with love. . . . You love, then you worship, then you honor. You never say a lie, you do your best to never betray that person. . . .

Everybody should be proud of me. My mother, God, how many mothers would have adored to have a child like me? No. And then I'm alone. . . . The revolution happened now in Paris, do you think my parents called, or my sister? Not once. . . . I've never had support from the people I care for the most. . . .

There are people born to be happy and people born to be unhappy. I am just not lucky. Frequently one asks, "Why should this be? Am I that wrong? Am I that bad a person? . . . When my main ambition is being honest with people. What's wrong with that? Is that such a peccato, a sin? This is what I've been asking myself lately. . . .

I didn't need this mess lately. I didn't need that kind of kicks. I've had too many kicks in my life. So my eyes were opened to a husband who was a pimp [meaning that Meneghini bartered her in the music world]. . . . I've opened my eyes to that. They [meaning Onassis] have opened them for me. To have what in return? What? This. Nothing. Not even a good friendship. . . . If for nine years you have been living a hidden life and a humiliating life, if you're a person like I am, it gets you, and you are not cured in two months.

That is my main worry. I don't have all that much time to get cured, because next year I've got to sing. . . . These are all things which have been brought into my mind . . . fear, you know, just fright. . . . I'm quite sure he did not do it on purpose. No one could be that cruel. . . . The hurt's there, and I can't get rid of it. I put in nine years. I've given up a hell of a career . . . for nothing.

It takes time. . . . when serious, strong people promise or guarantee relative happiness, then they have to live up to that. It's too easy to say, 'Well, you know . . . I mean . . . we did our best to be happy.' Well, thank you very much . . . for nine years. 'Well, ain't that sweet,' as they say vulgarly. What does it leave me? At least a friendship? Not even that. The way things have gone I can't be friends. How can he be my friend? Humiliating me that way . . . my mother and now this.

I've got to sit back and take it and try not to say anything, for whatever I do say will be to my disadvantage. Whatever I say, it will be undignified for me, not for them. . . . So, not even a friend I have. Why? After nine years, not a child, not a family, not a friend. That's very little, you know. And you say, "God, why? Why should these things happen?" . . .

I'm proud. I don't like to show my feelings. . . . I never ask for something for fear of also being disillusioned. . . . Frankly I'm terrified about going home. It's like the beginning of a performance. . . . If I could have a medicine that could give me strength, mental and physical. . . . I don't think that my health . . . could stand so much tension. I'd be pleased for one year, one good year coming back to what I was in 1958. . . .

I wonder, will I ever be happy, or will I pass my life always struggling to survive, even though I survive beautifully, let's not complain. I would rather hope for the worst and have the best. Frankly, for nine years I thought I would have, and I found out. . . . How can a man be so dishonest? So— I don't know—so crazy? Poor man!

At that point John Ardoin said, "But in terms of marriage you're still young," and Maria replied:

Oh no, I've had enough of these ups and downs. I'd rather stay down. . . . Damn it all, what does one do? Sit in the four walls? . . . The day is easy to go by. What about the evening? What about when you shut the door to your bedroom and are all alone. . . . There's lots of times I can't sleep. . . . At night you get lots of funny ideas, pessimistic ideas. And I'd like to shake them. Can you go for a walk, really walk your feet off, get tired, do something? A woman can't do it. . . . What does a woman do?

This outburst—tearful, bitter, proud, angry—must have served at least as a catharsis for Maria. Nevertheless, she had driven Mary Carter to the limit of her patience; in an attempt to escape, at least for a time, the exhausting problem of Maria, Mrs. Carter announced that she had to take her fourteen-year-old daughter, Lainie, "up East to school."

To Carter's despair, Maria immediately replied, "Of course you do. When do we leave?" So they flew with Mary Carter's daughter to New York. Mary put Maria up at the Sherry-Netherland, where friends had an apartment. An aunt of Carter's had an apartment there too, where the mother and daughter stayed. Even the young girl could not escape the spectacle of Maria's suffering. Lainie would later tell her mother, "I can't bear watching her pain. I hope I never, never care so much about anyone."

It was during this stay in New York that Callas made her celebrated reconciliation with her rival, Renata Tebaldi, who was singing in *Adriana Lecouvreur* at the Met's season opener on September 16. According to Mary Carter: "John Coveney, head of Angel Records [which later merged with Capitol], was a close friend of Maria's, and he took us all out to dinner. He suggested that we all go to the opening of the Met, and Maria, anxious to show she wasn't devastated by the loss of Onassis, which of course she was, agreed."

Maria was determined to make a grand entrance on this occasion; one that would play to her advantage in the press. According to John Ardoin, she called Harry Winston and asked to borrow some important jewels. He

Callas, wearing the famous emeralds Ari would later give Jackie, upstages her rival Renata Tebaldi at the Metropolitan Opera. Mary Carter is at her right.

volunteered to lend her a pair of magnificent earrings—a teardrop central emerald surrounded by diamonds—and a ring and bracelet of emeralds and diamonds to go with her green velvet gown.

After the performance, John Ardoin later recalled, "Mr. Bing took her backstage. It was the first time she and Tebaldi had met face-to-face, and there were pictures all over the press the next day of Maria wearing these earrings. She returned them to Mr. Winston, and about a year or so later, Mr. Onassis went to Winston's to buy a gift for Mrs. Kennedy, and guess what he bought her? The earrings! One of the magazines took a picture of Maria wearing them, and then one of Mrs. Kennedy wearing them, and put them side by side, and the cut-line read, 'What does he do, buy them by the dozen?' "

An Associated Press wirephoto shows Maria entering the opera house that night. The diamond and emerald pendants of the earrings are the size of pigeon eggs, and as she held her hand to her heart, acknowledging the applause of the crowd, everyone could see the huge matching emerald and diamond dinner ring and bracelet on her left arm. Glowing at the cheers of the crowd, Maria appeared ecstatically happy, determined not to betray her inner state, as Mary Carter and John Coveney trailed in her wake.

After the performance, Callas went backstage and the once dueling sopranos fell into each other's arms. Most reporters said that Maria had tears in her eyes, but photos suggest a carefully staged media appearance by Callas, who if nothing else was still a great actress. For the performance, according to Mary Carter, they sat in the special box belonging to the president of the Metropolitan Opera Association, George Moore, and when Maria entered, everybody went wild, applauding and shouting at her to perform again. "Renata Tebaldi was completely outshadowed. She was furious! We went backstage afterwards and she smiled and embraced Maria and put on a show, but we found out later from her colleagues that she was fit to be tied."

Within days, Maria learned that Onassis was in New York, squiring Jackie Kennedy everywhere. Mary Carter recalls that as soon as Maria learned Onassis was staying in his apartment at the Pierre, she wanted to call him, but Mrs. Carter and Anastasia Gratsos both emphatically warned her not to do anything of the sort. "But one night, when neither of us were with her, of course she called him. They spoke to each other, but he was not very warm to her and Maria was crushed. After that conversation, she resigned herself to the fact that he wasn't going to ask her to come back. . . . In a way, she may even have been relieved. She now knew clearly and firmly that it was over." She immediately booked herself on a flight from New York to Paris.

On September 25, Aristotle Onassis and André Meyer met in the banker's luxurious apartment in the Carlyle Hotel to settle the prenuptial agreement. The meeting was long and vitriolic. It was late when Onassis returned to the office of Costa Gratsos at 647 Fifth Avenue, which he used as his own when he was in town. Gratsos' secretary, Lynn Alpha Smith, was still there, and Ari brusquely asked her to find the bottle of Johnnie Walker Black Label that they kept there and pour him a double shot.

Then Onassis dictated to her a memorandum summarizing what he had thrashed out with André Meyer, which she typed and hand-delivered to the Carlyle. The memorandum never refers to Mrs. Kennedy by name but only as the "person in question." In a dig at Meyer, who had demanded the lump-sum prepayment, one of the clauses dictated by Onassis read: "The sum of twenty [million] indicated in the meeting, as a capital, apart from the fact that in the final analysis would be futile, due to gift, income, and other taxes that it necessarily would entail, apart from being detrimental to the feelings of either party, it might easily lead to the thought of an acquisition instead of a marriage."

As part of the contract Onassis got Jackie to waive her rights under Greek law called *nomimos mira* whereby Onassis would be required to leave at least 12.5 percent of his estate to his wife and 37.5 percent to his children. In exchange for the waiver, he guaranteed Jackie $3 million for herself and $1 million for each of her children at his death. He would be responsible for her expenses as long as the marriage lasted, and after his death she would receive $150,000 per annum for life—just as she would have continued to do under the terms of the Kennedy trust. "His American lawyers pushed the agreement, not knowing it had no legal standing under Greek law," says Stelios Papadimitriou, then a legal adviser to the tycoon and now the head of the Alexander S. Onassis Public Benefit Foundation.

Still, once this paper was signed, the wedding plan, which had begun as a mere rhetorical question in May, was now moving forward with irresistible momentum.

The writer Doris Lilly had been hissed, booed, and shoved by Jackie fans when, in mid-August, she predicted on the *Merv Griffin Show* that the former first lady and Onassis would marry. In September, to counteract these rumors, Onassis took Earl Wilson, the gossip columnist for the *New York Post,* aside at El Morocco and gave him an exclusive interview "to set the record straight." On September 20 Wilson wrote: "We think we can tell you with comparative assurance that Aristotle Onassis is not likely to be marrying Jackie Kennedy or anybody else. . . . 'Aris' had a drink or two with Maria [Callas] just before she flew back to Paris yesterday. . . . The night before, he had dinner with Jackie. . . . He feels he's 'not worthy of either of them.' His friends are a little offended that columnists keep harping on his friendship with Jackie, trying to make a romance out of it; their family friendship goes back several years. Onassis furthermore says to his friends that he doesn't expect to marry again for the simple enough reason: He's already been married."

It was a valiant attempt to slow down the avalanche, but it didn't work. Too many people were already in on the news. As for Maria's having a drink with Onassis before flying back to Paris, Mary Carter believes it never happened, that their only contact at the time was Maria's pathetic phone call, during which he treated her with devastating coldness. It's true that Maria could have snuck out to meet Aristo without her friends knowing it. But it's more likely that Onassis made up the meeting to reinforce the image he was trying to sell to Earl Wilson—that of a man pursued by two famous and desirable women—a man who had no intention of marrying either and who modestly claimed he was "not worthy of either of them."

Before the news of the impending wedding hit the front pages of the world press later that autumn, John Ardoin received a letter from Maria in Paris thanking him and the other members of their small group of pilgrims for supporting her during her summer of wandering around the West. It was dated September 27, 1968, and said in part:

> I came back quite exhausted—too many emotions, I suppose—I am so fragile under this so-called control.
>
> I do so want to be worthy of you all, & of course myself.
>
> It is still a long life to live and I must be worthy of so much bestowed upon me.
>
> Yours affectionately, Maria Click

Six days later, Maria wrote a letter to Elvira de Hidalgo recounting her painful fall during the American odyssey, and her letter had the same stoic tone: "But it is necessary to take life as it comes. I'm much better and in excellent spirits. I have been liberated from a nightmare called love, destructive from every point of view."

Jackie Kennedy, meanwhile, requested and received a two-hour-long audience with Richard Cardinal Cushing of Boston, the beloved, now terminally ill prelate who had officiated at her wedding to Jack and at the funeral of her small son. She promised Cushing that her children would keep their Catholic faith, the family name, and their close relations with the Kennedys. The cardinal, who had been badgered by the Kennedy family to discourage the match, told her that, though he could not speak for the Vatican, he personally would do nothing to dissuade her or criticize her decision.

But the more Jackie pushed ahead, the less certain Onassis grew. Lilly Lawrence, the daughter of Dr. Reza Fallah, head of the Iranian Oil Syndicate, was an Onassis friend privy to the complex marital negotiations. She later said, "Ari told me that he had begun to have second thoughts. He wanted to reconsider. He wanted more time. Jackie couldn't afford to let him off the hook. A reversal on his part would have permanently besmirched her reputation. Now that she had spoken to Cardinal Cushing, now that it had been in the press, she insisted he go through with it."

Cold feet or no, there was nothing Onassis could do to change the plans once it became known in mid-October that the *Boston Herald-Traveler* planned a front-page revelation. The bombshell exploded into the public consciousness on October 17 when the paper, quoting a "completely knowledgeable source," reported that the wedding could take place before the end of October, and "at all events, it will take place before Christmas." But even before the story ran, Onassis was back in Greece wrangling with the military dictatorship over Project Omega. Jackie called him to report that their secret was out and added her opinion that they should marry as quickly as possible.

(Mary Carter believes that the Kennedy family leaked the news to the *Boston Herald-Traveler* in order to force Ari's hand. "We heard later that Teddy Kennedy called Onassis to say that the *Herald-Traveler* was going to break the story that Onassis and Jackie were practically living together and they had to announce their marriage. Of course, this was all a setup. The Kennedys and the *Boston Herald*? Give me a break!")

By this time the train had left the station and Onassis was on it. "If I try to get out of the marriage now, it will cause a terrible scandal," he told close friends, including Yiannis Giorgakis, chairman of Olympic Airways in Athens, and Costa Gratsos. "I can't do that to Jackie. She's a mother with two young children."

Giorgakis later noted, "He had subjected his own children to such a scandal when he left his wife to pursue Maria and he wasn't going to let that happen again."

After hearing that the news was going to break, Onassis ordered Giorgakis to come to Glyfada. He told him to find a priest to conduct the ceremony on Skorpios "who understands English and doesn't look like Rasputin," so as not to unduly frighten Mrs. Kennedy's children. Onassis called his two children to the house in Glyfada. At the dinner table, he and Artemis, who was ecstatic about the union, informed them that he was going to wed Jacqueline Kennedy. Christina, then seventeen, burst into tears. Alexander, twenty-one, leaped up from the table in a rage and stormed out of the house. He spent the rest of the night speeding aimlessly around Athens in his Alfa Romeo.

As soon as the *Boston Herald-Traveler*'s story appeared, a feeding frenzy began among the world press. The *New York Times* tracked down Richard Cardinal Cushing in Sioux Falls, South Dakota, where he was doing a consecration. He said, "No comment. My lips are sealed. No comment at all," but then, according to the *Times*, "he prophesied that an official announcement of the marriage 'may be coming up tonight—tonight or tomorrow.' "

He was right. At 3:30 p.m. on the afternoon of the seventeenth, Jackie Kennedy's social secretary in New York, Nancy Tuckerman, made the following press announcement: "Mrs. Hugh D. Auchincloss has asked me to tell you that her daughter, Mrs. John F. Kennedy, is planning to marry Aristotle Onassis sometime next week. No place or date has been set for the moment." Under the barrage of hysterical questions from reporters, Nancy Tuckerman pleaded that she had no answers: "I didn't even know until a half hour ago."

That same day, in downtown Athens, Onassis was mobbed by reporters who discovered him having a drink with a friend in the lounge of the Grande Bretagne Hotel. He told the crowd, "She accepted my proposal by telephone. I've just come from having a physical checkup and my doctor says I'm in perfect health. Yes, it is true, I'm marrying her tomorrow or within three days at the latest. . . . I have so many family problems in my head to settle, please leave me alone now and give me your blessings." He then left the hotel by a rear entrance and rode in a limousine toward Glyfada. Later in the afternoon Artemis announced that the wedding was to take place on Skorpios and that her family was "extremely happy over the match."

As Jackie's social secretary was making her announcement, the Olympic pilot who was preparing to fly the scheduled 8:30 p.m. flight from New York to Athens was being told that the flight had been canceled, the 707's ninety-three passengers bumped. He was advised to be ready to take off early, at 6:00 p.m., and head for Andravida, a Greek military base in the Peloponnesus 145 miles from Athens and only 80 miles from Skorpios. The pilot soon discovered the identity of his eleven passengers: Jackie Kennedy, her two children, their nanny and Secret Service agents, her mother and stepfather, and her Kennedy sisters-in-law Jean Smith and Pat Lawford. The 707 arrived at Andravida at about 10:30 a.m. Athens time the next morning. There, after the gathered newsmen were all locked in a waiting room, Onassis greeted Jackie with a kiss on the cheek, and in his private DC-6 he flew with her and her children to Aktion on the west coast of Greece, where a helicopter was waiting to transport them to Skorpios.

On Friday, October 18, as the Kennedy contingent was settling into their quarters on the *Christina,* in the harbor of Skorpios, Onassis was making a phone call to Paris. According to Ferruccio Mezzadri, Maria's butler, "Two days before he married Jackie, Onassis called Madame from Greece. I answered the phone. And he asked her to come to Athens and save him."

When I asked Ferruccio how Maria was supposed to "save him," he replied, "Onassis told her that if she came to Athens, Mrs. Kennedy would get angry and go back to America. And Madame told him: 'You got yourself into this, you get yourself out of it.' "

The *New York Times* ran the news of Jackie's wedding plans on the front page, reporting as well: "Last night in Paris, where she is now living, Miss Callas refused to comment on the announcement of the marriage." The *Times* did, however, manage to get a comment out of the former deputy secretary of defense Roswell L. Gilpatric, a married lawyer in New York who had been one of Jackie's close friends and was often rumored to be a romantic interest. Gilpatric told the *Times:* "No, I didn't know about it. I wish her every happiness. She once told me that she felt she could count on him [Onassis]. It was an attribute she looked for in all her friends. One of the things she is looking for for herself and her children is a private life—not being in the public eye all the time—and he can afford to give her that privacy and protection."

Later that day the actor Richard Burton, at the Plaza-Athénée in Paris, called Rex Harrison and asked him to invite Callas to the party planned that night for the Paris opening of Harrison's film *A Flea in Her Ear.* Burton, who had come to know Maria well when he and Liz Taylor sailed on the *Christina,* said, "She'll need a bit of cheering up, I fancy."

18

THE JACKIE JINX

One must not tie a ship
to a single anchor
Nor life to a single hope.

Epictetus, *Discourses*

It was raining in a steady drizzle on Skorpios at 5:15 p.m. on Sunday, October 20, as the bearded Archimandrite Polykarpos Athanassiou (whose bushy, dark beard did, contrary to instructions, evoke Rasputin) chanted the Greek marriage service in the tiny white chapel of the Virgin Mary: "The servant of God, Aristotle, is betrothed to the servant of God, Jacqueline, in the name of the Father, the Son, and the Holy Spirit." Greeks consider rain to be good luck on a wedding day, but Artemis, taking no chances, tucked a charm under the mattress on the *Christina* where the newlyweds would sleep.

It was Artemis who had been asked to be the *koumbara,* or sponsor, of the marriage, with the responsibility of exchanging the white crowns of flowers on the couple's heads three times and then following them three times around the altar in the "Dance of Isaiah" as the guests showered them with flower petals. Caroline and John Kennedy, Jr., trailed the newlyweds around the altar too, carrying lighted candles and looking bewildered. In a corner, Onassis' children, Alexander and Christina, glowered and whispered. Afterward Alexander offered the following assessment of the event: "It's a perfect match. My father loves names and Jackie loves money."

As the roughly twenty-five guests invited to the ceremony crowded into the chapel, an army of press floated a thousand yards off shore on a motley armada of vessels rented, purchased, and commandeered for the occasion.

The rather somber wedding party and priest on the Christina *after the ceremony, in a rare photograph found on board the yacht*

The previous day, Mrs. Kennedy had issued the following announcement: "We know you understand that even though people may be well known, they still hold in their hearts the emotions of a simple person for the moments that are the most important on earth—birth, marriage, and death. We wish our wedding to be a private moment in the little chapel among the cypresses of Skorpios, with only members of the family present, five of them little children. If you will give us those moments, we will so gladly give you all the cooperation possible for you to take the pictures you need."

Despite this touching and carefully worded request, a landing force of more than thirty journalists had stormed the island before the ceremony and had been driven back by Onassis employees with the help of the Greek navy. As a compromise, a small group of newsmen were allowed to attend the church ceremony to relay news to their colleagues. One of them was Mario Modiano, the Athens correspondent for *The Times* of London, whose account included these lines:

> *The tiny chapel of Panayitsa ("Little Virgin") set among bougainvillea and jasmine was packed with relatives from both sides. Jackie looked drawn and concerned. . . . Jackie's glance kept turning anxiously towards Caroline. The Onassis children seemed grim. . . . There was no holding of hands, no kiss when it was over. Jackie seemed oblivious of her second husband but terribly aware of Caroline. Later, on the* Christina, *the closest she came to showing affection was to take his arm. Their hands never touched. One observer said, "It was like a business transaction."*

The wedding ceremony was followed by a party on the *Christina,* and the feasting and Greek dancing continued until dawn. Jackie was wearing a huge new heart-shaped ruby ring encircled by diamonds (with matching earrings), and at one point, while she was showing it to her mother, Janet Auchincloss, little Caroline Kennedy took it and tossed it into the air. Kiki Feroudi Moutsatsos, an Onassis secretary, wrote that she later paid the bill for the ring—$1.25 million dollars. She also described how, two weeks later, Jackie discovered the bauble missing, setting off a two-hour search all over the *Christina* and the island of Skorpios until a maid found it under a rug.

While Ari, Jackie, and their guests were dancing the *syrtaki* on board the yacht, Maria Callas was in Paris. The evening of Friday, October 18, a day after the *New York Times* had obtained her "no comment," Maria made an eloquently dazzling public appearance in a brightly printed gown and diamonds, smiling radiantly, first at the premiere of Georges Feydeau's *A Flea in her Ear* and later at the seventy-fifth anniversary party for Maxim's restaurant.

An Italian reporter wrote:

> *Maria Callas took advantage of a society event to show off her captivating elegance to all Paris, whose members probably were already enjoying the possibility of gossiping about her absence. This opportunity to show the world that she hadn't lost her morale at the news of the Kennedy-Onassis*

A loveless marriage on Skorpios (above), and
a brave face in Paris as Maria enters Maxim's (opposite)

marriage came in the form of a premiere of the movie "A Flea in Her
Ear" . . . held at the Marigny Theater during a gala evening. Not content
to have stunned all present by appearing in the brightly lit hall, Callas
exceeded all possible expectations by taking part after the film showing
in the gala dinner party at Chez Maxim's offered to celebrate their
75th anniversary. Her presence caused that of Liz Taylor to go almost
unnoticed.

The reporter quoted Maria as saying: "I knew all about this some time ago. Onassis had already told me every detail," and, "As far as I'm concerned I'm happy and cannot help but be happy about others' happiness." Despite insisting on her happiness, however, when asked the inevitable questions by the press corps, Callas, like Alexander Onassis, had a zinger prepared: "Mrs. Kennedy did well to give a grandfather to her children." Twisting the knife she added, "Onassis is as beautiful as Croesus."

It was a bravura performance—Callas at her best—but it was, as the Italians put it, only putting up a *bella figura*, a good face. Nadia Stancioff, who became one of the diva's close friends shortly after the Onassis-Kennedy wedding, wrote that in late-night conversations, Maria often fumed, "He lied. Do you understand? He duped me. What I'll never forgive him for is that he denied everything two days before! How could she marry a man who had had an affair with her sister?"

By "denied everything two days before," Maria was undoubtedly refer-

ring to the conversation—revealed to me by her butler, Ferruccio—when Onassis phoned her in Paris and desperately pleaded with her to come to Athens to "save him." Hearing his eagerness to foil the marriage may have convinced Maria that he wouldn't really go through with it, and so it was perhaps all the more shocking when she read the details of the fait accompli in the Paris newspapers. Her conviction that until the very last minute Onassis didn't really intend to marry Jackie was also reflected in an interview she gave in November of 1970 to Judy Klemsrud of the *New York Times,* in which she said, "Frankly, I didn't know about the wedding, and frankly, I don't think *he* knew about the wedding. You'll have to ask her. . . ."

Maria's true feelings, as opposed to the serene countenance she presented to the public, are indicated by a letter she wrote to Elvira de Hidalgo nine days after the ceremony:

Dear Elvira

Thank you for your comforting letter. It's cruel, isn't it, but they'll both pay, I can assure you of that. The worst thing is that he didn't tell me anything about his getting married. I think he had an obligation to do so after nine years together, then at least I wouldn't have found out from the newspapers. But, I think of him as a madman and therefore am putting him out of my mind as such. . . .

I'm pretty well considering the circumstances, and thank you for your affectionate concern for me.

This letter indicates that Maria still clung to her faith that God would look after her and exact justice for her mistreatment. Such fatalism is common among Greeks, but usually finds expression in pre-Christian terms: *moira*, or destiny, is thought to punish anyone guilty of *hubris*—a pride that can have fatal consequences.

Almost every Greek who knew Onassis—except possibly his sisters—soon began to talk about Onassis' marriage in relation to *moira* and *hubris*. Though many of them didn't like Maria, the crew of the *Christina* and his corporate employees, especially, felt he should have married her, that she was the only right match for him—to do otherwise was to resist his destiny. When the Boss, known as much for his good fortune as for his skill and acumen, began to suffer a series of crippling reversals that affected not only his business but also his family and ultimately his health, those in his service looked at one another knowingly. It wouldn't be long after Ari wed the former American first lady that whispered comments and rumors began to circulate around the offices of Olympic Airways and the staff quarters of the *Christina*, with references to what would come to be known as the "Jackie jinx."

Many books have reported that immediately after the ceremony, Ari and Jackie flew off on an Olympic plane that had been outfitted as a giant bridal suite. The accounts linger over the details of the satin sheets and the story of a confused steward who mistakenly opened some curtains and witnessed to his shame thrashing naked limbs as the amorous couple were being flown toward an exotic honeymoon destination.

The much-less-romantic truth is that Jackie remained on Skorpios, after sending her children and other family members back home, while Onassis flew to Athens to spend the first day of his honeymoon with Colonel George Papadopoulos, the head of the military junta that had seized power in Greece the year before. The world might be obsessed with every detail of his wedding, but Ari was involved in a much more important transaction: the birth of Project Omega. It had taken him a year to get to this point with the colonels. (Some of his associates remarked that only Onassis could conduct two honeymoons at once.)

Onassis made the hop to Athens again four days later, to firm up the last details. He rode from the airport beside Colonel Papadopoulos in the back of an armor-plated Mercedes-Benz, escorted by 350 armed police, to the dictator's home in an Athens suburb.

As the colonel's mistress poured Greek cognac from a thermos flask specially secured against assassination attempts, Onassis and the dictator prepared a joint statement announcing the launch of Project Omega, which

Onassis would later describe as "the biggest deal in the history of Greece." The $400 million investment program (around $4 billion today) included the construction of Greece's third oil refinery, an alumina refinery, an aluminum smelter, a power station, shipyards, and a new air terminal. The oil refinery would keep Onassis' fleet of tankers busy at a time when most others were idle. He would handle the oil production from beginning to end. As for the alumina complex, Onassis believed he could make a deal with an American company like Reynolds or Alcoa. Best of all, he had worked out a plan for financing the entire project with Other People's Money, his signature modus operandi in business.

A press conference took place on November 1. Announcing this deal on the heels of his marriage to Jackie Kennedy was a huge public relations coup. Many observers, journalists, and Greek patriots would criticize Onassis for getting into bed with the despised colonels at the same time he was getting into bed with America's sainted first lady. But Onassis was in the grip of hubris, or at the least was intoxicated by his triumphs: he had just married the most famous woman on earth and concluded a deal of unprecedented proportions in his homeland, leaving his rival, Stavros Niarchos, in his dust. "On that day," said one of his associates, "Onassis was the Sun King. He had everything."

One American Alcoa executive would comment less flatteringly, "After his marriage he just lost all sense of proportion. His must-win mentality tipped over into pure megalomania. His terms were not terms, they were commandments. . . . He seemed to think that we'd agree to just about anything for an invitation to dine with him and Jackie aboard the *Christina*. It was obvious that he saw that marriage as a good career move."

The colonels, and especially Papadopoulos himself, were less blasé about Ari's new bride. To butter up the dictator, Onassis offered him use of his estate at Lagonissi, a $40,000 new wardrobe for his wife, and—most exciting of all to the career officer who had grown up in a poor village in the Peloponnesus—an invitation to dinner in Glyfada with his bride, Jacqueline Kennedy. On that evening Jackie wore a long black dress and a diamond necklace, and before the guests arrived she told her sister-in-law, Artemis, "I am so glad that I can be a help to Aristo in his business matters."

With all his wildest ambitions finding fulfillment at once, Onassis could have hardly imagined that his fortunes would soon go into a precipitous decline that would reduce him, five years later, to a shattered man who had no desire to go on living.

For now, however, there was nothing he felt he couldn't accomplish. According to Ferruccio Mezzadri, Onassis tried to get his mistress back into his life even before the public announcement of Project Omega and Jackie's dinner with the dictator. Ferruccio told me: "A week after the marriage he was outside the door at Georges Mandel shouting, whistling for Madame to let him in. He called from the corner and I spoke to him myself, exactly a week after the wedding. He got married on Sunday and the next Sunday he was in Paris, trying to see Madame. But she wouldn't let him in. Sometime later she did. Then he was in Paris all the time. Every four or five days. He would tell her how miserable he was, everything he was doing. He shared everything with her. Even when Mrs. Kennedy was in Paris, he would go to dinner with his wife but would come first to Madame to have a drink with her and talk."

Bruna Lupoli confirmed the abrupt arrival of Onassis outside Maria's window shortly after the wedding, but said that it may have been more than exactly seven days after the ceremony. "Certainly it was one or two weeks after the wedding," she said.

Maria was in no mood to entertain Onassis when he turned up at Avenue Georges Mandel to cajole her. After she denied him admittance, he called from the bistro on the corner, then threatened to drive his car through her gate. But as she had indicated to Hidalgo, she intended to cut him out of her life. (She later wrote to her friend Dorle Soria: "As for Daddy O, what is over is over. Sagittarians are like that.")

Despite her assertions, however, Callas was observed dining with him at Maxim's in November, allegedly to celebrate the fact that they had won the final appeal in the Vergottis case. (This verdict was announced on October 31, 1968, eleven days after the wedding.) Maria was also seen with Onassis at a dinner party in Paris given by Maggie van Zuylen in late December, shortly after he had spent his first Christmas with Jackie on the *Christina*. But Callas would not entertain him at home or agree to be alone with him until many months had passed. She was not about to forgive Onassis for what he had put her through, and her manner with him was angry, stiff, and sullen. She was determined to concentrate on reviving her career and to put him out of her mind. Her *philotimo* demanded she see Aristo only enough to show him that she didn't need him in her life.

From the moment the wedding was announced, Maria had been besieged by directors, producers, and impresarios. She toyed with a proposal to do a new production of *Traviata* at L'Opéra in Paris, directed by Visconti, but in the end she panicked at the thought of singing again on stage, particularly in such a demanding vehicle. She asked for an outrageous number of days of rehearsals with the orchestra and chorus, knowing the Paris Opéra would never agree to it, and the deal fizzled out.

Callas on the set in Turkey during the filming of Medea

Callas had taken to heart Aristo's advice that the best medium to maintain her fame was the screen. The proposal that appealed to her most was a nonsinging movie version of *Medea,* to be produced by Franco Rossellini and directed by Pier Paolo Pasolini. Pasolini announced that Maria was the only woman he envisioned for his Medea because she was "in one sense the most modern of women, but there lives in her an ancient woman—strange, mysterious, magical, with terrible inner conflicts." Naturally he was aware that the world would be drawing parallels between Medea's murderous passion for Jason, who abandoned her to marry the daughter of a king, and Maria's famous, doomed affair with Onassis.

Callas flew to Rome in May of 1969 to discuss costumes and contracts for *Medea.* She was met at the airport by Rossellini and a half-American, half-Bulgarian woman named Nadia Stancioff, who had been hired by the producer to be Maria's personal assistant. Later Nadia wrote a memoir,

Maria Callas Remembered, which chronicles the diva's emotions, words, and behavior during this difficult time.

In June, Nadia accompanied Maria to Turkey on what would be another picaresque journey, this one leading from Rome to Ankara to Goreme, in the heart of Cappadocia—a land of surreal rock formations, where the film was shot under a broiling sun. At the end of July the film crew moved to northern Italy for a month and then back to Rome. Maria threw herself into becoming a film actress with all the intensity she had brought to her singing. Pasolini and the crew were astonished that she almost never required more than one or two takes to get a scene right.

Everyone had expected clashes between the slight director with the ravaged but handsome face and the statuesque, temperamental diva, but the opposite seemed to happen. He wrote Maria poems, drew portraits of her, and courted her like a suitor, and when, at the end of filming, he gave her a ring set with an antique Turkish coin, Maria showed it to her assistant, Nadia, with childlike excitement. "Do you think this means he is in love with me?" she asked. "The other day he told me that, besides his mother, I am the only woman he has ever loved. He even said that if he could feel desire for a woman, it would be me." In fact, the iconoclastic Marxist director never hid his homosexuality. His male Italian lover traveled with him to Turkey, and according to Nadia, Pasolini often invited Italian waiters and peasant boys into his quarters.

Like Larry Kelly, Pasolini evidently filled a deep need in Maria to be admired by a man. She was so insecure about her own attractiveness since the breakup with Onassis that she constantly needed to see adulation in male eyes and hear compliments from everyone around her.

Onassis did not let Maria's new career and the distance between them discourage his efforts to thaw their relationship. According to Stancioff, he pursued her by phone throughout the filming of *Medea,* but she was still deeply angry. On June 4, the eve of the first take, Nadia was in Maria's room when the telephone rang. The operator said, "The United States calling. Mr. Lupoli on the line." Nadia handed the phone to Bruna, knowing that Lupoli was her surname, but Maria realized it was Onassis, who often used this pseudonym. Through clenched teeth she said, "No! I will not take that call. Nadia, tell Mr. Lupoli that Madame Callas does not wish to accept the call."

Onassis called back and was refused once again. Nadia reports that Maria flew into a rage, saying: "Why doesn't that old man leave me alone? He's got what he wanted. He got the social status he was itching for. What more does he want? He's not happy? Bored with the first lady? That's too bad. One pays for everything in life. The gods will make sure he pays."

Callas couldn't calm down, couldn't bear to be left alone, until she took some sleeping pills.

The four-week stay in Cappadocia, not unlike Maria's western journey during the previous summer, was filled with bizarre misadventures. The only available water in her accommodations trickled down the rock wall of her room at the brand new Club Méditerranée, which had been carved out of local geological formations. The taps in the bathroom provided only running sand. Yet Maria remained good-natured through it all. She frequently treated the crew to recitals, accompanied by her poodles, whom she'd trained to howl operatic arias along with her. Nadia writes of these "somewhat depressing exhibitions" that "it was strange to witness 'the voice of the century' taking part in their weird circus act."

Every day Callas made Nadia find English or Italian newspapers, through which she'd page just to read her horoscope before tossing them away. Her superstitiousness was as strong as ever, and dealt her an unsettling blow one day when there was no shooting and she and Nadia visited a bazaar in a remote village. A gypsy grabbed Callas' hand and indicated she wanted to tell her fortune. Callas asked her driver to translate the gypsy's words, but at first he refused. "After a lot of prodding from Maria," wrote Nadia, "the driver stammered out, 'She says you are going to die young, madame. But you will not suffer.'

"The color drained from Maria's face. For a moment she leaned against the candy stall. That evening at dinner she spoke at length of the power of the occult. She was distant, preoccupied."

Acting in *Medea* had given Maria a new raison d'être. All her life she had been unable to rise until noon, but now she was up at 6 a.m. and ready to go on the set. She insisted on watching the filming of every scene, whether she was in it or not, and she studied the rushes obsessively, according to Rossellini, who recalled, "I kept telling her, 'Come on, Maria, let's go and have dinner, or let's go to sleep,'" but she would not budge. When a journalist asked her if she didn't find it exhausting to shoot the same scene over and over, Callas replied, "No, it's futility that exhausts me, not work. . . . There will be a great void when it's all over."

In early July the entire cast returned to the north of Italy, which was even hotter than Cappadocia and was infested with mosquitoes. During the last days of shooting, Maria was suffering from her chronic low blood pressure, and during one scene, when she had to run back and forth in a dry riverbed under the midday sun in her heavy costume, she fainted. When she came to, she apologized incessantly for holding up production. Nevertheless, the film remained on schedule, and eventually the cast moved to Rome to finish the last scenes in the studios of Cinécitta.

According to Nadia, "She told everyone she loved her new career, wanted to do more films and hated to see the *Medea* experience come to an end." She believed she had successfully resurrected the Callas legend after her terrifying failures on the opera stage.

That year Mary Carter's and Maria's paths crossed again. Mary and her husband, Bob Mead, were vacationing in Southern Europe, and when he flew back to the States, Callas met her at the airport. Maria immediately told her old friend the story of Onassis's theatrics outside her apartment in Avenue Georges Mandel. "She was standing there at the bottom of the escalator, like Medea. She told me how, days after Onassis married Jackie, he called her in Paris, came around to the apartment and started whistling the sailor's whistle, then he went to the bistro nearby and called her from there. She still refused to see him, but he persisted on every trip to Paris and later she agreed to have dinner with him," Mrs. Carter told me. "She refused to let him come to her apartment so they went to Maxim's. He told her he missed her terribly and wanted to continue their friendship. He said, 'You're the only woman I've ever loved.' She laughed and told him he had a very original way of showing it. She loved the whole scene, she confessed, but she refused to sleep with him. She told me she never slept with him after she left the *Christina,* and I believe her. I know others say she did, but she would have told me if she had. She told me everything."

By July, when Maria was completing her filming, Onassis had spent ten months parsing the adage "Marry in haste, repent at leisure." Four weeks after the wedding, the former Mrs. Kennedy had flown back to New York to rejoin her children. She would continue to spend most of her time either there, at her sister Lee's home in London, or visiting friends in Palm Beach, Florida—despite having declared after Bobby Kennedy's funeral, "I've got to get out of this country." Jackie and Ari did spend Christmas on the *Christina* at Skorpios (she and Caroline attended the Orthodox service at the little Church of the Virgin Mary in the nearby town of Nidri on the island of Lefkas), and in April the couple also took the yacht on the annual Caribbean cruise, sailing from the Canary Islands to Trinidad. Just a year earlier, at the same time, the *Christina* had been in Jamaica and the woman sunbathing by Onassis' side had been Maria Callas.

During their first year of marriage, Onassis traveled often to New York for short visits with Jackie. Those occasions—on which he escorted her to P. J. Clarke's and Elaine's and to a dinner given by David Rockefeller in honor of the newlyweds—were duly recorded in the press. The couple seemed happy, everyone said, and they had their little jokes, like the way Ari grabbed the pack of cigarettes out of Jackie's hand each time she reached for a smoke.

Jackie's fortieth birthday, July 28, was spent on Skorpios. Ari gave her a gift he had designed himself, a pair of earrings commemorating the Apollo 11 moon landing on July 20, 1969, eight days earlier. Each earring represented the moon and earth—the spheres were of twenty-two-karat gold and were encrusted with rubies, sapphires, and diamonds—linked together by a chain of golden spaceships. Jackie would wear the garish, heavy baubles only once. She told the Greek actress Katina Paxinou that Ari "felt they were such trifles. But he promised that, if I'm good, next year he'll give me the moon itself."

(What he actually gave her on her next birthday, according to the *New York Times,* was a pledge to order a spectacular new yacht in Japan, "the best yacht in the world, to be completed by the same date next year." It was to be named *Jacqueline,* but apparently Ari did not feel she had behaved well enough to deserve it, for it was never built.)

With Jackie and Onassis on Skorpios that summer of 1969 was the physical therapist Korinna Spanidou. Having spent the summer with him and Maria five years earlier, she had a unique opportunity to compare Onassis' intimacy with both women.

"He was more considerate with Jackie than he was with Maria," Mrs. Spanidou told me, "although I saw him explode at Jackie as well. But he was never as warm, as relaxed, as passionate with her as he was with Maria. He would sit in front of her [Callas] on his haunches and tell her stories about his years in Smyrna and Argentina for hours on end, and he was so alive, so contented. There was no comparison with what he was like when he was with Jackie. Or any other person, for that matter."

Also with Jackie and Onassis were her children. Their stepfather knew their trust would not come automatically, and in an effort to win them over, Onassis gave Caroline a twenty-foot sailboat emblazoned with her name. Worried that her brother would be jealous, Ari presented the eight-year-old with a red speedboat with JOHN painted on its stern. One chronicler of the year's largesse reported that he also stocked the island with Shetland ponies, routinely flew the children's beloved Coney Island hot dogs in from New York, and once brought John's pet rabbit across the Atlantic under the eye of a "very nervous" Olympic Airways pilot.

According to Niki Goulandris, who cruised with Jackie and Ari on the *Christina,* Onassis took John Jr. on his knee and explained the Greek myths to him. As a gift to her new husband, Jackie memorialized these moments with a book of photos she had taken of him on Skorpios, posing as his hero Odysseus, and she wrote in its pages English translations from Homer's

Odyssey. For his part, Onassis arranged for his bride to have a personal guided tour of Odysseus' island of Ithaca and Heinrich Schliemann's archaeological excavations there.

After the first couple of summers, Jackie found long stretches on Skorpios wearing and often invited friends and relatives, including her sister, Lee, to visit her. Lee Radziwill has not commented publicly about her sister's marriage to Onassis or about her own relationship with the tycoon. But friends say she felt lingering resentment toward both, although she continued to see the couple after their marriage and even spent most of a summer with them on Skorpios. Another guest on the island that summer was Peter Beard, the photographer and conservationist, who was a close friend of both Lee's and Jackie's. "Lee admired Onassis for what he accomplished and for the way he lived his life to the fullest," Beard told me. "Onassis was smart and powerful, but primitive in a way, and she liked all that about him. I remember once Lee made graphic remarks about him, his sexual prowess, his oriental tastes in that area.

"The relationship between Lee and Jackie was often tense," Beard continued. "Jackie played the big sister to the hilt and Lee didn't like that very much. There was an underlying resentment on Lee's part, and I think Onassis was one factor. Naturally, since Lee knew Onassis first, she didn't like it when Jackie attracted him away from her. She was upset with Onassis, too. I think she felt he had used her to get to Jackie. But by the time I was on Skorpios they got along all right; there wasn't any great hostility apparent."

The hostility by then was between Onassis and Jackie, according to Beard. "I can't tell you how many meals I sat through, when Onassis would scream at her," he said. "He used to make insulting comparisons, right to her face, between Jackie and Callas. He said Jackie was superficial and Callas was a 'real artist.' Jackie just sat around and took it. Ari was nicer to her in London and New York, but in Greece all the macho in him came out. When he exploded, everybody ran for cover. I remember once John Jr. and I hid in a shower during one of his outbursts."

One reason for his outbursts was Jackie's spending. At the very beginning of their marriage, Onassis gave his new wife carte blanche to redecorate the neoclassical Pink House on Skorpios. Jackie threw herself into the project with a passion, and flew her friend the interior designer Billy Baldwin to Greece to help her. As usual, the only corner of Onassis' domain that was off limits was the interior of the *Christina,* which Baldwin found appalling. (He did, however, exempt from his aesthetic indictment Ari's study, which he loved for its strong masculine character, noting that it "almost made up for . . . the rest of the ship.")

Working at full speed, Baldwin finished the Pink House before Christmas. But when I toured the island in 1998, Captain Kostas Anastasiades told me that Onassis quickly did away with Baldwin's pricey fantasia of flowered chintzes and returned the villa to a more appropriately spartan Greek-island decor.

The new Mrs. Onassis also studied the gardens of Skorpios with an eye toward improvement. She deplored the artificial look of all the plants that Onassis and Callas had brought back from their Caribbean cruises. To one visitor she remarked, "Look at all those snapdragons. They shouldn't be on this island. It looks like a Burpee's catalogue."

But if the improvements on Skorpios seemed extravagant, they were nothing compared with the notorious spending records Jackie set shopping for clothes in Manhattan. She spent an estimated $1.25 million on her wardrobe during the first year of her marriage, prompting *Women's Wear Daily* in 1969 to declare her the "retailer's best friend": "Jackie O continues to fill her bottomless closets." The article marveled, "She is making Daddy O's bills bigger than ever with her latest shopping spree. She is buying in carload lots."

In public, Onassis adopted a laissez-faire attitude toward his wife's demand-side economics. "God knows Jackie has had her years of sorrow," he reportedly said. "If she enjoys it, let her buy to her heart's content." But in private he was seething, particularly after he discovered her purchases were largely a ruse to increase the thirty-thousand-dollar monthly tax-free allowance he gave her over and above wardrobe costs. The thirty thousand was disbursed on the first of every month to Jackie's aide Nancy Tuckerman (who was also on the Olympic payroll) by Creon Broun in Onassis' New York office. But Jackie would often deplete the entire amount by the fifteenth and would send Miss Tuckerman to ask for more.

At first the sympathetic Broun complied, until Ari put a stop to the practice. Jackie was forced to fall back on the money-laundering scheme she had first developed during her marriage to Jack Kennedy. After wearing her new clothes once or twice or not at all, she would sell them to up-market resale houses, especially her favorite, Encore, at 1132 Madison Avenue, a convenient three blocks from her apartment. Sometimes she would demand a fixed price for an Yves St. Laurent or Valentino frock; other times she would accept whatever the market would bear.

Jackie would have the amount of the sale paid to one of her employees, who would then give the cash to her. Her bookkeeper, Mary Gallagher, told the columnist Jack Anderson that even as first lady, Jackie had "resold [clothing] under my name and home address. . . . Encore's check would come to me and I would deposit it in my personal account. At the same time, I would write out a check for the same amount to be deposited in Jackie's account." As Telis' new bride, Jackie expanded her resale business, according to Anderson, by also selling trivial old possessions like picture frames and John Jr.'s nursery furniture at auction through New York's William Doyle Galleries and Sotheby Parke Bernet (the auctioneers for the famous posthumous sale of her possessions in 1996).

Ari started to notice that Jackie's clothing bills were beyond extravagant. When one for nine thousand dollars came from Valentino he shouted, "What does she do with all the clothes? I never see her in anything but blue jeans." A few years later, particularly after he learned that she had lost $300,000 of her prenuptial payment investing in the stock market against his advice, Onassis got fed up and scaled her allowance down to twenty thousand dollars a month, according to Anderson. Responsibility for disbursements and management of her funds was reassigned to his Monte Carlo office so he could keep a closer watch.

While Onassis coped with the hidden costs of his marriage, he was also suffering unprecedented setbacks in his business dealings. Other shipowners had always considered him to be incredibly lucky because he had lost only one ship in more than three decades, but in the year after his marriage to Jackie, four of his vessels suffered major mishaps. At the same time, his precious Project Omega was also encountering rough seas and his new wife was rarely around to offer consolation.

Stavros Niarchos was not about to let Onassis walk off with the biggest business deal in the history of Greece. In March of 1969 he made a counteroffer, presenting the colonels an investment package worth $500 million that included a $150 million long-term low-interest cash loan.

The colonels stuck by Onassis, but when the deal was finally signed in the spring of 1971, it included fewer projects, under much less advantageous terms, than he had first proposed. Niarchos was appeased by a provision allowing him to expand his refinery and shipyard. When oil prices began to soar the following summer, the Omega deal collapsed. Under his agreement with the colonels, Onassis could not pass on the higher prices for crude oil to the state, and the projected losses threatened to ruin him financially. He was forced to abandon the deal in the fall of 1971. To get back his seven-million-dollar guarantee, Onassis was forced to waive any claim for damages.

Later a former Omega coordinator in Athens said of Onassis, "Watching him doing his number, keeping track of it all in that little notebook of his, it was kind of sad. He was a dinosaur. It was all over for him. The conviction began to grow even on Papadopoulos that everything Ari now touched was going to be a mess, a disaster."

Even his legendary bravado could not help him once the setbacks started. When four armed Palestinians hijacked an Olympic Airways flight from Beirut on July 22, 1970, Onassis personally went to the Athens airport, walked in the scorching heat to the beleaguered aircraft, and offered himself as hostage in place of the eighty passengers and crew. Although his net worth probably exceeded that of all the passengers combined and he was married to the former first lady of the United States, the hijackers turned him down. In the end he had to capitulate and ask the Greek junta then in power to agree to their demands—the release of four Palestinians in Greek prisons—to secure the release of the hostages.

Those closest to Onassis, including his intimate friends and top executives, whispered among themselves that the old man was losing his touch, and many of them were quick to blame it on the "Jackie jinx."

19

REUNION

We pardon to the degree that we love.

La Rochefoucauld, Maxim 330

In the first years of the marriage, Onassis' main complaint to his associates was not that Project Omega was faltering, but that his wife spent so little time with him in Greece, where he was obliged to remain to watch over his business deals. Jackie's friends and her children's schools were in New York, and she soon discovered that that was where she felt most at home. But each time she flew back to New York from Skorpios or Athens, Onassis felt he was being abandoned. On their first anniversary, October 20, 1969, someone calculated that Ari and Jackie had spent 225 days together and 140 apart. During the next year, their record would be much worse.

Three days after that anniversary, Jackie Onassis appeared at the charity premiere of the film *Giselle* at Lincoln Center in New York. She was escorted by Oliver Smith, the co-director of the American Ballet Theater. Her husband, who did not share her keen appetite for the arts, was not present. Eight days earlier he had accompanied her and her children to the World Series opener at Shea Stadium, but he slipped away early, leaving Jackie, Caroline, and John Jr. alone for the last innings.

On October 23, while Jackie's arrival was causing the crowd at Lincoln Center to part "like the Red Sea," as the *New York Times* put it, Onassis was flying to Paris. The first anniversary no doubt provided Ari occasion to contemplate what he had given up to marry Mrs. Kennedy. He could not have been pleased with his wife's near-pathological extravagance or the amount of gratitude and devotion she had expressed for his generosity during the past year, especially his many lavish gifts. Whatever Onassis was thinking, only days after celebrating a year of marriage to Jackie, he was on the phone with Maria saying he wanted to see her.

As soon as she hung up the phone, Maria begged Nadia Stancioff, who was visiting Paris, to escort her back to Rome: "I've got to get out of this city and find a place where he can't reach me." Later that afternoon Maria called Nadia back, saying that Onassis was already on his way. "He says he'll find me wherever I go and will plague me until I give in. . . ."

Nadia advised her to receive him at a small dinner at her house. "You need to be surrounded by friends who will protect you and an ambience you feel comfortable in. You can't go to Maxim's! He's just publicity-crazy and wants the whole world to know that he's won you back." Maria assented and invited a handful of friends who had shared the Onassis-Callas years. The guest list included Hélène Rochas of the French perfume family; Francesco Chiarini, an old friend from Italy; François Valéry, an ambassador to UNESCO and one of her closest male friends; Maggie van Zuylen, a socialite who was one of her closest female friends in Paris; and Nadia, the only one who didn't know Onassis. As the dinner hour approached, Maria, in a white and gold caftan, was so nervous, said Nadia, "she couldn't sit still. She fidgeted, ruined the flowers by rearranging them, cuddled the dogs, and talked nonstop."

As everyone began to be infected by Callas' anxiety, the doorbell rang, and Ferruccio, in livery and white gloves, escorted Onassis in. The tycoon embraced Maria, who pulled back nervously and told the group somewhat disingenuously, "Aristo has just arrived from New York."

Although Nadia found him "the opposite of the word handsome," she soon "felt some of his attraction and began to understand Maria's fascination for him. . . . During that evening, he acted as if he were dining in his own home. He was totally at ease, which I think annoyed his friends, who had expected a small sign of repentance, and while we sat stiffly in our evening clothes, Aristo shed his jacket and pulled his red tie down to half-mast without even consulting the hostess."

Maria jumped to attend to Aristo's every wish, François Valéry told me. The diva showed him piles of photographs of herself with Pasolini and her handsome leading man, working on the set of *Medea*. She prodded Nadia to relate all the adventures of those months. Onassis sat next to Maria on the couch and occasionally offered a monosyllabic comment through a cloud of cigar smoke. "We all observed how vulnerable Maria still was to every word Aristo uttered," Nadia recalled.

His hand found its way to Maria's lap and rested on her upper thigh. He took his cigar out of his mouth long enough to exclaim, "Ah, that feels good!

It's great to feel Maria's big fat thighs again. I've really missed them. Jackie is nothing but a bag of bones."

Maria's expression was one of embarrassment and delight, while the rest of us avoided each other's eyes and feigned amusement.

By the time our party left Maria's apartment, there was a crowd in front of 36 Avenue Georges Mandel. The press had followed Onassis from the airport and the news was out. Onassis and Callas were back together.

In December of 1969, Maria went back to Rome to review the first cut of the film with Pasolini before traveling with the director to Argentina to present *Medea* at the Festival of Mar del Plata. She was full of hope for the film—hope that it would launch her into a successful and lucrative new career.

On January 28, 1970, *Medea* was unveiled at a gala premiere at L'Opéra in Paris with Madame Pompidou in attendance. Also present were the Aga Khan, Maurice Chevalier, Mrs. Sargent Shriver (wife of the American ambassador to France and sister of John F. Kennedy), various Rothschilds, and ambassadors from eleven countries. Aristotle Onassis had reserved a box for four, but the reservation was canceled at the last minute; the excuse was that Mrs. Onassis would not be able to arrive in Paris in time.

(An English newspaper reported that Onassis stayed away to avoid embarrassing Maria but was "with her and director Pier Paolo Pasolini at Miss Callas' home until the very moment she had left for the premiere. . . . He also booked three seats on a plane to New York for the same evening, but these seats also remained empty. Instead he later attended a dinner at the Avenue Foch home of Baron and Baroness van Zuylen, at which Miss Callas was the guest of honour. . . . As for the film, Mr. Onassis had his own private show three days before the big premiere.")

The critics were kind to the film but the audience was cool. Janet Flanner, in *The New Yorker,* opined that "*Medea* turned out to contain the greatest acting performance of Callas's career." The film would prove a *succès d'estime,* but *Medea* would never make any money, nor would it launch Maria into the stratosphere of film stardom.

In February of 1970, a month after the disappointment of the film's cool reception, the growing cracks in the Kennedy-Onassis marriage were revealed to the world. The disclosure came with the publication of some letters that Jackie had written to a former suitor, the attorney Roswell Gilpatric, who had served as deputy secretary of defense in the Kennedy administration. The letter that caught everyone's eye, especially that of Aristotle Onassis, had been written from the *Christina* during the honeymoon:

Dearest Ros—I would have told you before I left—but then everything happened so much more quickly than I'd planned. I saw somewhere what you had said and I was touched—dear Ros—I hope you know all you were and are and will ever be to me—With my love, Jackie

This note—and the others—had reportedly been tossed into the trash by Gilpatric, had been discovered by an employee in his law firm, and had then been offered for sale to the Manhattan autograph dealer Charles Hamilton. In the history of billets-doux, it is hardly the most compromising, but it was affectionate enough to stir suspicions. When Mrs. Gilpatric sued for a separation the day after its publication, things began to look more ambiguous. For Onassis, the poster boy for Mediterranean machismo, the letter was a crushing blow.

"My God, what a fool I've made of myself!" Ari exclaimed to Costa Gratsos. He feared that the world would think he had been cuckolded—indeed, that only days after his marriage to the widow of Jack Kennedy, she had been sitting on his yacht writing love letters to an old flame. It was for him not merely a matter of pride but of business. Onassis believed that his success as a tycoon depended on his personal mystique and potent image. To be cast as a betrayed husband would shatter not only his ego but his reputation as the perpetual winner—equally unbeatable in both love and deal making.

Ari felt he had to take steps to remedy the damage that had been done. The first step was to go to Maria and pour into her sympathetic ear all his complaints about Jackie's profligate spending habits, her coldness, her shallowness, and her lack of understanding of his needs. As he contemplated his abandonment and betrayal by his new wife, his friends later said, Ari came to believe that only three women in his life had ever truly loved him: his mother, Penelope (who was long dead); his sister Artemis (who still refused to hear a word against Jackie); and Maria Callas, who found herself listening to his woes during hour-long phone calls.

Whenever Onassis came to Paris, he assigned his friend and adviser Miltos Yiannakopoulos to arrange the time and place for his meetings with Maria. (Yiannakopoulos also served as Ari's intelligence operative, with responsibilities for bugging phones and assigning private detectives, and so was feared by many Onassis employees.) In 1998, Yiannakopoulos told me that it was Maria who made Ari happy, not Jackie. "After the first few months [of marriage to Jackie] he didn't care if she existed. He saw [Callas] every chance he got, the first time within weeks of his marriage. . . . He would have me track her down and set up the meetings. Even when he just talked on the phone to Maria, he lit up afterwards."

Despite Maria's persistent anger over his betrayal, the attachment between herself and Onassis remained deep and enduring, according to Ferruccio Mezzadri: "She filled his life like no one else; you could see it. Madame adored him, that's for sure, and he too was strongly bound to her. You could see it in the way he was with her, the way he laughed with her, teased her, joked with her. Even when he fought with her, you could sense the passion in it."

In April of 1970, the *Christina* made its annual Easter cruise to the Caribbean with Andrew and Geraldine Spreckles Fuller as guests. (Ari had dated Geraldine Spreckles in the early 1940s.) Jackie joined the yacht in Puerto Rico, and seemed as bewildered as the others when the boat kept circling Haiti without making progress. Geraldine later described to the Onassis biographer Peter Evans the odd interaction she observed between the shipowner and his wife. Ari seemed at once angry with Jackie and anxious to placate her. For her part, Jackie alternately taunted her husband and behaved seductively, at one moment remarking coyly to him, "I went upstairs, darling, and I put perfume wherever Mr. Lanvin told me to put it, and you never came up. I put perfume *everywhere!*"

Geraldine said that Ari finally confessed to her that they were hanging out around Haiti because he was trying to persuade Jackie to slip ashore for a quickie divorce in Port-au-Prince, with the understanding that they would remarry the following day. The putative aim of this was to dispel rumors of problems in the marriage and demonstrate that they really did love each other. But Geraldine observed, correctly, that it was a highly unconvincing proposition. "You damn fool, Ari, she'll never buy that. Never!"

Onassis replied with a laugh, "Yes, but I was hoping." He also told her that he had offered Jackie a big payoff to end the marriage. (After the death of Onassis, the *New York Times* would report, on April 12, 1975: "Rumors of a divorce between Mr. and Mrs. Onassis date as far back as 1970, although they were always denied. In 1970, however, Mrs. Onassis speculated to her own friends and family that in time, Mr. Onassis would divorce her.")

In May of 1970, Onassis began a highly visible courtship of Maria in Paris. A French reporter who specialized in shadowing him, Henri Pessar, reported that the tycoon left the Georges Mandel apartment between 12:30 and 1 a.m. on four successive nights, on each of which the couple had earlier been seen dining together, though not always alone. Someone alerted the press that the pair would be at Maxim's on May 21, and they were duly photographed at an intimate table (accompanied by Baroness Maggie van Zuylen, who had acted as go-between and counselor for the lovers from the start of their reborn affair). The next day, a furious Jackie flew from New York to Paris and that night she and Onassis dined at Maxim's at the very same table. Afterward, they lingered at Régine's until two-thirty in the morning, by which time Mrs. Onassis must have been near collapse from the effects of jet lag.

Ari may have been amused by this public one-upmanship, but for Maria, the little duel had near-fatal consequences. It's impossible to know what Aristo told her during their four nights together, but he must have indicated his anger and frustration with Jackie and his desire to obtain a divorce from her. Maria, still hopelessly in love with him, must have believed that his marriage was nearing an end. But when she saw photographs in the French papers of Ari and Jackie at the very table where she had sat with him the night before—in the restaurant that had always been "their place"—Maria must have felt herself drawn once again into the perilous cycle of exultant optimism and crushing disappointment. She began to fear that Aristo would never break from his famous wife—that he would only continue to lie to her.

Three days later, on Monday, May 25, Maria invited to her home the conductor Carlo Maria Giulini and his wife, Marcella. They became concerned about her anxious and despondent manner throughout the evening. When they got up to go, Maria begged them, "Don't leave me alone. Please stay." The next morning when Mrs. Giulini called to enquire how Maria was, she was told that Callas had been taken to the American Hospital in Neuilly at 7 a.m. That same morning, it was announced on Radio Luxembourg that "Maria Callas has attempted to commit suicide by taking an overdose of barbiturates."

(Also on May 26, according to the *New York Times*, Mrs. Aristotle S. Onassis in Athens deflected a question about reports that her marriage was under strain: "Oh, my God. What will they think of next?" The same article reported, "She and Mr. Onassis arrived in Athens two days ago to prepare for their next party—a week-long cruise of Greek islands early next month aboard their yacht, the Christina, for three United States astronauts and their families and other prominent guests. They left Paris Sunday in the wake of reports in British newspapers that the . . . millionaire's renewed Paris appearances with the primadonna Maria Callas had brought his wife, the widow of President John F. Kennedy, from New York and had led to arguments.")

Later, Maria issued a statement that she had gone to the hospital for only a routine checkup. When a French tabloid repeated the suicide story, she instructed her lawyer to sue both the paper and Radio Luxembourg. (Ultimately she would be awarded twenty thousand francs in damages.)

Callas herself later said to Nadia Stancioff, "The press cooked up a dramatic story about my having attempted suicide. What nonsense all that was! . . . I admit I was depressed, but you know as well as I do, I would never have done anything stupid like that." It seems likely that Callas' alleged suicide attempt was in fact another miscalculated effort to quiet her nerves during a crisis and find solace in sleep. It was not the first such episode, nor would it be the last.

Only weeks before Maria's overdose, another woman well known to Onassis had swallowed twenty-five Seconal tablets and had succeeded in killing herself. On the evening of May 3, 1970, Eugenia Livanos Niarchos, the older sister of Tina Onassis and the wife of Stavros Niarchos, died on her husband's private island of Spetsopoula after writing him an incoherent suicide note. Eugenia had become distraught over a telephone call she overheard Niarchos making. (There are conflicting rumors about the nature of the call and the identity of the other party.) When a doctor was summoned after midnight, he found Eugenia's body bruised, with multiple contusions, and she was bleeding internally. Niarchos claimed that the injuries occurred during his strenuous attempts to revive his wife. Some, including Onassis, raised the question of why Niarchos had sent for his own physician to come by helicopter from Athens, a trip that took ninety minutes, when there was a doctor on Spetses, only three minutes away. Eventually, after three postmortems on Eugenia, the Greek public prosecutor recommended that Niarchos be charged with causing bodily injuries leading to his wife's death.

Throughout his life, Onassis' hatred for Niarchos, who was then still vying with him for control of Project Omega, never flagged, but on this occasion, according to Miltos Yiannakopoulos, Ari's intelligence adviser, he chose to help his archrival. "After the death of Eugenia," Yiannakopoulos told me, "Niarchos was found culpable in her death by the investigating magistrate. But Eugenia's mother, Arietta, came to Niarchos' aid because she was afraid that if he went to prison, his financial empire would be destroyed and her grandchildren would suffer, so she did everything possible to save Niarchos, even asking Onassis to use his influence. Aristo asked me if I could help, and it happened that I knew some of the key officials in the case and I was able to talk to them. A lot of money was passed around by Niarchos and of course that helped. Even Apache helicopters were bought for the Greek army. Onassis had the chance to finish Niarchos off then, but he didn't do it, because he knew it would hurt Tina, her mother, and the Niarchos children."

When I asked George Livanos, Eugenia and Tina's brother, about the death of his older sister, he said, "There was a lot of talk that he [Niarchos] was responsible, psychologically if not physically, but that's a lot of bull. . . . Anybody who's unhappy and wants to commit suicide, you can't say that the other person drove them to commit suicide. . . . We were called to testify by the prosecutor and there were never any indications that I, or my sister, or my mother, blamed Niarchos."

While Onassis was campaigning in Athens to save his enemy and brother-in-law from criminal charges, Maria, accompanied by Nadia Stancioff, was vacationing on Tragonisi, the private island of the shipowner Perry Embiricos, not far away. Embiricos, who had never been married, was a great fan of Callas', and in the evenings after sunset they would often sit on his terrace and listen to Maria's finest recordings. One evening, Nadia recalls, Maria was visibly moved by her own voice and sighed, "Brava! La Callas will never sing like that again."

They were joined on Tragonisi by Pier Paolo Pasolini, who still worshiped Maria and spent his time sketching her. He incorporated real flowers and seawater in his artworks. Callas took the opportunity to visit Meligala, her father's native village in the Peloponnesus, where the villagers wept and kissed her hand. She also traveled by helicopter to the island of Skiathos to visit Merope Konialidis, Onassis' half sister.

Nadia returned to Rome, leaving Maria behind to enjoy the sun and sea and to meditate on the beautiful music that was no longer within her power. Maria swam as naturally as a mermaid and loved to spend hours in the water, diving for seashells, sunbathing—just as she had during the years on the *Christina*.

On August 15, 1970, the feast day of the Virgin Mary, Maria reclined in a lounging chair under a large umbrella on Embiricos' beach. Her skin was bronzed, her face was innocent of makeup, her long hair was pulled back in a pony-tail. There was a buzz overhead, at first indistinguishable from the drone of the cicadas in the heat. Then the sound grew louder and a great shadow loomed over the sand. The roar of an engine grew deafening, the sand began to blow in the wind stirred by the propellers. Like an immense dragonfly, a helicopter alighted on the beach.

Maria shaded her eyes with one hand to watch as the helicopter's door opened. She did not get up as Onassis stepped onto the sand and walked toward her. It was Maria's name day, which they had always celebrated together, and although she did not expect him, she was not surprised at his arrival.

A photographer out of view in a small boat at sea captured the moment with a telephoto lens as Onassis came up to Maria, leaned over, and kissed her passionately on the lips. She accepted his kiss as naturally and as lovingly as if they were a long-married couple who had been apart for only a few hours. Then Onassis pulled a small box from his pocket and handed it to her. After she opened the gift—a pair of antique earrings—Aristo even kissed the poodle, Djedda (which he had given her).

Ari (married to Jackie) kisses Maria under an umbrella during a surprise visit to the private island where she was vacationing.

Eventually Maria stood up and the couple walked up the beach alone, hand in hand, talking quietly and intensely, trailed by the poodle. When they finally strolled back to the beach umbrella, Onassis greeted Maria's companions, Anastasia and Costa Gratsos, who had been watching the tender reunion.

Onassis sat and talked with Maria for more than an hour. Then he kissed her good-bye, walked to the waiting helicopter, and flew off as suddenly as he had come. Callas returned to the beach chair with a smile both sad and content, leaving the others to ponder the spectacle of the modern Odysseus dropping out of the sky to embrace his faithful Penelope and to wish her the traditional name-day blessing *"Chronia polla"*—Many years—before resuming his wanderings.

The intimate scene was manna for newspapers and magazines around the world and triggered another immediate response from Jackie. *Time* magazine put it this way: "No sooner does Aristotle Onassis lay one rift rumor to rest than he starts another. There was Jackie in New York, there was Ari in Athens, and there was Old Flame Maria Callas vacationing at the nearby isle of Tragonisi. One day Maria decided to throw a beach party. Ari dropped in by helicopter, greeted Maria with a kiss and picnicked away the golden hours with Maria and two other guests. Responding like a Dalmatian to the fire bell, Jackie flew back to Greece, to Onassis, to the yacht *Christina,* and to squelch rumors."

Callas, meanwhile, gave most reporters her usual careful, noncommittal comment: "I have great respect for Aristotle and there is no reason for us not meeting here since Mr. Embiricos is a mutual friend." But to another reporter, Judy Klemsrud of the *New York Times,* who interviewed her in November, she spoke with a good deal more candor (and a certain cattiness): "He [Onassis] is my best friend. He is, he was, and he always will be. . . . When two people have been together as we have, there are many things that tie you together. He knows he will always find cheerfulness, mutual friends, and honesty when he sees me. The scandal comes about because I have never met his wife. It's not wished on the other side."

Maria toasted the new year in Paris at a party given by Pierre Cardin's partner (Ari was in New York with Jackie), then in February traveled to Philadelphia, where she had agreed to lead a two-week master class. She found the eighteen students who awaited her so unprepared that she canceled the experiment and returned to New York to see friends. While she was there, Anastasia Gratsos took her to an eye doctor, who diagnosed incipient glaucoma. Maria's already severe nearsightedness was getting worse, and if she did not put drops in her eyes every two hours for the rest of her life she would go blind, he told her.

Not long after this, Onassis was rocked by two personal blows that inflamed his always volatile temper. He was on Skorpios with Jackie in July, celebrating her forty-second birthday, when he learned that his daughter, Christina, only twenty years old, had married, in Las Vegas, forty-eight-year-old California real estate executive Joe Bolker—a man whom she had met at the underground swimming pool of the Hôtel de Paris in Monte Carlo.

Onassis raged and spent hours placing international calls all over the world asking the question: "Who is Joe Bolker?" (Christina had described her husband to a friend as "a dinky millionaire in real estate.") Then Ari cut off Christina's trust fund and allowance, and announced that his daughter would never receive another penny as long as she stayed married. He even ordered a phone tap on Bolker's phone and sent Costa Gratsos out to California to grill the man. Bolker was thoroughly unnerved by his father-in-law's scrutiny: after he and Christina started divorce proceedings eight months later, he was quoted as saying, "When a billion dollars leans on you, you feel it."

Onassis blamed his ex-wife, Tina, for letting this wedding happen without his knowledge. Living in London, she had been absorbed in filing her own divorce suit against the marquess of Blandford ("Sonny") and in looking after the motherless children of Niarchos and her dead sister, Eugenia.

On October 22, only eighteen months after Eugenia's suicide, Tina secretly married Stavros Niarchos, her former brother-in-law, who had been suspected of causing her sister's death. The only guest at the wedding in Paris was her mother, Arietta. Tina's marriage to Sonny Blandford had soured early, and according to members of the family, she sounded out Onassis about getting back together before he married Jackie. When he demurred, Tina turned to Niarchos, who had always felt a strong attraction to her. Several family members told me that both the feelers to Onassis and the union with Niarchos were instigated by Tina and Eugenia's strong-willed mother, Arietta, who was anxious that all of the various fortunes in her family remain intact for her grandchildren. (Reinaldo Herrera told me that he received three letters from Tina during the years after they parted for the last time. In one, she related that she had married Niarchos—whom she had earlier viewed with derision—because, he said, "she saw her sister in a dream and Eugenia told her to marry him and look after the children.")

If his daughter's hasty marriage infuriated Onassis, his ex-wife's marriage to his despised rival drove him to the edge of madness. Feeling, perhaps for the first time, that he was losing control of all the aspects of his life—his marriage, his children, his business deals, even his ex-wife—he was determined to find someone to blame. It wasn't in his nature to shake his fist at the heavens and curse the gods—he had to find a human enemy, so that he could challenge and beat him. In a typically Greek manner, Onassis saw conspiracies and plots everywhere and when he sought to find a villain, he usually looked first in the direction of Stavros Niarchos. Having accused Tina, now under this devil's spell, of promoting her daughter's misalliance to keep attention off her own plans, he went on to allege that Niarchos had paid Bolker to marry Christina. (Tina had given Christina $200,000 after her father cut her off.)

Ari's twenty-three-year-old son took his mother's marriage to Niarchos even harder than his father did. Ari and Alexander had always had a difficult relationship—the father was never satisfied with the boy he had anointed his "alpha and omega," and the sensitive youth resented his father's criticisms and his womanizing. Alexander had always harbored the hope that his parents would reconcile, and he blamed first Maria Callas and then Jacqueline Kennedy for frustrating his dream.

At the same time, Alexander admired his father's accomplishments and

Maria and Vasso Devetzi in Moscow during the 1970 Tchaikovsky competition.
The woman on the left is the Soviet minister of culture.

had inherited Onassis' hatred of Niarchos. He, too, felt that his mother, in marrying his father's worst enemy, had committed the ultimate betrayal. The young man lost twenty pounds in the weeks after he received a registered letter informing him of his mother's remarriage. He never spoke to Tina again, and refused all her attempts to communicate with him.

Christina, still in Los Angeles with Bolker, reacted to her mother's marriage to Niarchos as she usually did when confronted with overwhelming bad news: she took an overdose of pills. The girl believed that Niarchos had killed her aunt Eugenia, and now she feared for her mother's life.

That fall Maria was in New York City, preparing for master classes she had agreed to give at Juilliard, which were to begin on October 11. The idea had originated in 1970, when she traveled to Moscow with the Greek pianist Vasso Devetzi to serve as president of the Tchaikovsky competition jury. Devetzi and Maria had been acquainted since Callas' first appearance in Athens in 1957, and after Maria moved to Paris, where Vasso lived, they became good friends.

On the Moscow trip, the Russian minister of culture invited Callas to conduct master classes for young Russian opera singers. On the plane back, Maria said to Vasso, "It's a great idea to give master classes, but why shouldn't I do it for my own country?" Even though she had given up her American citizenship, she still felt the United States was her homeland. On the same flight she discussed with Vasso the creation of a foundation to help young performers and asked, "Do you think Aristo will help?"

In New York City, in the fall of 1971, Maria was able to find young singers talented enough to profit from her teaching. She selected twenty-six students out of 350 who auditioned for her. The lessons were open sessions, and many celebrities came to watch them. (The lessons are the subject of Terrence McNally's play *Master Class,* but, contrary to his dramatic version, Callas did not at any time break into confessional monologues about her life and loves.) Larry Kelly later said, "The classes were really Maria's way of presenting herself to an audience for the first time in six or seven years. She needed an audience's reaction."

Maria flourished in the role of teacher and, also contrary to the stage portrayal, she was more helpful than harsh with the fledgling opera stars. When a student asked her, "What is the best way to interpret a piece of music?" she replied, "Love it."

The twenty-four master classes were spread out between October 11 of 1971 to March 16 of 1972. Callas was simultaneously working with a coach from the Metropolitan Opera every morning to improve her own voice. Her success on stage with her students, even though she would only sing brief passages of music to illustrate a point, emboldened Maria to feel that she might be able to sing professionally once again.

Mary Carter came from Dallas with a cousin to visit Callas while she was in New York. "The three of us went to Trader Vic's. Maria told me that Onassis had come to New York to see her. He wanted her back. 'You get rid of your wife and then we'll talk about it,' Maria told him." Mrs. Carter believes that Onassis began to try to force a divorce with Jackie by spreading rumors that their marriage had broken down, in the hope that she would leave him. Though some of the divorce rumors were actually spread by Costa Gratsos, she feels he was acting on Onassis' instructions. "Ari wanted to force the issue," Mrs. Carter said. "He was frantic to get rid of Jackie. Maria told me at that time, 'Now he talks to me about divorce the way he used to talk to me about marriage.' "

Although she never again withheld from Onassis her sympathetic attention and love, Maria would not sleep with him as long as he was married to Jackie. She declared this to Mary Carter and other friends, as well as to Miltos Yiannakopoulos, who continued to act as their go-between in Paris. "I got curious and asked her once if she was sleeping with him," he told me, "and she responded sharply, '*Poté!*' 'Never!' "

Kostas Pylarinos, a Greek politician who became close to Maria while he was in self-imposed exile in Paris during the junta years, also told me that after Onassis married Jackie, "He and Maria remained tied to each other. But the relationship was not sexual. She wouldn't permit it after he left her for Jackie."

When Maria tried to displace her romantic longings onto other relationships, it always led to regret. In New York, during the months of the master classes, Maria had a brief involvement with Peter Mennin, the head of the Juilliard School, who was married. "It's a pity . . . that happened," she wrote her godfather. John Ardoin, who visited Maria in New York at the time, told me, "It got very sticky for her because Mennin really fell for her and wanted to leave his wife and she wanted no part of anything like that."

Around Christmas of 1971, Maria received a dozen roses at the Plaza Hotel, where she was staying while doing the master classes. They were from Giuseppe di Stefano, the Sicilian tenor with whom she had had a tempestuous professional relationship in the 1950s. She was touched and called to invite him for a drink.

"I went to the Plaza and we started to talk, when the phone rang," he told me when I interviewed him at his home near Lake Como. "It was Onassis calling. She left the room to talk to him and I asked her afterwards: 'Why do you leave the room? I don't understand Greek, you know.' . . . Then Sander Gorlinsky heard we were seeing each other. And Gorlinsky, naturally, as an impresario, had the idea to put us together for a concert tour."

While Maria was beginning rehearsals for the ill-fated tour with di Stefano, Onassis was continuing his search to find a way out of his deteriorating marriage. His expectations about the union had run the full course from hope to utter disillusionment. He always knew Jacqueline would not make him the center of her life as Callas did, but he believed at the beginning that the benefits of marrying her would outweigh the advantages Maria offered him. At first he also thought that he could keep them both—juggling them as he had hoped to juggle Tina and Maria. "Onassis, being Onassis, thought he could have Jackie and keep Maria too," Yiannis Giorgakis, his close friend, told me in 1993.

Ari eventually realized that Maria would not give herself to him as long as he was married to Jackie. At first she wouldn't even take his calls, but after a year, having rebuilt her battered self-confidence by starring in *Medea,* she would at least dine with him, talk to him, listen to his problems, and commiserate. But the proud, religious, bourgeois Greek could not let herself sleep with her former lover after he had been married in the Greek church to the most famous widow in the world.

Jackie cared for Onassis and tried her best to please him during the limited time they spent together—especially at the beginning—but her primary devotion was to her children, and this continually led her back to New York. "So instead of having both women at once, he wound up with neither one the way he wanted her," said Miltos Yiannakopoulos.

As Jackie's absences grew longer and Maria showed no signs of wavering in her resolve, Onassis came to the conclusion that he would have to make a choice. He began trying to find a quiet, amicable way to divorce Jackie without any loss of face for either participant—a very tall order, considering that every detail of their marriage so far had received the rapt attention of the public.

Onassis' Athens lawyers were discouraging. "Under Greek law at that time you could not obtain a divorce without cause, even if both parties wanted it," said Stelios Papadimitriou. "I wrote several drafts of a divorce petition for him and each time I would ask him: 'What is the substance of your complaint? Does she insult you? Does she treat you badly? Does she betray you?' He said, 'No.' 'What then?' 'She doesn't stay with me.' 'Well,' I would tell him, 'you knew that her life was in the States. You knew that she had children whose father was a martyred president and they would be raised in the States. And if she goes to court and says, 'Yes, I don't spend as much time with my husband as I would like because I have a duty to my children,' what Greek court would tell her, 'Leave your children and go to your husband?' "

Mr. Papadimitriou smiled and shook his head as he recounted his discussions with Onassis about the difficulties of trying to divorce the former American first lady. "The trouble with him was that he wanted me to get a divorce without saying anything bad about Jackie, and that just could not be done then under Greek law, even for a man like Onassis."

Ari understood that if he tried to denigrate Jackie in order to divorce her, the public reaction would be fiercely against him, especially in the United States. That was not something he could risk in the early 1970s, because he was launching several major investments in the country and he would need all the goodwill he could get there.

But he was now convinced that the cost of having the most admired woman in the world was too high even for him to pay, and he had to find a way to recover what he had lost—the only woman who loved him unconditionally.

20

THE FALL OF ICARUS

This grave a father's hopes doth hide.

Callimachus, *Epitaph*

On January 4, 1973, Aristotle Onassis and his son had a dinner together in Paris that left the twenty-four-year-old Alexander feeling unexpectedly pleased and optimistic. Ari told him that he was going to consult New York lawyers to find a way to end his marriage, despite the difficulties of getting a divorce under Greek law. He was putting the case in the hands of the take-no-prisoners litigator Roy Cohn, and he even discussed with his son what kind of settlement he should offer Jackie. Father and son later recounted the exchange to trusted associates.

Onassis offered a second piece of news that pleased Alexander: he had decided to get rid of the outdated Piaggio amphibious plane on the *Christina* and replace it with a helicopter. The boy had long complained about the corroding "death trap." Now Onassis said that he'd had it overhauled, and on his annual winter cruise, he would transport the plane to Miami and sell it there. Accompanying him would be a new pilot whom he had hired to fly the Piaggio and then the new helicopter.

After the meal, Alexander called his longtime lover, Baroness Fiona von Thyssen, who was vacationing in Mexico with her two children. He told her triumphantly, "The old man is coming to his senses at last. He's divorcing the Widow and selling the Albatross."

The thorny relationship between Onassis and his son had been improving in recent years. Everyone who knew Alexander agreed that he had metamorphosed from a spoiled brat whose main pleasure was running down people with his various motorized vehicles into a sensitive young man who lived for flying. As he matured, his kindness and tact had endeared him especially to the Onassis employees with whom he worked.

His father had put Alexander in charge of Olympic Aviation, an air taxi and local charter service that included a fleet of small planes flying to smaller Greek islands, and the young man had made a respectable success of it. To Alexander's sorrow, his poor eyesight prevented him from ever becoming a commercial pilot, but at the age of eighteen he had qualified to pilot charter flights and on many occasions when someone was stricken ill in a remote spot in Greece in bad weather, Alexander would fly small air-craft in to carry the victim to medical aid when every other Olympic pilot refused to take the risk.

On one occasion, related by Maria Baroumi, a woman who worked with him at Olympic Aviation, Alexander interrupted a business meeting to fly to save the son of a fisherman who had blown off his hands fishing with dynamite and was bleeding to death. Later he told Ms. Baroumi that the young man's father had insisted on giving him a hundred-drachma tip (about thirty cents), which Alexander had accepted so that the father would not be insulted.

In many ways father and son were opposites. Ari had always been extroverted, voluble, able to enjoy himself anywhere and in any company. He loved to talk and to bask in the company of beautiful women. Alexander was shy and inarticulate—the only thing he could discuss with ease was machines—and despite his father's efforts to turn him into a playboy, he was monogamous, having been in love with Fiona since 1967, when he was nine-teen and she was thirty-five.

Ari stopped paying for Alexander's education when he flunked out of the French lycée at the age of sixteen. Instead he put the boy to work in his office in Monte Carlo and tried to browbeat him into becoming an ace wheeler-dealer. Alexander struggled to please him, but his performance was never good enough and he was overwhelmed by Ari's harangues and criticisms. He took to tape-recording his phone conversations with his father to prove to Fiona just how impossible the old man was. Stelios Papadimitriou, who shared an office in Monte Carlo with Alexander and Onassis, told me a story that reveals the dynamic between them:

"One day Alexander came in and said to his father, 'It's finished with Fiona. It's over between us.' "

" 'Oh yes,' the wily Anatolian said. 'That's good, good. Tell me some-thing. Are you having any physical problems? You can't get it up?'

"Alexander was embarrassed. 'No, I have no problem.'

" 'Ah, then, you found another girl?'

Alpha and omega: Aristotle and Alexander Onassis,
shortly before the heir's death

" 'No, I haven't found another girl. I've just broken up with Fiona,' Alexander told him.

" 'Go on, get out of here!' Onassis yelled at him. 'If your cock is still working and you don't have another girl, you'll be back with her in two or three days.'

"Sure enough, one day later they were back together again. You could never fool the old man," Papadimitriou concluded.

Despite their antagonism, the relationship deepened into mutual respect as Alexander became more confident and Ari began to recognize the young man's strengths. "He was a very, very bright kid," his uncle, George Livanos, told me. "He had all of his father's [best] traits—the character, the intelligence, the *poniria* [cunning], every bit of it."

Onassis was especially proud of his son's skills as a pilot. When they went together to the United States in 1972 to look over the new DC-10s ordered for Olympic Airways, Alexander flew one of them across the country with the ease of a veteran pilot. There is a photo of Onassis descending the stairs of the plane, beaming with pride as Alexander talks to the captain. "That picture shows Onassis on the happiest day of his life," said Nicholas Papanikolaou, who worked for him in the New York office. "He was so proud of his son, the kind of man he'd become."

On Monday, January 22, 1973, less than three weeks after the dinner in Paris with his father, Alexander was in Athens, having just flown a charter fight in from Monte Carlo. The next day he was to join Fiona and her children back in London for a wedding, but first he had to carry out a chore for Olympic—to test the new pilot hired to fly the Piaggio for Onassis until it was sold, and to acquaint the man, Donald McCusker, with the plane. Normally the assignment would have fallen to the retiring pilot, Donald McGregor, but he had just had an eye operation and was not yet cleared to fly, so he would ride in the back as a passenger while McCusker learned the ropes.

Stelios Papadimitriou says that he tried to discourage Alexander from making this quick trip to Athens. "I told him, 'Let someone else test the new pilot. Your position is not to test pilots or planes, but to learn shipping.'

" 'No, I've got to go,' he told me. 'I have to show my father I care for him.' "

Ever since Tina married Niarchos, Alexander had refused to take his mother's calls. That morning, before Alexander left Monte Carlo, Papadimitriou told me, "His mother called . . . and asked me to pass her on to Alexander. He shook his head and I told her he wasn't there. She said, 'Please tell him to call me. It's crucial that I speak to him.' He could hear her over the phone but he never called her back."

Shortly after 3 p.m. on the afternoon of January 22, 1973, Alexander, McGregor, and McCusker boarded the Piaggio at the Athens airport. Their plan was to make a short flight to practice sea landings and takeoffs between the nearby islands of Aegina and Poros. Alexander took the right-hand passenger seat, the new pilot McCusker sat at his left, in the pilot's seat, and the old pilot, McGregor, sat behind. At the last minute it was discovered that the preflight checklist for the Piaggio's takeoff had been left behind, but Alexander had done it so often he knew it by heart, and he ran through all the usual steps.

An Air France Boeing 727 had just lifted off when Alexander signaled the new pilot to start. The air controller instructed him to bank left as soon as he was airborne to avoid the wake left by the large French plane. Within two seconds of takeoff, when the Piaggio was only one hundred feet in the air, it suddenly banked right instead of left; it struck the ground with a float before it wing-tipped and began to cartwheel. Rescuers who ran to the wreckage found the two pilots were injured, but not fatally. Alexander was recognizable only by the monogram on his pocket handkerchief. The right temporal lobe of his brain had been crushed and he was covered in blood. He was rushed to the hospital, where he underwent surgery to remove blood clots from his brain and was put on life-support machines.

When Alexander crashed, Ari and Jackie were in New York, Tina and Niarchos were in St. Moritz, Fiona was in London, and Christina was in Brazil (where she heard the news on a car radio). Onassis immediately dispatched planes to fly the best neurosurgeons in the world from London, Boston, and Texas. The desperate father also called the archbishop of Athens, Ieronymos, who was a native of Tinos, and successfully pleaded to have the miraculous icon of the Virgin flown to Athens from the island where invalids flocked daily in search of divine intercession.

By the next morning, as family members and friends arrived at Alexander's bedside, where life-support machines were keeping him breathing, the doctors had reached the conclusion that Alexander had suffered "irrecoverable brain damage." Onassis told his sisters that he would wait until Christina arrived before deciding what to do.

All the money, the business deals, the yachts and villas and ships—his kingdom had been accumulated for this boy. For that reason Onassis often chided Alexander not to spend so much time thinking about the airline, because, "while airplanes are the leaves of the tree, the ships are the roots—the real money is in the ships."

Until now, Onassis had been able to solve nearly every problem in his life with large infusions of money. Money had gotten his father out of the Turkish jail in Smyrna. Money had turned an ignominious refugee into a bon vivant who enjoyed the company of celebrity friends and the most beautiful women in the world. It was inconceivable to Ari that money couldn't save his son. While Alexander's fate was still uncertain, Onassis called one neurosurgeon and asked him, "If I give you my entire fortune, can you save my boy's life?" The doctor told him the sad truth.

When Christina arrived, her father told her to go in and say good-bye to her brother, then said, "Let us torture him no more." After she emerged, sobbing, Onassis instructed the doctors to turn off the life-support machines.

As they waited, Christina walked over to Tina, who was standing nearby with her husband, Stavros Niarchos. Like her brother, Christina had been angry at her mother ever since the marriage to her father's rival, although she did not refuse to speak to Tina the way Alexander did. Now, as they waited for their son and brother to take his last breath, mother and daughter embraced each other in tears, according to Onassis' niece Marilena Patronikola, who was also at the hospital. "Christina then went over to Niarchos," Marilena told me, "and she said, 'I would like to stay with my mother tonight. Is it all right?' Niarchos refused to say anything to her but turned and walked away. Of course, she didn't stay with her that night."

When the end finally came, Onassis made a last, desperate effort to keep his son with him. He ordered an aide in New York to contact the Life

Extension Society in Washington to see if Alexander's body could be deep-frozen and kept in cryonic care until medical science could learn how to rebuild his brain. His friend Yiannis Giorgakis finally convinced Onassis that it was wrong "to impede the journey of Alexander's soul." (In the Orthodox religion there are a number of rituals intended to aid the soul's journey to paradise, a progress believed to take forty days. A soul prevented from leaving the earth is believed to become a *vrykolakas*—a kind of vampire—destined to wail in agony and haunt the living until it can find peace.)

The day after Alexander's death, Onassis held a press conference in his Athens office. His press relations aide, Helen Speronis, told me that she was surprised he would want to talk to the press, but on his orders she set up the conference in the sixth-floor conference room of Olympic Airlines on Syngrou Avenue. "He came in and his secretary, Amalia, and I both started crying. He kissed us both and then he sat down and started to talk to the reporters about Alexander. It was at seven p.m. on January twenty-fourth, exactly twenty-four hours after he died."

During the press conference Onassis said, "Above all, Alexandros loved the skies and flying. He became a perfect pilot in only three or four years. I have never seen a more careful, meticulous pilot. He also used his abilities to good ends. He had carried out a number of mercy missions. I, as a father, never stopped him from doing these things. He was a good boy, a promising boy."

As Onassis spoke, tears coursed down his face, until finally his secretary signaled to the security men to end the conference and herd the reporters out the door.

Onassis flew a Swiss plastic surgeon to Athens to repair Alexander's face for the viewing of his remains. He lay in state for three days in a gold-colored casket in the Athens cemetery chapel, where thousands came to pay their respects. Among them was the Greek prime minister and junta leader George Papadopoulos. President Nixon, President Pompidou, Queen Elizabeth, and exiled King Constantine of Greece all sent messages of condolence.

On the third day, after looking on his son's face for the last time, Aristotle Onassis emerged from the chapel along with a sobbing Christina, into the bright sunlight of the Athens cemetery, where a huge crowd was gathered. As he left the church, Onassis, overcome with grief, stumbled, and Christina tried to keep him from falling. At that moment someone in the crowd—a grizzled, leathery sailor—shouted, "Courage! Stand up, old man!" Onassis looked at the speaker, pulled himself up, raised his chin, and walked forward.

*Onassis and Christina emerge from Alexander's funeral.
With them is close friend Yiannis Giorgakis.*

Although he tried to maintain a stoic composure in public, he didn't hide his desolation from his friends. "Aristotle said to me, 'Couldn't it have been me who died?' " Lilika Papanikolaou recalled. Everything that Onassis had fought for and accomplished in his life, he had done with the intention that the family name and fortune would be perpetuated through his son, whom he referred to as his "alpha and omega."

Friends like Lilika had warned him about concentrating all his hopes on Alexander: "I said to him once, 'Have you gone crazy? Alpha and omega is Christ. It's not right to say such things about your son!' I saw that attitude in two people. The other was an English lord, and in both cases their sons died."

"Actually, Christina was much more like her father than Alexandros," Stelios Papadimitriou told me, "but the old man didn't see it. The boy's death devastated him, although he tried to keep going."

The day after Alexander's funeral, Onassis called a business meeting at the Olympic offices in Athens. Captain Kostas Anastasiades had come to deliver his condolences to the Boss, and Onassis left the meeting to speak to him. After expressing his sorrow over the death of Alexander, whom he had known since he was a small boy, Captain Kostas asked, "What do you want me to do now with the *Christina*?"

"Go ahead just as planned," Onassis told him. "Sail the boat down to Dakar and we will meet you there to sail across to the Antilles. Nothing has changed."

But for Onassis everything had changed. He had lost the reason for all that he did. Within days of Alexander's death, Aristo flew to Paris and was driven to 36 Avenue Georges Mandel. He entered the ornate iron gate and the wood-paneled lobby decorated with tapestries and busts of dead French kings. He slowly climbed the spiral staircase with its carved balustrades, past the stained-glass windows of stylized fan-shaped lilies. He stopped and knocked on the heavy wooden door of the third-floor landing. It was opened by Bruna. He walked into the grand salon, where Maria was waiting for him. Aristo embraced her, and as their tears mingled, he said, "My boy is gone. There's nothing left for me." Choked with emotion, she cried, "If only our son had lived!"

Bruna later described this scene to a close friend, the same person who posed to her my questions about the birth and death of the baby boy named Omero. Maria herself related the scene to Kostas Pylarinos. "When I saw Aristo after Alexander's death, he seemed to have aged ten years in a few days," Callas told him. Shortly after that she told Nadia Stancioff, "He's obsessed with Alexander's death and he keeps talking about tracking down those who killed him, although I'm certain it was an accident. Aristo has changed, Nadia. He really is an old man now."

After much speculation in the Greek press about where Alexander would be buried, his coffin was transported to the island of Skorpios and placed inside its chapel while a wing was built to serve as his tomb. On Friday, February 2, Yiannis Giorgakis issued a statement on behalf of Onassis: "It was a myth that there was any disagreement between Alexander's father and mother, Tina Niarchos, as to a final burial place. Alexander's casket has been placed in a church on the island of Skorpios, where he will finally be buried." He also denied rumors that Alexander had secretly married Fiona von Thyssen and that he had been highly insured. "This son who so often risked his life to help others wasn't insured for a single cent," Giorgakis said.

Almost a month after the fatal plane crash, on February 20, Alexander's body was formally laid to rest in the new wing of the little white chapel to the Virgin where Jackie and Ari had been married four years earlier. Only his mother, Fiona von Thyssen, and some close relatives were present. (His casket had been placed in a marble sarcophagus beside the chapel, because only saints could be buried in a church, and then a chamber was hastily added on to enclose it.)

Investigation of the wreckage of the Piaggio showed that the wires controlling the left and right ailerons had been reversed when a new control column was installed in the airplane shortly before the test flight. When the pilot tried to turn left, the plane turned right, and when he automatically tried to correct the error, he only made it worse. Onassis immediately suspected a conspiracy and offered a million-dollar reward to help him find the murderer ($500,000 to the person who fingered the culprit and another $500,000 to be donated to a charity of his choice).

Topping Ari's list of suspects was Stavros Niarchos, followed by the junta leader Colonel George Papadopoulos aided by the American C.I.A. "It's revenge for the Project Omega fuckup," he told friends.

The Greek air force, then Olympic Airways, and finally an English air-disaster detective hired by Onassis could find no evidence of a conspiracy. As it was only at the last minute that Alexander decided to fly the plane instead of the usual pilot, there would have been no time for anyone intending to kill him to switch the control cables. Nevertheless, Onassis refused ever to close the case, remaining hopeful that his million-dollar offer would unearth a killer. Typically, he desperately needed to believe that his son had been destroyed by a human enemy and not by a random mechanical—or fateful—error.

(It is one of the many heavy ironies of this saga that Jackie's son, John Kennedy, Jr., then only twelve years old and absorbed in piloting the speed-boat that Onassis had given him, would die twenty-six years later in a similar mysterious tragedy while piloting a private plane. Like Alexander, John Jr. was planning to attend a wedding the next day.)

After Alexander's death, Jackie made a concerted effort to get close to her husband again, to console him and to mend fences with his family. One of those she turned to was Marilena Patronikola, Onassis' favorite niece, who had, however, always favored Maria despite Jackie's dogged efforts since her marriage in 1968 to win the young woman over. "She called me all the time, wrote me letters, came to Memorial Hospital in New York when my father was there for treatment and brought him soup," Marilena told me. She described how Jackie would tell the nurses she had made the soup herself to inspire special treatment for the patient. "She brought gifts for my children, did everything possible to win my favor. But I kept thinking there was a reason for it, and I finally figured out that she did it because she knew Uncle Aristo liked me and she wanted me to tell him how nice she was. I know that now because, when the marriage turned sour, she never contacted me again."

Two days after Alexander's death, however, on January 25, Jackie wrote the following letter, on stationery that was imprinted with the address of the villa in Glyfada:

> Dear Marilena . . . Your letter came tonight—I am so touched that you would write to me. With all my heart I will try to console your Uncle Ari— I wonder if it is possible to console anyone for such a loss—but I will try.
>
> Do you know what I tell him all the time? (It causes a few battles— which you will understand!) I tell him that you are the example of what a young woman should be—that I want Caroline to be like you—that I wish for him that his life had not been so mixed up—so that Christina could be more like you—Even if I was not related to you by marriage I would think that.
>
> We may not see each other very often (in the transAtlantic life that one must lead with your Uncle Ari—) but I hope you always know the admiration and respect I have for you—And you are much younger than me—so to say that to a younger person really shows that I feel you are exceptional—which you are—
>
> . . . I hope—as years go on—that we will get to know each other really well—Thank you dear Marilena for all your love over all these years and especially now
>
> With great affection
Jackie

On the *Christina*'s cruise from Dakar to the Antilles, which began on February 11, 1973, Jackie tried hard to distract Onassis from his grief, inviting along Pierre Salinger, JFK's former press secretary, and his wife. Onassis seemed under control as he spent hours chatting with Salinger about politics, journalism, and philosophy, but after everyone else went to bed he would roam the lower decks, not returning until dawn to the master suite on the bridge deck that he shared with Jackie.

In the summer of 1973 the tanker business soared again and Ari ordered four supertankers from Japan and two ultralarge crude carriers from France. When his first cousin and top aide, Kostas Konialidis (Nikos' brother), congratulated him on the coup, Onassis astonished him by replying, "I can't get excited about it, Kostas. Perhaps I've used up all the excitement. Perhaps I don't need it as much as I thought I did."

Tina had been even more undone by grief than Ari. She always called Alexander her darling, her angel, yet he had refused to speak to her for the last years of his life. After his death, Tina began seriously abusing alcohol and prescription drugs and she looked shockingly older than her age of forty-four. "Tina took Alexander's death very badly . . . very, very badly," George Livanos told me. "She just started to drink, you know, and it affected her health very quickly. The boy's death hit her very hard. Onassis too."

In that summer, Ari went back to Skorpios for the first time since Alexander's body had been entombed there, and he began to behave in a way that unnerved Jackie and everyone else who saw him. Nearly every night he would wander the island, accompanied by a mongrel dog named Vana who had attached itself to him. He would be seen by employees walking and talking to the dog, which seemed to listen intently. The walks would always end at the tomb of Alexander.

Onassis would sit down on the grass and pull a bottle of ouzo and two glasses from his pockets. For hours he would sit and drink and talk to his dead son. The employees began placing a blanket on the grass every night so that their boss would not catch cold. Sometimes he would bring food and set out a plate for Alexander. He told his staff that he often heard his son's voice. "Eventually Artemis asked the bishop of Lefkada [the nearest large island] to talk to him and tell him that it's not right to disturb the dead and that Alexander should be allowed to continue his journey in peace," Captain Kostas told me.

To Jackie's surprise and dismay, Ari also invited Tina and her husband to come to Skorpios that summer to visit the grave of Alexander. Before the arrival of the Niarchos yacht, he restored Tina's portrait to its place of honor in his study. The two yachts met at sea and proceeded to Skorpios. Onassis led his former wife to the grave, where she collapsed in tears.

That summer, Maria was involved in preparing a series of concerts that she had been persuaded to do with Giuseppe di Stefano, the dashing Italian singer who had called on her in New York during the master classes.

In the 1950s di Stefano was considered one of the finest tenors in the world, but he sang with such animal intensity that he quickly wore out his voice. When they performed together during those celebrated years, he and Maria had often clashed in headline-making brawls, but now they found in each other not only a reminder of past triumph but also a kind of lifeline in a time of trouble. Like Maria, di Stefano had exhausted his gift and his fame and now desperately needed a way to revitalize his career, and teaming up with his former partner, he did just that. He encouraged her to sing in public again, and eventually they planned to make a world concert tour together in late 1973 and 1974.

Most of Maria's friends and admirers feel that her relationship with di Stefano was a disaster both professionally and personally, not least because he was married to a woman, also named Maria, whom Callas knew and liked. They had a nineteen-year-old daughter who was dying of cancer. But the liaison with the tenor did give Callas a chance to show the world (and especially Onassis) that she still could fascinate an attractive and talented man and excite the admiration and love of her public.

John Ardoin described to me the romance that grew between the handsome, macho, self-absorbed di Stefano and the neurotic and needy Callas: "It was really weird that they got together later. What makes it even weirder is that Maria was really a very moral woman in a peasant sense. And when they did those concerts together, they were having their affair and di Stefano's wife frequently traveled with them. That was really unlike Maria. That shows how really desperate she was to find an identity again after Onassis dropped her. The only identity she had was singing."

Kostas Pylarinos, who knew Maria well during this period, considers it a rather unromantic symbiosis: "He [di Stefano] had many affairs. All were known to his wife. He had economic reasons for his relationship with [Callas] and there was a period when Maria needed companionship. Each was going for specific things. Companionship for her and economic gain for him. His wife understood this. Maria was an easy victim."

Needless to say, di Stefano himself does not characterize the relationship this way. When I interviewed him at his home on the hills above Lake Como, he was charming and amusing, expansive and boastful.

"I first met Maria [in 1951] at a very rough moment of her career, in Rio de Janeiro," he told me. "She had an argument with the director of the opera house. She took a big inkwell, very heavy, and she was hitting him on the head with it. One of my colleagues stopped her or she would have killed him. Eloquent, no? . . .

"In 1972, when we met again, I needed my art. In this year I had my daughter very sick. Maria had her problems with Onassis. So we started to go on together and try to forget reality. It was welcome to be occupied. [The agent] Gorlinsky knew that. We had these big reasons to try to get away from life, from our sorrows."

Di Stefano told me that while he and Maria were rehearsing for their concerts in Paris, Onassis would often visit Callas' apartment. "Once we had dinner together at her home. Onassis was very curious about me. When he saw me he said, 'You are strong and young.' I said, 'And handsome.

Don't forget handsome!' He must have been jealous, but he was very *simpatico*. I liked him very much. We laughed a lot. We had oysters that night and he said, 'You have them. I don't need them anymore.' "

Maria, of course, was in heaven that evening to have Onassis beside her trading *badinage* with her new, younger lover. But before she and di Stefano launched their concert tour, which would prove the nadir of her singing career, she had struggled through a difficult year of losses of her own.

In December of 1972, Maria and di Stefano were in London, secretly recording with the London Symphony Orchestra. The rehearsals went very badly but the two falling stars were undaunted in their optimism. In the middle of these sessions Maria learned that her father had died in Greece on December 4 at the age of eighty-six, two days after her forty-ninth birthday. She was grief-stricken, though she had never forgiven nor spoken to him since his unannounced marriage to a family friend in 1965. Her sister begged her to come to Greece for the funeral, but Maria—who had a horror of attending any funeral—replied, "I can't come just now, I'm working again: recordings, can't interrupt them. You understand. Can you explain for me?" Earlier that year, Maria had also suffered the death of her dear friend Baroness Maggie van Zuylen.

Despite the intensity of her commitment, after completing the sessions with di Stefano, Maria would decide that the London recordings were not good enough to be released. Through it all, her perfectionism, if not her instrument, was still very much intact.

In April of 1973, Maria was hired to direct Verdi's *I Vespri Siciliani,* the first production to be staged at the elegant new Teatro Regio in Turin. She insisted that di Stefano be her co-director. But Maria, who could perform opera with unrivaled brilliance, had no idea how to direct one, and the entire production was a disaster. Di Stefano and Callas had never been responsible for sets, costumes, an orchestra or a chorus. Even the singers were left largely to their own devices. Raina Kabaivanskas, the soprano who starred in the production, told Nadia Stancioff, "She did it for di Stefano. . . . It's not for me to judge. We will never know how much he really loved her, but his seduction was very convincing. He gave her the courage to confront a new phase in her career."

The production, on April 10, was savaged by the critics. Maria's devotion to di Stefano did not waver, however, and she agreed to travel with him on a punishing schedule of concerts—eight countries in seven months. She was of course terrified of singing in public again. Onassis begged her not to go, she told friends. He wanted her nearby and he suspected the project would tarnish her reputation rather than restore it. He assured Maria that he was divorcing Jackie and soon they would be together again, just as they

Maria and her last lover, Giuseppe di Stefano

had been during the years on Skorpios. But Maria, still deeply injured, would not be convinced. "He speaks to me of divorce the way he used to speak of marriage," she told Mary Carter. "I'd be a fool to believe him until I hold the signed paper in my hand."

For Mary Carter, it was her friend's inability to believe in the seriousness of Aristo's resolve and repentance that elevated their relationship to the status of a Greek tragedy. "Again and again Aristo implored her to marry him. He was serious this time. He was ready to get a divorce, but Maria wanted it in black and white as proof. She was not a woman who forgot or forgave easily. So she went off with that horrid little man, Giuseppe di Stefano, believing that the tour was her salvation as an artist and a woman."

In May, a month after the disaster in Turin, Maria and di Stefano flew to Japan to conduct a master class there. In June they returned to prepare for the world tour, which was to begin in September. They rehearsed all summer in Paris and Milan, but as Gorlinsky excitedly told them that fans in every major city were clamoring for tickets—in London thirty thousand people were vying for three thousand seats—Maria became more and more nervous.

It was eight years since Callas had sung in public. "I'm scared stiff," she wrote her godfather, "but I hope that I will be calm and well by my first one on the twenty-second of this month, because the expectation is great and of course I am not what I was at thirty-five years—let's hope for the best."

Three days before the opening concert in London, Maria began to suffer excruciating pains in her eyes and had to put in drops every few minutes. On the advice of her ophthalmologist, she canceled the concert. It took a month for di Stefano to restore her courage. In their first recital, in Hamburg, Germany, on October 25, they sang six duets and one aria each. The moment Callas came onstage, the audience gave her a five-minute ovation. But when it was over, the critics were not so kind. A month later one compared her voice to "a monochrome reproduction of an oil painting."

At this time, Onassis was watching with disbelief as the bottom fell out of the world tanker market. In October, Egypt and Syria attacked Israel during Yom Kippur, and war once again engulfed the Middle East. The Arabs, angered by Western aid to Israel, cut off the world's supply of oil. Onassis' fleet of tankers was laid up and he was forced to cancel his order for the two ultralarge crude carriers. He took a loss of $12.5 million. Trying to recoup, he instructed Costa Gratsos, the head of his New York office, to scout for a site on which to build an oil refinery in the United States to profit from the huge American demand for gasoline free of the vagaries of the Middle East. But that project too would fail.

By now, the "Jackie jinx" had become common coinage, not merely among Onassis' employees but also with the Greek man on the street, who was seeing it mentioned in some tabloids. Never had Onassis suffered such a run of bad luck. Christina had always felt that the union with Jackie had brought a curse on the family; now she was certain of it and openly said as much to her father. Even Artemis, who bowed to no one in either her superstitions or her defense of her sister-in-law, felt it necessary to assure a guest at her dinner table, "It is just bad kismet. Jackie's not responsible for it."

But Onassis himself was not so sure, because he needed somebody to blame for his continuing troubles. Everything Jackie did was starting to annoy him: her spendthrift ways, her chronic lateness for appointments, her habit of being early to bed and early to rise while he stayed awake all night and slept till noon, the way she'd go off by herself on Skorpios to read or sketch and ignore his friends and business associates. Most of all he resented her unfailing absence during his darkest hours.

"Onassis was sorry he married Jackie, almost from the beginning," Yiannis Giorgakis told me two years after Ari's death, "but he was slow to move toward a divorce because the experience of divorcing Tina was so painful for him and the process of getting a divorce would have been difficult under Greek law. . . . On top of that, Maria was seeing that tenor, di Stefano, and it seemed easier to let things go along as they were. But the more time he spent alone, and the more things went wrong for him, the more determined he became to get rid of Jackie no matter what it took."

For the first time in his life, Onassis was finding himself powerless to control his fate. With the death of his only son, the future and the succession of his empire were in doubt. He was struggling to free himself from an alliance that had become painful to him and kept him from the woman he now wanted and needed. He was determined to wrest back control of his destiny, but the man who liked nothing better than a challenge had no idea of the forces that were gathering against him.

21

OMEGA

Even when I'm gone,
I shall pursue you with dark fires
And when cold death
Tears my soul from my body,
Wherever you are
My spirit will be there too.

Virgil, *Aeneid,* Book IV

In late 1973 Costa Gratsos found a site for the proposed American oil refinery—near Durham, New Hampshire—but state environmentalists and the local press launched a fierce campaign in opposition to the plant.

In December Onassis decided that he would personally fly to New Hampshire to improve his company's public relations in the state. As he flew over Durham, he saw that local residents had tramped huge letters on a snow-covered field: GET LOST ARI! At a press conference, Onassis' legendary charisma seemed to have taken a holiday. He made weak jokes that fell flat, beginning with "I am not a Greek bearing gifts," and when he was asked why his people were secretly buying up land, he brandished a bottle of the local staple and said, "Well, we certainly didn't come to say that we are going to build a distillery of maple syrup." Observers remarked that his speech was slurred and his body seemed "curiously floppy."

Onassis spent the time preceding the holidays of 1973 in New York. It was a lonely period for him. Nicholas Papanikolaou, Lilika's son, then twenty-four, whom Onassis had hired straight out of Columbia Business School a year earlier, found himself frequently summoned to the Boss's office after working hours to sit and chat. Evidently Onassis found some consolation confiding in a young man approximately the same age as his late son.

"He seemed to hate to leave the office and go home, apparently because there wasn't much to go home to," Papanikolaou recalls. "I remember once, close to Christmas, it was about eight p.m. and he said to me, 'All right now, go home. You've stayed long enough.'

" 'What are you going to do, Mr. Onassis?' I asked him.

" 'I'll probably go to El Morocco,' he told me.

" 'But it's almost Christmas. Aren't you going to go home?' I said, meaning home to Jackie.

" 'No,' he answered abruptly.

" 'Aren't you going to see Christina?' I then asked him.

" 'No.' He looked up at me and said, 'What are you going to do when your daughter is crazy and your wife is robbing you?'

"As time passed, he avoided seeing Jackie as much as he could. He looked for excuses to avoid seeing her. The death of his son really broke him. Until then there was, I would say, a semblance of a marriage with Jackie, but after that, everything she did seemed to bug him, and he talked about Maria all the time."

By the beginning of 1974, Onassis seemed exhausted by the battle over the refinery in New Hampshire and the continued problems caused by the Arab oil embargo. He told employees that he felt tired all the time, and one of them remarked that he looked "sick as a dog." Hoping some rest would help, he took a vacation with Jackie in Acapulco, where she had spent her honeymoon with John Kennedy. She was eager to buy a villa there and led Ari on a tour of available real estate, but this was the last place he wanted to live, and he was in no mood to indulge her reckless spending now that his empire was under pressure on several fronts.

The tensions between the couple broke out in arguments during the vacation. They were still bickering as they boarded their private Learjet on January 3, 1974, to fly back to New York. During the trip Ari got up, retreated to a corner of the plane, took out a pencil and a note pad, and began to write. He wrote for the entire six hours of the flight. He was composing his last will and testament. (In Greece, a will must be handwritten by the legator to ensure against challenges on the grounds of incompetence or senility.)

The document was addressed "To my dear daughter." Ari dispatched Jackie with a lifetime income of $250,000 a year. He noted that, in accordance with their prenuptial agreement, his wife had relinquished her right under Greek law to the standard 12.5 percent of his estate. He further stipulated that if she tried to overturn the terms of his will, his executors should immediately stop her annuity and block her efforts "through all possible legal means."

Onassis outlined a foundation he wanted established in memory of Alexander, who would have managed and controlled the bulk of his father's estate had he lived. Its endowment would be used to promote social, religious, artistic, and educational activities, mostly in Greece, and to make annual awards in these areas. Half of the assets of the Onassis business empire would finance the Alexander S. Onassis Public Benefit Foundation, and the other half would go to Christina. Both the foundation and Christina's half of the estate would be administered by a board of directors made up of Ari's inner cabinet of advisers, headed by his cousin Kostas Konialidis.

The will also provided $60,000 a year, indexed against inflation, for each of his sisters and for Kostas Konialidis. Nicholas Cokkinis, another cousin and aide, as well as Costa Gratsos and Stelios Papadimitriou, would receive $30,000 a year each, and $20,000 was allotted to other executives, including Costa Vlassopoulos, his chartering manager in Monte Carlo. Smaller amounts were bequeathed to his chauffeurs, chambermaids, housekeepers, and other staff.

Maria was not mentioned in the will. Long before, Onassis had arranged for the continuing payment of common charges on the flat he had bought for her in Paris and he knew that she would be well provided for by the investments he had helped her make (such as her share in the ship *Artemision II*) and the royalties she earned from the sale of her recordings. "He knew Maria was the only woman in his life who never wanted or needed his money," his aide Miltos Yiannakopoulos told me. "Putting her in the will would have caused all kinds of gossip and speculation and he didn't want to subject her to that."

When the jet touched down in Palm Beach to refuel before continuing on to New York, Onassis put down his pencil and pad and bought bacon, lettuce, and tomato sandwiches for himself and Jackie. He tried to pay for the fuel with a Shell Oil credit card, but the airport manager tactfully pointed out that it had expired.

As the flight continued, Onassis finished the lengthy document. He left his yacht to his wife and daughter. In the event they didn't wish to pay the $500,000 annual expense of maintaining it, he instructed that the *Christina* be offered as a gift to the Greek head of state. In a final flourish, and perhaps as a parting barb at Jackie, Onassis named as the executor of his will "Athina née Livanos-Onassis-Blandford-Niarchos, the mother of my son Alexander." (Oddly, he omitted to give her credit for producing Christina as well.)

It is clear, however, from a letter Onassis wrote to Christina eleven days later—a letter handwritten in English and never before published—that he intended his daughter to direct his estate and that she was very much on his mind as he prepared for his death.

> My darling daughter Christina
>
> This is my instructions as to what to do with my estate. I want the business to go on with a little more than half of my estate as a foundation for Alexander's memory. It is written in the form of "WILL" in Greek "DIATHIKI." For legal and tax and other reasons might be *better* not to disclose that I left a WILL in which case you just and simply *do not* disclose it and see that all the instructions are carried [out] fully. On the other hand it might do no harm and on the contrary might be advantageous to DECLARE THE "WILL." Mr. Papadimitriou knows all about it. A consultation between Mummy, your mother, Cokkinis, Papadimitriou, Costa Konialidis, Vlasopoulos and GRATSOS with you will decide which of the two, DISCLOSE IT OR NOT DISCLOSE IT, and just carry out the instructions, is the best course to take.
>
> > Last kiss
> > Daddy
> > January 14 - 1974,

This letter is a remarkable document, not only for its expression of tenderness, but also for its mere existence. Onassis feared being bound by his written word, and he almost never committed himself to paper. According to Stelios Papadimitriou, when he first went to work for Onassis in 1954 the Boss instructed him: "If you see me write anything, tell me immediately to stop. If I continue, I give you permission to grab the pen, and if I still insist, you have my irrevocable authority to bite my hand."

In late March of 1974, two months after Onassis' return from Acapulco, the New Hampshire state legislature finally rejected his refinery proposal, forcing him to cancel the project despite having pumped hundreds of thousands of dollars into lobbying and various public relations efforts to win its approval. Onassis was not a man to give up easily and everyone expected that he would mount an effort to overturn the decision. But he now felt no zeal to pursue the project, ordered his aides to abandon it, and turned his attention to growing health problems that had been troubling him. He checked into New York Hospital to find out why he had been feeling weak and dizzy and was having trouble keeping his eyes open. After a battery of tests, it was determined that he was suffering from myasthenia gravis, which he was relieved to learn is a nonfatal disease of the body's autoimmune system that can be controlled by drugs.

Onassis had always feared he would die of heart problems at an early age, like his father and his uncle Omeros. Since 1970, he had been consulting the eminent New York cardiologist Isadore Rosenfeld. When I interviewed Dr. Rosenfeld in 1999, he told me Onassis had an arrhythmia. "His heart problems weren't life-threatening, but he had palpitations, which got worse after his son died. He really fell apart after that. He lost his will to live, in my opinion."

Grief was a major factor in the rapid decline of his health, Dr. Rosenfeld believes. "You don't catch myasthenia gravis from anything. It's an autoimmune disorder produced by the body itself in the later years and often following an overwhelming emotional crisis," he said. "That was the case with Onassis after the death of his son. When he developed the first symptoms of this disease, I admitted him to New York Hospital under a pseudonym. They started him on a steroid program and it worked very well, relieving the myasthenia gravis considerably."

Onassis then inadvertently sabotaged the attempts to treat his illness, according to Dr. Rosenfeld. He went back to Greece and began to take a drug prescribed by Ana Aslan, a Romanian doctor who treated wealthy Europeans who were trying to keep encroaching old age at bay. "What she gave him was Procain, which she claimed improved everything—memory, sex drive, and energy," Dr. Rosenfeld said. "The Procain, which is not legal in the United States except in one state, really undermined all the positive results that the steroid treatment achieved and the myasthenia gravis returned stronger than before. Onassis came back to New York and told me that he'd been taking Procain and I stopped it immediately, but the damage was done. He did not respond to steroids like the first time."

Nicholas Papanikolaou visited his boss when he first entered New York Hospital for the tests. He remembers Onassis sitting up in a chair, monitoring devices attached to his chest, while Jackie was stretched out, lounging on his bed. It was not lost on the young employee—nor likely on Onassis himself—that a Greek wife would not be lounging but would be hovering over her husband, solicitously trying to make him comfortable. "As soon as Onassis saw me, he motioned to me to come in," Papanikolaou recalls, "and he turned to Jackie and said, 'Why don't you go home now?' He couldn't wait to find an excuse to get rid of her."

Dr. Rosenfeld remembers Onassis fondly ("I loved him. He was very open, very direct, unpretentious"). He told me that during the lonely days Onassis spent in New York after his second hospitalization, they would sometimes dine together several nights in a week. On the basis of conversations they had during these encounters, Dr. Rosenfeld confirmed that Onassis was planning to divorce his wife: "In fact, when he got sick, they were both seeing divorce lawyers. He was talking to Roy Cohn, and she was seeing Louis Nizer, I think. It wasn't that she wasn't spending enough time with him. That did bother him at the beginning, but in the end he didn't want to see her even when they both were in New York. He would stay at his apartment in the Pierre. He was not happy with her and was determined to get out of the marriage." Dr. Rosenfeld believes Onassis would have done so if his health had not failed.

While Onassis was battling the worsening symptoms of myasthenia gravis, Maria was struggling to fulfill the commitments of the eight-month world tour Giuseppe di Stefano had plotted for them. Beginning in Hamburg in October of 1973, they sang in Berlin, Düsseldorf, Munich, Frankfurt, Mannheim, Madrid, London, and Paris and ended the year's programs in Amsterdam on December 11.

Maria knew perfectly well how inadequate their voices were, but she pretended, for the benefit of di Stefano and the press, that everything was fine. When Peter Diamand, the former director of the Holland Festival and the Edinburgh Festival, went backstage to see her in London, she said, "Don't tell me anything. I *know*. Go to Pippo [her nickname for di Stefano]. Tell him something, anything to pep him up. Do it for me. . . ." Despite her concern for di Stefano, there were tensions between the two.

On January 20, 1974, the tour took them to Milan, where they performed privately for the patients at the hospital where di Stefano's daughter was being treated for cancer. Then Maria sang alone in Stuttgart. Di Stefano was suffering from "a sudden indisposition"—a circumstance that would become increasingly common as their relationship became more acrimonious. The tenor would abandon scheduled performances in anger and leave Callas to try to fill in for him somehow.

"While we were on tour, Onassis called Maria almost every evening and talked to her for hours in Greek," di Stefano recalled. "In many ways she still depended on him and his people. They booked hotels, arranged flights, renewed her credit cards, looked after her wherever she went."

They were scheduled to begin the U.S. leg of the tour in February at New York's Carnegie Hall. They would also perform in Philadelphia, Toronto, Washington, D.C., Boston, Chicago, New York, Detroit, Dallas, Miami Beach, Columbus, Ohio, and Brookville, Long Island, before returning to Carnegie Hall on April 15. But their first American concert, in February, presented by the famous impresario Sol Hurok, had to be canceled when Maria again overmedicated herself; the incident followed a quarrel with di Stefano that threatened to end the entire tour.

Di Stefano told me that Maria had given interviews in both Milan and

New York implying that she was having a romantic relationship with the tenor. The suggestion angered the family of di Stefano's wife, some of whom lived in New York. "Immediately I got calls," he said. "What was going on between Callas and me? I hated it. I'm Sicilian. So I called my wife in Italy and I said, 'You come to New York, because I want everything here to quiet down. We have a concert Sunday.' I realized all the paparazzi would be waiting. But Maria took this very bad. She didn't like that I called my wife and brought her over.

"She was taking pills—Mandrax," di Stefano continued. "You start with one, then you take two, and then three. Then you forget and take another three. At the beginning of the tour she didn't take them."

The doctor who announced the cancellation of the performance in New York attributed it to "the acute inflammation of Miss Callas' upper respiratory tract," but his credentials were in psychiatry. The fashionable crowd at Carnegie Hall became so angry at the news that police on horseback were called to quiet them.

Maria's recklessness provoked equally bad behavior in di Stefano. "After the furor in New York, I started to get mad, and when I get mad, I get a cold," he told me with a wry smile. "So I didn't go to Boston." Maria persuaded Vasso Devetzi to come to Boston as her pianist, and paid her the fee di Stefano was supposed to get, which further inflamed her partner.

Sol Hurok rescheduled the Carnegie Hall concert for March 5, two weeks later. On that day, while Carnegie Hall was flooded with calls inquiring whether Maria would actually manage to perform this time, Sol Hurok died of a heart attack on his way to a meeting. At first it was thought better to keep the news from Callas until the performance was over, but too many others knew, and she found out just before she was to go on.

Both Maria and di Stefano were certain that the stress of their escapades and cancellations had contributed to Hurok's demise, although he was eighty-five years old. That night at Carnegie Hall Maria's former record producer, Dario Soria, introduced the two singers and dedicated the concert to Hurok. Maria, speaking almost inaudibly, begged the audience's forbearance as the pair attempted to sing under the great emotional strain, retreating off stage after each song to regain their strength. Nevertheless, the crowd—"one of the most celebrity-filled audiences ever assembled there" according to the *New York Times*—cheered wildly as Callas and di Stefano soldiered on through the program.

At the end of the concert Callas spoke again. Now incoherent as well as inaudible, she seemed to be having a nervous breakdown right on stage. She rambled on, complaining about the way opera was produced in New York and bitterly attacking the Met. She pointed out how much more difficult it is to sing without an orchestra, costumes, and sets, as she had just done. Finally she wept. And the audience thundered its approval again.

Harold Schonberg's review for the *Times* excoriated di Stefano's singing as "indescribably coarse, self-indulgent and vulgar. . . . He was . . . going in for all kinds of dubious pianissimo and crooning effects, in general making an artistic mess of whatever he attempted." But of Callas he wrote:

> *It would be silly to pretend that Miss Callas has much voice left. But, unlike the tenor, she remains an artist. She gave her best, and every now and then the old Callas sound came out. . . . To the audience, nothing could go wrong. It was understandable that the concert was a representation to them of the singer that was, not the singer who is. And Miss Callas was able, even with her limited resources, to give an idea of the kind of temperament and musical understanding that never has deserted her. She looked not a day older than in her last appearance here almost 10 years ago, and everybody washed her with oceans of love. She, at least, deserved the tribute.*

As the days and cities whirled by, Maria took more and more pills. Sometimes she forgot the words of songs. Yet everywhere, the moment Callas took the stage she was applauded, cheered, bathed in the adoration of fans who had not heard her voice for so long. Everywhere too, music critics wrote of her ravaged voice, but they wrote also of the fanatical devotion with which she was received, and this became a story in itself. A critic who saw the Boston concert opined: "Callas has long commanded our attention, our respect, our gratitude, our awe. Now in her struggle and in her exhaustion, she asks and earns, at cost to herself and to us, what she had never before seemed to need, our love."

Maria spent a lot of time on the phone complaining to Gorlinsky. "Pippo" was indisposed again in Dallas and in Detroit. She insisted that di Stefano's wife be sent back to Italy, and by the time they reached the West Coast she was screaming into the phone, "I can't work with this man anymore."

Di Stefano recounted this story to me: "I said, 'Who do you think you are? You order my wife sent away? You have to ask *me* to do that!' And that was when the tour started to get fucked up. Then she started to take tablets again. One night in Seattle I went in to say good night and I couldn't find her. She had fallen out of bed and was on the other side of the bed, on the floor, unconscious."

They had a big fight in Seattle, he said, and "she called the tour manager. She was on the bed with three or four telephones. Calling Gorlinsky. Calling everybody. I said, 'When you decide, let me know.' The decision was that she would keep on singing, but I would have to leave the hotel and talk to her through the pianist. But instead of going to another hotel, I went to Las Vegas. I spent three days there. Then I came back. I was the employee now. She was the star. She wanted to put me in my place."

While performing selections from *Carmen* on the West Coast in what they agreed was to be their last concert together, Maria and di Stefano began singing insults to each other in French, to an audience oblivious of their departure from the libretto. The exchange became so funny to the two singers that they couldn't remain angry at each other any longer, and they made up and agreed to end the North American leg of the tour as scheduled in Montreal on May 13. There di Stefano had again summoned his wife to sit in the front row, "so Callas could see she's not the boss of my life, you understand. Then she became Greek again. A Greek tragedy. We escaped, and I didn't see her again until she called me at my house in San Remo [that summer] to make peace again."

Maria returned to Paris in the spring of 1974 and there Mary Carter saw her often during the summer. "She was getting calls from Onassis constantly," Mrs. Carter told me. Maria showed her a watch Onassis had given her for Christmas. "It wasn't much of a watch," Mrs. Carter recalls, "the kind you give a girl going off to college, but it obviously meant a lot to her."

Maria was also frequently calling Nadia Stancioff in Rome. "She spoke mostly of Onassis," Nadia wrote in her memoirs. " 'He's going downhill,' she said, 'and he has serious business worries. She's probably spending too much. All she knows how to do is spend, spend, spend! Clothes, antiques, jewelry, everything!' I was always amused by the anonymous 'she' Maria used when speaking of Jackie Kennedy Onassis."

Despite their volatile experiences and the mixed results of the earlier engagements, di Stefano persuaded Maria to accompany him to Korea and Japan that fall, where they performed nine concerts beginning in early October. During the tour Maria suffered a hernia and began bleeding internally. She would go home to Paris in terrible pain, but not before the final concert, on November 11, 1974, in Sapporo, Japan. It would be the last place that Maria ever sang on stage.

Callas was very ill when she returned to Paris. Even her mind seemed to be affected as her memory faltered, but slowly she began to regain her health, thanks to "a neurologist—a marvelous one!" she wrote to her godfather. "Now with his cure I am much calmer, my memory has come back—and I sleep well with his cure—Pills of course, but good ones, not heavy drugs," she declared with alarming false confidence.

By the fall of 1974, Onassis was losing ground to his disease and he was taking out his pain and frustrations over his business problems on his wife.

He was often seen berating Jackie for one thing or another—her taste in art and friends, her lateness to meals, her long absences. According to many acquaintances, his wife never screamed back at him during these arguments. She would simply leave the room or the house, sometimes in tears.

This response to Onassis' temper most likely only exacerbated matters; as Maria understood, when Onassis was being the brute, it was better to answer him with insults, curses, even fists. Miltos Yiannakopoulos told me, "Maria was the only one who gave it to him. When he yelled one thing at her, she yelled ten things back. While that drove him crazy at the time, he loved mixing it up with her. Once we were in Monte Carlo," Yiannakopoulos continued, "and Onassis exploded at Maria, 'Who the hell do you think you are? You're just a whistle that can't sing, a whore nobody wants!' "—an insult Onassis used publicly more than once. In the face of this crushing attack, "Maria just fired back with all barrels: 'If I'm what you say, what are you, what am I doing with you, you paunchy little *Tourkosporos*?' "—invoking the first insult that had ever caught his attention. "Suddenly Aristo burst out laughing and squeezed her thigh. 'What a woman!' He laughed, and you could see how good he felt being with her."

By the summer of 1974, Ari was back on Skorpios with Jackie, who was well aware that he was preparing divorce papers to get rid of her. Stelios Papadimitriou recalls a visit to the island during which Jackie said to Ari, "I don't want to divorce you, but if that is your final decision, I accept it in sadness. I'll never forget the good life we had together." But Onassis, already dwelling among the dead, was beyond the reach of any sentimental appeal. Hélène Gaillet, a friend of both, also visited Skorpios that summer and found Ari alone. He took her to see the tomb of his son and said, "Alexander is just as living to me as you are. He comes to me often. Unfortunately, till I die I cannot go to him."

From the time of Alexander's death Onassis had begun grooming Christina to take over his empire. She passed most of the summer in New York under the tutelage of Costa Gratsos and seemed to be working hard to master the intricacies of the family businesses. But in August of 1974, a month that she traditionally spent relaxing on Skorpios, Christina disappeared, then turned up in the public ward of a London hospital suffering from a huge overdose of sleeping pills. Her mother flew to her side from the South of France. After lying unconscious for two days, Christina was pronounced out of danger and moved to a private room.

By this time Tina had reached the end of her strength. Her reliance on alcohol and prescription drugs worried everyone around her, and Onassis enlisted several of his ex-wife's friends to travel from Athens to Paris to visit her and report back to him on her condition.

"I saw Tina shortly before her death and she looked awful," her friend Vivi Crespi recalled. "Her face was so swollen and she seemed so weak. 'I'm just falling apart,' she told me. The death of her son devastated her, of course, but so did her life with Niarchos. When she first told me she was marrying him, I asked her how she could do it after the way he treated her sister. 'I'm tougher than Eugenia,' she said. But Stavros proved much tougher than she anticipated. When I saw her after the marriage, she seemed frightened of him."

Shattered by the loss of Alexander and the way he and Christina had reacted to her marriage, Tina was unable to save herself. "I don't think Stavros was in any way responsible," her former lover Reinaldo Herrera told me. "He always adored her. But once Alexander died, she didn't want to live anymore. She started drinking and taking pills, which she never did when I first met her. It was so sad how it all ended for her."

On October 10, 1974, Tina's maid found her dead in her room at Niarchos' Paris mansion. She was forty-five years old. The cause of death was reported to be "a heart attack or a lung edema," the latter denoting an accumulation of excess fluid in the tissue. Christina immediately suspected that Niarchos was somehow responsible. She flew to Paris from New York and obtained a magistrate's warrant for a postmortem. Meanwhile, the newspapers were pointing out the eerie similarities between the fates of the two sisters, each married to the same man at the time of her premature death.

The perennial foes Onassis and Niarchos united a final time for the sake of the children and Tina's memory. They issued a joint statement saying that the two families "not only are not opposed to it [the autopsy] but on the contrary, welcome the decision." The two pathologists appointed by the public prosecutor's office announced that Tina had indeed died from an acute edema of the lung.

At Tina's funeral there were only a handful of mourners, and Ari was not among them. Niarchos had issued instructions that only immediate family members could attend. Vivi Crespi, who had known Tina since they attended school together, called and insisted on coming. She told me, "Her funeral was so sad. There were hardly a dozen people there. Besides her mother, her brother, and her daughter, the few friends who attended the service in the Greek church in Lausanne were Gloria Guinness, Eugenie Carras, and me." Christina broke down at the graveside and was comforted by Tina's second husband, Sonny Blandford, now the duke of Marlborough. She was heard to say, as she wept in the arms of her former stepfather, "My aunt, my brother, now my mother—what is happening to us?"

Angered by Christina's clear implication that he was at fault in Tina's death, Niarchos issued his own statement putting the blame on the girl. He revealed Christina's recent suicide attempt in London and said that it had happened "at a time when her mother still mourned the death of her son. Tina never recovered from the depression into which these blows plunged her."

In Paris, Maria Callas was mourning the death of her dear friend Larry Kelly, the man who had appointed himself her protector during the summer of 1968 and had persuaded her to leave the *Christina* and travel with him throughout the western United States. During the last weeks of Larry's struggle with cancer in Kansas City, Mary Carter had called Callas repeatedly and urged her to come. "She told me a lot of reasons she couldn't make the trip," Mrs. Carter told me, "but I knew the real reason was that she couldn't face death." When Kelly died, on September 16, 1974, Callas once again couldn't bear to attend the funeral of someone she loved.

After the shock of Tina's demise, Ari and his daughter returned to New York. He admitted himself to New York Hospital once again under an assumed name for further treatment of his myasthenia gravis. Onassis' facial muscles were now so weak that he had to tape his eyelids open. He tried to disguise his pathetic handiwork behind special glasses even darker than the ones he usually wore. The treatment of his disease consisted primarily of painful injections of cortisone, which not only made his face puffy, but further exacerbated his already volatile temper. Little wonder that Onassis' employees were reluctant to tell him, when he returned to the office, that his favorite "hobby enterprise," Olympic Airways, was in serious trouble ("Shipping is my wife, but aviation is my mistress," he would say when describing his attachment to the airline).

Onassis' anger and frustration at Jackie were now his chief animating emotions. He complained to Roy Cohn that his marriage had come down to a "monthly presentation of bills" and advised him to draw up divorce papers outlining his grounds. Onassis also hired detectives to shadow Jackie for any signs of misbehavior, and embarked on a campaign to undermine her public image.

The Washington columnist and Pulitzer Prize–winning investigative reporter Jack Anderson was invited to New York in December 1974 to lunch with Onassis at "21." After some vague complaints about his wife's extravagant spending on clothes, Ari escorted Anderson back to the office, where he introduced him to his aides, including Costa Gratsos, then mentioned another engagement and left them alone. Anderson was shown documents and told anecdotes describing Jackie's profligate spending and was informed that divorce proceedings were imminent.

*Onassis' myasthenia gravis destroyed his facial muscles
and forced him to hold his eyelids open with tape.*

Gratsos and the others gave Anderson the information "on background," or off the record, and Anderson's assistant made notes. Ari's grievances included not only his wife's inability to keep within a budget but also "the total incompatibility of jackie and ari and jackie's faggoty friends," he wrote. Ari was "very unhappy" over the marriage, and a "major factor was the 'odd people' around her." Her system of laundering money by buying and reselling clothes was also described in detail to Anderson, who later confirmed the charges by interviewing salespeople and employees of Mrs. Onassis.

When Anderson's articles were printed (in April of 1975) he wrote extensively about Onassis' desire to divorce Jackie: "What concerned Onassis the most, apparently, were the financial consequences, for he had quietly determined according to our sources that the Greek Orthodox Church would allow him to dissolve the marriage on the simple grounds of incompatibility.

"Apparently Jackie received the message that the marriage was on the rocks," Anderson continued. "While she was vacationing with friends on Antigua in the British West Indies, aide Nancy Tuckerman called Onassis to give a routine report on Jackie's doings and to ask how long she should stay. Sources with direct knowledge of the incident say he retorted, 'Tell her to stay indefinitely.' . . . One intimate summed up the Jackie-Ari relationship, after six and a half years of marriage, as 'total incompatibility.' "

As Onassis mustered his fast-ebbing strength to pursue the divorce from Jackie, he was distracted by the news that Olympic Airways was threatened with bankruptcy. The Arab oil embargo had hurt the airline badly, and when Ari left the hospital, his first cousin Kostas Konialidis, the president of the airline, summoned up the courage to tell his boss just how bad things were. The airline could no longer afford to keep its planes in the sky. This news reached him at the very time Onassis was christening his Olympic Towers, the new glass-walled, fifty-one-storey Fifth Avenue condominium with a cutting-edge security system, lavishly designed to attract the richest of occupants. On the verge of this high-stakes venture and with an international recession deepening, Onassis could not afford any conspicuous business failures.

Against his doctor's orders, Onassis flew to Greece in December of 1974, convinced that his old friend Constantine Karamanlis, whose party had just come to power, would bail him out with a large infusion of government money, but the prime minister refused to help. Onassis' former cronies, the colonels who had headed the military junta that seized power in 1967, were now cooling their heels in prison, and Karamanlis could not risk the political fallout of aiding someone who had been so close to them. Instead, he announced that the Greek government would buy the airline back from Onassis.

Already near exhaustion, Ari stayed up around the clock for many days, negotiating with the Greek government, quibbling over every point. On New Year's Eve he kept the negotiators working until almost midnight. He was described as being very pale, sweating profusely—probably from the cortisone—and sometimes speaking incomprehensibly.

While her husband was struggling through what some aides called the "worst weeks of his life," Jackie was celebrating the holidays in New York and then on a ski vacation in Switzerland. Della Garoufalia Rounick, a Greek who was then married to one of the imprisoned colonels, told me that when she came to Onassis' villa in Glyfada on Christmas Eve to beg him to try to help her husband, she was astonished to find Ari completely alone for the holidays with no plans to go anywhere.

On January 15, 1975, despite all his efforts at negotiating better terms, Onassis was forced to hand Olympic Airways back to the Greek government for cash and assets valued at $35 million, a fraction of its value. Though he had bought the money-losing Greek national airline TAE in 1957 for only $2 million, when it consisted of just twelve DC-3s and one DC-4, after the deal was done and Olympic's debts were settled, *Fortune* magazine opined, "Even thirty-five million dollars was not much of a return for the money and effort he had put into the business."

Onassis entered the new year alone in Glyfada, bereft of his pet enterprise and afflicted with a bad case of flu. He was also having trouble chewing and speaking clearly and soon had to support his chin with his hand to do either. He refused to eat despite the pleadings of Artemis, or to take the medicines prescribed for his myasthenia gravis. He was wasting away, and lost forty pounds in two months' time. In a desperate effort to bolster what was left of his fortune for his daughter, he elicited a promise from Christina to marry Peter Goulandris, heir to the world's fourth-largest shipping dynasty.

January 20 was Ari's seventy-first birthday. One of his gifts was a red cashmere Hermès blanket, sent from Paris by Maria Callas. (Bruna described it to me as a small coverlet.)

On Sunday, February 2, Onassis called his wife in New York and complained bitterly about being sick, in pain, and alone. The next day he collapsed with severe abdominal pains. Artemis put through a frantic call to Jackie, who immediately flew to Greece on a chartered plane, bringing with her Ari's cardiologist, Dr. Rosenfeld. Christina was already with her father in Glyfada when Jackie and the doctor arrived. Waiting downstairs were all Onassis' sisters, and at his bedside was a gastroenterologist, Professor Jean Caroli, whom Christina had called in from Paris.

"Christina had called and told me he had pneumonia," Dr. Rosenfeld told me, "but when I examined him I saw he didn't have pneumonia. He had developed a stone in the common bile duct that leads from the gallbladder to the intestine. The family had called a French doctor, Jean Caroli, and he recommended that Onassis be taken to the American Hospital in Paris and have the gallbladder removed. I felt he was too weak to survive such an operation and instead I recommended that he be flown to New York, where a local procedure would be performed to dislodge the stone and leave it to drain outside. When someone is old and weak and surgery poses a very high risk, that is the recommended procedure."

But Onassis did not want to go to New York. "Even though there was an Olympic 707 waiting to fly him there," Dr. Rosenfeld continued, "he didn't want to die in New York, I think for tax reasons."

Christina wanted her father to fly to Paris; she still believed that he

Onassis, struggling to walk alone, on his final trip to Paris

could be saved. Although Ari himself clearly did not, he acceded to his daughter's pleas and, having secured Stelios Papadimitriou's promise that he would always look after her, allowed himself, on Thursday, February 6, to be taken to France. But he repeated to several of his associates and his doctor that he would die there. It may have been, as Dr. Rosenfeld thought, that he didn't want to die in New York for tax reasons. Or he may have been influenced by the fact that Maria Callas was in Paris.

Onassis took with him the red Hermès blanket, Maria's last gift, as he made his final display of macho pride: he forced himself to walk unaided and unprotected past the gauntlet of reporters outside his door like a *palikari*—a warrior—as Papadimitriou put it.

On the plane, Onassis said to the French doctor, Professor Caroli, "You understand, doctor, the meaning of the Greek word *thanatos*—death? Well, please practice *thanatos* on me."

After the plane landed at Orly Airport, a limousine transported Onassis to 88 Avenue Foch. Again, he mustered his strength to walk alone through the crowd of reporters and photographers waiting outside his door—this time a veritable army, including five television crews. According to the *New York Times*, "Mr. Onassis said 'Good evening' to newsmen clustered around the gates and walked across the garden and into the building without assistance, his hands in the pockets of his blue overcoat. Mrs. Onassis and his daughter Christina arrived about 30 minutes later."

Once inside the apartment, Aristo took the first opportunity to make a surreptitious call to Callas at her nearby flat; she took the receiver from Ferruccio with trembling hands. He told her quickly that he was entering the hospital the next morning and "the Widow" was with him, but he would try to arrange a way for her to visit him.

When Jackie and Christina arrived, Ari lay down and slept for several hours, then took a stimulant so that he could discuss final business matters with his aides through the night. His public relations consultant, Johnny Meyer, described his shock at the emaciated appearance of his boss and old friend and later recalled that Ari roused himself from silence to say, "You know, Johnny, soon I shall be on Skorpios with Alexander."

On Friday, February 7, 1975, the kind of bright winter day that makes Paris look newly minted, Aristotle Onassis was taken by car to the American Hospital in Neuilly and was spirited in through a side entrance that served as a passage to both the chapel and the morgue. Meanwhile, reporters and photographers were distracted by the sight of Jackie and Christina arriving at the main entrance.

Onassis was given most of a corridor, according to his aide Nicholas Papanikolaou, who flew to Paris from New York at Christina's behest and arrived on the same day that his boss entered the hospital. He told me that they reserved the rooms on either side of Onassis so he wouldn't be disturbed.

Once her father was settled into the hospital, Christina moved out of the Avenue Foch apartment and into the Plaza-Athénée Hotel, because according to Papanikolaou, she didn't want to be left alone with her stepmother. "Christina and I were the only ones who were there at the hospital every day," he told me. "We would visit for three or four hours in the morning, then go back to the hotel and rest, then go back to the hospital in the afternoon for another three or four hours. Periodically his sisters and other friends and relatives came, but not Jackie. She was there at the beginning for four days, and then left to go back to New York."

Onassis was severely jaundiced, and the French doctor repeated his warning that without removal of the gallbladder the patient would not survive. According to Papanikolaou, "They gave him papers to sign for the operation and he threw them away, telling them he didn't care if he lived or died. Then they turned to Christina and asked her to sign the authorization. They explained to her that if they didn't do it, he most certainly would die within three to four days, but even if they did the operation there was a fifty-fifty chance he would die during the procedure. Christina went crazy.

'What am I going to do?' she asked me. 'How can I make a decision like this?' I told her since he was sure to die if the operation was not done, she had to authorize the operation despite the high risk, and she did."

"The operation should never have been performed," according to Isadore Rosenfeld; he had said as much when he flew to Greece with Jackie in early February. His recommendation was that Onassis be brought to New York for a local procedure that would dislodge the stone without removing the gallbladder and allow it to pass out of his body. But after Onassis elected to go to Paris, Dr. Rosenfeld sent a colleague, Dr. Louis Weinstein, now deceased, from Boston to Paris. "Lou Weinstein was the best specialist in the country on the gallbladder," Dr. Rosenfeld told me. "But Onassis had developed a very serious infection that didn't respond to antibiotics and there was nothing he could do against the infection. I believe that if Onassis had elected to come to New York instead of Paris, and avoided the gallbladder operation, he could have been saved."

On Sunday, February 9, when Onassis' gallbladder was removed, Jackie, Christina, and Artemis were by his side. A family spokesman announced that he was "feeling much better."

After being told that her husband was making "a slow but progressive improvement," Jackie flew back to New York and checked on his condition daily by phone. "She didn't want to spend any more time in the hospital than she had to, but wanted to be there in the end so she wouldn't be criticized," Papanikolaou told me.

When Jackie did return to Paris and her husband's bedside during the following weeks, she also found time to visit the Louvre and the cinema and to dine with friends almost every night. But she returned to New York at the end of February to watch a television documentary that her daughter, Caroline, had worked on. She came back to Paris and was seen on March 7, dining at an elegant restaurant on the Place de la Madeleine with the president of Air France. Three days later she returned to New York again, despite the warnings of two doctors that Ari's condition was deteriorating rapidly.

After Onassis' condition worsened, he was put in the last room on the corridor and Christina took a suite across from it. "That's where she and I stayed while we were in the hospital, going back and forth from his room to the suite," said Papanikolaou, who observed that Onassis showed little will to improve and implored Christina many times, "Let me die."

Maria, desperate for news of Aristo's condition, called the hospital every day. She also called Costa Gratsos, asking him to find a way she could visit Onassis' room, but, according to Papanikolaou, Christina refused permission. "At that time she still blamed Callas for breaking up the marriage of her parents."

Nevertheless, Maria found ways to keep herself informed about Onassis' health. By coincidence, Vasso Devetzi's mother was in the same hospital corridor suffering from cancer, and when Vasso visited her every day, she would ask nurses and relatives about Onassis' condition and then convey the news to Callas. Vasso's niece, Vicky Anthopoulou, told me, "My aunt met Jackie at the hospital and a kind of friendship developed between them because they both were big smokers and went out in the hallway to smoke. Jackie cautioned Vasso to cut down, but she couldn't do it herself."

Another source of information was Eleni Siros, a close friend of Bruna's who served as Onassis' housekeeper in the Avenue Foch apartment nearby (and later as maid and companion to Christina Onassis). "Even after the wedding to Jackie Kennedy in 1968, Eleni Siros would come over to Maria's apartment, bringing her the cheese pies that she loved," Vicky Anthopoulou told me. "I know she would never have done that if Onassis himself hadn't given her permission."

Although denied admittance to his hospital room, Maria spoke to him on the phone for as long as he was able to talk, and as his health deteriorated, she relied on her friends for information about his condition. Many who knew her believe that Callas also managed to visit Aristo one last time, evading the photographers that constantly lay in wait for her both outside her apartment and at the hospital. But the two people closest to her, who watched and attended her every move, deny that she ever went. Bruna and Ferruccio concur that, though Callas and Onassis spoke on the telephone many times—Maria increasingly upset by his feeble voice with each conversation—she never went to the sickroom.

Nevertheless, Callas herself told several people after Onassis' death that she did manage to sneak in during a period when Jacqueline Kennedy was not in Paris and Christina was away from the hospital. Among those who repeated her story were her friend and modiste, Madame Biki in Milan, her assistant, Nadia Stancioff, and the music critic Stelios Galatopoulos.

Nadia, in her memoir of Maria, wrote, "Only once, a few weeks before Onassis' death, did Maria manage to sneak into the hospital for a short visit unobserved by the press."

Madame Biki Bouyeure, when I interviewed her in her home in Milan shortly before her death in 1999, repeated to me what the diva told her while a guest at her home. Maria described how she entered the hospital room to find Onassis lying in the bed, pale and gaunt, but watching her approach with the same intense gaze that she remembered so well. Concealing her dismay at his appearance, she reached for his hand, which lay on the coverlet, cold and thin.

Callas said she had been warned by the doctors not to stay long and not to upset him. When she bent over to kiss Aristo good-bye, he managed to tell her that he loved her and to say the farewell that he had prepared while waiting for her visit. As Maria turned and left the room, she said later, she knew that she would never see him again. He was eager for the arrival of *thanatos,* and Maria, who never could bear to look death in the eye, wanted to leave Paris. Though they had spent so many happy days together there, the city would ever after remind her of her lover's last painful moments of life.

The music critic Stelios Galatopoulos, who wrote about his conversations with Callas, reports her description of their last meeting:

> *When I saw Ari on his deathbed at the hospital he was calm and I think at peace with himself. He was very ill and he knew that the end was near, though he tried to ignore it. We did not speak about old times or much about anything else, but mostly communicated with each other in silence. When I was leaving, he made a special effort to tell me, "I loved you, not always well, but as much and as best I was capable of. I tried."*

There are few people still alive who know if this moving farewell in the hospital room actually happened or if Maria made it up to tell friends for her own inscrutable reasons. In an effort to confirm the story, I tracked down the only survivor among Onassis' primary physicians in Paris, Dr. Maurice Mercadier, who had been quoted on the front page of the *New York Times* of March 16, 1975, as saying that the death was due to bronchial pneumonia which "resisted all antibiotics."

Through the doctor's son, a Paris lawyer named Robert Mercadier, I requested an interview with the elder Mercadier, but he refused, citing doctor-patient privilege. Then I asked whether he could simply say that he never saw Maria Callas visit Onassis in the hospital—a statement that would answer my question without revealing any confidential information about his patient. The doctor refused even to deny seeing Callas there, which leads me to suspect that she may indeed have managed to visit the hospital.

Five days after the gallbladder operation Onassis was rendered unable to speak at all. According to the *New York Times,* "Six main doctors and six consulting doctors at the American Hospital said in a communiqué that it had been necessary to put Mr. Onassis on a respirator. . . . They said there had been no blood transfusions nor any heart failure or change, despite the fact that the . . . patient's health had been 'compromised' by myasthenia gravis and subsequent cortisone therapy for it, heart fibrillation, pneumonia and severe gall-bladder infection with jaundice." It was then, according to Stelios Papadimitriou, after Onassis was hooked up to a kidney machine and a tube was forced down his throat, making speech impossible, that he seized a pencil and wrote to his daughter, in ever smaller letters: "PLEASE, Let me die!"

Longing to complete the odyssey that would finally lead him home to Skorpios beside his son, Onassis also begged his doctors and his sisters to end his life support, but no one would oblige him.

Before he reached this point, Christina had come to her father's bedside with Peter Goulandris—the young shipping heir whom Onassis had chosen as the ideal match for her. They exchanged rings before his eyes and asked for his blessing, which he gave. It was a desperate attempt to offer him something to live for, or at least to ease his mind as he slipped into the other world. But the gesture would prove entirely hollow, for the couple would break off the engagement shortly after his death.

March arrived in Paris draped in gray rainclouds. Jackie Onassis was in New York. Maria knew that she would never speak to Aristo again, nor even be allowed to see him, alive or dead. She decided to take the advice of friends in Palm Beach and to fly to Florida, where a house had been rented for her with the promise that she could buy it if it pleased her. She packed up Bruna, Ferruccio, her cook, Consuela, and the dogs and wrote a letter to her godfather dated March 7, 1975. She begged him to visit her in Palm Beach, knowing she would need support from the few people she trusted, now more than ever. She ended the letter, "All my love, dear Leonida. I hope to see you soon, soon."

On March 15, a day of relentless rain in Paris, Aristotle Onassis came to the end of his journey. Sleeping the sleep of morphine, with tubes attached to every part of his body, he arrived at last on the shore of his personal Ithaca.

Artemis woke Jackie in New York to tell her that her husband was dead. "Christina was with him when he left us," she said.

Maria learned the news of Onassis' death amid the walled villas, pristine sands, and swaying palm trees of Palm Beach. When Mary Carter called her from Dallas, Callas responded to her words of sympathy by saying slowly, heavily, "Ah, Mary, it's over. It's all over now."

When Nadia Stancioff called from Rome, Maria told her, "Nothing matters much anymore, because nothing will ever be the same again without him."

John Coveney, the director of classical music for Angel Records, went to see Callas in Florida a short time later, on a day when she received a parcel of letters and telegrams of condolence that had been forwarded to her.

She started to show him the letters, then stopped and said, "All of a sudden, I am a widow." It was a bitter irony for the woman who had never been considered by the world to be her beloved's wife or known to be the mother of his child.

In the shaky handwriting of an old man, Maria's godfather, Leonidas Lantzounis, made a note at the bottom of Callas' March 7 letter that she had phoned him from Palm Beach on March 11, the day after she arrived, and had called him again on March 15, the day of Onassis' death. He didn't indicate what she said about her loss, but he recorded another call, a week later, pleading with him to go to her, and he noted that on March 22 he promised to go.

"Officially, Jackie was his widow, of course," Captain Kostas told me, "but for those of us who had been with him for a long time, the one we grieved for was Maria. She was the one who loved him best and with whom he seemed to enjoy life the most."

Of all the testimonials offered by Onassis' famous friends after his death, the one most quoted by the press came from Prince Rainier of Monaco, who had once welcomed the tycoon as the savior of Monte Carlo but later forced him to sell his interests in the principality.

"There will be no more men of such stature," he said. "Death deprives us of an unpretentious and good man who was remarkably clever. He was also a discreet and faithful friend. He built his economic empire with only the qualities of his mind and his ability."

Aristotle Onassis was surely a fortunate man. But Solon of Athens, on learning the nature of his death, might not have called him a happy one.

22

DEATH IN PARIS

Vissi d'arte
Vissi d'amore.
(I lived for art
I lived for love.)

Giacomo Puccini, *Tosca*

On the day after Onassis died, his official widow, Jacqueline Kennedy
Onassis, arrived at Orly Airport in Paris wearing a black Valentino dress
and a black leather coat. She flashed an incongruous and automatic smile at
the crowd of photographers and read a statement she had composed on the
plane: "Aristotle Onassis rescued me at a moment when my life was
engulfed with shadows. He meant a lot to me. He brought me into a world
where one could find both happiness and love. We lived through many
beautiful experiences together which cannot be forgotten, and for which I
will be eternally grateful."

Jackie then visited the hospital chapel where her husband lay in state
with a Greek Orthodox crucifix on his chest. She stayed seven minutes and
then reportedly asked to speak to Onassis family members, but was
rebuffed. Christina, under heavy sedation, was in no condition to speak to
anyone.

On March 18, an Olympic Airways 727 arrived at the airport in Aktion,
Greece (the harbor on the Ambracian Gulf where Antony and Cleopatra
were defeated by Octavian, after which they fled to Egypt to die). The plane
carried Ari's body in the hold and thirty-four family members and friends
on board. Jackie supported a sedated Christina as they emerged into the
tumult of photographers' lights and shouts. Again the widow flashed her

reflexive grin. Christina's face remained etched with the lines of the ancient Greek mask of tragedy.

The funeral cortege drove through the countryside toward Nidri, the fishing village that was the point on the coast nearest Skorpios, past flowering cherry trees and herds of sheep and goats. In the first limousine behind the hearse were Jackie, Christina, and Ted Kennedy, and in the second rode Onassis' sisters. Only a few minutes into the drive, Christina later told friends and family, Ted Kennedy leaned toward her and said, "Now it's time to take care of Jackie."

"Stop the car!" Christina shouted at the driver. To everyone's surprise, the funeral cortege came to a halt as she leaped out and ran back to join her aunts in the second limousine.

Two launches took the casket and the immediate family from Nidri to Skorpios, while other mourners were transported by ferry. On the mainland, black-scarved village women holding bunches of wildflowers crossed themselves as the casket passed. On Skorpios, the dozens of Onassis employees and the *Christina*'s crew members, all in their work clothes, held lighted yellow mourning candles as the casket was carried up the winding path to the chapel by six pallbearers. The simple, closed walnut casket with four silver handles was set into a concrete sarcophagus on the side of the chapel opposite the chamber housing the tomb of Onassis' son, Alexander, whose corpse had been carried up the same path only twenty-five months earlier.

Onassis had told his sisters that he wanted his burial to be as simple as possible, and he had chosen the exact spot where the coffin would rest—in the shade of a large cypress tree beside the chapel. Greeks plant the tall, straight evergreens in cemeteries as a symbol of the resurrection, and Onassis had particularly loved the trees ever since seeing them sheltering his mother's grave in Smyrna. As he lay dying, Aristo instructed architects to build a second chamber around his tomb, like the one they had created for Alexander, but on the other side of the chapel. Onassis told them to take care not to disturb the cypress tree that had comforted him when he visited his son's grave.

(When I visited the chapel and the grave sites in June of 1998, the same cypress rose through the roof of the white structure, which now consists of the original small chapel with two adjoining chambers. The wing on the left as you face the chapel contains the marble sarcophagi of Aristotle Onassis and his sister Artemis and the one on the right, the identical tombs of his two children. The marble lid of each tomb is carved with the name of the deceased in Greek letters and the dates of birth and death, and each is deco-

At Onassis' funeral, his sisters pushed Jackie Onassis far into the background.

rated with a marble cross and a white marble vase, which the staff on Skorpios keep filled with fresh flowers. The white walls of the chambers are hung with icons that gleam golden, reflecting the light of the oil lamps on the hanging silver chandeliers.)

As the funeral procession climbed the road on Skorpios and the mourners walked behind the casket toward the chapel, Jackie continued to smile nervously for the photographers. Onlookers said that Onassis' sisters deliberately crowded together and linked arms, pushing the widow and her fourteen-year-old son to the back of the procession. Christina Onassis wept inconsolably and had to be supported by her aunts, as the village priest, Father Apostolos Zavitzsianos, intoned the words of the Greek funeral service:

> *All mortal things are vanity, since after death they are not. Wealth*
> *remaineth not, glory goeth not with us. Death cometh suddenly and all*
> *these things vanish utterly. . . . Where is the yearning for the world?*
> *Where is the pomp? Where are the gold and the silver? Where are the*
> *tumult and rush of servants? All is dust, all is ashes, all shadow. . . .*

Onassis' tombstone on Skorpios, bearing an incorrect birthdate

Let us give the last kiss to him who hath died; for he is gone from his kinsfolk and hasteneth to the tomb, and no longer hath a care for the things of vanity and our much-toiling flesh.

At the end of the service, the mourners approached the casket one by one and leaned to kiss the icon that lay atop it. As they turned away and began the slow procession back down to the harbor, a few drops of rain spattered the walnut coffin and the hundreds of white lilies that encircled the chapel's courtyard. In the bay below, the *Christina* lay at anchor with its flag flying at half-mast.

After Onassis' death, Maria began to drift aimlessly. She debated buying the Palm Beach house, twice agreed to do it, then twice changed her mind. She went back to Paris in April, but could think of nothing to do to occupy herself. She became reluctant even to leave her apartment. Callas was often glimpsed during this period peering warily out from behind the curtains of her French windows, gazing toward "her" chestnut tree and the little park beyond.

*Callas, withdrawn after Ari's death, felt more secure watching
the days pass from behind a window pane.*

Maria did make an effort to focus on her career, agreeing to undertake one project and then another, but each time she eventually canceled, with excuses as flimsy as "I need a more glamorous role." She tried to find some solace in her relationship with di Stefano, but as her letters to her godfather from that time demonstrate, the affair seemed as pointless as the abortive attempts at singing:

June 26, 1975

I'm working hard because this year I either have to be much better or nothing. . . . I'm still with Pippo. I cannot find anyone better.

July 18, 1975

I have come to a big decision. I'm stopping singing. I'm fed up with the whole business. . . . My nerves can't stand the strain anymore. Of course now I have to find something to do—to keep active. I don't know what! Right now I'm resting here in Paris.

August 22, 1975

I've gained weight and I've lost my will power to diet—isn't that terrible? . . . I am peaceful, no great love on my behalf. I think I prefer life this way. Pippo, of course, is in love and I also up to a certain point, maybe through years of habit, and nothing else as temptation. Men, real men, are difficult to find.

October 29, 1975

I know I have to work but what—maybe start practicing again and recording on my own. . . . Di Stefano is deeply in love with me, but I'm cooling off because—well—who knows, only I want him to realize it little by little. His daughter's death gave him a terrible blow. He already knows I'm not the same with him.

Clearly Maria found it hard to make a clean break with the tenor, however much she wanted it. Di Stefano told me of an incident in 1976 when Maria called him in Rome and asked to see him. He took a plane to Paris and called her from the airport.

"It was in the evening and I talked with Bruna, who said, 'Oh yes, you come. I'll fix your bed in the studio,' " he told me. "I used to sleep in the studio when Maria practiced. So I go there, to Georges Mandel, and I call and Bruna said, 'I'm sorry, Mr. di Stefano, Madame can't see you. She's sleeping.' When I heard that, I go back to the airport and go back to Milano.

Maria didn't say anything because at that time she was in the hands of this Devetzi woman."

Others say that Maria herself discouraged the servants from letting di Stefano in and that he was the one who called and insisted on seeing her. Kostas Pylarinos, the Greek politician who lived in Paris during those years, told me, "She wanted to cut off relations with di Stefano. One time she asked me to come to her apartment because she was afraid of him. That afternoon he was threatening her and she feared he would force himself into her apartment."

By 1976 the affair with di Stefano had run its course. Maria wrote to her godfather: "The relation I had is definitely finished. All I have to do is ask for my few belongings in his home at San Remo—but I don't even want to do that." Her very reason for being with him in the first place had disappeared. As John Ardoin told me: "Onassis was the whole meaning in her life, and after his death she felt there was no point in going on—because everything she had done after they separated was to prove to him that she still meant something. The concerts were to prove to him that she could still sing. The affair with di Stefano was to prove that men still found her desirable."

In the first year after she lost Onassis, Maria was battered by the news of three more friends' deaths: di Stefano's young daughter, Luisa, of whom she had been very fond; Maria's mentor and friend, the stage and film director Luchino Visconti; and her director in *Medea*, Pier Paolo Pasolini, who was gruesomely murdered in November of 1975. A youth he had picked up on a beach near Rome ended the evening by clubbing Pasolini and then running over him with the director's own car. Maria was particularly grief-stricken by the senselessly cruel end of the dear friend who used to celebrate her with poems and drawings. "I've only known one Pasolini," she said, "so sensitive, full of concern. . . . His ideas on art, on life were so powerful and original that you could not remain unmoved by them."

Callas became reluctant to leave the security of her own apartment. She sat inside, watching television around the clock, primarily westerns. Many visitors to 36 Avenue Georges Mandel were offended that Maria would keep switching the television on and off while they were there. (Dorle Soria recalled, "The television was on. We offered to switch it off. 'No, I never turn it off,' she said sharply. 'Do you?' ") It comforted her to lose herself in the simple, reassuring world of cowboy films, where justice always triumphed and evil was always punished. Nadia Stancioff reports the embarrassment of going with her to see *Midnight Cowboy*, which Maria expected to be a standard genre piece, only to have the diva, shocked and

Maria's butler, Ferruccio, escorting the bereft diva near the end of her life

confused, ask loud questions throughout the film and disturb the others in the audience.

Maria's friends didn't exactly desert her, but many became frustrated and alienated by her habit of making plans with them only to cancel at the last moment for the most trivial reasons. Gaby van Zuylen, the daughter-in-law of Maria's old friend Maggie van Zuylen, complained, "She would call and say, 'Gaby, shall we meet tomorrow to go shopping?' Then she would call back, 'Shall we go to the movies instead?' The next day she would call again and cancel altogether. You had to be endlessly available."

One of the few friends willing to indulge this behavior was François

Valéry, the French ambassador to UNESCO, who would escort Maria to the cinema. She confided to him many of her intimate thoughts about Onassis, including how much pleasure he had given her. "He really did love me," she told Valéry. "You can't lie in bed."

The sense of loss Maria felt without Onassis was all-consuming. Prince Michael of Greece recalled that he attended a dinner party in Paris at this time, when he overheard Dame Margot Fonteyn speaking to Maria about her trials as an aging dancer having to support her husband, who had been paralyzed by an assassin's bullet. Maria looked at her compassionately and replied, "For all your miseries, I envy you!"

Maria would beg Ferruccio and Bruna to sit up late at night and play cards with her—sleep had become ever more difficult, despite the pills. On Sunday, the servants' day off, she would invent reasons for them not to go out. When friends came to visit she clung to them, begging them not to leave. Often she would telephone them late at night for long rambling conversations, without apologizing for the hour. One of the people she often called was her sister Jackie in Athens, to whom she began to send small checks, as "a present."

Jackie Callas was astonished by Maria's first call after Onassis' death. Then, after telling Jackie she had sent her a gift, Maria added, "You can do something for me too—I can't sleep and all that helps is Mandrax, but they've stopped them here. Send me some if you can."

Mandrax (methaqualone) was Maria's drug of choice, and it was illegal in most countries, but not in Greece. Jackie told me that she had no trouble procuring it in Athens at the pharmacy on the corner, called Bekas.

Jackie complied with the request and continued to receive phone calls from her sister in Paris. "There was no routine, I never knew when the calls might come," she wrote in her memoir. "Sometimes they were very brief, as if she only wanted to check that I was still there, available at the end of the line. Sometimes she only wanted to ask for more Mandrax. . . . On other occasions there were long late-night calls full of rambling talk about her loneliness, the betrayal of everything she'd lived for, the loss of Onassis."

There's little doubt that, after Onassis' death, Maria's addiction to the drugs that helped her sleep grew more dangerous. After her death, Ferruccio told her sister sorrowfully, "Madame was tired. She seldom went out and she couldn't sleep, so she took tablets. It was the tablets that weakened her, she took so many, they were so strong. She had many people send them to her. I told Madame Devetzi once but she just shrugged. 'If she wants them, let her have them,' she would say, so what could I do?" Hearing this, Jackie Callas "thought of Bekas handing me the packets of Mandrax, and I wondered who else had joined in this bizarre network of death." Only later would she discover that Maria "had been taking pills to sleep and pills to revive herself the next day. . . ."

Renzo Allegri and his son Robert, in the book *Callas by Callas,* an accumulation of Maria's published words, cite a "diary" she kept in her last months which confirms that even she was aware of the magnitude of the problem. According to the Allegris, it consists of approximately 150 pages of letterhead (with Callas' Paris address printed in the top right corner) on which Maria jotted down in French her thoughts and emotions and events that concerned her.

On her death, according to the Allegris, the diary came into the possession of "a friend of Callas, the lawyer who administered her business affairs," who proclaimed, "As long as I live, this diary will never be published." These pages changed hands several times and "are currently owned by an Italian doctor, Ivano Signorini, who, having read them, in turn decided to keep them secret. . . . We have been able to read photocopies of some of these sheets of paper."

The Allegris write that the diary contains "messages of terrible despair. Short, concise, desolate sentences, jotted down in firm handwriting, with just one or two comments on each page . . . like a cry for help." He quotes some of the despairing inscriptions: "I know of no affection or esteem for me: I am infinitely alone." "Callas: but Maria?" "I have never depended on anyone in my life: Today I am the slave to a bottle of pills." "I think that, for me, ending this life will be a joy: I have no happiness, no friends, only drugs." At times, he notes, she complains because the person who should bring her the drugs is late.

In the summer of 1976, a year after Onassis' death, after Maria spent the day reminiscing about Aristo, Vasso called their mutual friend Kostas Pylarinos in Greece and said that they had to do something to cheer her up; she badly needed rest. Pylarinos organized a vacation for the two women, a two-week stay in August at the Eagle's Palace Hotel near Ouranoupoli ("City of Heaven") on the Chalkidhiki Peninsula, near Thessaloniki, where he was serving as prefect. Pylarinos told me, "Maria was so depressed that Vasso said, 'I had to carry her on my back every day.' "

Maria, who even in the worst of times would still never venture out the door without applying full makeup, was becoming self-conscious about the pounds she had gained in the past months. She looked forward to this trip as a chance to swim every day, and shed some weight as well as worries. According to Pylarinos, "Close to the sea, close to friends whom she trusted, Maria was once again happy. She explored, she laughed, she rested.

She swam like a young girl, with fins and a special mask made for her so she could see in the deep despite her myopic eyesight. She sunbathed next to her [latest] little poodles, Djedda and Pixie. She celebrated her name day on August 15."

The first eight days of the vacation were everything that Maria had hoped, but then the press discovered her in Chalkidhiki and the town where she was staying was overrun with paparazzi. Maria locked herself in her small room in the Eagle's Palace Hotel, closed the shutters, and, suffering in the stifling heat, consoled herself with chocolate and the Greek sweets called "submarines" (*ipovrihio*)—vanilla cream submerged in ice water. She longed for the beach and the sea but she feared being photographed in a bathing suit and doing further damage to the diminishing aura of La Callas.

Callas returned to Paris in anger and frustration and once again took refuge within the walls of her apartment. Friends who visited her there in the last year of her life suggest that she may in fact have been suffering from bouts of agoraphobia. In December of 1976 Maria wrote to her godfather rather plaintively, "I am here in Paris, peaceful and doing nothing. I don't even feel like singing for the time being. I think I've done enough singing in my life to last. Anyway maybe next year will be more exciting. . . . Are you going on a holiday for Xmas? I'm staying here—I'm comfortable at home."

When Nadia Stancioff called on New Year's Eve she was astonished to find Maria answering the phone herself. When asked what she was doing home alone, Maria replied, "No one dares ask me out on New Year's Eve. I guess they feel they'd have to take me to some fancy ball. Silly people. All I want is someone to take me to the movies. Never mind, I have Pixie and Djedda and my TV."

In a letter to her godfather in February of 1977 Maria describes her declining health and dangerously low blood pressure. "Dear Leo," Maria wrote, "I received your letter a few weeks ago—but did not answer sooner because I was not well—Low blood pressure—80 max.—50 min. Now I'm having injections, etc. It makes me feel low and without desire for anything—but in a week I'll be back to normal. . . ."

Maria never returned to "normal," but she made one last abortive try to sing again. A friend offered her the Théâtre des Champs-Elysées so she could practice singing on a stage, but a reporter from *France Dimanche* managed to sneak into the theater while she was working, snapped some photos, and then wrote a cruel article describing the terrible condition of Callas' voice.

She sued the newspaper and eventually won—but posthumously. The experience robbed Maria of her last shred of confidence and any hope of ever singing in public again. She did, however, at least consider the impre-

One of the last photos ever taken of Callas

sario John Tooley's proposal that she sing *Cavalleria Rusticana* with Placido Domingo. Franco Zeffirelli also suggested *The Merry Widow*, but Maria dismissed that as "too undignified." ("Callas, in musical comedy? Me in an operetta?" she exclaimed.) The closest she would come to performing again was a Zeffirelli production of *Traviata*, but the director later reported that Callas would not accept modifications in the first act aimed at compensating for her diminished range.

In his autobiography, Zeffirelli describes visiting Maria in Paris for these discussions:

> *I had noticed that her once beautiful hands now looked transparent; you could see the veins below the skin. Then, as I walked her back to her apartment after lunch, I was appalled to realize that she was actually afraid. She kept close to me, terrified that she would come into contact with passers-by, she hesitated at crossings, looking wildly about her until I led her firmly forward. This was partly due to her usual problem of being unable to see without her spectacles, but now it went deeper. She kept on talking about how*

dangerous the world had become, that terrorists were everywhere and she would never go back to Italy because of all the kidnappings. From time to time she gave a little involuntary shiver. It was beyond any normal distress at the present state of the world, it was paranoia.

While considering *Traviata,* Maria read *Camille* by the younger Alexandre Dumas, which was the inspiration for Verdi's opera. (Dumas *fils* based his sensational novel about a beautiful courtesan who dies of consumption on the true story of a Parisian woman, Marie Plessis, whom he had known before her death at the age of twenty-two.) *Camille* contains a gruesome scene in which the bereaved lover, Armand Duval, has the dead courtesan, Marguerite, disinterred from a temporary grave in Montmartre Cemetery and removed to a permanent, larger plot which he has bought for her. Dumas includes a graphic description of how the young woman's beauty had vanished in the tomb:

It was terrible to see, it is horrible to relate. The eyes were nothing but two holes, the lips had disappeared, vanished, and the white teeth were tightly set. The black hair, long and dry, was pressed tightly about the forehead, and half veiled the green hollows of the cheeks; and yet I recognised in this face the joyous white and rose face that I had seen so often.

Traumatized by this passage, Callas marked it in the book and showed it to Vasso Devetzi, saying, "I never want to be buried in the ground and eaten by worms! I couldn't stand the thought of this happening to my body. I want to be cremated."

At the beginning of 1977, Maria seemed to be preoccupied with the thought of death, as her conversation with Devetzi suggests. Some biographers report that in the summer of 1977 she made a pilgrimage to Aristo's tomb on Skorpios. Kiki Feroudi Moutsatsos, an Onassis secretary, claims in her book *The Onassis Women* that she personally arranged the visit without consulting any members of the Onassis family. She was not, however, able to provide me with any substantiation for the account, and all the caretakers of Skorpios, including Captain Kostas Anastasiades, told me it would have been impossible for Maria to go there without their knowledge. Furthermore, both of Callas' servants, Bruna and Ferruccio, stated unequivocally that she never left Paris in the summer of 1977. "Impossible," Ferruccio told me. "We were with her every day. She never went out except to a restaurant or to shop for a few hours. This could not have happened."

Before she died, Vasso Devetzi, Maria's companion during the last months of her life, annotated a copy of Arianna Stassinopoulos' biography of Maria with comments in four languages, written in red ink. Next to the sentence "Her last pilgrimage was to Skorpios; she spent hours kneeling in front of Aristo's tomb praying," Vasso has written *"pas possible!!!"* Kostas Pylarinos, who married Devetzi's niece in 1993, also told me, "Maria wanted to come back to Greece in 1977—Vasso was performing at Herodes Atticus Theater—but she didn't come. The last time she was in Greece was at Chalkidhiki in 1976."

In the fall of 1977, Mary Carter spoke to Maria for the last time—by phone, when Mrs. Carter was in Italy around the first of September. "We talked for hours and Maria wanted me to come by Paris on the way back." But she was traveling with Richard Hubert, the dean of continuing education at Hunter College in New York, and he had persuaded her to hurry back to New York in time to teach a course called "Ultimate Chic" at Hunter. To her great eventual regret, Mary Carter told Maria she didn't have time to stop in Paris.

"I told her about the course I was going to teach and she got huge giggles out of that," Mrs. Carter recalls. "I told her I wanted her to come to New York and be a guest speaker and she agreed, but said she had to lose weight first, because she'd gotten a bit heavy. She sounded good when we talked and she was amused by my teaching gig, but it was obvious she had not gotten over the loss of Onassis. 'We do the best we can, Mary,' she said at one point. 'We just go on and do the best we can.' "

At the end, only a few faithful friends still came regularly to see her. La Divina had vanished, and Maria Callas was very much alone. In July of 1977, the opera commentator Alan Sievewright went to Paris to try to persuade Maria to do a discussion evening at Covent Garden, to talk about her career. When she heard his proposal, Maria shook her head and said, "Everything they want to know about me is there in the music. . . . Callas is dead."

According to Sievewright, "Maria was stroking the little white poodle on her lap: 'She is getting very old, you know,' she said. 'I always replace them when they die. I've always thought we should do the same with human beings, but I've discovered we can't.' "

In the course of my research about Maria's last days, I came upon a bit of information that throws new light on a possible cause of her death. Several friends, including Mary Carter, mentioned that Callas was eager to lose the weight she had gained. Then Kostas Pylarinos alluded in passing to a conversation that Maria had on the night before she died with Yiannis De-vetzis, Vasso's brother, who lived in Athens.

"Maria called Vasso's brother late on the night of September 16, 1977, a few hours before her death," Pylarinos told me, "and she said, among other things, 'You can't believe how much weight I've lost! It's a miracle!' He replied, 'Why are you staying in Paris then? Come and show us your body. Vasso has just finished her recital and is preparing for a few days' vacation in Cyprus. Will you come?' And she agreed."

I called Yiannis Devetzis in Athens and he confirmed this conversation. "Of course it was a long time ago," he said, "but I can tell you that all the reports that she killed herself are totally wrong. She was very upbeat, full of plans, and really pleased with herself that she had lost weight. We talked about going to Cyprus, where my wife has family, and she said she really wanted to go. She sounded better than she had in years."

If Maria had complained to Mary Carter in early September about hav-ing to lose weight before she could be seen in public, and then, less than two weeks later, was exulting to Yiannis Devetzis about "a miracle" of how much weight she had lost, it's possible that she may have taken some sort of diet medication to effect a quick weight loss and that the interaction of this medication with the Mandrax on which she was dependent may have had fatal consequences for her already frail heart.

(Both Callas and Onassis' daughter, Christina, had taken diuretics to lose weight and did so surreptitiously because of Aristo's disapproval, according to the physical therapist Korinna Spanidou and others. Both Maria and Christina died at an early age after a period of stringent dieting and weight loss. Christina was only thirty-seven when she was found dead in her bathtub; the cause of death has never been determined.)

On the last night of her life, after calling Yiannis Devetzis in Athens, Maria courted sleep by paging through a French television guide. She found no program of interest but lingered over a short cover article on Gina Lollo-brigida in which the actress declared she was through with films and was devoted to her new profession as a reporter-photographer. It includes the sentence: *"Elle estimait qu'une actrice devait terminer sa carrière au som-met de sa gloire"* (She thinks that an actress must end her career at the height of its glory). Putting down *Tele Sept Jours,* Maria picked up *Spy/Counterspy,* the autobiography of Dusko Popov, "one of the master intelli-gence officers of World War II," published in England by Weidenfeld & Nicolson, but her interest in Popov's saga lagged on page 90, where she put a silver bookmark on a page with a passage describing a brawl in a night-club. She closed the book and turned off the light.

Maria Callas died on the morning of September 16, 1977. According to Bruna, she awoke late, was served her breakfast in bed, then got up and took a few steps toward the bathroom. She crumpled to the floor, falling against a bureau. Bruna and Ferruccio rushed in and helped her back into the bed. Her lips were blue. Bruna tried to revive her with three spoonfuls of coffee. Meanwhile, Ferruccio was frantically phoning Maria's doctor, but the line was busy. The emergency number at the American Hospital was also busy. Then Ferruccio called his own doctor, who rushed to the apartment. But by the time he got there, Maria Callas was dead. The Turkish fortune-teller had accurately predicted that she would die young, but without suffering. She was fifty-three years old.

In an appraisal after her death, the *New York Times* music critic Harold C. Schonberg wrote: "Her career was short and toward the end she was displaying only the shreds of a voice. . . . But for some 15 years after 1947 she was a symbol fired into the very psyche of the opera-goer. . . . She drove her audiences wild; she had a kind of electrical transmission that very few musicians have ever approached. . . . Callas, dead at 53, blazed through the skies and was burned out very early. But what years those were!"

Maria Callas devoted her life to art and to love, as she sang in *Tosca,* and she did it with such intensity that she was consumed by them and perished too soon.

23

EPITAPHIOS

Death is not the end of everything.

Propertius, *Elegies,* Book IV

"Can you imagine what my funeral will be like?" Maria said to Nadia Stancioff while they were vacationing on a Greek island in 1970. "Hundreds of people pushing and shoving, all saying they loved me and we were best of friends. . . . I wonder how many people will be there who really love me? Four? Five? Anyway, I'm going to enjoy myself. I'll be hiding behind a column watching the performance."

If Maria Callas lived life on an operatic scale, soaring on some occasions to high tragedy and stumbling on others to opera buffa, then her death and the ensuing drama are worthy of a gothic novel, filled with hints of suicide, murder, grave-robbing, even cannibalism. Maria, who was a firm believer in reincarnation, may have been an interested observer of the bizarre misadventures that followed her death, as she predicted. Whether or not she enjoyed the show, it was quite a performance.

Vasso Devetzi was preparing for a performance at the Herodes Atticus Theater in Athens when she received Bruna's brokenhearted message, *"Madame est morte."* Still, Devetzi took charge of all arrangements and gave detailed instructions by telephone. She also called upon her longtime companion, Jean Roire, a Parisian executive with Le Chant du Monde, a major recording studio in France, to supervise the funeral arrangements until she could return to Paris.

The entire world courted admittance to 36 Avenue Georges Mandel to see the great diva lying in state. Reporters and photographers crowded outside the building and offered large sums of money for the privilege of photographing La Divina in death, but, even shaken by grief, Bruna maintained her firm control, carefully selecting who would be allowed in to pay their respects.

Among the chosen was Peter Andry, the head of the classical division of EMI, who described Callas lying on her bed on the day of the funeral, dressed in a gray gown, with a cross and a rose resting on her bosom, her long auburn hair tumbled on the pillow around her white face. "Her hair was so rich, so full of life," he said, "I shuddered at the thought that in a few hours it would all be ashes. I felt a strong urge to touch her, to cut a lock to preserve it forever. . . . I wish I had."

Both Franco Zeffirelli and Jackie Callas later wrote that the sight of Maria's body immediately made them think of the tragic and ethereal heroine of *La Traviata,* who died so picturesquely of consumption. Zeffirelli's description of Callas in death paints a vivid picture:

> *The cold body on that bed had been two people: Maria the woman who wanted to be loved and Callas the diva who was a Vestal at the altar of her art. They had seemed to battle it out within her and in the end both lost; all that had been left in those last years was little more than the shell which was laid out in that darkened room. Her maid, Bruna, stood by her body, obsessively fussing over her dead mistress: first she would gently comb her long tresses, then she would smooth her precious lace nightdress or brush away some imagined speck, then she would stop for a while and pray a little, then she would begin again, combing, combing, combing. It was a sublime image of the dead Violetta.*

It's a haunting scene that Zeffirelli describes, one worthy of the stage: the mistress, tragic and lovely in death, the faithful maid, obsessively grooming the body as she weeps. But Franco Rossellini, the producer of Callas' film *Medea,* later reported that in fact Bruna had refused to let Zeffirelli in when he called. "She said La Signora would turn over in her grave if he stepped into the house," Rossellini recalled. And when I asked her, Bruna herself replied, "Categorically no. Zeffirelli did not come to the house after her death. Things were not good between them."

Jackie Callas was informed of her sister's death by Jean Roire's call from Paris, although she had no idea who he—or Vasso Devetzi—might be and she had not laid eyes on her sister for sixteen years, despite talking to Maria frequently and supplying her regularly with Mandrax. Jean Roire arranged for Jackie Callas to fly immediately to Paris (where she'd never been) to represent the family at the funeral. Maria's mother, Evangelia, who

Princesses Grace and Caroline of Monaco being mobbed at Maria's funeral in Paris

now lived with Jackie in Athens, was suffering from diabetes and was too ill to travel.

The funeral was held on Tuesday, September 20, in St. Stephen's Greek Orthodox Church on Rue Georges Bizet. (Friends of Callas' organized memorial services on the same day in Milan, Rome, New York, and London.) At four-thirty in the afternoon, more than two thousand mourners tried to push into St. Stephen's as the priests began to chant and reporters, photographers, and television crews jostled for a good view of the illustrious mourners and the catafalque in the aisle.

The hysterical press drowned out the words of the service, elbowing mourners, friends, and family, and ultimately even shoving Maria's casket aside in an effort to get a photograph of Princess Grace and her daughter Caroline as they left the building. There was little sign of order or dignity as the coffin was carried out, but when it reached the street the onlookers burst into cries of "Brava Maria, Brava Callas!" Many were weeping.

The funeral cortege left the crowds behind as it headed toward Père Lachaise cemetery. Vasso Devetzi had informed the presiding Greek prelates, including Metropolitan Meletios, the head of the Greek church in France, of Maria's wish to be cremated. But the clerics reminded her that the Orthodox church forbids the practice. There are no facilities for cremation within Greece, but in foreign countries it is sometimes permitted if it was the express wish of the deceased.

Kostas Pylarinos, one of the handful of friends who accompanied the body, asked the bishop to officiate at the cemetery, but he refused, citing church law. Finally, Pylarinos told me, the prelate, after he "pressured him a bit," agreed to come as far as the cemetery but "refused to be present at the cremation."

Jackie Callas, in her memoirs, expresses her horror that Maria was to be cremated, but allows that she was too frightened to object. She describes waiting in a "gaunt stone building," while Maria was taken away to be incinerated.

> *I don't think I have ever been so cold: it was like a tomb. It seemed hideously ironical that somewhere nearby they were burning my sister while I froze to death in that barren ante-chamber. . . . When the doors creaked open they revealed an official coming forward with a plain metal box. It was so small and Mary had been such a tall woman. Whatever that little box contained was all that was left of her. . . . I had never had anything to do with a cremation before, and the object in front of me looked like nothing so much as a dull metal cash-box, no handles, no inscription, anonymous. The very idea of a cremation nauseated me but the reality was ten times worse. I felt uncontrollably faint. Pylarinos and Roire were quickly beside me. "Take the ashes," [Vasso] said. "On behalf of the family."*

Many critics, including Maria's ex-husband, Meneghini, have pointed out the irregularity of the body's having been cremated immediately after the funeral service, because in France it is standard to wait for twenty-four hours. The haste and the unorthodox method of disposal of the remains have led to insinuations that Devetzi and others may have been trying to hide the cause of Maria's death by preventing an autopsy. The doctor who first arrived in Maria's flat had written the words "heart attack" on the death certificate. "The funeral was so hastily arranged and shrouded in mystery that everyone was amazed . . . ," Meneghini wrote. "I also learned from the director that the cremation was not done the day after the arrival of the body, as is customary, but immediately. Thirty minutes after the bier arrived at the cemetery, the body was cremated. Why such haste?"

Meneghini eventually developed a theory, which he outlined in his book, that Maria had committed suicide. This was based on a scrap of old blue notepaper from the Hotel Savoy in London that he found in a prayer book beside her bed, on which she had scribbled the opening lines of an aria from *La Gioconda* which begins with the word *"Suicidio!"* Battista believed that the note was a last message to him from Maria because in one corner it bore the letters "*a T*," which he interpreted as meaning "for Titta"—her nickname for him.

Stelios Galatopoulos disputes this theory, pointing out that although the note is in Callas' handwriting, "The paper was several years old—before the London telephones were given a new code—and the date, as well as the words '*a T*' ('for Titta'), are slightly smaller than the other letters in the note. In other words they could have been forged, and the whole thing might have been another effort on Meneghini's part to convince himself and show the world that Maria's last message was for him."

Nearly everyone who knew Maria discounts the idea that she would have killed herself on purpose. Kostas Pylarinos told me: "I'm sure the pills she took over the years contributed to the death. But there is no possibility she committed suicide, because she had a fear of death. She never wanted to talk about it." And then there is Yiannis Devetzis, who on Callas' last evening spoke by phone with her and found her "very upbeat because she had lost weight" and "full of plans." He, too, is convinced she did not commit suicide.

John Ardoin is another friend who doesn't believe she died on purpose: "I don't think that for a second, because I don't think she would have wanted anything to have gone to either her family or Meneghini. She would have prepared better if she had designed her death. But I think she gave up on life and that contributed to her death. Onassis was the whole meaning in her life and after his death she felt there was no point in going on."

Because no will was found among Maria's possessions (although a number of friends say she had spoken to them about taking care of Bruna and Ferruccio and setting up a foundation to encourage young singers), Callas was considered to have died intestate, her only beneficiaries her mother and sister. Then, on October 18, 1977, before the passage of the forty days that the Orthodox church believes necessary for the soul's migration to paradise, Battista Meneghini turned up in Paris accompanied by a lawyer and clutching a will that Maria had written and signed in 1954 that left everything to her husband. (In *My Wife Maria Callas,* he describes a series of almost supernatural coincidences which led him to find this piece of paper in a deceased former lawyer's messy files—beginning with an alleged dream in which Maria said to him three times, "Battista, remember the will.")

Meneghini, who never ceased hoping for Maria's return, had suffered a serious heart attack on May 1, 1977. Four months later, he was still convalescing at his home in Sirmione when his housekeeper, Emma Brutti Roverselli, called his doctor to the house to inform Battista of Maria's death. The physician refused to give permission for him to travel to the funeral, so Meneghini tried to send Emma in his place, but when she phoned Bruna, she was told not to come: "It is not possible to see the body. Try to remember her as she was in life." A month later Battista had managed to locate the twenty-three-year-old will and to convince the doctor he was well enough to go to Paris.

Since the Italian courts did not then recognize divorce, Meneghini presented himself as her only heir. As a result, the French authorities sealed off the rooms of her apartment with wires and gray legal seals, which meant that Bruna and Ferruccio were confined to the servants' quarters. Nadia Stancioff, who visited at this time, described a poignant scene: "Bruna looked older and lifeless. In her arms she cradled a trembling Pixie, whose cataract-covered eyes blankly searched my face for recognition. . . . We stood in the bare entrance talking. After a few moments Bruna sat down on the black-and-white marble floor and motioned me to join her. 'I'm sorry I can't offer you a chair,' she said, 'but I can't take you in there.' "

After Meneghini's arrival, Vasso Devetzi immediately summoned Jackie Callas back to Paris from Athens. Jackie and her mother signed over to Vasso their power of attorney, giving her control of the fate of Maria's work, including her recordings, and also Maria's *droit moral*—the right under the Napoleonic Code to protect one's reputation, which passes to the next of kin upon death.

A short while later Meneghini capitulated and agreed to meet and discuss a settlement, and Jackie was called back to Paris again. On that visit, she learned to her astonishment "that Bruna and Ferruccio had never been given a regular income. Maria had fed and housed them, sent small sums to their families in Italy, given them gifts from time to time and that was it. . . . There, so near, were those cupboards filled to bursting point with silks and furs and here was Bruna with only the clothes she stood up in. Amazingly, she didn't seem to mind."

In the end, Meneghini and Maria's mother and sister agreed to a fifty-fifty split of the $8 million estate with an award of $500,000 each for Bruna and Ferruccio. Jackie also agreed to Vasso's suggestion that they set up a foundation to help young singers, and make Devetzi the director.

Jackie would return again to Paris on January 6, 1978, to divide the movables in Maria's apartment. The heavier items—furniture, pictures, rugs, and so on—would be auctioned off later and the proceeds shared like the rest of the estate.

"We all met at the apartment," Jackie wrote, "Vasso and myself on one side, Meneghini on the other, though by then it was all perfectly amicable.

Meneghini had brought Signora Roverselli, the maid I had met on that visit to his home near Lake Garda, and his notary." (Signora Roverselli looked after Meneghini until his death in January 1981 and then became his heir and thus a half owner of all Maria's royalties and the proceeds from her estate.)

Jackie describes in her book, *Sisters,* the bizarre partition of Maria's possessions that ensued. "We wandered round, not unlike naughty children in a parents' bedroom. . . . We opened cupboards and pulled out drawers, fascinated by the sheer quantity of things, often still in the wrappers they were bought in. . . . Eventually Vasso came to tell me that . . . the jewellery that had been bought during the Meneghini era would revert to him, that of the Onassis period would be Mother's and mine. Everything else would be simply divided into two halves and parcelled up. . . . Everything seemed, inexplicably, to be in two hundreds—two hundred blouses, two hundred pairs of shoes, two hundred silk nightgowns."

In the end, according to Jackie, "Piled high were one hundred and ninety-four large parcels—ninety-seven for Meneghini and ninety-seven for the family. Vasso said she would take our share to her apartment for safekeeping and the jewels would all be sent to the Union de Banques Suisses in Geneva." Some time later, Jackie wrote, when she and her mother came to Paris and asked for their parcels, Vasso delivered only seven. When pressed for the other ninety she said that Meneghini must have driven off with them, according to Jackie.

Nevertheless, in June of 1978 Jackie Callas transferred $300,000 to Vasso to establish the Maria Callas Foundation. The final sum, delivered incrementally, she says, amounted to approximately $1,250,000.

(The foundation was formally established in 1980, with Vasso serving as president. Since her death in 1987, it has been headed by the Greek publisher Christos Lambrakis. The goal of the foundation, according to Kostas Pylarinos, its vice president, is to promote Maria's legacy, to provide scholarships to talented music students under a fund established in Maria's name and to recognize new talent in opera through the Maria Callas Awards, which were initiated in 1986. Among the artists so honored early in their careers have been the sopranos Aprile Millo and Anne-Sophie von Otter and the baritones Thomas Hampson and Paata Burchuladze. The foundation has also organized celebrations of Maria's career on her sixtieth and seventieth birthdays in Europe in 1983 and 1993 and on the tenth and twentieth anniversaries of her death in 1987 and 1997 in Athens.)

At Vasso's suggestion, Jackie also bought out Meneghini's half interest in the Paris apartment, for $420,000, and then handed over to Devetzi for safekeeping the bearer shares representing both halves of the apartment. Much later, according to Jackie, Vasso sent her a check for $80,000, saying that the rest had gone for estate taxes.

In a macabre twist, the urn holding Maria's ashes mysteriously vanished from the vaults of Père Lachaise cemetery on the day after Christmas in 1978, leading to Vasso Devetzi's appearance on television to plead for its return. When the urn was found the next day in a random corner of the cemetery, Devetzi decided the ashes would be safer in a bank vault.

More of Maria's relics were dispersed on Wednesday, June 14, 1978, when the furniture, statues, paintings, rugs, and even the Steinway piano from her apartment were sold at auction at the Hôtel George V in Paris. Many who attended the public auction had the distinct impression of Callas' presence in the hotel. According to John Ardoin, despite the still, airless summer day, a pair of tall doors from a hallway suddenly burst open, knocking over and breaking a commode and hurling a painting to the floor. Then, as the auction commenced, a runner held up a mirrored tray and the glass shattered unaccountably, with a sound like a rifle shot. As her cherished possessions were graveled away to the highest bidder, one could not help imagining that Maria was unhappy with the proceedings.

Ardoin was among those vying for such treasures as her seventeenth- and eighteenth-century Italian paintings, ancient Chinese vases, and the Rococo painted Venetian furniture of her boudoir, as was Battista Meneghini. Bidding frantically, he told the press, "I came here to save my memories." His acquisitions included the eighteenth-century marriage bed on which Maria had died. Ardoin told me, "He bought more than two hundred thousand dollars' worth of things, saying he intended to set up a museum on Maria's career at Sirmione, which of course he never did. I didn't buy anything."

The final scene of Grand Guignol took place a year later, on June 3, 1979, when Vasso Devetzi removed Callas' ashes from the bank vault and took them in a box to Greece. She had coaxed permission from the Greek government to conduct a ceremony during which the ashes would be scattered from a naval destroyer into the Aegean Sea under the auspices of the Greek Ministry of Culture.

The best description of Maria's final disposition was given by Jackie Callas, who came again to represent the family: "I wasn't at all sure about this; it seemed too far from what Maria would have wanted, just like the cremation itself. . . . If asked, I am certain she would have wanted to be buried beside Ari but it is unlikely the family would have agreed to such a thing."

The actual casting of the ashes into the sea as Jackie describes it was as dramatic as any scene from Maria's life:

The warship bucked and heaved in a brisk Aegean swell and the wind howled in the turret. It was evident to me that Maria definitely did not approve of this business. . . . Vasso held the casket, that same grim box that had so upset me in the cold vault. . . . She handed it to the minister [of culture, Dimitris Nanias] and for a moment they both wrestled with the lid. The priest intoned a prayer and then the minister approached the rail and tipped the contents over the side. Precisely at that moment, the worst gust of wind of the whole day blew in from the sea and just as Maria's fluffy grey ashes left the receptacle they were instantly blown back over us all. Vasso received most of the fine powder full in her face, and as she had her mouth wide open in order to catch her breath in the driving spray, a great deal went straight down her throat. She began to splutter and retch. Indeed we all got some in the face and mouth and were forced to spit and cough it up. The wind howled in the turret. The ship's horn was sounded in mournful tribute, though it appeared more like the moan of an anguished spirit. Rubbing my lips with my handkerchief I looked around at the illustrious party and realised that we were all swallowing Maria's remains. We were helplessly eating my sister; the greatest diva of the century was being consumed by those who had thought to placate her spirit.

At the beginning of her career Maria had described herself as very fortunate and favored by God, but near the end she said to John Ardoin, "There are people born to be happy and people born to be unhappy. I am just not lucky." If she would have been displeased by the public sale of her belongings, she would have raged about the people chosen as her heirs—the beneficiaries of all the wealth her recordings and her image would generate after her death. As John Ardoin explained to me, "The estate was split between her mother and sister and her ex-husband, Meneghini. When he died he left it to his housekeeper, and when she died she left it to her nephew. So Maria's money today goes to her sister, which she would have hated, and to the nephew of her ex-husband's housekeeper, which she would have hated even more. Maria's ashes are spinning in the Aegean somewhere."

Battista Meneghini died in January of 1981. Maria's mother, Evangelia, died August 20, 1982, at the age of eighty-three. Maria's sister, Jackie, married Dr. Andreas Stathopoulos, twenty-four years her junior, on December 16, 1983, and they now live in an Athens apartment filled with Callas memorabilia. Vasso Devetzi died of a heart attack in 1987 at sixty-two.

Onassis, unlike Maria, had the foresight to leave a detailed will, but a part of his estate, too, was disposed of in a manner completely contrary to what he

Maria's ashes being tossed into the Aegean in a hard wind

would have wanted. He had spent his life and all his energy trying to establish and protect the world's largest shipping fortune for the benefit of his son. After Alexander died, Ari tried to safeguard the family empire for his daughter, Christina, by making sure in his will that Jackie Kennedy Onassis would inherit no more than their prenuptial agreement dictated.

When Onassis died, according to former aides, he left assets valued at more than $1 billion, including $426 million in cash and securities; fifty-seven ships; a half interest in the Olympic Tower in New York; five other prized real estate properties on the same block, including the Cartier building; the Banque de Depot in Switzerland and other holdings in half a dozen countries; as well as the island of Skorpios. His outstanding liabilities totaled almost $421 million, mostly bank loans on the ships. The net value of his estate, therefore, was estimated at more than $500 million on the basis of 1975 market prices for the ships and real estate, according to Stelios Papadimitriou, who came to head the foundation Onassis established in memory of his son.

The estate was then divided into two equal lots, A and B, and Christina, the only surviving child of Onassis, was allowed to choose which one she wanted, Papadimitriou told me. She chose Lot B, and Lot A was assigned to the Alexander S. Onassis Public Benefit Foundation.

The management of both lots had been assigned by Onassis in his will to the directors of the foundation, perhaps because he didn't trust his daughter to administer it wisely, but Christina, showing that she was her father's daughter, immediately moved to gain control of her portion and eventually prevailed in the Greek courts.

Christina then turned her attention to her father's widow. A month after Onassis' death, on April 18, 1975, the *New York Times* reported that Onassis had been trying to divorce his wife, using Roy Cohn as his lawyer. Jackie immediately called Christina in Monte Carlo and within four days the *Times* ran another story headlined: MISS ONASSIS DENIES HER FATHER PLANNED DIVORCE.

A few days later, Christina and Jackie flew separately to Skorpios to attend the traditional Greek Orthodox service held on the fortieth day after a death, when the soul is presumed to arrive in paradise. Jackie took advantage of the occasion to remove her personal effects from the island as well as a priceless jade Buddha from the yacht; Christina, who didn't want to disturb Jackie until her claims to the Onassis estate were settled, let her take it with her.

Three months later, Jackie made an effort to show family unity by flying to Glyfada to attend Christina's wedding and announcing to reporters, "I so love that child. At last I can see happy days ahead for her."

Aside from that public relations effort, Jackie and Christina avoided each other's company while their lawyers thrashed out a settlement between them over Ari's estate. Although Onassis had specified that his widow was to receive $200,000 a year for life, Christina feared her stepmother might challenge the provision and sue for the 12.5 percent of the estate that she, as the surviving spouse, would have customarily received under Greek law despite her having waived the right. Christina told Papadimitriou to begin negotiations with Jackie's attorney, Simon Rifkind, and they eventually reached a settlement of $26 million. (I disclosed this settlement in an article for the *New York Times* on September 20, 1977—the first story I wrote when I was sent by the paper to Athens as its correspondent in the eastern Mediterranean.) The settlement surprised Onassis associates because Jackie could have received more than twice that amount had she turned to the Greek courts.

After Onassis' death, his widow returned permanently to New York City and became a working editor for Doubleday. She began a relationship with Maurice Tempelsman, a wealthy, married diamond merchant who helped her invest the money she had received from the Onassis estate. Despite the hostile negotiations with Christina, Jackie remained friends with Onassis' sister Artemis, who died in 1984, and occasionally visited her former sister-in-law's home in Glyfada during trips to Greece. But when she was invited to join the board of the Alexander S. Onassis Foundation, she declined, according to its president, Stelios Papadimitriou.

When Jackie died of cancer on May 19, 1994, at the age of sixty-four, she left an estate estimated at more than $200 million. (Two years later, Sotheby's auctioned off 1,195 lots from the estate of Jacqueline Kennedy Onassis, including many gifts Onassis had given her, such as the "moon landing" earrings. The auction brought in an additional $34,461,495 for her two children.)

After the original settlement with Jackie, Christina turned her attention to her father's nemesis, Stavros Niarchos, with a fervor worthy of her family name. Niarchos argued that since Tina had left no will, as Tina's last husband, he was entitled to 75 percent of her estate, then valued at $77 million, but Christina fought him and he settled for only 17.5 percent, according to her former aides. "Onassis always thought that Alexander was most like him and should run his empire after he died, but Christina had much more of her father in her when it came to business," Stelios Papadimitriou told me.

"When her personal life was stable, she could be very sharp," commented Nicholas Papanikolaou, who worked closely with Christina in New York, "but when things went wrong for her in her private life, it was hard to get her to focus on business."

Unfortunately, she was much less astute in her romantic affairs, a weakness that not only distracted her from running the family empire but also left her vulnerable to the kind of fortune hunters her father had feared would prey on her. Christina parted from the man to whom she was betrothed beside her father's deathbed, the shipping heir Peter Goulandris, and took up with the scion of a Greek banking family, Alexander Andreadis. She married him an impolitic four weeks after their first meeting and only three months after her father's death. Fifteen months later the marriage was over and Christina was involved with the man who would be her next husband, a Russian bureaucrat (and rumored KGB operative) named Sergei Kausov. She married him in a Moscow "wedding palace" on August 1, 1978, but the Soviet capital proved too much for Christina and she was soon back on Skorpios. She gave Kausov a tanker as part of his divorce settlement. In March of 1983 she married Thierry Roussel, the heir to a French pharmaceutical fortune. They wed at the Paris town hall and celebrated afterward with a dinner at Maxim's for 125 guests.

Roussel, who suffered heavy losses trying to start his own business career, became the father of Christina's only child and Aristotle's only grandchild. Athina (named for her maternal grandmother) was born on January 28, 1985, in the American Hospital in Paris, where her grandfather had died ten years before. But Christina soon learned that her husband had also impregnated his mistress, a Swedish model named Gaby Landhage, with a child—their second together—who was born shortly after Athina. Roussel and Christina divorced in May of 1987.

Christina Onassis died in November of 1988 in Buenos Aires at the age of thirty-seven, from "acute pulmonary edema of the lung which had produced a heart attack." An edema is often the result of an overdose of barbiturates, and this was the same description given for her mother's death. Although friends were well aware of Christina's lifelong use of barbiturates and amphetamines and her wild weight fluctuations, no precise cause of the edema was ever determined. Upon Christina's death, her three-year-old daughter, Athina, the last direct descendant of Aristotle Onassis, became the sole heir to the Onassis fortune.

Roussel took the child to live with him and Gaby and their (by now) three children in Switzerland. They proceeded to launch a legal battle in both Swiss and Greek courts to wrest supervisory control of Christina's estate from the directors of the Alexander S. Onassis Public Benefit Foundation. The Swiss court ruled in 1999 that supervision of the estate should be taken over by a Swiss fiduciary company, KPMG Fides in Lucerne, and the foundation complied. Athina is scheduled to receive direct control of her inheritance, currently some $800 million, when she turns eighteen on January 28, 2003.

At least part of Onassis' bequest has been fulfilled—the Alexander S. Onassis Public Benefit Foundation has disbursed $250 million in his son's memory since its inception in 1975. Some of these funds ($80 million) were used to build a state-of-the-art hospital for heart diseases in Athens, and the rest to provide more than two thousand merit scholarships and fellowships for Greek students to pursue postgraduate studies abroad, to offer grants to non-Greek scholars to study in Greece, to fund modern Greek studies chairs in Europe and the United States, to support Greek communities in Eastern Europe, to finance international competitions in the arts every four years, and to award international prizes valued at $250,000 every two years for lifetime achievement in cultural, environmental, and social endeavors to individuals from around the world.

The other half of the Onassis empire, however, will be turned over in 2003 to his only grandchild, Athina, who will then likely be the richest teenager in the world. When she comes of age at twenty-one, Athina will probably attempt to become head of the foundation, as her mother was until her death, but this is certain to be resisted by its board, since, contrary to the terms of Christina's will, the girl has not been taught to speak Greek or to worship in the Greek Orthodox church, nor has she been allowed to spend time alone with her Greek family.

More recently, Roussel has made an effort to improve relations with

The author with Athina, Onassis' granddaughter and only heir,
and her father (left), Thierry Roussel, as Athina greets a guest
at the wedding of her second cousin in 1999

Athina's Greek relatives. Over the past two years he has brought his daughter to several Onassis family gatherings, including the marriage of her second cousin, George Drakos, on August 3, 1999, which I also attended at the invitation of the groom's family. (Drakos is the son of Marilena Patronikola, the daughter of Onassis' sister Kalliroe.) I was introduced to the attractive, willowy, and strikingly timid fourteen-year-old at this event and watched as she chatted in French with her grandfather's two aged half sisters and a number of her cousins. She rarely left her father's side, and whenever they are seen in public, she cowers fearfully behind him.

Though Skorpios is kept fully staffed and ready in case Athina chooses to go there to visit the graves of her mother, her uncle Alexander, her great-aunt Artemis, and her grandfather Aristotle, the girl has only visited her island kingdom twice in the last four years. "The only direct descendant of Aristotle Onassis is being raised in total ignorance of the language, history, and culture that were such a part of who he was and that he valued so much that he gave half his fortune to help promote them," laments Stelios Papadimitriou, still head of the foundation's board.

Maria's recordings are now supporting her sister and the nephew of her ex-husband's housekeeper, and Onassis' beloved island paradise stands permanently ready for a granddaughter who doesn't visit it. There is no child left to light a candle to honor the memory of either Onassis or Callas. Jackie Callas ended her book about Maria with these words: "She always told me she longed for children." It was Aristo and Maria's shared tragedy that the one child resulting from their love died the day he was born. If a novelist had invented their history, he would be accused of ladling on the irony with too heavy a hand.

Almost everyone who knew them felt that Onassis and Callas were fated to be together, that each was the great love of the other's life; yet though Maria realized this from the beginning of their affair, Onassis didn't understand it until it was too late. As Papadimitriou explained it, "Callas was madly in love with Onassis and gave herself totally to him. Onassis loved her but did not give himself completely to her, or to anyone else, for that matter. Onassis loved, but he never fell in love. He had the oriental view that a real man does not allow himself to be conquered by love. Maria, on the other hand, flooded Onassis with her love, surrendered totally, even after he abandoned her for Jackie."

When, after he married Jacqueline Kennedy, a crippling series of setbacks convinced Onassis that his happiness could only be found with Maria, fate and ill health blocked him from freeing himself to spend his last years with her. Their love affair was a modern version of the ancient tragedies in which the protagonist, doomed by fatal ignorance, realizes in the end that he has brought upon himself an inexorable fate that will destroy him.

When Onassis decided that the gods had turned against him, he lost the will to fight. When he died, Maria, too, lost her purpose in living, withdrew into herself, and gave up. The tragedy of their relationship was that Onassis failed to recognize until too late that he and Maria were meant to be together, like the two halves of the same soul described by Aristophanes in Plato's *Symposium:* "This becoming one instead of two, was the very expression of an ancient need," Plato wrote, "and the reason is that human nature was originally one and we were a whole, and the desire and pursuit of the whole is called love."

In the end such happiness evaded Onassis and Callas. But it is not impossible to imagine that after Maria's remains were consigned to the sea, the tides of the Aegean carried those ashes in a southerly direction, around Cape Sounion, below the cliff crowned by the temple to Poseidon, through the Corinth Canal, where the yacht *Christina* passed so often, to the Gulf of Corinth and into the Ionian Sea. In a world where the winds and tides brought Odysseus home to Ithaca after ten years of wandering, it's not hard to envision the last relics of Maria Callas finally coming to rest on the green shores of Skorpios, still flowering with the oleander and jasmine that she and Aristo brought there from the Caribbean. In the birthplace of myths, legends, and mysteries, it is not difficult to suppose that her ashes might even have washed up on the sands of their private cove, below the white chapel to the Virgin where Aristotle Onassis lies. In a land where love is immortal although the body is not, it's even possible to imagine that on this island, completing the journey they began in 1959, they are finally together and at peace.

> *Keep Ithaca always in mind.*
> *Arriving there is what you are destined for. . . .*
> *And if you find her poor, Ithaca won't have fooled you.*
> *Wise as you will have become, so full of experience,*
> *you will have understood by then what these Ithacas mean.*

Acknowledgments

This story of Maria Callas and Aristotle Onassis was written with the help and in some instances the literary collaboration of my wife, Joan Paulson Gage, whose insight, critical judgment, and support were as important to me as her assistance. I'm grateful to her as well as to my editor, George Andreou, and my agent, Joni Evans, for their help and encouragement.

I want to express my gratitude also to the relatives, friends, and associates of both Aristotle Onassis and Maria Callas who agreed to be interviewed, many for the first time, for this book. They include Onassis' sisters, Merope Konialidis and Kalliroe Patronikola; his niece, Marilena Patronikola; his former brother-in-law, George S. Livanos; his former son-in-law, Alexander Andreadis; his legal adviser and the last manager of his shipping operations, Stelios Papadimitriou, now president of the Alexander S. Onassis Public Benefit Foundation; his special assistant and intelligence chief, Miltos Yiannakopoulos; his physician, Dr. Isadore Rosenfeld; the captain of the *Christina,* Kostas Anastasiades, and his wife, Genevieve, who tutored Onassis' children; the *Christina*'s chief engineer, Stefanos Darousos; the ship's alternate captain, Panayiotis Zigomalas; Onassis' Smyrna classmate George Katramopoulos; his houseman, Panayiotis Konidiaris; Onassis' friend Lilika Papanikolaou, and her son, Nicholas, who served as an executive in his New York office; his and Callas' physical therapist, Korinna Spanidou; his press aide at Olympic Airways, Helen Speronis; his wife's friends Reinaldo Herrera, Peggy Scott Duff Kertess, and Vivi Crespi; his son's friends Constantin and Nikos Vernikos; and especially his guests on the fateful 1959 cruise when he and Maria fell in love, Anthony Montague Browne, Lady Sargant (the former Nonie Montague Browne), and Winston Churchill's granddaughter Celia Sandys Perkins.

I'm equally indebted to three close friends of Onassis' who are no longer with us: Costa Gratsos, director of Onassis' U.S. operations and his confidant since his early days in Argentina, whom I visited regularly in the early 1970s in his New York office at the Olympic Towers to sip ouzo and listen to his colorful and often ribald tales of his adventures with Onassis; his Athens friend and adviser, Yiannis Giorgakis, with whom I lunched at least once a week during the years I was the *New York Times* correspondent there and on every visit to Greece afterward until his death in 1994; and the great Greek actor and director Alexis Minotis, one of Onassis' favorite companions on his late-night visits to the *bouzoukia,* who became my close friend after I interviewed him for the *Times* in 1976. As a Greek-born journalist, I was often asked to write articles about Onassis, so I recorded whatever his friends told me about the tycoon in my notebooks after our conversations. Their recollections and insights proved invaluable in the writing of this book and I deeply regret that I can't convey to them my appreciation. *Eonia tous e mnimin.*

On Maria Callas' side, I am grateful to her close friend Mary Reed Mead Carter, who spent long hours with me in New York, Newport, and Cuernavaca recalling her journeys, misadventures, and conversations with Maria; the noted mezzo-soprano Giulietta Simionato, Callas' colleague and confidante, who trusted me enough to reveal for the first time important secrets about Callas' personal life; Kostas Pylarinos, Maria's adviser, friend, and host during her last summer in Greece; his wife, Vicky Anthopoulou, who related to me the recollections of her aunt, Maria's close friend Vasso Devetzi; the critic John Ardoin, Maria's friend in good times and bad, whose personal help and published works on Callas were invaluable to me; Nicola Rescigno, who conducted some of Maria's most successful performances; Sue Blair and David Stickelbar, Maria's companions during the first part of her 1968 odyssey through the western United States; Yiannis Devetzis, who talked to her the night before she died; her loyal friend in Paris, the diplomat François Valéry; her friends in Italy, Biki Bouyeure, Carla Verga, and Giovanna Lomazzi; and her Greek friends Amalia Karamanlis Megapanou, Prince Michael of Greece, and his wife, Marina Karella.

I also want to thank Callas' former leading man, the tenor Giuseppe di Stefano, who spent several hours with me candidly recounting both his personal and his professional relationship with Maria; her sister, Jackie Callas Stathopoulos, who told me about Maria's early life in New York and Athens during several interviews; Jackie's husband, Dr. Andreas Stathopoulos, who let me study and copy important documents that came into their possession after Maria's death; and Nikos Petsalis-Diomidis, who generously shared with me information he collected about Maria's early career in Greece for his forthcoming book, *The Unknown Callas.*

I am especially grateful to Maria's loyal attendants, Bruna Lupoli and Ferruccio Mezzadri, who broke their silence for the first time and agreed to answer my questions (through an intermediary in the case of Bruna) about their famous employer and friend as they watched her from a close and privileged perspective.

Finally, I want to thank my friends Fabrizio Cerina, Sylvie Rais, and Susan Williams for serving as guides, researchers, translators, and wise counselors for me in Milan, Paris, and Rome, respectively, and Andreas Fryganas, the Greek consul in Smyrna (now Izmir), the birthplace of Onassis, for helping me research the tycoon's early life.

Many of the people mentioned above—including Mary Carter, the Montague Brownes, Celia Sandys Perkins, Captain Kostas, Marilena Patronikola, Maria's sister, Jackie, and Jackie's husband, Andreas, Stelios Papadimitriou, Reinaldo Herrera, John Ardoin—and others who don't want to be singled out, generously gave of their time, recollections, and personal interest, even searching their diaries, letters, and logbooks to help fill in details about the history of Callas and Onassis. Their help was a great gift to me. Without it I would never have uncovered the facts about these lovers disclosed in this book, which reveal them as both human in their failings and extraordinary in their strengths.

Notes

Most of the sources for my information are mentioned in the text itself. In the following notes I am providing information that I could not include in the main text. Publishing information on the works cited in the notes can be found in the bibliography.

Foreword

PAGE

xiv "During the ten years . . .": Attila Csampai, *Callas,* p. 11

xx "Only my dogs will not betray me": Quoted by Arianna Stassinopoulos in her biography of Callas, *Maria: Beyond the Callas Legend,* and corroborated to me by John Ardoin, the noted music critic and friend of Callas'.

xvi The 1960 loss of the parakeet is reported in Anthony Montague Browne's memoir, *Long Sunset,* page 312. Churchill was playing bezique with Montague Browne and Toby was strutting about the room, chattering away, when the bird was startled and flew out an open window. Churchill and Onassis offered large rewards for his return but he was never seen again. Two years later, in June of 1962, in the very same suite, Churchill fell, breaking his hip and beginning his long descent into death. He elicited a promise from Montague Browne: "Remember, I want to die in England. Promise me that you will see to it." On the journey back, Churchill, despite being heavily sedated, made one remark: "I don't think I'll go back to that place. It's unlucky. First Toby and then this."

xxi The disclosure about the son born to Maria in 1960 is based on documents that come from Callas' private papers and from official files in archives of the city of Milan and from interviews with individuals who knew about the birth, including her maid, Bruna Lupoli.

1 *The Last Deal*

4 Details of Aristotle Onassis' last trip to Paris are based on interviews with his lawyer, Stelios Papadimitriou; his doctor, Isadore Rosenfeld; his houseman, Panayiotis

Konidiaris; his associate, Nicholas Papanikolaou; and Maria's butler, Ferruccio Mezzadri, as well as articles from Greek, French, and American newspapers.

2 *A Meeting in Venice*

9   Background information on Elsa Maxwell is drawn from her autobiography, *R.S.V.P.,* and her *New York Times* obituary.

12 Information about the 1957 Venice ball where Callas and Onassis met is based on Elsa Maxwell's own columns in the *New York Journal-American* and other articles in Italian and American newspapers.

14 Onassis told friends, including Yiannis Giorgakis and Alexis Minotis, about his first meeting with Maria, and she also recounted the story to several friends, including Mary Carter.

3 *The Rules of the Game*

17 The background on the marriage of Tina and Aristotle Onassis is based on interviews with several of their friends and relatives, including his half sisters, Merope Konialidis and Kalliroe Patronikolas; his legal adviser, Stelios Papadrimitriou; Tina's brother, George Livanos; and Tina's former lover Reinaldo Herrera.

23 "In business, we cut each other's throats": Joachim Joesten, *Onassis: A Biography,* p. 42.

26 Onassis told the story of his assignation with Eva Perón often, and it is recounted in several books about him, including *Ari,* by Peter Evans.

4 *Life at the Top*

29 My account of Maria's first visit to Dallas is based on interviews with Mary Carter and from published accounts.

30 Elsa Maxwell's unrequited passion for Maria is described in her letters to the singer, copies of which I have obtained.

32 Maria's problems with her career in 1957 and 1958 are based on newspaper and magazine articles from the period; on statements made by her husband, Giovanni Battista Meneghini, in his memoir, *My Wife Maria Callas;* on interviews with her friends, including Giulietta Simionato; and on discussions with music critics and opera scholars, including John Ardoin.

38 "I am a passionate artist . . .": Renzo and Alberto Allegri, *Callas by Callas,* p. 74.

46 Maria's growing disenchantment with her husband was described to me by her friends Giovanna Lomazzi, Mary Carter, and Biki Bouyeure.

5 *Weighing Anchor*

54 The account of the first meeting of Onassis and Churchill has been related in several books, including Montague Browne's *Long Sunset,* and two biographies of Onassis: *Ari: The Life and Times of Aristotle Onassis,* by Peter Evans, and *Onassis: A Report Without an End,* by Willi Frischauer.

55 The gathering of guests for the 1959 cruise is based on recollections of several participants, including Nonie (now Lady Sargant) and Anthony Montague Browne and Celia Sandys, as well as crew members, including Captain Kostas Anastasiades and the chief engineer, Stefanos Darousos.

57   The description and history of the *Christina* is based on information provided by its captain, Kostas Anastasiades, and on several visits to the yacht I made while it was being restored in Greek shipyards during 1999.

6 *Cities on a Hill*

63   The account of the activities on board the *Christina* as it set out on the cruise and the tour of Portofino are based on interviews with surviving passengers and crew members, including Nonie Montague Browne (now Lady Sargant), Celia Sandys, Anthony Montague Browne, Kostas Anastasiades, and Stefanos Darousos.

66   Maria's close friend Giulietta Simionato and her sister, Jackie Callas, confirmed that the major reason for her dramatic weight loss was a tapeworm that she voluntarily ingested.

71   "In Monte Carlo, where the cruise began": Quoted by Stelios Galatopoulos in *Maria Callas: Sacred Monster,* p. 406.

7 *Passage to Delphi*

81   The details of Maria's childhood in New York and youth in Athens are based on recollections offered by Callas herself in several newspaper and magazine interviews; on interviews with her sister, Jackie; and on accounts provided by her friends, relatives, and neighbors in Athens, collected by the Callas scholar Nicholas Petsalis-Diomidis.

     Petsalis, fifty-six, is an art dealer and historian who lives in a neoclassical villa in the Athens suburb of Kifissia. In 1990 Petsalis sold his art gallery to concentrate all his energy on researching Maria Callas' years in Greece. (In one of those coincidences that would never be allowed in a work of fiction, his wife was born in Argentina, her name was Lydia Onassis, and her grandfather was Alexander Onassis, the beloved uncle of Aristotle, who was hanged by the Turks in 1922.)

     Petsalis' home and gardens contain many paintings and statues of Callas, and the basement is a virtual museum to her: here, her clothing, shoes, coats, furs, dresses, lingerie, photographs, handwritten notes, and sheet music, as well as voluminous files of documents pertaining to her, are displayed and archived. Petsalis, who says he bought his Callas memorabilia from Maria's sister, even has a jar that contains a large hank of Maria's hair, cut off when Onassis convinced her that she would look better with a short bob.

     Of all the Callas devotees in Greece, Petsalis is certainly the most scholarly, and he has exhaustively chronicled the years Maria spent in Athens until she sailed to the United States in 1945 at the age of twenty-one in his book *I Agnosti Kallas* (The Unknown Callas), which will be published by Amadeus Press in the spring of 2001.

90   "More than her artistic talent . . .": Quoted by Willi Frischauer in his authorized biography, *Onassis,* p. 217.

97   The description of the dinner at Anavisos for the Greek prime minister was provided by his former wife, Amalia Karamanlis Megapanou, Anthony Montague Browne, and the former Mrs. Montague Browne.

100   "Don't ever believe . . .": Quoted by Nadia Stancioff in *Maria Callas Remembered,* p. 144.

8 *Dinner for Two*

103   "If you can't trust . . .": From a recorded interview with Maria made by John Ardoin.

105   The descriptions of the various stops of the *Christina* in the Cyclades Islands are based on interviews with surviving passengers and crew members cited previously.

107 The background of Artemis Garofalidis recounted here is based on information provided by her half sister, Merope Konialidis, and her niece, Marilena Patronikola.

111 The history of Stavros Livanos is derived from information provided by his son, George, and by Greek shipowners who knew him.

112 "In a thousand months . . .": Quoted by Nicholas Fraser, Philip Jacobson, Mark Ottaway, and Lewis Chester of the *London Sunday Times* in their book *Onassis,* p. 80.

9 *Visions of Smyrna*

117 Sources for the tribulations of the Onassis family during the Smyrna holocaust include Ari's half sisters, Merope and Kalliroe; his niece, Marilena Patronikola; his grandniece Monica Onassis de Arizu; his classmate George Katramopoulos; and published interviews with Onassis himself. He was not always truthful in the details he provided, however, so I have used only information I could verify through independent sources.

127 "You told me, Sir Winston . . .": This conversation is reported by Churchill's physician in his published diaries, Charles Moran, *Churchill: Taken from the Diaries of Lord Moran,* p. 818.

128 "Mademoiselle, you are indecently . . .": Fraser et al., *Onassis,* p. 11. Onassis told several friends about his youthful sexual exploits, and some of the tales have been recounted by his biographers, including Peter Evans and Willi Frischauer.

130 "Although he was getting out of life . . .": Quoted in Galatopoulos, *Maria Callas: Sacred Monster,* p. 407.

10 *At the Crossroads*

134 The events in Istanbul are based on eyewitness accounts from surviving passengers and crew members who have been previously cited and on reports published in Turkish newspapers, especially *Hurriyet.*

143 In addition to Mary Carter and Nadia Stancioff, the friends with whom Callas later discussed the visit to Istanbul included Giovanna Lomazzi and Vasso Devetzi.

145 "It was as if a fire was devouring them both": Arianna Stassinopoulos, *Maria: Beyond the Callas Legend,* p. 176.

146 The quotations from Plato's *Symposium* are from a translation by Benjamin Jowett.

11 *The Journey Back*

150 The difficulties Onassis encountered upon his arrival in Athens and his trip to Constantinople to try to free his father were described to me by his half sister Merope, his niece Marilena Patronikola, and several friends from that period, including the actor and director Alexis Minotis. I conducted interviews with him in the 1970s for the *New York Times* when he was executive director of the Greek National Theater.

152 "You know how it is, people forget quickly . . .": Evans, *Ari,* p. 46.

12 *Pas de Quatre*

163 The major sources for this chapter are the diaries of Giovanni Battista Meneghini; his memoir, *My Wife Maria Callas;* private letters from Meneghini and Callas that I obtained; Italian, Monegasque, and American newspapers; and interviews with

Reinaldo Herrera and Peggy Kertess, who were witnesses to many of the events described.

170   "Did you forget to feed your dog": The comment was told to me by Peggy Kertess.

13 *Going Public*

185   "To the disappointment of her Spanish audience . . .": *Time,* September 21, 1959, p. 58.

186   Information on Maria's conflict with her mother came from Maria's sister, Jackie Callas Stathopoulos; her colleague and friend Giulietta Simionato; and from letters she wrote to her godfather, Dr. Leonidas Lantzounis.

188   The account of Maria's separation hearing in Brescia is taken from contemporary Italian newspapers and from Stancioff, *Maria Callas Remembered.*

14 *The Secret Son*

197   Most of this chapter is based on documents from Maria Callas' private papers that I was able to obtain. I confirmed the authenticity of the papers through individuals who saw them shortly after Callas' death on September 16, 1977.

198   "I have news, Ari . . .": Terrence McNally, *Master Class,* Act II, Scene 1.

"At first I couldn't believe he was serious": Stancioff, *Maria Callas Remembered,* p. 161.

199   "Unable to conceal his tears . . .": Galatopoulos, *Maria Callas: Sacred Monster,* p. 405.

207   "the book of remembrances she wanted to write . . .": Vasilis Vasilikos, *To Sfrato* (The Eviction). The selections quoted were translated into English by me.

15 *The Good Years*

215   The early years of Maria's relationship with Ari are drawn from the recollections of eyewitnesses, including friends and employees of both of them and relatives of Onassis. They include his half sisters, Merope Konialidis and Kalliroe Patronikolas; her sister, Jackie Callas; his niece Marilena Patronikola; the captain and the chief engineer of the *Christina,* Kostas Anastasiades and Stefanos Darousos; their physical therapist, Korinna Spanidou; and his friends Yiannis Giorgakis, Alexis Minotis, and Costa Gratsos, with whom I talked often about Onassis and Callas before their deaths.

225   "In this case Aristo is the lucky one": This comment is reported in Korinna Spanidou, *O Onassis, Opos Ton Ezisa* (Onassis As I Knew Him), but she does not identify the speaker in the book other than to say it was a dinner guest of Onassis'. When I interviewed her in 1998 she disclosed that the statement was made by his cousin and brother-in-law, Nikos Konialidis.

227   After her second appearance at Epidaurus, Maria again donated her fee to the Maria Callas Scholarship Fund, which has supported young Greek musicians ever since.

236   "Four years ago . . .": Evans, *Ari,* p. 195.

16 *Cold Wind in Eden*

242   The picture of life on Skorpios in this chapter comes from guests and employees of Onassis' who spent time on the island in the first few years after he bought it. Especially informative were Korinna Spanidou, a physical therapist who spent the sum-

mer of 1964 on the island; Captain Kostas Anastasiades of the *Christina;* and Captain Panayiotis Zigomalis, who replaced him for eight months in late 1964 while he was on another assignment for Onassis; Ari's niece Marilena Patronikola; and various friends of the tycoon's and Maria's.

252   "Franco, don't you think I look pretty . . .": Franco Zeffirelli, *Zeffirelli: An Autobiography,* p. 209.

256   Maria's renunciation of her U.S. citizenship and her assumption of Greek citizenship are reported from the legal documents that Callas signed to conclude both actions, which were found in her private papers after her death. I obtained copies of the documents from individuals who now have them.

257   The description of Maria's apartment is based on photographs found in her private papers, some of which I have obtained. The documents showing that two Onassis companies owned the shares in the apartment were also found in her private papers. Copies were given to me by her sister's husband, Dr. Andreas Stathopoulos.

260   The legal battle with Panaghis Vergottis is recounted from contemporary newspaper articles and from court papers.

17 *On the Road*

265   Jackie Kennedy's Caribbean cruise on the *Christina* in May of 1968 was described to me by two of the three people who met her on St. Thomas: Captain Kostas Anastasiades and First Engineer Stefanos Darousos.

271   Maria's decision to break off with Onassis in 1968 was recounted to me by Mary Carter and John Ardoin, who got their information from the man who persuaded her to make the fateful move—Larry Kelly. He died at forty-six on September 16, 1973, exactly three years before Callas.

272   Maria's odyssey through the western United States in the summer of 1968 was described to me by individuals who joined her in the journey at various points, including Sue Blair, David Stickelbar, John Ardoin, and especially Mary Carter.

      Mary Carter was going through her own emotional crisis at the time. The daughter of a prosperous furniture dealer in Dallas, she was in love with Larry Kelly, but was married to the Dallas businessman Robert Mead. Her attraction to Kelly began in 1957 when he came to Dallas to establish the city's first opera company; at the time, she was married to her first husband, William Reed, whom she divorced in 1960.

      In 1973 Mary Carter divorced Robert Mead, and a year later she had a brief three-month marriage that was annulled. She married the retired intelligence officer Rudolph "Foxy" Carter in 1981 and was widowed in 1994. Although she lives mostly in Manhattan, Mary Carter also spends time every year in Newport and Cuernavaca, Mexico, where she often entertained Callas. She has two children, Lainie and Max, from her first marriage.

281   Maria's outburst to John Ardoin was recorded by him with her permission, and I'm grateful to him for providing me with both a recording of it and a transcription.

288   Virtually every book that cites the *Boston Herald-Traveler* story on the pending marriage of Jackie and Onassis gives October 15 as its dateline, but an examination of the original front-page article shows it appeared two days later.

18 *The Jackie Jinx*

293   "Maria Callas took advantage of a society event . . .": *Gente* magazine, October 30, 1968, pp. 15–16 (translated for me by Susan Williams).

294   The disclosure by Ferruccio Mezzadri, Maria's butler, that Onassis called her two days before his wedding was made in Italian during an interview with him that was interpreted for me by a Milanese friend, Fabrizio Cerina, an international banker who graciously volunteered to assist in my investigations.

297   I interviewed Onassis about the Project Omega deal in the fall of 1968 for the *Wall Street Journal* at the Olympic Airways offices in Athens. Part of the deal involved the construction of a third refinery near Athens. I asked him why he didn't build it outside the capital, which was overly congested and polluted, and suggested northwestern Greece, since a refinery already existed in the northeast region, near Thessaloniki. "The main market is in the Athens area," he told me. "It will add a dollar a ton to transport the refined products to the Athens market if we build it in the north."

I pressed him. "But gas prices are fixed by the government and you have a built-in profit, so what is a dollar less to a wealthy man like you?"

"I'm a businessman," he responded candidly. "I'm in it to make every dollar I can. Don't forget, the price I'll get for crude under my agreement with the government is three dollars less a ton than is paid for the Salonika [Esso Papas] refinery and three dollars less than was paid for the state-owned refinery when Niarchos was running it. They got seventeen dollars a ton. I'm getting fourteen."

What impressed me most about Onassis was that he could recall without any notes or memos every detail about the deal and every price and cost figure related to it.

I interviewed him in an empty room with only two chairs in it, which he and I occupied. Shortly after the interview began, his press aide, Helen Speronis, came into the room, and before I could even stir he stood up and gallantly offered her his chair, as if an important guest had walked into the room rather than one of his employees. It quickly became apparent, despite his unimpressive looks and physique, why he was so attractive to women, even in his mid-sixties.

303   The Apollo 11 earrings were among the personal belongings of Jacqueline Kennedy Onassis auctioned by Sotheby's in New York during the week of April 19, 1996, at the request of her children. They were valued by the auction house at $1,000 to $1,200 and sold for $112,500.

19 *Reunion*

311   The "Dear Ros" letters were offered for sale by a former employee of Roswell Gilpatric's law firm who said he found them in a wastebasket in their office. After Mr. Gilpatric filed a complaint with the Manhattan district attorney's office, the letters were returned to him.

316   "No sooner does Aristotle Onassis . . .": *Time* magazine, September 7, 1970, p. 26.

317   "He [Onassis] is my best friend": *New York Times,* November 30, 1970, p. 52.

321   Yiannis Giorgakis, who died in 1994, often reminisced about Onassis during the dozens of times we met for lunch and dinner on my visits to Athens and on his trips to New York.

20 *The Fall of Icarus*

323   The last days of Alexander Onassis were recounted to me by his mentor, Stelios Papadimitriou, and his friend Constantin "Totis" Vernikos.

327   The reactions of Onassis to his son's injury and death were described by his half sis-

ters, Merope Konialidis and Kalliroe Patronikolas; his niece Marilena Patronikola; his former brother-in-law, George Livanos; the captain of the *Christina,* Kostas Anastasiades; and his legal adviser, Stelios Papadimitriou.

328 The information about the press conference Onassis held after his son's death was recounted to me by his press aide, Helen Speronis, and by several Greek journalists who attended.

330 Onassis' trip to Paris to see Maria Callas after Alexander's death was described to me by Maria's butler and her maid, Ferruccio Mezzadri and Bruna Lupoli, and her friend Kostas Pylarinos, with whom Maria spent her last summer in Greece.

332 Jacqueline Kennedy Onassis wrote several letters to Marilena Patronikola, who generously allowed me to read and copy them.

334 Maria's relationship with Giuseppe di Stefano was recounted to me by di Stefano himself and several of her friends, including Mary Carter.

21 *Omega*

339 The doomed effort of Onassis to build a refinery in New Hampshire was described to me by the man assigned to oversee the project, Nicholas Papanikolaou; several other Onassis aides in New York; and New Hampshire political figures who opposed the project, including Chris Spyrou.

343 Ari's deteriorating relationship with Jackie and his plans to divorce her were recounted by his aide, Nicholas Papanikolaou; his doctor Isadore Rosenfeld; his late friends Costa Gratsos and Yiannis Giorgakis; and Tom Dolan, a partner of Roy Cohn, the New York lawyer he hired to handle the divorce.

344 The account of Maria's concert tour with di Stefano is based on interviews with the tenor and with Maria's colleague Giulietta Simionato and on articles from newspapers in the cities where they performed.

348 The decline and death of Tina Livanos was described to me by her brother, George, and her friend Vivi Crespi.

350 There has been some controversy as to whether the damaging information about Jackie given to Jack Anderson by Costa Gratsos originated with Gratsos because he disliked Jackie and wanted Ari to return to Maria, or because Onassis asked him to do it. Although Stelios Papadimitriou, the legal adviser to Onassis and now president of the Onassis Foundation, insists Gratsos acted on his own, the overwhelming majority of Gratsos' aides and friends say he would never have taken such action unless instructed to do so by Onassis, a view supported by friends of Onassis' as well. It is telling that Onassis was present at the beginning of the first meeting with Anderson and then left Gratsos alone to outline the complaints against Jackie.

353 Sources who described Onassis' declining health include his half sisters, Merope and Kalliroe; his niece Marilena Patronikola; his doctor Isadore Rosenfeld; his houseman, Panayiotis Konidiaris; and news reports on his hospitalization.

22 *Death in Paris*

361 The description of Onassis' funeral is based on recollections of family members and friends who were present, and contemporary newspaper articles.

364 Callas' reaction to Onassis' death was recounted by her friends and staff: Ferruccio and Bruna, Mary Carter, Kostas Pylarinos, Nadia Stancioff, François Valéry, and Prince Michael of Greece.

369 Mandrax (methaqualone) is described in medical literature as a barbiturate that was developed to treat sleeplessness, anxiety, tension, high blood pressure, and convulsions but was found to produce dependence; its short-term effect is to slow down activity of the central nervous system. A small dose relieves tension, but a large dose produces blurred vision, impaired thinking, slurred speech, impaired perception of time and space, slowed reflexes and breathing, and reduced sensitivity to pain. Overdoses cause unconsciousness, coma, and death. Regular use results in tolerance, making increased doses necessary to produce the desired effect. Since tolerance increases with use, the margin between an effective dose and a lethal dose gradually narrows.

370 Maria's 1976 vacation on the Chalkidhiki Peninsula was described to me by her host, Kostas Pylarinos.

Despite published assertions by Kiki Feroudi Moutsatsos, an Onassis secretary, that Callas went to Skorpios to visit Onassis' grave in the summer of 1977, there is no corroborating evidence that she did. Maria's maid, Bruna Lupoli, her butler, Ferruccio Mezzadri, and her closest friends all say she never left Paris that summer. When I questioned Ms. Moutsatsos about the visit, which she says she personally arranged, she at first told me Maria flew from Athens to the closest airport to Skorpios on an Onassis Learjet, but when I asked her to give me the name of the pilot, she changed her story and said Maria actually flew on a regular Olympic flight but she couldn't remember which one. No one who was on Skorpios that summer remembers Maria coming to the island, and the staff say it would have been impossible for her not to be seen if she had come.

375 The description of Maria's activities the night before her death is based on reading material found on her night table next to her bed after her death and made available to me.

376 The description of Maria's death is based on information provided by her maid, Bruna Lupoli, and her butler, Ferruccio Mezzadri, who were with her at the time.

23 Epitaphios

377 Jean Roire is still alive in Paris but refused to be interviewed. Some Paris friends of Vasso Devetzi's believe that when Vasso died, she left to him whatever she had of Maria's possessions and papers.

379 The description of Maria's funeral is based on testimony of participants, including her sister, Jackie, and her friend Kostas Pylarinos, and on contemporary newspaper accounts.

381 "The paper was several years old . . .": Galatopoulos, *Maria Callas: Sacred Monster,* page 459.

382 The financial details of Maria's estate were provided by her sister and beneficiary, Jackie, and Jackie's husband, Dr. Andreas Stathopoulos. For details of the Onassis estate, the primary source was Stelios Papadimitriou, the president of the Onassis Foundation.

383 When Jackie Callas married Dr. Andreas Stathopoulos in 1983, he questioned Vasso Devetzi's use of the money that Jackie had given her to set up the Maria Callas Foundation, and had Jackie withdraw her power of attorney as well as the *droit moral.* Later he charged that Vasso had squandered most of the money Jackie had given her for the foundation and that it was not providing the kind of scholarships and programs that Maria had envisioned for it. The directors of the foundation have denied the charges and point to its programs as evidence that the accusations are baseless.

384   The dispersal of Maria's ashes over the Aegean was described to me by eyewitnesses, including her sister, Jackie, her friend Kostas Pylarinos, and the then Greek minister of culture, Dimitrios Nanias.

389   The Onassis Foundation originally awarded four prizes of $100,000 each every year. When its first president, Yiannis Giorgakis, left in 1991, the prizes were reduced to three every two years but enhanced in value to $250,000 each.

Bibliography

Allegri, Renzo, and Roberto Allegri. *Callas by Callas: The Secret Writings of "la Maria."* New York: Universe, 1998.

Andersen, Christopher P. *Jackie After Jack: Portrait of the Lady.* New York: William Morrow, 1998.

Ardoin, John. *The Callas Legacy.* London: Duckworth, 1977.

Ardoin, John, and Gerald Fitzgerald. *Callas.* New York: Holt, Rinehart & Winston, 1974.

Bing, Rudolf. *A Knight at the Opera.* New York: G. P. Putnam's Sons, 1981.

Brady, Frank. *Onassis: An Extravagant Life.* Englewood Cliffs, N.J.: Prentice-Hall, 1977.

Cafarakis, Christian. *The Fabulous Onassis, His Life and Loves.* New York: William Morrow, 1972.

Callas, Evangelia, with Lawrence G. Blochman. *My Daughter Maria Callas.* New York: Fleet, 1960.

Callas, Jackie. *Sisters: A Revealing Portrait of the World's Most Famous Diva.* New York: St. Martin's Press, 1989.

Csampai, Attila. *Callas.* New York: Stewart, Tabori & Chang, 1996.

Davis, L. J. *Onassis: Aristotle and Christina.* New York: St. Martin's, 1986.

Dedichen, Ingeborg. *Onassis Mon Amour . . . Mémoires Recueillées par Henry Pessar.* Paris: Pygmalion, 1975.

Dempster, Nigel. *Heiress: The Story of Christina Onassis.* London: Weidenfeld & Nicolson, 1989.

Dobkin, Marjorie Housepian. *Smyrna 1922: The Destruction of a City.* Kent, Ohio: Kent State University Press, 1966.

Evans, Peter. *Ari: The Life and Times of Aristotle Onassis.* New York: Summit, 1986.

Fraser, Nicholas; Philip Jacobson; Mark Ottaway; and Lewis Chester. *Aristotle Onassis.* New York: J. B. Lippincott, 1977.

Frischauer, Willi. *Onassis: A Report Without an End.* London: Mayflower, 1968.

Galatopoulos, Stelios. *Callas: La Divina—Art That Conceals Art.* London: J. M. Dent, 1963.

———. *Maria Callas: Sacred Monster.* London: Fourth Estate, 1998.

Gobbi, Tito. *My Life.* London: Hamish Hamilton, 1984.

Harewood, George Henry Hubert Lascelles. *The Tongs and the Bones: The Memoirs of Lord Harewood.* London: Weidenfeld & Nicolson, 1981.

Hemingway, Ernest. *The Short Stories of Ernest Hemingway.* New York: Charles Scribner's Sons, 1938.

Heymann, C. David. *A Woman Named Jackie.* New York: Lyle Stuart, 1989.

Jellinek, George. *Callas: Portrait of a Prima Donna.* New York: Dover, 1986. This is a slightly corrected republication of the work originally published by the Ziff-Davis Publishing Company, New York, in 1960, with a new preface and epilogue added and the discography omitted.

Joesten, Joachim. *Onassis: A Biography.* New York: Abelard-Schuman, 1963.

Kennedy, Rose Fitzgerald. *Times to Remember.* Garden City, N.Y.: Doubleday, 1974.

Klein, Edward. *Just Jackie: Her Private Years.* New York: Ballantine, 1998.

Lilly, Doris. *Those Fabulous Greeks: Onassis, Niarchos and Livanos.* New York: Cowles, 1970.

Limberopoulos, Dimitris. *I Dynasteia Onassi* (The Onassis Dynasty). Athens: Vasdekis, 1989.

Linakis, Steven. *Diva: The Life and Death of Maria Callas.* Englewood Cliffs, N.J.: Prentice-Hall, 1980.

Lowe, David A., ed. *Callas As They Saw Her.* New York: Ungar, 1986.

Marchand, Polyvios. *Maria Callas.* Athens: Gnosi, 1983.

Maxwell, Elsa. *The Celebrity Circus.* New York: Appleton-Century, 1963.

———. *R.S.V.P.* Boston: Little, Brown, 1954.

Meneghini, Giovanni Battista (with Renzo Allegri). *My Wife Maria Callas.* New York: Farrar Straus Giroux, 1982.

Montague Browne, Anthony. *Long Sunset: Memoirs of Winston Churchill's Last Private Secretary.* London: Cassell, 1995.

Moran, Charles. *Churchill: Taken from the Diaries of Lord Moran.* Boston: Houghton Mifflin, 1966.

Moutsatsos, Kiki Feroudi, with Phyllis Karas. *The Onassis Women.* New York: G. P. Putnam's Sons, 1998.

Pearson, John. *The Private Lives of Winston Churchill.* New York: Simon & Schuster, 1991.

Petsalis-Diomidis, Nikos. *I Agnosti Kallas* (The Unknown Callas). Athens: Ekdosis Kastanioti, 1998.

Rasponi, Lanfranco. *The Last Prima Donnas.* New York: Alfred A. Knopf, 1982.

Rémy, Pierre-Jean. *Maria Callas: A Tribute.* New York: St. Martin's Press, 1978.

Scott, Michael. *Maria Meneghini Callas.* Boston: Northeastern University Press, 1991.

Smith, Michael Llewellyn. *Ionian Vision: Greece in Asia Minor, 1919–1922.* London: Hurst and Company, 1998.

Spanidou, Korinna. *O Onassis, Opos Ton Ezisa* (Onassis As I Knew Him). Athens: Estia, 1996.

Spoto, Donald. *Jacqueline Bouvier Kennedy Onassis: A Life.* New York: St. Martin's Press, 2000.

Stancioff, Nadia. *Maria Callas Remembered.* New York: E. P. Dutton, 1987.

Stassinopoulos, Arianna. *Maria: Beyond the Callas Legend.* London: Weidenfeld & Nicolson, 1980. (Published in New York in 1981 by Simon & Schuster as *Maria Callas: The Woman Behind the Legend.*)

Vasilikos, Vasilis. *To Sfrato* (The Eviction). Athens: Gnosi, 1987.

Verga, Carla. *Vita di Maria Callas.* Lucca: Lim, 1995.

Wright, William. *All the Pain That Money Can Buy: The Life of Christina Onassis.* New York: Simon & Schuster, 1991.

Zeffirelli, Franco. *Zeffirelli: An Autobiography.* New York: Weidenfeld & Nicolson, 1986.

Index

Page numbers in *italics* refer to illustrations.

mances, 36, 43–6, 180, 188, 227, 232, 239–41, 247, 249, 251, 254, 335, 337, 344; in *Lucia di Lammermoor*, 10, 33, 190, 191; in *Madame Butterfly*, 269; marriage to Meneghini, 8–10, 34, 38–49, 64, 65–6, 68–72, 75–6, 106, 130–2, 138–9, 142–5, 157–60, 168, 178, 186, 199–200, 213, 257; master classes given by, 317, 319–21; Elsa Maxwell and, 9–13, *13*, 14–16, 28–33, 40, 43, 47–8, 50–2, 177–80, 189–90, 223; in *Medea* (film), 299, *299*, 300–302, 309, 310, 321; in *Medea* (opera), 37, 40, 43–6, 180, 190, 192, 196, 218, 227–30, 232, 240, 247; Meneghini as business manager of, 8–10, 32, 35, 41, 46–7, 130, 145, 166, 177, 185, 202; Mexico trip with her mother, 186–7; Milan home, 65, 163–9, 172–3, 175–6, 189–90, 192, 194–6, 203, 257, 267; New York performances, 10, 33, 37, 40, 75, 248–50, 344–6; on 1959 *Christina* cruise, 46–9, 52–3, *53*, 54–69, *69*, 70–9, 80, 90, 92–5, *95*, 96–8, *98*, 99–101, *101*, 102–12, *112*, 113–14, 123–36, *136*, 137–61, *161*, 162, 163; in *Norma*, 10, 31–3, 42, 101, 102, 217–21, 224, 240–1, *241*, 242, 247, 249–51; obesity, 8–9, 34, 48, 51, 64, 65–7, *67*, 85, 222, 229, 252, 274, 310, 370, 374–5; in Palm Beach, 359–60; Paris apartment, 64, 257, *258*, 259–60, 298, 302, 309–13, 319, 330, 334, 347, 364, *365*, 366–73, 376, 377, 382–4; Paris debut, 40–2; Paris performances, 40–1, *41*, 42, 240–2, 344; performance cancellations and walkouts, 12, 28, 32–3, 91, 217, 218, 251, 337, 344, 345; performances in Greece, 11–12, 91, 97, 101, 102, 217–21, 227–30; personality, 29, 77, 139, 217, 246; in *Il Pirata*, 35; in *Poliuto*, 223–4, *224*; pregnancy and death of premature son, 197–203, *203*, 204–5, *206*, 207–14, 215, 330, 390–1; press on, 10, 12, 29, 33, 36, 40, 41, 44, 46, 53, 64, 68, 76–7, 100, 110, 160–4, 168–70, 173–88, 201–3, 215, 219, 223, 232, 233, 239–42, 250, 260, 261, 276–7, 280–5, 290, 293–4, 310–17, 335, 337, 345–6, 371, 376, 378, 379; professional debut, 86; in *I Puritani*, 36, 38, 187; Lee Radziwill and, 233–7, 238–9, 248; recordings, 37, 38, 177, 181, 217, 221, 240, 335, 341, 390; relationship with her father, 240, 335; relationship with her mother, 7–10, 37, 39, 8–90, 129, 143, 153, 185–8, 203–4, 213, 221, 232–3,

378–9; relationship with her sister, 91, 221–3, 228–9, 369–70, 378, 380, 382; religion, 137–44, 149, 200, 221, 257, 296, 379; Rome Opera debacle, 31–3, 34; scandal with Onassis, 163–81, *181*, 182, 183–96, 260, 288; separation and divorce from Meneghini, 142–5, 159–60, 162, 163–73, 176, 178–82, 183, 188–92, 195–6, 215, 232, 233, 251, 256–7, 382; sexuality, 129–30, 143–5, 172, 191, 201, 255, 310, 320, 369; as shipowner, 248, 249, 255–6, 260, 341; singing voice, 10, 36–40, 221, 242, 246; in *La Sonnambula*, 12, 16, 65; in Soviet Union, 319, *319*; superstitiousness, 145, 166, 296, 301, 377; - Tebaldi rivalry, 283–4, *284*, 285; temper, 10, 246–7, 253–5, 269, 348; in *Tosca*, 10, 33, 37, 42, 87, 239–41, 249–52, 376; in *Traviata*, 33, 36, 37, *67*, 240, 298, 372; vision problems, 35, 84, 192, 230, 317, 337, 372; in *Die Walküre*, 38; weight loss, 9, 36, 65–7, *67*, 245–6, 375; working style, 35–40; *see also* Callas-Onassis relationship

Callas, Vassili, 81

Callas (Maria) Awards, 383

Callas (Maria) Foundation, 383

Callas-Onassis relationship: "back-street complex" of Callas, 189–90; birth and death of their premature son, 197–203, *203*, 204–5, *206*, 207–14, 215, 330, 390–1; Callas disliked by Onassis' children, 158–9, 225–6, 243, 318, 356; Callas' mothering role in, 215–16, 309; Callas' Parisian apartment, 257, *258*, 259–60, 309–13, 330, 334, 347; death of Alexander Onassis, 330; as destiny, 145–6, 165, 296, 391; early 1960s happiness, 215–37; effect on Callas' career, 36, 164, 172, 185, 191, 195–6, 202–3, 216–33, 241–2, 246–52, 270, 272; end of 1959 *Christina* cruise, 160–1, *161*, 162, 163; first meetings, 7–13, *13*, 14–15, *15*, 16, 27, 29, 40–9; first seduction and sexual liasons, 45–6, 129–30, 132, 142–6, 156–7, 160; Greekness, 90–1, 130, 141, 145–6, 182, 218, 230, 254; Kennedy-Onassis relationship and, 46, 198, 199, 211, 213, 234–6, *236*, 237, 239, 248–50, 260–1, 264–9, 279–80, 284, 285–90, 293–300, 309–13, 317, 320, 347, 391; after Kennedy-Onassis wedding, 297–300, 302, 309–16, *316*, 317–21, 330, 334–5, 347, 352, 355–9; London *Medea*

Cyprus, 55, 134, 142, 375
Czechoslovakia, 277

Daley, Richard, 277
Dalitz, Moe, 274
Dallas, 272, 273, 274, 277, 279, 280–3; Callas'
 performances in, 29, 37, 40, 190–2, 218,
 227, 280, 344; Kennedy assassination, 237
Dallas Morning News, 280
Darousos, Stefanos, 265
Davis, Bette, 225
Dedichen, Ingeborg, 8
de Gaulle, Charles, 97
Delos, 148
Delphi, 94–5, *95,* 96, 148
Devetzi, Vasso, 130, 140, 204, 207–9, 212, 319,
 319, 320, 345, 357, 369, 370, 373, 374, 375,
 377; Callas' death and, 377–85
Devetzis, Yiannis, 375, 381
Diamand, Peter, 46, 177, 344
Dimitriadis, Colonel Petros, 82
Disneyland, Callas at, 275, *275*
di Stefano, Giuseppe, 210, 212, 321, 333; Callas
 and, 321, 333–6, *336,* 337, 338, 344–7, 366–7
di Stefano, Luisa, 367
Dizikes, John, *Opera in America,* 39
Domingo, Placido, 372
Don Carlos (opera), Callas in, 65
Doyle (William) Galleries, 306
Drakos, George, 390
Drown, Joe, 274
Dumas, Alexandre, *Camille,* 373
Düsseldorf, 344

Echeverria, Luis, 277
Eden, Anthony, 88
Edinburgh Festival, 12, 16, 177, 344
Ednam, Lady Stella, 169
Egypt, 5, 337
Eisenhower, Dwight, 277
Ekmekzoglou, Nikos, 121
Elizabeth, Queen of England, 328
Embiricos, Miltos, *84,* 85, 88, 222
Embiricos, Perry, 315
EMI, 177, 228, 378; Callas' recordings for, 177,
 181, 217, 221
England, 14, 15, 43–6, 113, 115, 117, 134, 188,
 226–7, 232, 251; World War I, 131; World
 War II, 72, 86–9; *see also* London
Epictetus, *Discourses,* 291

Epidaurus (ancient Greek theater), Callas'
 performances at, 101, *101,* 102, 217–21, 223,
 224, 227–30
Ethnos, 24, 223
Euripides, 218
Evangheliki Scholi, Smyrna, 124–5, *125*
Evans, Peter, 25, 45, 52, 120, 160, 266, 312

Fairbanks, Douglas, Jr., 43, 45
Fallah, Dr. Reza, 287
Farouk, King, 57
Feydeau, Georges, 293
Fields, Gracie, 78
films, Callas in, 230, 248, 253–5, 299, *299,*
 300–302, 309, 310, 321
Flanner, Janet, 310
Flea in Her Ear, A (film), 290, 293, 294
Florida, Jaime Campo, 169
Fonda, Henry, 16
Fonteyn, Margot, 43, 225, 369
Foreman, Carl, 230
France, 97, 115, 212, 240–2, 257, 332, 380;
 see also Paris
France-Soir, 201
Franco, Francisco, 70
Frischauer, Willi, 131, 141, 193, 260
Fuller, Andrew, 312
Fuller, Geraldine Spreckles, 312

Gabor, Madame Joli, 185
Gage, Nicholas, *210, 222, 390*
Gaillet, Hélène, 348
Galatopoulos, Stelios, 71, 130, 131, 199, 201,
 221, 255, 358, 381; *Maria Callas: Sacred
 Monster,* 199–200
Gallagher, Mary, 305
Galsworthy, John, *Over the River,* 147
Garbo, Greta, 21, 24, 27, 43, 51, 56, 61, 74, 169,
 170, 225, 234
Gardner, Ava, 56
Garofalidis, Artemis Onassis, 3, 4–5, 22, 92–4,
 107–8, 121, 126, 135, 151, 169, 182, 204, 217,
 229, 244, 247, 265, 311, 353, 356, 362, *363;*
 Callas disliked by, 107–8, 146, 225–6; Jackie
 Kennedy and, 265, 280, 288, 289, 291, 297,
 337, *363,* 387; on 1959 *Christina* cruise,
 92–4, 99, 107–8, *136,* 140–2, 149, 153–4
Garofalidis, Theodore, 92, 93, 94, *98,* 99, 101,
 108, *136,* 140–2, 153–4, 185, 204, 217, 229,
 247

Mussolini, Benito, 85
Mykonos, 148, 158
mythology, Greek, 60, 79, 95–6, 101–2, 148, 218, 231, 236, 303–4, 391

Naples, 76
Nassau, 263, *264*
National Conservatory, Greece, 84
National Lyric Theater, Callas at, 86
New York, 7–8, 10–11, 15, 17, 21, 24, 25, 77, 81, 113, 185–6, 188, 190, 192–3, 195, 203, 233, 240, 261, 271–2, 283, 285, 317, 319, 339–44, 353, 374, 379; Callas' childhood in, 7–8, 81–5; Callas' performances in, 10, 33, 37, 40, 75, 248–50, 344–6; Callas as teacher at Juilliard, 319–21; as home of Jackie Onassis, 302–3, 304, 308, 387–8; late 1960s, 262, 267; Onassis-Livanos wedding in, 17–18, *18*; Onassis in New York Hospital, 342–4, 350
New York Daily News, 17
New Yorker, The, 310
New York Herald Tribune, 123
New York Journal American, 184
New York Post, 266, 268
New York Times, 10, 189, 235, 239, 250, 272, 277, 303, 308, 317, 345, 346, 354; on Callas' death, 376; on Kennedy-Onassis wedding, 288–90, 293, 295; on Onassis' death, 120, 358, 387; on troubled Kennedy-Onassis marriage, 313, 317, 387
Niarchos, Eugenia Livanos, 17, 18, 23, 27, 112, 184, 318, 349; death, 314–15, 319
Niarchos, Stavros, 14, 17, 18, 22, 27, 111, 149, 184, 226, 314, 318, 333, 388; marriage to Tina Onassis, 318–19, 326, 327, 349–50, 388; -Onassis rivalry, 22–5, 54, 230, 297, 306, 314, 318, 331
Niarchos, Tina, *see* Onassis, Tina Livanos
Nixon, Richard, 277, 328
Nizer, Louis, 344
Norma (opera): Callas in, 10, 31–3, 42, 101, 102, 217–21, 224, 240–1, *241*, 242, 247, 249–51; Epidaurus production (1960), 101, 102, 217–21, 224; Paris performances, 240–1, *241*, 242, 247, 249, 250–1
Nureyev, Rudolf, 265

Oberon, Merle, 14
Oberon (opera), Callas in, 85

O'Donnell, Ken, 238
oil, 19; Arab embargo, 337, 352; Middle East, 24–5, 337, 352; Onassis' U.S. refinery proposal, 339, 340, 342; Project Omega, 266, 288, 296–8, 306–7, 308, 331
Olympic Airways, 24, 138, 185, 211, 216, 218, 230, 255, 277, 296, 324, 325, 329, 331, 350; 1970 Palestinian hijacking, 307; Onassis' loss of, 352–3
Olympic Aviation, 324–7; Alexander Onassis' fatal plane crash, 326–32
Olympic Chivalry (ship), 238
Olympic Maritime, 22
Olympic Tower, New York, 352, 386
Onassis, Alexander S. (son of Onassis), 3, 19, *21*, 204, 205, 294, *325*; aviation interests, 158, 323–8; birth, 20; Callas disliked by, 158–9, 225–6, 243, 318; childhood, 20–2, 56–7, 96, 100–101, 108–9, 134, 158–9, 161, 163, *171*, 176, 179, 192, 194, 195, 225–6; education, 324; fatal plane crash, 326–9, *329*, 330–3, 338, 339; Jackie Kennedy disliked by, 288, 318, 323; his mother's remarriage and, 318–19, 326; relationship with his father, 159, 204, 243, 288, 318–19, 323–5, *325*, 326–33; Skorpios tomb of, 330–3, 348, 358, 362
Onassis, Alexander H. (uncle of Onassis), 117, 119, 120, 125, 205
Onassis, Aristotle Socrates, *18, 21, 44, 53, 54, 98, 101, 112, 127, 156, 161, 181, 224, 236, 264, 292, 294, 316, 325, 329, 351, 354;* airline business, 24, 138, 185, 216, 218, 230, 307, 323–7, 329, 350, 352–3; in American Hospital, Paris, 4–6, 353–9; appreciation of opera, 220, 228, 242; in Argentina, 120, 153, 155; art collection, 24, 58; birth, 120–1; business setbacks of 1970s, 306–7, 337–40, 342, 347, 350, 352–3; childhood and adolescence, 114, 115–28, 150; *Christina* beloved by, 57–62; Churchill and, 54, *54*, 55, 59, 61, 63, 70–4, 77, 92, 94–6, 99, 113, 127, 131, 134, 135, 141, 148, 149, 203, 217, 233; complaints about Jackie Kennedy, 287–90, 295–8, 303–6, 308, 310–14, 320–2, 337–8, 343, 348–52; courtship of Jackie Kennedy, 234–6, *236*, 237, 239, 248–50, 260–1, 264–9, 279–80, 284–8; death, 120, 359–60; death of son Alexander, 326–9, *329*, 330–3, 338, 339, 348, 358; death of Tina Onassis, 349,

Trenton Inversion Company Inc., 259

Trovatore, Il, 42

Truman, Harry, 191

Tsarouchis, Yiannis, 227

Tuckerman, Nancy, 288–9, 305, 351

Turin, 335, 336

Turkey, 23, 62, 92, 111; *Medea* filmed in, 299, 300, 301; 1922 Smyrna massacre, 14, 115–25, 128, 149–53; 1955 Istanbul pogrom, 134–5, 142; 1959 *Christina* cruise to, 114, 123–8, 132–6, *136*, 137, 140–4, 147

United Press International, 183

United States, 19, 21, 113, 115, 248, 319, 322; Callas' immigration to, 7–8, 90, 153; Callas' tours in, 29, 37, 40, 190–2, 248–50, 344–7; JFK assassination, 237–9; RFK assassination, 267; King assassination, 262, 263; late 1960s, 262, 263, 266–7, 277; 1968 Callas' road trip, 263, 271–5, *275, 276, 276*, 277–8, *278,* 279, 280–4, *284,* 285, 287; Onassis' refinery proposal in, 339, 340, 342; space program, 262, 303

U.S. Maritime Commission, 19

Valentino, 305, 306, 361

Valéry, François, 309, 369–70

van Zuylen, Gaby, 368

van Zuylen, Baroness Maggie, 228, 250, 298, 309, 310, 312, 335, 368

Vasilikos, Vasilis, 207–8; *The Eviction (To Sfrato),* 208

Venice, 8, 27, 48, 163, 169, 171, 173–5, *175,* 177–80, 217; Callas-Onassis meeting in, 9–13, *13,* 14–15, *15,* 16, 27, 29; Callas' performances in, 38; Maxwell balls, 9, 12–13, *13,* 14, 42, 177–80

Verdi arias, Callas' recording of, 217

Vergottis, Panaghis, 232, 236, 247–8, 249, 253, 255–6; Callas-Onassis lawsuit against, 256, 260, 298

Verona, 8, 138, 179, 256

Vespri Siciliani, I (opera), Callas' direction of, 335

Vickers, Jon, 40

Vietnam War, 262

Virgil, *Aeneid,* Book IV, 339

Virgin Islands, 265

Visconti, Luchino, 223, 298, 367

Vlassopoulos, Costa, 341

Volpi, Count, 16

von Karajan, Herbert, 254–5

von Otter, Anne-Sophie, 383

von Thyssen, Baroness Fiona, 323, 324–5, 326, 327, 330, 331

Voulgarides, Yianni, 121

Walküre, Die (opera), Callas in, 38

Washington, D.C., 37, 344

Washington Post, 233

Webster, David, 251

Weinstein, Dr. Louis, 356

Westchester Corporation Ltd., 259

Wilson, Earl, 286

Wilson, Meredith, 275, *276*

Windsor, Duke and Duchess of, 9, 11, 24, 40

Winston, Harry, 283, 284

Women's Wear Daily, 305

World War I, 92, 112, 131

World War II, 8, 19, 72, 78, 85–9, 94

Yeats, William Butler, "Sailing to Byzantium," 133

Yiannakopoulos, Miltos, 271, 311, 314, 320, 322, 341, 348

Zavitzsianos, Father Apostolos, 363

Zeffirelli, Franco, 37, 38, 39, 219, 224, 252, 372–3, 378; Callas directed by, 239–42, 250, 254, 372; *Tosca* film project, 253–5

Zeno, 7

Zigomalas, Panayiotis, 216, 243, 271

Illustration Credits

A Note About the Author

Nicholas Gage, a former investigative reporter for the *Wall Street Journal* and the *New York Times,* is the author of six previous books. His native Greece is the subject of half of them, including *Eleni,* which received the National Book Critics Circle's nomination for best biography, was awarded first prize by the Royal Society of Literature of Great Britain in 1984, was a Book-of-the-Month Club Main Selection, and was made into a motion picture. Mr. Gage lives in North Grafton, Massachusetts, with his wife, Joan, who is also a writer. They have three children, Christos, Eleni, and Marina.

A Note on the Type

This book was set in a typeface called Bulmer. This distinguished letter is a replica of a type long famous in the history of English printing that was designed and cut by William Martin about 1790 for William Bulmer of the Shakespeare Press. In design, it is all but a modern face, with vertical stress, sharp differentiation between the thick and thin strokes, and nearly flat serifs. The decorative italic shows the influence of Baskerville, as Martin was a pupil of John Baskerville's.

Composed by
North Market Street Graphics, Lancaster, Pennsylvania

Printed and bound by
Quebecor Printing, Fairfield, Pennsylvania

Designed by Ralph Fowler